Experimental General Chemistry

W. T. Lippincott
University of Arizona
Tucson, Arizona

Devon W. Meek
The Ohio State University
Columbus, Ohio

Kenneth D. Gailey
University of Georgia
Athens, Georgia

Kenneth W. Whitten
University of Georgia
Athens, Georgia

In collaboration with:

Jason Manchester
The Ohio State University

Steven Brown
University of Arizona

Violet I. Meek
Ohio Wesleyan University

Frank H. Verhoek
The Ohio State University

Saunders College Publishing
Harcourt Brace Jovanovich College Publishers
Fort Worth   Philadelphia   San Diego
New York   Orlando   Austin   San Antonio
Toronto   Montreal   London   Sydney   Tokyo

Experimental General Chemistry   ISBN: 0-03-060463-x

Copyright ©1984 by Saunders College Publishing

Printed in the United States of America.

45 066 1514131211

CONTENTS

MOLECULAR BEHAVIOR

SOLUTION BEHAVIOR

CHEMICAL EQUILIBRIA

ELECTROCHEMISTRY

OXIDATION-REDUCTION REACTIONS (POTENTIOMETRIC TITRATION)

CHEMICAL DYNAMICS (Kinetics)

THERMODYNAMICS

INORGANIC SYNTHESES AND REACTIONS

COORDINATION CHEMISTRY

INORGANIC QUALITATIVE ANALYSIS

PREFACE

Chemistry is an experimental science. This means that the final authority in chemistry is the experiment. The source of our information, our concepts, and theories in chemistry is right here in the laboratory. This laboratory text is designed to show some ways in which chemists synthesize compounds and how they obtain information by experiment and then use the collected data to draw conclusions about the properties and behavior of matter. It is planned to help students learn not only to perform essential laboratory operations, but also to observe, to correlate and interpret data, and to think and act in laboratory situations. It is also intended to help students, almost all of whom are voting age citizens, realize just how much care, forethought, and skill are needed to produce accurate, reproducible experimental results.

This text is designed to serve the needs of chemistry courses for students at several different levels. One choice of a set of experiments will serve a course for chemistry majors, whereas a different set of experiments will serve a broader group of students who may be planning majors in other sciences; a third set of experiments will serve a course for students with little previous background in science. Obviously, this laboratory text contains more experiments than could be completed in any one year-long course. With the large number provided, it is possible to select a different group of experiments in successive years or to give students a choice of experiments during one year. Several of the experiments require more than one three-hour laboratory period for completion.

Approximately one half of the experiments consist of more than one part, any or all of which may be assigned by the instructor or elected by the student. This format provides the opportunity for individualized assignments and for some students to spend more or less time on a given experiment than others do. Thus, one student may complete three or four parts of a single experiment, while others in the same laboratory are working on different parts of related experiments. For example, many students, having learned a new and moderately complicated technique such as measurement of vapor pressure, would like to continue to use this technique in more challenging ways; other students prefer to move on to other experiments rather than repeat a learned activity. Such options in several variations are included in combinations of experiments.

Two features of this laboratory text are the **Prelaboratory Questions** for each experiment and the **Techniques Section** in the front of the manual. Even at those schools that have developed their own specific experiments for a special section of the course, we believe that the **Techniques Section** will provide a very useful support for those special experiments. We also hope that this section will continue to be useful to students in other courses after they complete the general chemistry course.

Because lecture and textbook presentations often emphasize the results rather than the details of experiments, each experiment in this manual begins with an introduction, which gives background information needed to bridge the gap between lecture presentation of the topic and laboratory study of a small segment of it.

The 34 experiments include portions of a variety of topics, including separations, identification, stoichiometry, qualitative and quantitative analysis, coordination chemistry, chemical equilibrium, electrochemistry, thermodynamics, organic chemistry, and biochemistry. They were selected to illustrate both modern and traditional techniques and to provide teachers and students with a large number of options in choosing experiments to be used and in determining the amount of time and study to be given to any one experiment.

Among the techniques included are: use of an analytical balance; paper and thin-layer chromatography; spectroscopic and spectrophotometric methods; qualitative analysis of inorganic cations, anions, and simple organic substances; precipitation, ion exchange, and solvent extraction quantitative separations; colorimetric, gravimetric and volumetric analysis, including acid-base, precipitation, oxidation-reduction, and complexometric titrations; use of a pH meter, measurement of vapor pressure, vapor density, enthalpy change, free energy change, equilibrium, reaction rate, and electrochemical data; and certain aspects of inorganic and organic synthesis.

All experiments are designed for students with little previous laboratory experience, but students are expected to work carefully and to learn good laboratory habits. The apparatus and instruments used are, with few exceptions, inexpensive and simple to operate. All experiments have a **Report Sheet** and a **Question-Problem** section from which questions may be chosen. In addition, some instructors may require a written report, and there is a section dealing with record-keeping in the laboratory notebook. Because the evaluation of numerical data is essential in many experiments, special sections on errors of measurement and their treatment, use of significant figures (Experiment 34) and graphical representation of data are provided (Techniques Section).

Most of these experiments have been used in the general chemistry laboratories at The Ohio State University, University of Arizona, and University of Georgia for several years. They have been scrutinized by thousands of students and hundreds of instructors. Pre-laboratory films prepared to accompany certain of these experiments also have been used for several years at Ohio State and Arizona. They increase significantly the speed and efficiency with which students learn the experimental techniques.

No laboratory experiments that have been developed over a period of time can be considered to be the work of the authors alone. To the students and teaching assistants, to those who have shared their experiences through the literature, and especially to our colleagues at Ohio State, Arizona, Georgia, and elsewhere who have used or examined this laboratory program, we acknowledge with grateful appreciation our debt for their assistance and advice. The authors are grateful to Professor William Hohman, Marietta College, for proofreading several of the experiments and especially to Roberta Swenton for the creative and expert typing of this camera-ready copy.

W. T. Lippincott

D. W. Meek

K. D. Gailey

K. W. Whitten

TO THE STUDENT

It may come as a surprise to you, but many chemists first became seriously interested in chemistry because they enjoyed the laboratory. Most of us have a fond memory about the first time we made a compound that no one else had ever made or the first time we realized that we could obtain good, reproducible results from an analysis or even the first time an experiment in the laboratory made a lecture topic clearer. **Enjoyment** may not be the word you would use to describe chemistry laboratories, but they can be fascinating places--if your remember to ask "Why?" often enough. **Enjoyment** or **fun** is not synonymous with **easy**. Anything complicated enough to be worth doing takes thought, planning, and care. However, the rewards and learning can be great. We hope that the experiments in this laboratory text will help you learn and will give you some new facts and experiences. Also, we hope that they will help you understand, at least in part, why we have found the study of chemistry so interesting and compelling all these years.

There are some things you can do to help make your progress through the course smoother. For example,

1. **Study** the experiment **before** you come to the laboratory. We have provided prelaboratory questions and problems with each experiment. Your instructor may require that you turn in the prelaboratory exercise at the beginning of the experiment. Even if they are not required for admission to the laboratory, the discussions will help you focus your thinking on that experiment, so write the answers before the laboratory period.

2. **Plan** your work ahead of time. For example, if you need boiling water for an experiment, start heating the water before you actually need it and while you are doing another part of the experiment.

3. **Listen** to your instructor. There may be some modification to the procedures listed in this manual or other special instructions about the location of special equipment or reagents.

4. **Write** the results of the experiment in your notebook, at least in preliminary fashion, while they are still fresh in your mind. Your instructor may ask you to turn in a copy of your results (data) before you leave the laboratory. If not, start the report as soon as possible thereafter. For one thing, a prompt start on the report will give you a chance to ask questions and find information before the report deadline.

In planning an introductory course, most chemical educators elect to present the important principles of the science in the lecture portion of the course and to illustrate some of these principles with appropriate laboratory exercises. In addition to illustrating principles in a quantitative manner, we have attempted in this laboratory program to incorporate some new techniques, manipulative skills, and ingenuity into the experiments and methods of experimentation. For example, Experiment 14 illustrates the methods by which vapor pressure data of a liquid can be obtained and the way these data can be used to determine the heat of vaporization of the liquid. In this case, a value for a property--specifically, the heat of vaporization of the liquid--is obtained without actually measuring that property. Since it is often difficult or impossible to measure certain properties of matter directly, such techniques are employed frequently.

Several of these laboratory experiments are sequential. For example, in Experiment 2 you separate a mixture and determine its quantitative composition. Then in Experiment 3 you identify qualitatively the organic and inorganic salt components of the mixture. In Part A of Experiment 11, you prepare and standardize a sodium hydroxide solution and then use the solution in Part B to determine the equivalent weight of an unknown acid. Thus, both Parts A and B must be performed carefully to obtain the correct equivalent weight. Similarly, Experiments 29, 30, and 31 involve three different quantitative analyses of the same unknown.

Many of the experiments have a quantitative basis; consequently, you will generally be asked to determine a value or to make calculations based on your data. Thus, careful, efficient work is required throughout the laboratory program.

Finally, a word about safety. Safe laboratories result from planning and caring. Read the **Safety and Laboratory Rules** in the following section of the manual, and then THINK about safety--**all the time.**

Think. Ask why and how. And enjoy.

SAFETY AND LABORATORY RULES

The experiments and procedures in this laboratory text were chosen with your safety as a primary consideration. If you follow the directions written in this manual and those of your instructor, there is no reason for you to be apprehensive about your safety. However, there are good reasons to <u>plan</u> for your safety. Safe laboratory practice is compounded from equal parts of common sense and caution. We can discuss safety in terms of preventing or minimizing accidents and of responding to accidents that do occur.

Remember: The most effective safety device in any laboratory is the fully functioning human mind.

ACCIDENT PREVENTION

1. **Techniques for Preventing or Minimizing Injury**

   a. WEAR SAFETY GLASSES AT ALL TIMES. Contact lenses are a hazard in the laboratory and should be avoided. They are forbidden in some chemical laboratories; the soft lens types are especially dangerous to wear in the laboratory because of absorption of vapors.

   b. Read the labels on chemical bottles to be sure that you have picked the correct reagent or item. Particularly, check to see that solution concentrations match those specified.

   c. Always add concentrated acids to water, never the reverse.

   d. Use a towel to protect your hands when cutting glass tubing.

   e. Always fire polish rough ends of glass tubing. Also, remember that hot glass looks just like cold glass. Be careful where you touch it.

   f. Use glycerine, soapy water, or other lubricant to facilitate the insertion of glass tubing, funnels, or thermometers into stoppers or rubber tubing. Use a towel to protect your hands. When inserting a bent piece of tubing, never use the bend as a handle. It will break.

   g. Wipe all spills as soon as they occur.

   h. Point test tubes being heated away from yourself and other people.

   i. Smell vapors cautiously by fanning them toward you with your hand and **only** if directed to do so.

   j. Do not taste chemicals unless directed to do so by your instructor.

   k. **Wear suitable clothing.** Clothing is a protection against spilled chemicals or flammable liquids. Dress which exposes large areas of bare skin is a laboratory hazard and may, on a purely esthetic basis, affect the concentration of your classmates. Open-toed shoes or sandals are an invitation to maimed feet. **Footwear must be worn in the laboratory at all times.**

   l. **Do not pipet by mouth.** Always use a rubber bulb or rubber tubing connected to an aspirator to fill your pipet. Never fill the pipet by using your mouth.

   m. **Call loudly** for help when an accident occurs. Even when the accident seems minor, notify your instructor immediately.

   n. Never eat, drink, or smoke in the laboratory. These activities are strictly forbidden.

o.   Never rub your eyes unless you are absolutely sure that there are no chemicals on your hands.

p.   Never work alone in a laboratory.

q.   Always keep doors to lab desks and laboratory drawers closed except when you are placing something into or removing something from your drawer or desk. Open doors and drawers obstruct the aisle--such obstruction may cause serious accidents.

2.   Safe Experiment Design

In the first place, **DO NOT ATTEMPT UNAUTHORIZED EXPERIMENTS.** If you would like to try an extension or a different experiment, check with your instructor first. In a chemical laboratory, ignorance is downright dangerous.

Examine all experiments for safety hazards before you begin. In other courses or once you are on your own, proper examination will also include checking the properties of unfamiliar compounds whether they are reactants or possible products. Some further points to consider are:

a.   Make sure the experimental apparatus is solid and well supported. Major pieces of glassware should be clamped individually. Hose connections should be wired to make sure they are tight.

b.   Decide in advance how to stop the reaction if something starts to go wrong. This may be as simple as turning off a burner--or it may not be.

c.   Make sure you know how to trap any noxious gases which may be evolved and how to dispose of any dangerous or unpleasant residues left at the end of an experiment.

d.   Read the directions when using an unfamiliar instrument. Instruments must be kept in top operating condition. Otherwise, everyone's time and results are affected.

RESPONSES TO CHEMICAL ACCIDENTS

In addition to standard first-aid measures, there are a few procedures peculiar to chemical accidents. In general, call your instructor when something goes wrong and allow him or her to deal with the trouble. In some cases, however, immediate action or reaction means the difference between a serious injury and a minor inconvenience.

1.   **Safety equipment.** Memorize the location of the safety showers, safety sprays, fire extinguishers, and fireblankets. If you need them, you may not have time to look for them, and you may be unable to.

2.   **Fires.** Most small fires in beakers or flasks can be smothered simply by putting a watch glass or nonflammable plate over the top of the vessel. Since those fires which do occur in general chemistry often involve organic solvents which do not mix with water, avoid water as a smothering agent. In any case, most of the equipment in the laboratory is relatively nonflammable. This means that there will be time to get the instructor and the fire extinguisher. There is no need for foolish heroics. The most important thing is to make sure that the fire does not reach personal clothing. If this does occur, use the nearest safety shower or fireblanket (or safety spray for small fires). NEVER RUN; this only fans the flames. In this connection, students with long hair should tie it back, beyond the reach of burner flames.

3.   **Chemical burns.** Water is the first line of defense for all chemical burns. Specific antidotes can come later; the first thing is to get rid of as much of the chemical as possible. Your safety in the laboratory may someday depend on how instinctively you react by getting the affected area under water. Yell for help while you are washing. Contaminated clothing should be removed immediately. Your modesty will suffer only slightly, and you may save considerable portions of your skin! After the bulk of the chemical has been washed away, the remainder may be neutralized: acids with sodium

bicarbonate and bases with dilute acetic acid (5%). <u>Never</u> attempt this for injuries to the eye; in that case, use copious quantities of plain water and consult a physician. **Bases are especially injurious to eyes. Every precaution should be taken to avoid their entering the eyes.**

4. **Nonchemical burns.** For small burns where the skin has not been broken, a most effective treatment is to hold the affected area under cold running water until the pain stops. This may take as long as 15 to 20 minutes.

LABORATORY ETIQUETTE

When large numbers of people use the same equipment and chemicals, a few rules are needed to promote the general welfare.

1. Clean up spills and always leave a clean desk when you are finished.

2. Do not put paper or solids in the sinks.

3. Clean the area around the balance and other instruments after you use them.

4. Never put your own spatulas or medicine droppers into stock chemicals. Contamination is bound to occur.

5. Never return chemicals to stock bottles. Again, the problem is contamination.

6. Never put the stoppers of stock bottles on the desk top.

7. Leave reagents on the shelves. Do not carry reagent bottles to your desk. This is a matter of courtesy to the other students in the class, and it minimizes the possibility of contamination of the reagent. Obtain the required quantities of chemicals from the reagent shelf by taking clean test tubes or beakers to the reagent area. Take the amount you need and return the bottle to the shelf. Make it a practice not to take much more material than is required for the experiment because many chemicals are quite expensive.

8. Use the hood. Any experiment involving the use of or production of objectionable gases must be performed in the hood.

THE LABORATORY NOTEBOOK AND REPORT

The laboratory notebook is a running record of what actually occurs in the laboratory. The tradition grew from the daily journals of the early experimentalists and modern notebooks still appear somewhat like diaries. This is particularly true of the notebooks of working scientists. Since a notebook is a record of the actual course of the work, it will also contain a record of mistakes and missteps. This is to be expected. It is essentially dishonest to keep two records books--one for use and one for show--because the "good" notebook does not accurately report what has occurred. It is also dangerous to employ this system since the first record tends to be a piece of scrap paper which is easily lost. Another, and perhaps greater, danger of this system lies in the fact that what looks like a mistake or an unproductive path at first might, on later reflection, be found to be correct. Finally, this system is just wasted work since no one expects any scientist to work entirely without error.

The format of a notebook is determined to a large extent by the nature of the work being recorded. We will make some further modifications for class use. However, most notebooks use the following general outline.

1. **The book.** Normally, notebooks are hardbound blank books with numbered pages. Pages are never torn out. If it is acceptable to your instructor, a spiral-bound notebook is convenient for class use because it folds back when open and uses less space on the laboratory bench.

2. **Table of contents.** The first few pages of a new notebook are usually left blank; the names and page numbers of the experiments are entered as they are performed.

3. **The experiment proper.**

   a. **Title.**

   b. **Date.** The date should appear at the beginning of each new experiment. During the course of the experiment, the date should be recorded at the beginning of each day. Enter the work accomplished in each laboratory period under that day's date, and add nothing to these entries at a later date. If you discover on Wednesday that something additional should have been recorded on Monday, write it under Wednesday's date with a note that it should have been a part of Monday's record.

   c. **Description of method.** For a research experiment, this can be a fairly long section, describing what is to be done in some detail. It generally contains references to the original literature. For our general chemistry purposes, a one-sentence reference to the experiment in the laboratory manual will be sufficient.

   d. **Data and experimental.** The criterion of an acceptable laboratory notebook is that the record should be so complete that a second person, with the notebok at hand, could repeat your experiments exactly as you did them and would know the reason you selected the particular procedure you followed. So this section will include things like weighing information, temperature, gas volumes, etc. Especially in synthetic experiments, it will contain observations of color changes, evolution of gases, and formation of precipitates. This should be arranged as logically as possible. Consult the report pages of this manual for examples of the arrangement of data. In this section, be specific in your references to the method section of your own notebook or the laboratory manual so that you will know what you did. [Our mythical second person is important but you are the one who must write the report.] For example, a three-line entry that appears as

$$1.2463$$
$$0.8297$$
$$0.4166$$

is meaningless to a second person (and will become meaningless to you, too, after a few days or weeks have passed). But an entry such as the following

weight of crucible and salt	1.2463 g
weight of empty crucible	0.8297 g
weight of salt	0.4166 g

is perfectly clear (provided that the salt is described elsewhere). The weights given should have been recorded at the balance; take the notebook there, and copy the balance reading directly.

There are two additional points. First, it is better to record too much data than too little. When in doubt, RECORD IT. Second, if a mistake is made, simply draw a single line through the affected data, and note the reason. Do not attempt to obliterate any data. For example, if a weighing was ruined because a gremlin knocked over the weighing vessel, just say so. Think of it as an exercise in the attainment of humility.

e.   **Calculations.** These should be kept in the notebook for the simple pragmatic reason that it is easier to check calculations if you can find them. These need not be done in the laboratory. Many laboratory workers find it convenient to use the right-hand pages for recording procedures, observations, and data and to use the left-hand pages, opposite the data, for calculations based on those data. Again, no calculation is too trivial to record; if you are to weigh 0.10 mole of KCl, show on the left-hand page your addition of the atomic weights of potassium and chlorine to find the weight of 1 mole and your multiplication by 1/10 to determine the weight required.

f.   **Summary.** Every experiment should be concluded with a neat, orderly summary of the data and a discussion of the results. For class use, this may be the laboratory report itself. Follow your instructor's directions.

g.   **Signature.** When several people work on the same project and use the same notebook, they normally sign their own entries. Industrial chemists who must be concerned about patent rights may sign each page of the notebook. Analysts usually sign their analyses, thus taking responsibility for the work. Other cases are determined by the circumstances.

4.   **Form.** The record is kept in ink. It has been traditional to avoid the use of personal pronouns. This is done to reemphasize that the results of an experiment should not depend on the identity of the experimenter. The rule is less firm these days, especially when the experimenter is expressing a personal decision or observation, e.g., "I heard a loud, popping noise just before I..." In any case, the notebook record is generally more informal than the final laboratory report.

5.   **The Laboratory Report.** A formal laboratory report can follow the same format as the notebook. Your instructor may make modifications for specific experiments and, of course, the nature of the work being reported will also affect the format somewhat. A general format is given below:

a.   **Title**

b.   **Object.** See the experiments in this manual for examples.

c.   **Description of the method.** For a class report, this is a 1-3 sentence reference to the method in the laboratory manual.

d.   **Data.** This should summarize the data in the notebook in tabular form. For example, in 3d above, you would give only the weight of the salt--**identified by name**--not the actual weighing data.

e.   **Calculations and Results.** Carefully labeled sample calculations should be included for each significant type of calculation. Then display all of the calculation results in tabular form. If the experiment has only a few numerical results, make sure they are clearly labeled and set apart so they are easy to find.

f.   **Interpretation of Results and Summary.** What did you find? This is also an appropriate place to discuss any errors inherent in the method and their effect on the results.

COMMON LABORATORY EQUIPMENT

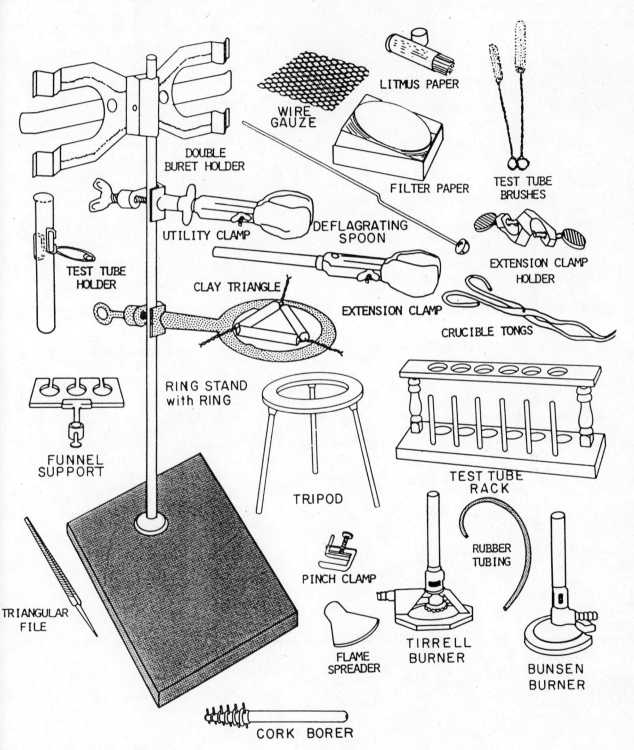

DOUBLE BURET HOLDER

WIRE GAUZE

LITMUS PAPER

FILTER PAPER

TEST TUBE BRUSHES

UTILITY CLAMP

DEFLAGRATING SPOON

TEST TUBE HOLDER

EXTENSION CLAMP HOLDER

CLAY TRIANGLE

EXTENSION CLAMP

CRUCIBLE TONGS

FUNNEL SUPPORT

RING STAND with RING

TRIPOD

TEST TUBE RACK

PINCH CLAMP

RUBBER TUBING

TRIANGULAR FILE

FLAME SPREADER

TIRRELL BURNER

BUNSEN BURNER

CORK BORER

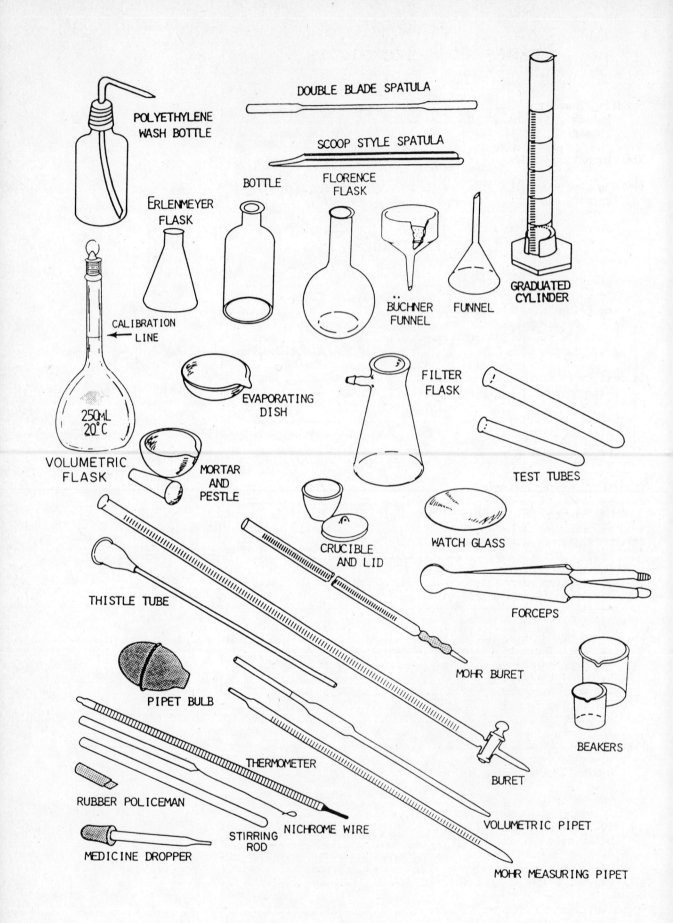

POLYETHYLENE WASH BOTTLE

DOUBLE BLADE SPATULA

SCOOP STYLE SPATULA

BOTTLE

FLORENCE FLASK

ERLENMEYER FLASK

BÜCHNER FUNNEL

FUNNEL

GRADUATED CYLINDER

CALIBRATION LINE

250 mL 20°C

VOLUMETRIC FLASK

EVAPORATING DISH

FILTER FLASK

TEST TUBES

MORTAR AND PESTLE

CRUCIBLE AND LID

WATCH GLASS

THISTLE TUBE

FORCEPS

MOHR BURET

PIPET BULB

BEAKERS

THERMOMETER

RUBBER POLICEMAN

BURET

NICHROME WIRE

STIRRING ROD

VOLUMETRIC PIPET

MEDICINE DROPPER

MOHR MEASURING PIPET

LABORATORY TECHNIQUES

LABORATORY TECHNIQUES

The following sections contain descriptions of some common laboratory techniques and practices. For the most part, it is written for you to read by yourself without your instructor. Read the first sections (pp. 1-7) carefully at the beginning of the term. Skim the rest to become familiar with the topics covered, and then reread them as the techniques are used in the experiments. Thoughtful reading of this section will help prevent time-consuming mistakes.

HANDLING CHEMICALS

Solids

Solid chemicals are usually stored in wide-mouth bottles. ALWAYS CHECK THE LABEL CAREFULLY BEFORE REMOVING ANY CHEMICAL. Remove the lid or stopper, place the lid or stopper so that it will not be contaminated, tilt the bottle, and roll it back and forth until the desired amount of solid falls from the bottle into the appropriate container. Replace the lid or stopper, and return the bottle to its proper location. Spatulas should not be placed in solid reagent bottles. If a solid reagent is compacted or "caked," ask your instructor for assistance. Neither solid nor liquid chemicals should be returned to the bottles from which they were removed--discard any excess in the appropriate waste container.

Liquids

Many commonly used laboratory reagents are solutions, while others are pure liquid compounds such as alcohol or acetone. Liquid reagents are stored in a variety of bottles such as those shown in Fig. 1.

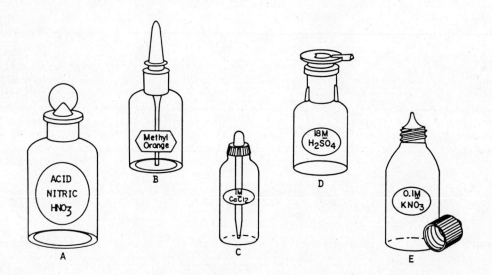

Figure 1. Liquid reagent bottles. (A) Standard reagent bottle. (B-E) Dropper bottles

Dropping bottles are used when very small amounts of the liquids are required in experiments. When larger amounts of liquids are required, standard reagent bottles are often used. Fig. 2 illustrates the transfer of a liquid from a standard reagent bottle. YOU SHOULD ALWAYS CHECK THE LABEL ON A REAGENT BOTTLE CAREFULLY BEFORE YOU REMOVE ANY LIQUID FROM THE BOTTLE. CAREFUL CHECKING OF LABELS PREVENTS MANY ACCIDENTS.

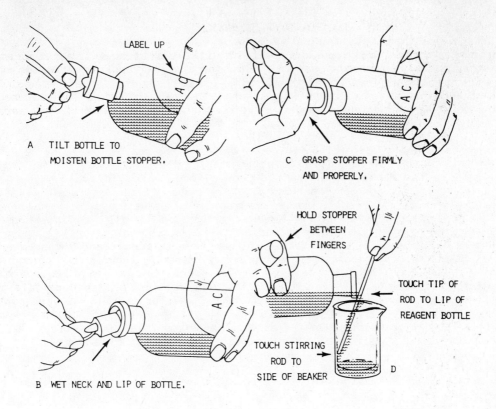

A TILT BOTTLE TO
MOISTEN BOTTLE STOPPER.

LABEL UP

C GRASP STOPPER FIRMLY
AND PROPERLY.

HOLD STOPPER
BETWEEN
FINGERS

TOUCH TIP OF
ROD TO LIP OF
REAGENT BOTTLE

TOUCH STIRRING
ROD TO
SIDE OF BEAKER

D

B WET NECK AND LIP OF BOTTLE.

Figure 2. Transfer of a liquid from a standard reagent bottle

THE LABORATORY BURNER

This section will be read most profitably in the laboratory with your burner at hand. Small burners are used for most common laboratory heating. Their flames will melt soft glass but not Pyrex. (This is handy since beakers and flasks are Pyrex.) The small burners used in many laboratories are actually Tirrill burners although they are usually lumped together with all small burners and called Bunsen burners by everyone except the authors of freshman texts. Other larger burners such as the Meker and Fisher burners can be used to obtain higher temperatures with somewhat larger flames.   These will not be discussed since the operating principles are essentially the same as for the small burners. The maximum temperatures attainable with Bunsen or Tirrill burners are about 1000-1100 $^{\circ}$C; with Meker burners the maximum is about 1200 $^{\circ}$C.   The temperatures inside covered Pyrex or porcelain vessels may be 200-300 $^{\circ}$C less than that, however.

1.   **Construction.**   Burners have three main components: a gas inlet, an air inlet, and a mixing chamber. The mixing chamber is simply the barrel of the burner. At the base of the barrel of Tirrill burners is a perforated sleeve which can be rotated. Rotating this sleeve will screw it onto the base of the burner, thus increasing or decreasing the amount of air that can enter the barrel. The gas intake is conrolled by means of a needle valve at the base of the burner. Unscrew the barrel of the burner and notice the small hole in the circular top of the remaining portion of the burner. If you put your finger over it lightly, and turn the screw at the base of the burner, you will be able to feel the "needle" moving up or down in the hole. This valve is what regulates the flow of gas into the burner.

2.   **Operation.**   (Reassemble the burner.) Shut off the air supply by rotating the sleeve until the air holes are completely covered. Now turn on the gas and light the burner. Notice the sooty, yellow flame. The soot, of course, is just

unburned carbon from the gas. This means that there was not enough oxygen available for complete combustion and that the flame temperature was less than the maximum attainable. Now gradually rotate the sleeve and barrel to admit more air. A blue cone will begin to appear in the center of the flame. At the same time, the yellow color will begin to disappear. A good flame will have a small, pale blue cone in the center surrounded by a larger pale purple cone. The blue region is the reducing part of the flame, and the purple region is the oxidizing portion. The hottest part of the flame is just at the tip of the inner cone.

3. **Adjustments.** The sizes of the two cones of the flame can be varied by adjusting the amounts of both air and gas used while keeping the proportions of the two the same. Thus, the flame can be varied from a long, fairly diffuse ribbon to a short, stubby cone. For most heating, a fairly stubby flame is more efficient and less likely to be blown out. The two most common misadjustments of the burner are obvious from the appearance of the flame. If the flame is tipped with yellow and the inner blue cone is missing or small, there is too much gas relative to the amount of air. Open the air intake. If the flame is purple and burns down the top of the barrel, turn down the gas. (What is happening here?)

4. **Use of the wing top.** The wing top for the burner is used to spread the flame, usually for glassworking. The flame should be adjusted so that the blue portion of the flame extends a short way above the top of the wing top. This portion of the flame should be nearly flat and as intense as possible. Don't forget that the hottest portion of <u>this</u> flame is the line at the top of the blue region.

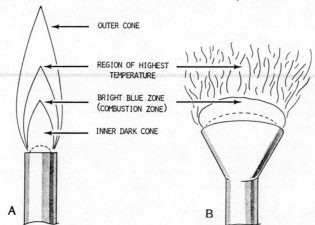

OUTER CONE

REGION OF HIGHEST TEMPERATURE

BRIGHT BLUE ZONE (COMBUSTION ZONE)

INNER DARK CONE

A   B

Figure 3.   (A) Properly adjusted Bunsen burner flame.
(B) With a wing top (flame spreader)

WORKING WITH GLASS

Cutting Glass

Glass tubing or rods can be broken quickly, smoothly, and safely by following a few well-established procedures.

1. The piece of glass tube or rod should be placed on a flat surface and held firmly while a scratch is made with a triangular file or a laboratory glass cutter (a small piece of steel with one serrated edge). The scratch should be made by a single firm stroke--there is no need to saw the glass.

2. ONE OR TWO THICKNESSES OF A CLOTH TOWEL SHOULD BE PLACED BETWEEN THE GLASS AND YOUR THUMBS. THE TOWEL HAS BEEN OMITTED FROM THE FIGURE FOR THE SAKE OF CLARITY. The piece of glass is then grasped firmly as shown (Fig. 4) with the scratch exactly opposite your thumbs. Your index fingers should be approximately 1 1/2 inches apart and your thumbs approximately 1/2 inch apart.

3. Pull and bend the glass quickly for a clean break. Some people find it easier to think about pushing <u>out</u> with their thumbs. It takes a little practice.

4

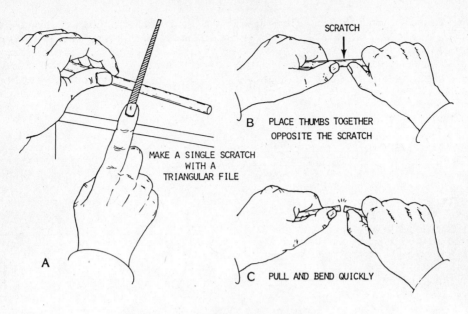

Figure 4. Cutting glass tubing

Fire Polishing Glass

The edges of cut or broken glass are quite sharp and must be fire polished to eliminate sharp edges. The burner flame should be adjusted so that the flame is as hot as possible. The cut end of a piece of glass should be warmed by bringing it near the flame <u>slowly</u> while the glass is rotated. After the end of the glass is warm, it should be held at the top of the hottest part of the flame (rotating the glass constantly) until the sharp edges have melted and become smooth (Fig. 5).

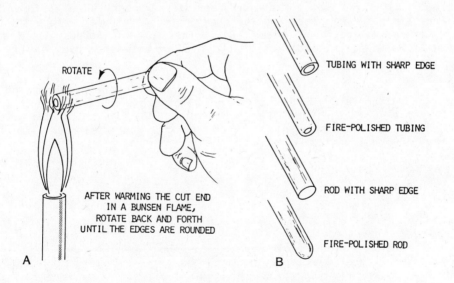

Figure 5. Fire polishing cut glass

Bending Glass

Glass tubing is bent by rotating it constantly and heating in a properly adjusted flame (see Fig. 3). When the glass tube begins to sag, remove it from the flame, and bend it to the desired angle (Fig. 6). Place the bent glass on a surface such as a wire gauze until it cools. CAUTION: HOT GLASS LOOKS EXACTLY LIKE COLD GLASS. DON'T PICK UP A PIECE OF HOT GLASS.

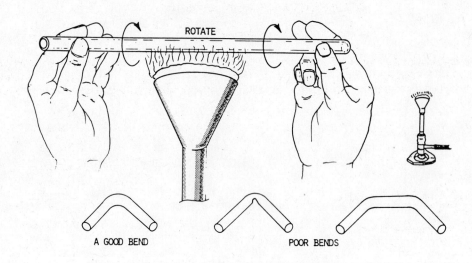

A GOOD BEND

POOR BENDS

Figure 6. Bending glass tubing

Inserting Glass Tubing, Thermometers, and Funnel Stems into Corks and Rubber Stoppers

Glass does not slide into corks and rubber stoppers easily. Therefore, it is necessary to lubricate both the glass and the cork or rubber stopper before inserting glass tubing, thermometers, and funnel stems. Glycerin is one of the best lubricants-- it is readily soluble in water, and excess glycerin can be washed away easily with water.

Place a drop of glycerin in the hole in a cork or rubber stopper and then place 2 or 3 drops of glycerin on the end of the piece of glass to be inserted. Spread the glycerin over the surface of the glass with your index finger. Use a towel to shield your hands. Grasp the piece of glass and the cork or rubber stopper firmly with

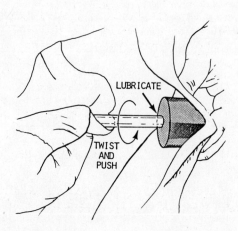

LUBRICATE

TWIST AND PUSH

Figure 7. Inserting glass through stoppers

a towel (Fig. 7) and slowly, with a rotary motion, insert the glass into the cork or rubber stopper. HOLD THE PIECE OF GLASS AS NEAR THE END BEING INSERTED AS POSSIBLE. DON'T FORCE A PIECE OF GLASS--IT MAY BREAK AND CUT YOUR HANDS. After the glass has been inserted, wash the excess glycerin away with water.

DETERMINATION OF MASS AND WEIGHT

Types of Balances

Most laboratories have several types of balances. Two of these--the platform balance and the triple-beam balance--are illustrated in Fig. 8. Although the features of different brands of balances differ somewhat, the general characteristics are shown.

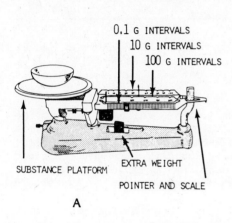
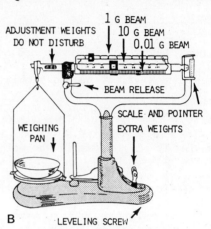

Figure 8. Two kinds of laboratory balances. (A) Platform balance for rough weighing. (B) A triple-beam balance for weighing quantities to ± 0.01 g

Platform balances are used (1) when a large mass or weight must be determined or (2) when only an approximate mass or weight is required. Triple-beam balances may be used when it is necessary to determine a mass or weight to within ± 0.01 gram.

Balances are delicate instruments and must be used properly. Your instructor will provide specific instructions for the balances in your laboratory.

Some of you will have access to direct reading electronic balances that are accurate to ± 0.001 g. Others will have access to analytical balances accurate to ± 0.0001 g (i.e., a tenth of a mg). The analytical balances are used when we wish to determine mass or weight as accurately as possible.

Since there are many kinds of analytical balances in general chemistry laboratories, it is not practical to provide operating instructions for all brands and models. Your instructor will provide more specific directions for the use of the balances in your laboratory.

Experiment 1 deals with the use of the balance and is designed to help you develop good weighing techniques. Since good weighing techniques will be pointless if the balance has been abused and is not in good order, a few points should be reiterated.

1. Never place chemicals directly on the balance pan. Use a beaker, a flask, or weighing paper.

2. Clean up spills immediately. This means transporting the spilled substances all the way to the appropriately labeled waste container.

3. Never weigh liquids in unstoppered flasks in closed balance cases. Nonvolatile, noncorrosive liquids may be weighed unstoppered on triple-beam or other rough balances, if desired.

4. Never place hot objects on balance pans.

5. Never load or unload the balance unless the beam is arrested.

6. Never remove the pans of the triple-beam balances. THEY ARE NOT INTERCHANGEABLE.

7. Never overload a balance.

8. Always arrest the balance beam at the completion of weighing. Remove all weights.

Weighing Techniques

1. **Direct Weighing.** This method is used for samples that are stable in air. It is fairly commonly used for single weighings on the rough balance. It is usually used on analytical balances only when a specific, exact weight of a substance is desired.

   In this case, a clean, dry vessel is weighed empty. Then weights equal to the desired weight of the substance are added to the balance. That is, the balance reading is now the sum of the weight of the empty container and the desired weight of the substance. Finally, the substance is slowly added to the empty container until the balance comes into balance. Near the end, it may be necessary to add the substance in very small quantities, e.g., a crystal at a time.

2. **Indirect Weighing.** This method is used for air-sensitive substances. This includes substances that must be kept dry during the course of a weighing. It is also the method of choice for serial weighings.

   In this case the sample substance will be in some sort of covered container (weighing bottle) to protect it from the air. This will include almost all quantitative experiments since it is essential that the substance not absorb any water. If this technique is used simply to speed a set of multiple weighings, sufficient sample may be placed in a small flask. The weighing bottle or flask containing the sample is first weighed. Then a small amount of the sample is transferred by pouring, if possible, into the vessel in which it will be used. Obviously, whatever goes out of the weighing bottle must end up in that vessel. The weight of the weighing bottle is then checked to see if enough sample has been removed. When it has, the accurate weight of the bottle is recorded. The difference in the initial and final weighings of the bottle represents the weight of the sample. It is good practice to underestimate the amount of sample slightly on the first trial since more sample can easily be removed. It is bad practice to return sample to the weighing bottle. If more than one portion of the sample is to be weighed, note that the final weight of the bottle for the first portion becomes the initial weight for the second portion. Thus, only one more weighing-- after the second portion has been removed--need be made. This means that n portions of sample can be weighed with only $(n + 1)$ weighings required. To weigh the same number of samples individually would require $2n$ readings.

3. **Sample Size.** Generally, there is a fair leeway in the amount of sample required. A set of directions may read: "Take between 4.6 and 5.4 g of NaCl..." or "Take 5 g of NaCl...". These are equivalent, and in neither case must the weight of NaCl be exactly 5.0000 g. The only requirements are that you know the actual weight of the NaCl and record it to as many significant figures as the experiment requires. Thus, a perfectly acceptable weight for the above example might be 4.876 g of NaCl.

SEPARATION TECHNIQUES

Filtration

Filtration is one means of physically separating a solid from a liquid. This means that at the end of a successful filtration, there will be very little solid in the liquid and very little liquid on the solid. Before filtration, the liquid standing on top of the solid is called the <u>supernatant liquid</u> or the <u>supernate</u>. After filtration, the solid is still called the solid or a suitable pseudonym like precipitate, but the liquid is called the <u>filtrate</u>. Three possible cases can be distinguished.

1. **Only the solid is to be collected.** In this case, all of the solid must end in the filter funnel. The solid should be washed free of the supernate with some other liquid <u>in which the solid is insoluble</u>. It is desirable that the wash liquid evaporate quickly. (Choices in general chemistry experiments could be acetone or ethanol.) Since the original liquid is to be discarded, it doesn't matter what gets mixed with it.

2. **Only the liquid is to be collected.** In this case, the solid can be anywhere as long as it is not in the filtrate. The solid usually is not washed unless all of the liquid must be recovered and then is washed only if the addition of the wash liquid will not interfere with the intended use of the filtrate.

3. **Both the solid and the liquid are to be collected.** In this case, the wash liquid is usually caught in a container other than the one containing the first filtrate.

Gravity Filtration (via a Long-Stemmed Funnel)

1. **Folding the filter paper.** Filter paper is available in several diameters; choose a size such that the precipitate occupies approximately one-third or less of the filter paper cone. The filter funnel should be of comparable size so that the folded cone comes to within 1 to 2 cm of the top edge of the funnel; the filter paper should <u>never</u> extend over this edge.

    Fold the filter paper as illustrated in Fig. 9A. Make the second fold so that the edges do not quite overlap, and tear a small corner at the outside to give a better fit at the fold (Fig. 9B). Make the creases lightly, especially near the point. Otherwise, the paper will be weakened, and tragedy may ensue during the filtration. When the paper is folded in this fashion, it fits the funnel snugly around the top of the paper but not nearer the point. This leaves an air space between the glass and the paper which allows a free flow of the filtered liquid.

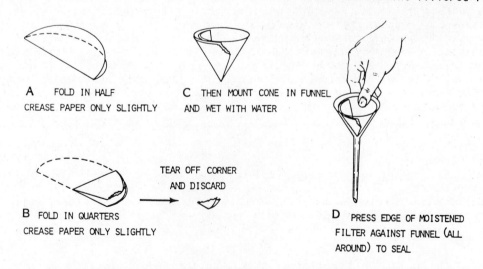

A   FOLD IN HALF
CREASE PAPER ONLY SLIGHTLY

C   THEN MOUNT CONE IN FUNNEL
AND WET WITH WATER

TEAR OFF CORNER
AND DISCARD

B   FOLD IN QUARTERS
CREASE PAPER ONLY SLIGHTLY

D   PRESS EDGE OF MOISTENED
FILTER AGAINST FUNNEL (ALL
AROUND) TO SEAL

Figure 9.   Folding and placing the filter paper in the funnel

2. **Preparing for the filtration.** Insert the folded paper cone into a <u>clean</u> funnel. The paper should not extend above the top of the funnel. The stem of the funnel should touch the wall of the receiving vessel (usually a beaker) so that the filtrate does not splash into the vessel as it is collected. The stem of the funnel should not be immersed in the filtrate. Wet the filter with a liquid as similar as possible to the supernate, i.e., water for aqueous solutions, alcohol for alcoholic solutions, etc. Press the moist upper edge of the cone of filter paper gently against the sides of the funnel with your fingers. This should ensure a good, tight seal. If everything has been done properly, the stem of the funnel should fill with a column of the liquid when the filter paper is filled with liquid. Filtration will be most rapid under these conditions. Sometimes if the stem of the funnel is greasy or too wide, a column of liquid cannot be maintained. In this case, hold your finger over the end of the stem until it does fill and allow the trapped air to escape from the top by temporarily breaking the seal at the three-thickness side of the paper. If that doesn't work, start over with a new filter cone, and this time, clean the funnel.

3. **Filtering and Washing.** Because it is more efficient to wash a precipitate in a beaker than on a filter paper, washing by decantation is usually advisable. Allow the precipitate to settle in the beaker, and then pour the supernatant liquid through the filter, leaving as much of the precipitate in the beaker as possible. Use a stirring rod to guide the stream of liquid and to prevent splashing (Fig. 10-B). Add wash solution to the beaker, stir it, allow the precipitate to settle, and decant the wash solution as before. This washing may be repeated as often as necessary; the wash solution should be tested by collecting a small portion of the solution that runs through the filter and adding a reagent that will produce an observable sign if the unwanted contaminant is still present in the washings. Sometimes the first portions of a mother liquor leaving the filter are cloudy; these should be poured through the filter after its pores have become clogged by larger particles of precipitate. The possibility that refiltration might be necessary indicates the need for collecting the filtrate in a clean beaker, even though the filtrate will be discarded later. Several washings with small volumes of solution are more effective than a single washing with the same total volume of solution.

When washing is completed, the precipitate is stirred with a portion of wash solution and poured down the stirring rod without allowing the precipitate to settle. Final residues are transferred by means of a stream from a wash bottle The last traces of precipitate adhering to the glass are removed by rubbing the glass with a moist rubber policeman; the policeman is in turn cleaned with a stream from a wash bottle or wiped gently with a scrap of moist filter paper, and the precipitate thus removed is added to the precipitate on the filter. Use a specific policeman for each sample; do not interchange them.

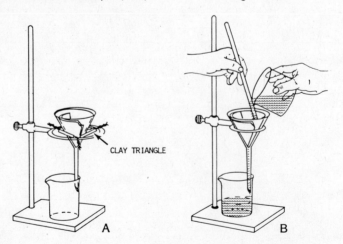

CLAY TRIANGLE

A   B

Figure 10. Filtration. (A) Set-up for filtration.
(B) Pouring solution down a stirring rod

Vacuum Filtration

This is a much more rapid means of filtration since the liquid is pulled through the filter funnel by a vacuum. The receiver--the filter flask--is a heavy-walled Pyrex flask connected by heavy-walled rubber tubing to a water aspirator. Since aspirators have a notorious tendency to back-up and send water back through the connecting tubing, it is the better part of valor to put a trap between the aspirator and the filter flask (Fig. 11A). The filter funnel we will use most often is the Büchner funnel which is used with filter paper. Other types of funnels, designed for use without paper, can also be used (see Fig. 11B).

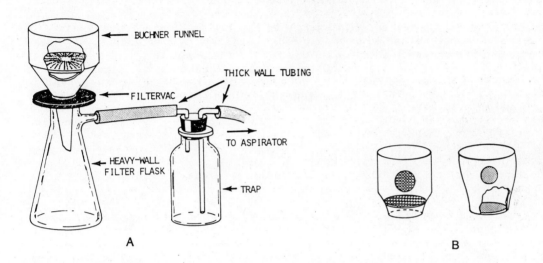

BUCHNER FUNNEL

THICK WALL TUBING

FILTERVAC

TO ASPIRATOR

HEAVY-WALL FILTER FLASK

TRAP

A

B

Figure 11. (A) Vacuum filtering apparatus (Büchner funnel). (B) Two kinds of filter crucibles used to collect precipitate for gravimetric determinations

1. **Preparation.**   The filter paper should cover all of the perforations on the bottom plate of the Büchner funnel. The diameter of the paper should not be any larger than the inside diameter of the funnel. If the filter paper does not fit correctly, cut it with a scissors until it does. Wet the filter paper with liquid exactly as you would for a gravity filtration. Then turn on the aspirator gently. If the system is tight, there should be no way for air to enter except through the filter paper. To check this, cover the top of the funnel with your hand. You should be able to feel the suction. If not, check the connections for leaks and make sure there are no wrinkles or channels in the filter paper.

2. **Filtration.**   The procedure here is essentially the same as for gravity filtration. The chief difference is that washing the solid once it has been collected on the filter paper is more common and less hazardous for beginners than in gravity filtration. To wash a solid on the filter, first draw off as much of the original liquid as possible with suction. Then interrupt the vacuum by pulling the rubber tubing off the aspirator. (If you just turn off the aspirator, water will back-up into the trap bottle.) Pour a small amount of wash liquid onto the solid. Stir them together gently so that the wash liquid comes in contact with all of the solid. (CAREFUL: DO NOT TEAR THE FILTER PAPER!) Reconnect the vacuum and draw off as much wash liquid as possible. Repeat as needed.

Filtration with Fluted Filters

Fluted filter paper is used to speed filtration when suction filtration is not feasible for some reason. This is most often a part of a purification procedure--recrystallization--for a solid. Suppose you have the solid substance you want to collect, but it is contaminated with some other substance. The technique then is to find a solvent in which your product is soluble at high temperatures--i.e., the solvent boiling point--and in which it is insoluble at low temperatures. Ideally, the contaminating substances should not be soluble in this liquid at all. (There are other

11

variations on this theme, but they do not involve fluted filters.) The contaminated product is then heated with enough of the chosen solvent so that all of the desired product dissolves. The problem then is to complete the filtration fast enough to catch all of the insoluble contaminants before the solution has cooled enough for any of the product to begin to reprecipitate. The apparatus is just the same as for gravity filtration. (Why will vacuum filtration not work?) The filter funnel itself is often heated prior to filtration so that contact with the cold glass of the funnel does not cool the hot liquid. The main difference, however, is that the paper is folded in such a way as to increase the amount of surface area in contact with the hot liquid. Once the fluted filter paper is inserted into the warm funnel, the hot liquid is poured through the dry filter paper as fast as possible. If it is necessary to pour the liquid in two portions, keep it warm during the waiting period.

To fold a fluted filter, fold the paper exactly in half and then exactly in fourths. With the paper folded in half, fold it (flute it) just as you would to make a paper fan. Use the crease you made when you folded the paper in fourths as a guide to keep the folds of about equal size. Open the paper to make a cone. There will be two flat sides--the former ends of the fan; crease each of these down the center so that the points of contact with the glass funnel will be the edges of the creases in the filter paper.

Figure 12. Folding a fluted filter

Centrifugation

Another way to separate a solid and liquid is with a centrifuge. A centrifuge is a small machine (with several test tube holders) that rotates rapidly. When a mixture of a liquid and solid is placed in a test tube and then placed in a centrifuge, the solid can be "packed" into the bottom of the test tube by the rotary motion of the centrifuge so that the liquid can be decanted (poured) into another container, leaving the solid behind. Sometimes we use a capillary pipet to withdraw the liquid and leave the solid in the test tube.

Before the centrifuge is turned on, a balance tube must be placed opposite the test tube of interest to prevent excessive vibration which will destroy the centrifuge. The balance tube should be the same size as the test tube that contains the mixture to be separated, and it should contain a volume of water equal to the volume in the other test tube.

Extraction

The most common use of this technique is to separate substances of different polarities. If a reaction has both organic and inorganic products, the organic products will tend to be more soluble in a solvent of low polarity such as ether, and the inorganic products will be more soluble in a polar substance such as water. Thus, if the reaction products are treated with a mixture of two solvents <u>which are insoluble in one another,</u> the polar products will be concentrated in the polar solvent and the nonpolar products in the nonpolar solvent. Take the specific example of water and ether. At the completion of the reaction, water is added, and this is followed by the addition of small volumes of ether. After each addition, the ether and water are shaken in a separatory funnel (Fig. 13a and b) to allow the organic product to dissolve in the ether. The mixture is then allowed to stand so that the ether and water layers can separate (Fig. 13c and d), after which the ether layer is removed and saved. A second small volume of fresh ether is then added to the water layer, the mixture shaken, the layers allowed to separate, and the ether layer again removed and combined with the previous ether extract. Using two or three small volumes of ether in separate extraction operations will remove the product more efficiently than a single extraction with a large volume of ether. This procedure is illustrated in Fig. 13.

The product can be removed from the ether solution by distillation if it is a liquid or by crystallization if it is a solid.

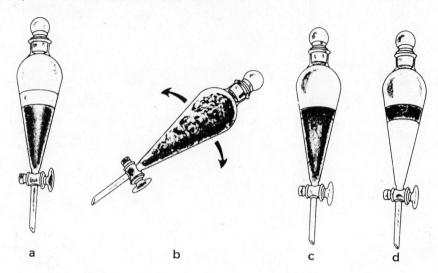

a   b   c   d

Figure 13. Extractions using a separatory funnel.

(a) The solution containing the material to be extracted is added to the separatory funnel; the immiscible extracting solvent is carefully poured into the funnel.

(b) The funnel and its contents are shaken to bring about contact among solvents and the material to be extracted. Pressure created by evaporating solvent or released gas must be relieved frequently during shaking by opening the stopcock when the funnel is inverted.

(c) and (d) After shaking, the liquids again separate, but the material to be extracted may now be concentrated in the extracting solvent.

TREATMENT OF PRECIPITATES

Ignition of Crucible and Precipitates

Some precipitates must be heated to high temperatures to remove water completely. Such precipitates are usually collected by gravity filtration on ashless filter paper, i.e., paper that contains almost no inorganic substances so that no ash (inorganic residue) is left when the paper is burned. In other cases, we heat apparently "dry" compounds, which are in fact hydrated compounds, to remove the water of hydration. High temperatures are often required.

In both cases we use porcelain crucibles. If there is danger of spattering or if we wish to exclude as much air as possible, the crucible is covered. A clean crucible and its cover must always be heated before the sample is placed in it to remove any water or other volatile matter that adheres to the crucible. The process is illustrated in Fig. 14. Ordinary burner flames produce sufficient heat to heat porcelain until it is dull red. At this temperature, water and other volatile materials are vaporized (and expelled) completely. Hot crucibles and their covers should always be handled with crucible tongs. Never place a hot crucible on a cold surface--it may crack. Also, never place a hot crucible on a painted or wooden surface; the wood will burn and the crucible may gain weight from the burned material.

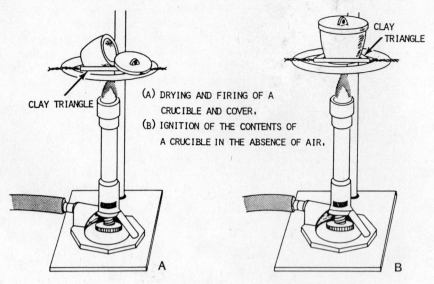

(A) DRYING AND FIRING OF A
CRUCIBLE AND COVER.

(B) IGNITION OF THE CONTENTS OF
A CRUCIBLE IN THE ABSENCE OF AIR.

CLAY TRIANGLE

CLAY TRIANGLE

A

B

Figure 14

Ignition of a Precipitate

Ignition is the process of heating a crucible to incipient redness followed by cooling and weighing. It is first accomplished with the empty crucible so that a precise value for the tare weight may be obtained. When a filter paper and precipitate are present, the heating should follow a definite program as follows.

Drying and Charring the Paper. Support the covered crucible containing the wet filter paper and precipitate on a clay triangle in a slanted position. Heat it with a small flame, touching about the middle of the underside. Do not hurry the drying by using too hot a flame.

When the paper is dry, lift the cover slightly to allow access of air, and increase the heat to char the paper, moving the flame toward the bottom of the crucible. The paper must not be allowed to burst into flame which might cause particles of precipitate to escape with the gases. If a flame appears, immediately close the cover to smother it. Take care that complete combustion occurs in the burner flame so that reducing gases from it are not swept onto the precipitate.

Igniting the Precipitate. When the paper is completely charred, remove the cover from the crucible, and increase the heat gradually until the bottom of the crucible is a dull red. It may be necessary to rotate the crucible occasionally to remove soot and tars that may have condensed during the charring. When the dark organic material has completely burned away, set the crucible upright and continue heating it for 10 minutes.

COLLECTING GASES

Testing for Odor

In some experiments you will collect gases and determine their odors. Extreme caution should be exercised in testing the odors of gases, pure liquids, or aqueous solutions from which gases are being evolved. NEVER BRING SUCH A SUBSTANCE UP TO YOUR NOSE AND INHALE BECAUSE MANY GASES ARE POISONOUS AND OTHERS ARE QUITE CORROSIVE. You should hold the container some distance from your face, and gently waft the vapor toward your face as illustrated (Fig. 15).

14

WAFT THE VAPOR
TOWARD YOUR FACE GENTLY

Figure 15.   Testing a substance for odor

Collection of Gases

1.   **By displacement of air.**   Often we wish to collect samples of gases to use in experiments.   In most such cases, there is no requirement that the sample of gas be absolutely pure.   If the gas is more dense than air, it may be collected by displacement of air as illustrated in Fig. 16.   If the gas is less dense than air, the bottle is inverted and the tube from the generator is turned upward. POISONOUS OR IRRITATING GASES MUST ALWAYS BE GENERATED AND COLLECTED INSIDE A FUME HOOD.

2.   **By displacement of water.**   Often we wish to collect all of a gas that is produced in a chemical reaction.   If the gas is insoluble in water, it may be collected by displacement of water as illustrated in Fig. 17.   Obviously, gases that react with, or that dissolve in, water cannot be collected quantitatively by this method.   A pneumatic trough (a metal pan with an overflow attachment), a plastic pan, or a larger beaker may be used to hold the water (depending of course on the amount of gas to be collected).   The generator may also be a test tube, for

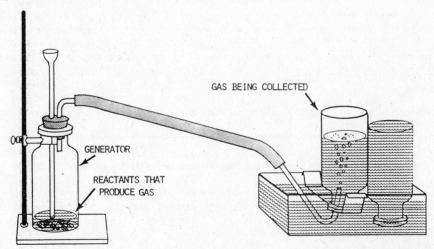

GENERATOR

REACTANTS THAT
PRODUCE GAS

GAS BEING COLLECTED

Figure 16.   Collecting a non-
toxic gas that is
more dense than air

Figure 17.   Collecting a gas
by displacement
of water

example. If the volume of the gas must be determined, it is important that you know the pressure inside the flask as well. The easiest way is to make it equal to the atmospheric pressure by raising or lowering the collection bottle until the water level is the same inside as outside. Atmospheric pressure can be read on the laboratory barometer.

An Improvised Fume Hood

If the fume hood system in the laboratory is inadequate, your instructor may ask you to construct a simple device that will prevent noxious vapors that are soluble in, or react with, water from being discharged into the laboratory. Fig. 18 shows how this can be accomplished when irritating vapors are given off (by a sample being heated in an evaporating dish).

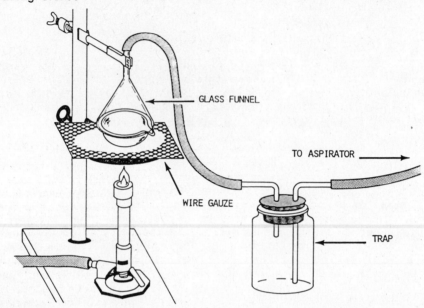

Figure 18. An improvised fume hood for removing irritating vapors

USE OF VOLUMETRIC GLASSWARE

Volumetric glassware is used, as the name implies, for the very accurate measurement of volumes of liquids or solutions. Some pieces, notably burets and pipets, are calibrated "to deliver" a specified volume of liquid. They are labeled T.D. Other pieces such as volumetric flasks are labeled T.C. for "to contain." The two terms are not interchangeable. For example, a good 250-mL volumetric flask will contain 250.0 ± 0.1 mL (± 0.04%) of liquid. On the other hand, not all of the 250 mL can be poured from the flask. As much as 2 or 3 mL may be left on the walls. Even though graduated cylinders barely qualify as volumetric equipment, it is worth pointing out that most graduates are calibrated to contain.

Care and Cleaning Volumetric Glassware

Volumetric equipment is even more vulnerable than most glassware to the effects of misuse. For example, the tips of pipets and burets are easily chipped; they are virtually useless as volumetric glassware once that happens. The stopcocks of burets are another danger point. Make sure they are securely in place and are not dropped. Strong heating of volumetric glassware is apt to set up strains which may cause breakage and will surely destroy the accuracy. Never heat volumetric glassware with a burner or a hot plate. Some of the smaller pieces may be dried in the oven at 110 °C; this should be done in ovens reserved for glassware only.

The use of dirty volumetric glassware is an exercise in futility. Clean, rinsed glassware drains smoothly with no spots of water forming. There are several strong chemical solutions which can be used to clean glassware. Their use in general chemistry laboratories is seldom required. Ordinary dishwashing detergent or the soap provided is usually sufficient. These cleaning agents may be supplemented with organic solvents occasionally. Consult your instructor if ordinary washing techniques fail. The actual cleaning is just like any other dishwashing; use hot water, plenty of soap, a brush, and elbow grease. After the final rinse, the glassware should be rinsed with distilled water (no spots!) and allowed to drain dry. When washing burets, be careful not to push the brush up onto the stopcock. This will spread grease all over the inside of the barrel. In addition, the brush will get grease all over the next buret it touches. It is not strictly necessary for the outside of volumetric equipment to be clean, but it does make it somewhat easier to tell whether the inside is.

Reading Volumetric Equipment

In all cases, your eye should be exactly level with the mark you are attempting to read. This will eliminate parallax error. It is sometimes easier to locate the meniscus of a liquid if a white card with a heavy, <u>straight</u>, horizontal, black line on it is held behind the glassware. The top of the black line is positioned just at the bottom of the meniscus.

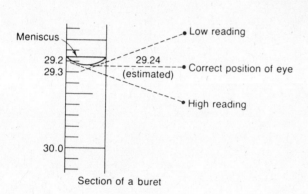

Figure 19.

Estimation of a buret reading to the nearest 0.01 mL. The two etched marks nearest the bottom of the meniscus are for 29.20 and 29.30 mL. Visually divide the distance between the two into 10 equal parts, and estimate on which of these imagined divisions the meniscus is. In this figure, the bottom of the meniscus appears to be on the fourth division, and the reading is 29.24 mL.

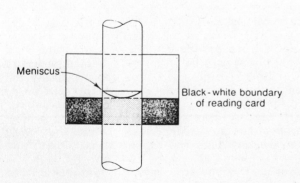

Figure 20.

Proper position for the reading card

Use of Volumetric Pipets

Volumetric pipets are used <u>to deliver</u> specific volumes of liquids quite accurately. The pipet is rinsed with distilled water and then with small portions of the liquid to be measured. A small amount of the liquid is drawn into the pipet (ALWAYS USE A PIPET BULB), the pipet is held nearly horizontal and rolled so that the liquid comes in contact with the entire interior surface, and finally the liquid is allowed to drain through the tip. After the pipet has been rinsed three times with the liquid to be measured, liquid is drawn into the pipet until the liquid level stands above the calibration mark. The tip of the pipet is wiped with a <u>clean</u> tissue to remove the liquid on the outside, the liquid level is allowed to fall slowly just to the calibration mark, and the hanging drop is removed by touching the tip of the pipet against the wall of the waste beaker. The specified amount of liquid is then allowed to drain into a new container. When the liquid appears to have drained from the pipet, wait ten seconds, touch the tip of the pipet to the inside surface of the container to remove the hanging drop, and remove the pipet. DO NOT BLOW OUT THE LAST BIT OF LIQUID IN THE PIPET. When the above instructions are followed, the pipet will deliver the specified volume. Pipets are available in a variety of sizes--commonly, 5, 10, 25, and 50 mL. Fig. 21 illustrates the use of volumetric pipets.

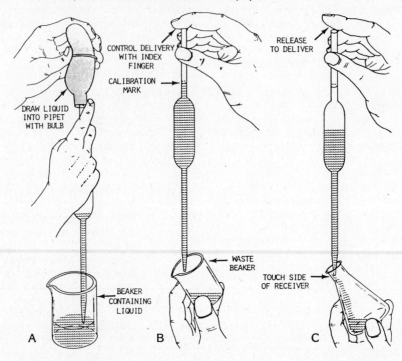

Figure 21. Volumetric pipets (A) draw the liquid into the pipet with a rubber bulb, (B) control the delivery of liquid with the forefinger, and (C) deliver the liquid with the pipet touching the side of the receiver

Use of Volumetric Flasks

The following procedure may be used in dissolving a solid and diluting to a specified volume in a volumetric flask. The solid should be in a small beaker, usually the one into which it was transferred in an indirect weighing. Dissolve or suspend the solid in a minimum volume of the solvent, and transfer it to the volumetric flask using a funnel whose stem extends <u>below</u> the calibration lines. Any solid in the beaker should not stick to the inside neck of the flask. If the solid is difficult to dissolve, this part of the procedure may be repeated several times. When the solid (solution) has been transferred, pour more solvent into the beaker to rinse it, and then pour the rinse liquid through the funnel. Then pour more solvent through the funnel to wash it. Remove the funnel and carefully add solvent. If the neck of the flask has come in contact with the solution (probably), use this added solvent to rinse the neck of the flask. Fill the flask to within 1 mL of the mark, using a long medicine dropper as the liquid starts to fill the neck of the flask. Let the sides drain for about a minute, and then dilute to the mark with the medicine dropper. Be careful not to get any solvent above the mark at this point.

The very shape of the flask makes mixing difficult. Swirl the flask gently until all of the solid has dissolved. Add the stopper, invert the flask, and shake it to mix. Insert and shake the flask at least ten times to be sure of good mixing.

Finally, return the volumetric flasks when you are finished since they are expensive and the stockroom has only a limited number.

Use of the Buret

Stopcock lubrication. Begin by removing all of the old lubricant from both the plug and barrel of the stopcock. If your instructor permits, you may use chloroform, ethyl ether, or petroleum ether for this cleaning. The plug and barrel will dry to an even luster if clean. Grease the stopcock by applying a narrow band of lubricant around the upper (thick) end of the plug. Hold the plug so that the hole is horizontal. At the narrow end, apply two short, narrow strips on the top and bottom of the plug, stopping short of the hole itself. Insert the plug in the barrel and rotate the plug slightly to spread the lubricant evenly. A well lubricated stopcock will be transparent with no striations visible. Beware of using too much grease; the hole will become plugged!

Some burets are equipped with Teflon® stopcocks (white opaque material), which require NO grease.

Mounting the buret. The buret should be mounted vertically (not at a slant), using a buret holder if possible. The vertical mounting is very important. Otherwise, the reading will be in error, due to parallax, as shown in Fig. 19.

Reading the buret. If the buret is clean but not dry, place a small amount (5 mL) of the solution to be used in the buret. Roll this solution around inside the buret, and then drain it through the stopcock. Repeat the rinsing procedure three times. This will prevent the dilution of the solution to be used for titration. Fill the buret with the solution to a point above the zero line. Let some of the liquid drain through the stopcock until there are no bubbles either in the stopcock or in the tip of the buret. Release more solution so that the liquid level is at or slightly below the 0.00-mL mark. Let the sides of the barrel above the solution drain about a minute. Then take the initial reading. The initial value need not be 0.00 mL; in fact, it is better if it is not since a value different from 0.00 mL discourages subconscious fudging. For example, 0.27 mL would be a perfectly acceptable initial reading. After the desired amount of solution has been released from the buret, e.g., at the end of a titration, again allow the barrel above the liquid level to drain about one minute. Then take a final reading. Your instructor will demonstrate the correct way to hold a stopcock and some of the techniques involved in delivering very small quantities of solution such as half drops.

Storage. Burets are a bother to clean, so once they are clean, try to keep them that way. The best way to store them, given the space limitations of a teaching laboratory, is filled with distilled water, corked, and labeled in a desk buret drawer. At the end of the term, for more permanent storage, the buret should be drained and washed if needed. All grease should be removed from the stopcock plug and barrel. A narrow strip of paper should be inserted in the barrel along with the clean plug. The plug should be held in place with a rubber band if necessary. This procedure will prevent the plug from freezing in the barrel.

Titration techniques. The sample to be titrated is usually placed in an Erlenmeyer flask (the receiving flask). The stopcock (rubber tubing and glass bead on Mohr burets) is used to control the rate at which the liquid in the buret—the titrant—is added to the receiving flask (Fig. 22C). The receiving flask is rotated gently during the titration to ensure thorough mixing. A piece of white paper should be placed under the receiving flask so that the indicator color change can be detected easily. Near the endpoint of the titration (the color fades slowly), the inner wall of the receiving flask should be "washed down" with distilled water so that all of the titrant comes into contact with the solution being titrated.

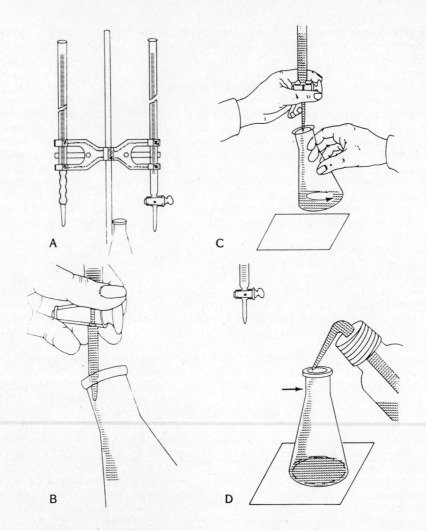

Figure 22.   **Titration. (A) Titration apparatus. (B) Operation of a stopcock with the left hand. (C) Adding titrant. (D) Washing wall of receiving flask during titration**

Calibration

Volumetric equipment should be checked to make sure that it does contain or deliver the amount of solution it is supposed to, within tolerance. Particularly, with student-grade glassware which has been much used, it is important to determine the actual volume of solution contained or delivered. In more advanced courses, these calibration procedures serve more to check student technique than to check equipment.

1.   **Calibration of volumetric flasks.**   Clean and dry the flask. Weigh it and its stopper to the nearest mg, or 0.1 mg for small flasks. Fill the flask to the mark with water of known temperature, stopper, and weigh again. From the density of water at the given temperature, calculate the volume of water contained.

2.   **Calibration of volumetric pipets.**   These pipets, also known as transfer pipets, are calibrated to deliver one volume only, e.g., a 10-mL pipet. For graduated (Mohr) pipets, follow the procedure given for burets. Clean and weigh to the nearest 0.1 mg a small, stoppered Erlenmeyer flask. Fill the pipet to the mark with water of known temperature. Drain the pipet into the Erlenmeyer, stopper it, and reweigh. Again, calculate the volume of the water delivered from its density at the known temperature. This may be repeated as a check simply by adding another pipetful of water to that in the flask and weighing again.

3. **Calibration of burets.** Read the section on burets before attempting this procedure. In calibrating burets, the volume of solution delivered at various readings is important. Begin as before by weighing a small, clean, stoppered Erlenmeyer flask to the nearest milligram. Fill the buret with water of known temperature, take an initial reading, and deliver a precisely known volume of about 10 mL into the flask. That is, the volume need not be exactly 10.00 mL, but you must know exactly what it is, e.g., 9.51 mL. Stopper and weigh the flask. Repeat this at about 10-mL intervals until the buret capacity is reached. Again, given the density of the water at the known temperature, calculate the volume of water actually delivered at each reading. Calculate the buret corrections at each reading. For example, if the volume read was 9.51 mL and that delivered was 9.47 mL, the correction is − 0.04 mL. Plot these corrections in hundredths of mL (y axis) against the buret reading in mL (x axis). Connect the points with broken lines. (This is one of the few fever chart graphs you will ever draw.) Use these corrections whenever you use the buret.

4. **Relative calibrations: 10-mL pipet vs. 50-mL volumetric flask.** It is sometimes less important to know how much a volumetric flask actually holds than it is to know that one pipetful represents a known fraction of its volume. In this case, the 10-mL pipet will be 1/5 the volume of the flask. Since both the pipet and the flask markings may be slightly in error, this usually requires marking the flask with a special filling mark. Clean and dry the 50-mL volumetric flask. Fill the 10-mL pipet to the mark with water; transfer the water to the flask. Do this a total of five times. Place a label on the neck of the flask so that the top of the label marks the bottom of the liquid meniscus. Put your initials on the label, and cover it with cellophane tape.

MELTING-POINT DETERMINATION

The melting behavior of a compound is often a simple test of its purity because an impure compound melts over a range of temperatures and usually at a lower temperature than does the pure compound. Consequently, a chemist is frequently called upon to determine the melting point and melting range of compounds he or she prepares in the laboratory.

To determine the melting point, a small quantity (0.0001 to 0.0002 g) of the powdered compound to be examined is placed in a melting-point capillary, and the capillary is fastened to a thermometer by use of a rubber band or a slice of rubber tubing (Fig. 23A). The thermometer and capillary are then inserted to the immersion mark into a beaker containing a liquid that is heated gradually with constant stirring while the material in the capillary is watched carefully (Fig. 23B). The thermometer is read at the first sign of collapse of the solid material in the capillary and again at the exact temperture at which the last of the solid disappears. For substances with unknown melting points, it is often convenient to make a preliminary determination by rapidly heating the bath liquid to obtain an approximate melting point, letting the

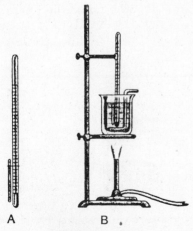

A   B .

Figure 23. Simple apparatus for
determining melting points

Figure 24. Melting point
tube, Thiele

bath cool a few degrees, and heating the bath much more slowly (i.e., about one degree per minute) for the accurate determination of the melting point of the compound, using a second capillary. In place of the beaker and stirrer, a Thiele melting-point tube may be used (Fig. 24). Heating the side arm with a small flame produces convection currents in the liquid which heat the thermometer slowly and evenly.

To fill the melting-point capillary, crush or grind a small portion of the crystalline sample on the watch glass with a spatula, scrape the powder into a mound, and scoop it into the capillary by pushing it against the spatula. Shake down the material by gently tapping the capillary, supported in an upright position, on a hard surface. Add material until you have enough to see easily, i.e., until you have a column equivalent to one-half to three-fourths the length of the thermometer bulb tightly packed in the bottom of the capillary.

Mixed Melting Point

The mixed melting point technique is particularly useful for identification of organic compounds since the technique is simple and the determination is rapid. The technique simply involves mixing (by grinding thoroughly) approximately an equal amount (~10 mg) of the unknown compound with each of 3-4 known possible compounds that have melting points close to the unknown and determining the melting points of the resultant 3-4 mixtures. If the unknown is the same as one of the known compounds, the mixed material will still be a pure substance, and it will melt at the characteristic melting point of the compound. However, if the mixed material contains two different compounds, the melting point of the mixture usually will be lower than for either of the individual pure components. That is, an impurity depresses the melting point of a compound. Thus, by comparing the melting points of the different mixtures with the melting point of the pure unknown compound one may determine which added compound gives no depression of the melting point.

Drying Crucibles or Samples; The Desiccator

A desiccator provides a closed container of dry air. The atmosphere in the desiccator is kept dry with a chemical, called a desiccant or drying agent, that absorbs water. The desiccant generally used in general chemistry is Drierite (anhydrous calcium sulfate).

The desiccator can be used either to dry a moist chemical preparation or to aid in the ignition of a crucible to constant weight. A warm crucible is placed in a desiccator to cool to room temperature so that moisture does not absorb on the crucible during cooling. Adsorbed moisture would increase the weight of the crucible to a varying degree, thus making the weight measurement less precise.

An inexpensive student desiccator can be constructed by use of a wide-mouth glass jar with a screw-on lid and a Pyrex watch glass (illustrated below). Remove the watch glass and pour the previously used Drierite into the container marked "Used Drierite." This used Drierite will be recycled. Pour fresh Drierite into the jar

**Research Chemists'
Desiccator**

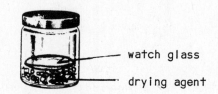

watch glass

drying agent

**An Inexpensive
Student Desiccator**

until the layer of Drierite is 1-2 cm deep. Place the watch glass (concave side up) on top of the Drierite. Place the object to be dried on the watch glass; then screw the lid on the desiccator.

Desiccators should remain closed as much as possible to avoid the unnecessry introduction of moisture from the laboratory.

You should change the Drierite each time a new experiment is begun.

SEMIMICRO TECHNIQUES

The procedures described below employ a technique known as semimicro--or very small scale--analysis. They are most often used in general chemistry in qualitative analysis. These methods are faster and more conservative of materials than are the macro methods you will be using for most of the experiments. Small (4-mL) test tubes are used for most of these reactions. Reagents are added dropwise using a medicine dropper (or a similar dropping tube). Filtering is replaced by first centrifuging the reaction mixture, thereby causing the precipitate to settle to the bottom of the test tube, and then removing the clear solution above the precipitate with a micro pipet or dropping tube. Precipitates are transferred using small spatulas (Fig. 25). A brief description of some important semimicro techniques follows.

Transfer of Reagents

Since liquid reagents are added in drops, micro pipets and dropping tubes (Fig. 25) must be both readily available and kept absolutely clean. A drop from a dropping tube has about twice the volume of one from a 15-µL pipet. In the procedures that follow, a drop refers to that from a dropping tube. If the 15-µL pipets are used, the number of drops should be doubled. Tubes should be <u>thoroughly rinsed immediately after each use</u>. Otherwise, residues of previous uses may remain on the walls of the tubes, causing contamination of the sample and misleading or incorrect results.

Great care should be taken to avoid adding a large excess of any reagent since this frequently displaces the chemical equilibria in solution so as to cause analytical difficulties. However, reagents must be added until precipitation appears to cease, that is, until an added drop of reagent fails to produce further precipitate as it diffuses through the reaction mixture. Fig. 26 illustrates the transfer of a reagent.

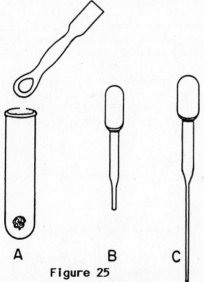

Figure 25

(A) Transfer of a precipitate using a small spatula.
(B) Medicine dropper. (C) A micropipet

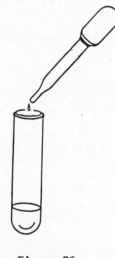

Figure 26

Transfer of a reagent
using a dropping tube
or a micropipet

Heating Solutions

Solutions can be heated by placing the test tubes in a beaker of hot or boiling water. If a flame is used, the test tube should be moved around the edge of the flame so a large area of the tube is being heated. Point the tube away from your neighbor's face, and take care to avoid over-heating the small test tubes to prevent the sudden ejection of liquid from the mouth of the tube.

Decantation

This consists of centrifuging, followed by removal of the decantate (the clear liquid) from the precipiate.

Centrifugation is the most rapid method of separating a precipitate from a solution. Power-driven centrifuges (Fig. 27) are easy to operate, but certain precautions must be observed in using them. The centrifuge must first be balanced. This is done by placing a second test tube containing an equivalent volume of water in the holder opposite the tube containing the mixture to be centrifuged. Care must be taken to avoid catching ties, hair, apron strings, etc., in the centrifuge.

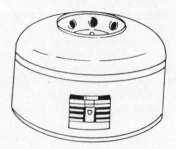

Figure 27. A power-driven centrifuge

Most mixtures require no more than a minute of centrifugation to separate a precipitate from the decantate. After centrifugation, the clear liquid can be withdrawn from the precipitate using a pipet with a long stem.

Washing Precipitates

Following removal of the decantate, the precipitate must be washed to remove from it any ions adsorbed from the solution from which it was separated. Washing usually consists of adding 1 or 2 mL of distilled water to the precipitate, agitating the mixture with a stirring rod, centrifuging it, and removing the wash water with a pipet.

Dissolving Precipitates

When possible, precipitates are dissolved in the test tubes in which they are formed, using the smallest possible volume of dissolving reagent. Large amounts of precipitate frequently are transferred to casseroles which can be manipulated easily.

Adjusting the pH of a Solution

To make acidic solutions basic or basic solutions acidic, the appropriate solution is added dropwise until, based on your knowledge of the situation, you feel the pH is close to that desired. Stir the mixture well with a stirring rod, and then touch the end of the rod to a piece of pH paper. Add reagent to the mixture, and repeat the test until the pH reaches the desired point.

GRAPHICAL DISPLAY OF DATA

This section is divided into two distinct parts. In the first section, we go once over (very) lightly on the mechanical steps necessary for you to produce a graph which is acceptable in polite company, e.g., to your instructor. The second section treats the subject in more detail and more mathematically.

Simple Graphing

A graph is a pictorial way of representing the relationship between two variables such as the solubility of a substance in a solvent and the temperature of the solution. In order for that relationship to be as clear as possible, there are a few practical matters to remember.

1. **Every graph needs a name.** There is no need to be fanciful about this. For the solubility example we used above, the heading might be "The solubility of barium nitrate in water" or "The temperature dependence of the solubility of barium nitrate in water."

2. **Axes must be labeled.** Obviously, for the graph to be meaningful, one needs to know which direction represents temperature and which represents solubility. One also needs to know the <u>units</u> in which the variables are expressed. It is important to know whether temperature is given in $^{\circ}$C or K or $^{\circ}$F, for example.

3. **The scale must be clear.** In the physical sciences, this is most often indicated by marking the scale units just below or beside the axis. As you will see on the sample graphs, the markings need not appear at every division, just often enough to make the scale clear and the reading easy. The markings must extend the full length of the axis or at least as far as you have data or intend to extrapolate.

4. **The choice of scale should be rational.** For example, if the temperature readings have been made only to the closest tenth of a degree, it makes little sense to choose a scale which allows you to express thousandths of a degree. On the other hand, unless the graph is purely for display purposes, you might think twice about a scale that only allows you to express temperature to the nearest degree. (Compare Figs. 31 and 32.) In most cases, the scales for the two axes can and should be chosen independently. It is worth noting that the axes need not begin at (0, 0); they need only cover the region of interest.

5. **Data points should not be obscured.** As you can see on the samples, the points representing experimental data are enclosed in circles (or squares or triangles, etc.), and the curve connecting the points is drawn only to the edge of the circle and <u>not</u> through the points. In more advanced work, the size of the circle or square is chosen to indicate the magnitude of the uncertainty in the measurement.

6. **The data points should be connected by the best smoothed curve possible.** Your graphs should seldom if ever look like fever charts with straight lines connecting the individual points. The best smoothed curve (or line) is the one that comes closest to the greatest number of points. There are mathematical techniques for determining the best curve, but they need not concern us here.

Serious Graphing

Data Tables. The data from an experiment often appear as a pair of quantities giving the value of one measurement when the value of a second has been set at a particular magnitude. A second experiment under another condition gives another pair of values, and other experiments give other pairs, so that a table like Table T-1 can be made. Here, an experimenter measured the number of grams of barium nitrate that 100 g of H_2O will dissolve when the temperature is 0 $^{\circ}$C and again at 10 $^{\circ}$C, and so forth.

Table T-1. Solubility of Barium Nitrate in Water

Temperature ($^{\circ}$C)	Solubility (g/100 g of H_2O)
0	5.0
10	7.0
20	9.2
30	11.6
40	14.7
50	17.1
60	20.3

Graphs. Although a table of this sort reports the data, the trend in the solubility as the temperature is changed can be assessed more readily if the data are plotted on a graph. It is evident that the solubility is a <u>function</u> of the temperature, and, as in algebra, we plot the <u>dependent variable</u> as the <u>ordinate</u> (along the vertical axis) and the <u>independent variable</u> as <u>abscissa</u> (along the horizontal axis) on a pair of lines at right angles to each other (Cartesian coordinate axes). Each axis must be assigned a <u>scale</u> so that a certain distance along the axis corresponds to a certain value of the variable. For a plot of the data of Table T-1, for example, we might choose to let 10 $^\circ$C be represented as a distance of 20 mm and 5 g of $Ba(NO_3)_2$/100 g of H_2O be represented also by 20 mm and prepare a piece of graph paper for plotting as in Fig. 29. The positive directions of the axes are taken from left to right and from bottom to top; this rule holds also for negative numbers so that -15, for example, lies on the horizontal axis to the left of -10 and, similarly, -4 is below -2 on the vertical axis.

Independent and Dependent Variables. The independent variable in a scientific measurement usually can be identified as the quantity over which the experimenter has control. In the solubility measurement, for example, the experimenter has control of the temperature; he or she may choose to measure the solubility at 9 or 22 $^\circ$C instead of at 10 and 20 $^\circ$C. Hence, the temperature is the independent variable and is to be plotted horizontally (as abscissa). The solubility at the temperature he or she has chosen, however, is a fact of nature that he or she cannot alter; the solubility is thus the dependent variable and is plotted vertically (as ordinate). We speak of plotting the dependent variable <u>against</u> the independent variable; therefore, the direction to "plot the solubility against (or versus) the temperature" means that the temperature is to be the abscissa.

To plot the data of Table T-1, we plot the paired values (temperature, solubility) as coordinates of experimental points. For the second line

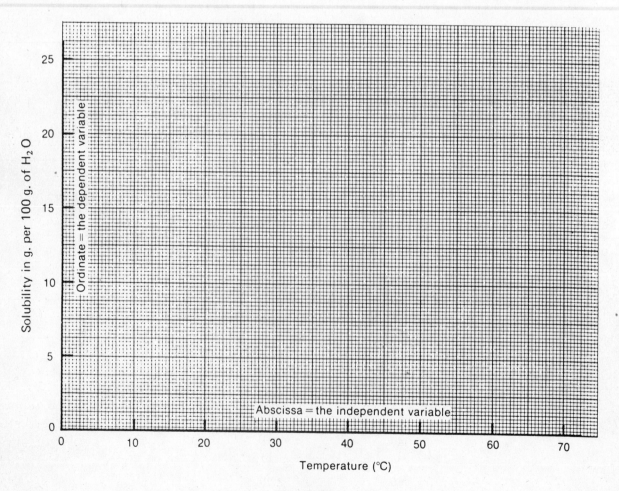

Figure 29

of the table, for example, the coordinates are (10, 7.0), and we move horizontally to the scale reading corresponding to 10 $^{\circ}$C and then vertically to the position corresponding to 7.0 and mark a point. We proceed similarly for other points: over to 20 and up to 9.2, mark a point, and so forth. It is usually convenient to draw a small circle around the point, for better legibility. The plotted data will then look like Fig. 30.

Note that the points are plotted as exactly as possible, dividing by eye, the distance between lines on the graph into smaller divisions as necessary. There is no line on the graph paper that corresponds to 9.2; the nearest line represents 9.25. Hence, the distance between 9.00 and 9.25 is considered to be divided into five parts, and the point for 9.2 is placed four-fifths of the distance from 9.00 and 9.25. It is not necessary that all graphs start at the origin (0, 0). Had the measurements been made only between 50 and 100 $^{\circ}$C, for example, it might have been convenient to mark the intersection of the axes as (50, 15) and increase from those values.

Drawing the Curve. Fig. 30 properly records the experimental data of Table T-1. The advantage of a graphical display, however, is that it enables us to predict values of the dependent variable for values of the independent variable at which experimental measurements have not been made. To make this prediction, we rely upon experience which tells us that things in nature usually change gradually from one value to another. (They do not always change gradually; consider, for example, the quantum jumps in energy that occur in the electronic excitation of an atom.) If the change is gradual, we connect the experimental points of a graph by a smooth curve, representing a continuous function which will have no abrupt changes of direction. (Note that abrupt changes of direction sometimes do occur.) If nature demands a smooth curve, apparent deviations from a smooth, nonbumpy curve must be the result of experimental error, and our curve may not actually touch all of the experimental points. Thus, in completing the graphing of the data in Table T-1 as in Fig. 31, we reject exact contact

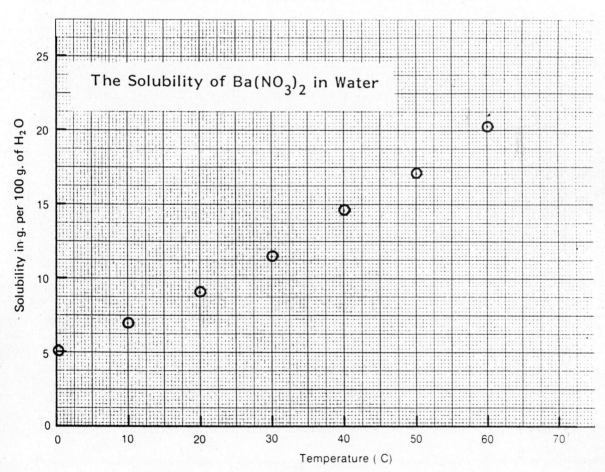

Figure 30. The solubility of Ba(NO$_3$)$_2$ in water

with the points at 40 and 50 °C in favor of making a smooth curve. Although the curve
may be drawn free hand, it is better to use a ruler (for straight lines) or to draw
against the edge of a properly bent flexible spline or a plastic French curve placed at
successive positions to fit the points.

**All graphs should be titled, the scale numbers marked, and the axes labeled
with correct units.**

Choice of Scale. In plotting Figs. 30 and 31, the scale was chosen to
correspond to the precision of the data. Since the data are measured to one decimal
place, we want to plot them in such a way that two points differing by a few decimal
places will appear at recognizably different places on the graph. It would be possible
to plot the data as in Fig. 32, but this small scale shows only the gross trend of the
data and does not do justice to the care with which the measurements were made. The
precision of the data for both ordinate and abscissa should be considered in deciding
upon a scale.

Comparison with Theory. Graphs of data are often used to compare the data
with a prediction from theory. A common procedure is to cast the prediction into a
form that can be graphed as a straight line, $y = mx + b$. In this equation, y is the
dependent variable, x the independent variable, m the _slope_ of the line, and b the
intercept on the y axis. The intercept is the value of y when $x = 0$, and the slope of
a straight line is obtained from the coordinates of any two points on the line--

(x_1, y_1) and (x_2, y_2)--by setting up the quotient $\dfrac{y_2 - y_1}{x_2 - x_1}$. The value of this quotient

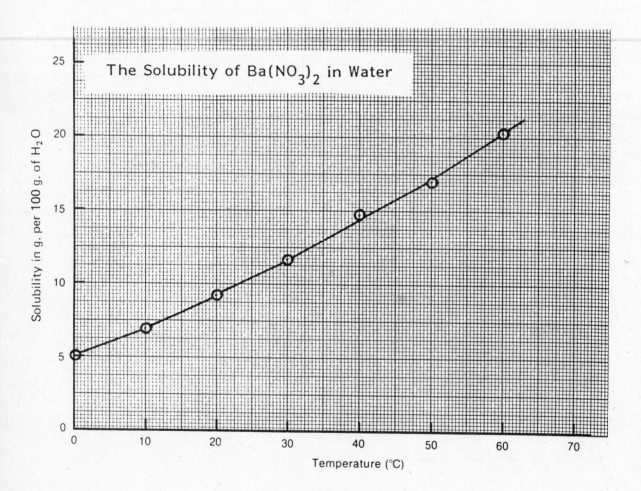

Figure 31

28

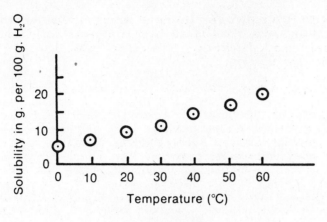

Figure 32

is the slope, m. Note that (x_1, y_1) and (x_2, y_2) are points <u>on the line</u>; if experimental error causes the measured points to lie off the line, their coordinates should not be used in determining the slope, but new coordinates should be read from the best straight line through the experimental points. The <u>best</u> straight line is the one that is drawn as closely as possible to as many of the points as possible. If theory predicted, for example, that the data of Table T-1 should fit a straight line (the theory does not make such a prediction), this straight line would be drawn as the solid

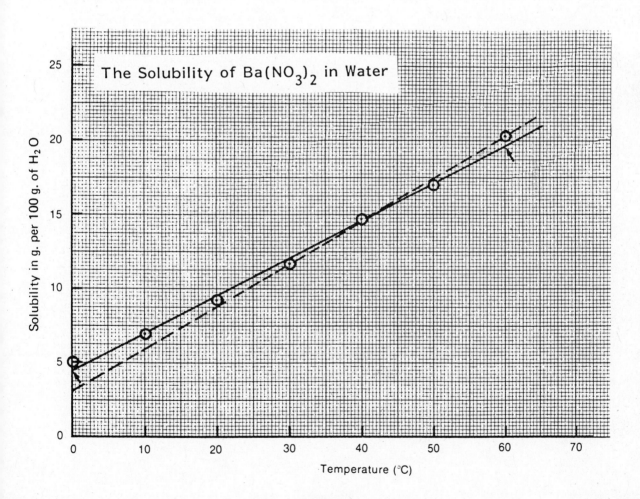

Figure 33

29

line of Fig. 33 and not as the dotted line. The slope of the solid line may be obtained from the marked points as

$$\frac{19.75 - 4.35}{60.0 - 0.0} = 0.267 \text{ g per 100 g per degree.}$$

Derived Functions as Variables. Often the dependent and independent variables to be plotted are not the quantities that are directly measured but quantities derived from them by mathematical manipulations. Thus, in Exp. 14, the measured quantities are pressure and temperature. The theoretical equation to be tested, however, is

$$\log p = A - \frac{B}{T}.$$

The quantities to be plotted are, therefore, the logarithm of the pressure against the reciprocal of the temperture. The reciprocal of the temperature remains the independent variable and is plotted as abscissa because the temperature is the quantity over which the experimenter has control, while log p is plotted as the ordinate. In plotting logarithmic quantities, it should be remembered that the logarithm of a number less than 1 is negative.

A.   USE OF THE SINGLE-PAN ANALYTICAL BALANCE

B.   DETERMINATION OF THE DENSITY OF A LIQUID

Objective

To learn to weigh precisely; to learn to compare the reliability of weighings of the same objects made on balances of different sensitivities; to determine the density of a liquid

Equipment Needed

Single-pan analytical balance with a sensitivity of 0.0001 g; porcelain crucible with lid; crucible tongs; top-loading or triple-beam balance with a sensitivity of 0.01 g; 10-mL volumetric pipet; two 50-mL Erlenmeyer flasks

Reagents Needed

NaCl solutions for unknowns for Part B

PART A: USE OF THE SINGLE-PAN ANALYTICAL BALANCE

INTRODUCTION

The measurement of mass is one of the fundamental operations performed in any chemical laboratory. Balances are mechanical devices for determining the mass of an object; they are constructed in several styles and sizes and can measure a variety of mass ranges. Laboratory balances vary from rather rough devices (platform or triple-beam balances) sensitive to 1 or 0.1 g to precision analytical instruments sensitive to 1 part in 10^{-6} g.

Single-pan analytical balances with a sensitivity of 0.0001 gram (0.1 milligram) are now common. For objects weighing approximately 10 g, this sensitivity means there is an uncertainty in the mass measurement of 1 part in 100,000, or 1 part in 10^5.

Modern single-pan analytical balances occur today into two dominant types. One type uses a hybrid of mechanical and electronic forces, whereas the more recently developed electromagnetic force balances use electronically generated forces entirely. In both cases, a null indicator is used to determine when the internal force balances the gravitational force of the sample.

The mechanical single-pan balances employ the principle of substitution weighing and utilize an optical level mechanism or an electronic digital readout to record the small increments of mass ranging from 0.1 mg to as much as 0.1 g.   The balances are simple to operate because no weights are transferred outside the balance cover by hand. Instead, the weights are located inside the balance housing and are normally never seen by the operator. The operator manipulates the weights by turning a series of dials on the outside of the balance. Associated with each dial is a scale that records the mass of the weights manipulated. When the weighing is completed, the mass of the object on the pan is read directly from the scales of the balance.

A hybrid analytical balance is identical to the mechanical balance described above, except that the balance beam is never allowed to swing widely. When a sample is added to the balance, a servo-controlled electromagnetic force is applied to the beam to minimize the displacement motion and to restore the beam to a predetermined reference position.

For the electromagnetic force balance, the force associated with the sample being weighed is mechanically coupled to a servomotor that generates the opposing magnetic force. When the two forces are balanced, the average electric current in the servomotor coil is proportional to the force that is holding the mechanism at the equilibrium reference position. The balance readout (digital or optical scale) is proportional to the amount of current passing through the coil when the equilibrium position is established.

An excellent discussion (with color pictures) of the different types of analytical balances is given by Schoonover in reference 1.

Pictures and operating instructions for some typical single-pan balances are given in Appendix I. Your instructor will provide specific operating instructions for the analytical balances available in your laboratory.

In order to weigh masses accurately to within 0.0001 g, it is necessary to use careful techniques to insure the safety of the instrument and to obtain maximum reliability and reproducibility in the measurements.

Errors in Weighing

Moisture. Condensation of water vapor from the atmosphere onto dry samples, glassware, and precipitates may add several milligrams to the weight of the sample. Precipitates should be weighed rapidly if they are open to the air; a preferable procedure is to weigh the dry sample in a stoppered bottle that has been stored in a desiccator.

Temperature. All weighing should be done at room temperature. Hot objects, such as heated crucibles (Experiment 4), set up convection currents which tend to push up the pan of the balance and reduce the apparent weight.

Static Electricity. A static charge can be set-up on the surfaces of glass vessels when they are rubbed with a dry cloth, especially in the low humidity conditions of the Southwest or on cold, dry winter days. The charge may cause the balance to behave erratically. This effect usually does not present a major problem except with very large objects.

Buoyancy. According to the principle of Archimedes, a large container will be buoyed by the air in the balance case. The true weight of the object (i.e., its weight if weighed in a vacuum) will be greater than the weight obtained in air by the net buoyancy on the object. The buoyancy effect on the weights partially cancels the buoyant effect of the air on the object. The net buoyancy on the object being weighed is the difference between the buoyance experienced by the object (because of its displacement of a volume of air) and that experienced by the weights. The larger the volume of the object and the smaller its density, the greater will be the buoyancy effect. In most cases, buoyancy effects are not significant because the volume and density of the object being weighed are such that they result in an insignificant buoyancy correction. When objects are weighed in large containers, one usually takes the difference between the weight of an empty container and the weight of the container with the object. In such cases, the buoyancy effect of the large container is offset.

Care of the Balance

Analytical balances are expensive, precision-made instruments and do not function properly if abused. **Each student is responsible for cleanliness, knowledge of proper operating steps, and adherence to the following rules whenever he or she uses the balance.**

Rules for the Analytical Balance

1. Never move the balance. Check to see that the balance is level, as indicated by the leveling bubble. If it is not level, ask the instructor for assistance.
2. Be sure that the beam arrestment control is in the arrest position before placing the object to be weighed on or removing it from the pan.
3. Always move the arrestment control gently. Avoid a sudden jar, which might damage the mechanical parts of the balance.
4. Always close the balance case before adjusting the weights. Air currents must be avoided for accurate weighing.
5. Do not overload the balance. The balances in the laboratory are designed for maximum loads ranging from approximately 100 to 200 g. (See your instructor for specific operating instructions for the type of analytical balance that you are using.)
6. Never weigh any chemical or moist object directly on the balance pan. Clean up any material that is spilled on the pans or within the balance case immediately, making sure the beam arrestment control is in the arrest position.
7. Never place a hot object on the balance pan; its apparent weight will be incorrect because of convection currents set-up by the rise of heated air.
8. Avoid using your fingers to handle objects that are to be weighed. Do not touch the balance pan or the pan support. Care must be taken to prevent weight changes caused by absorption of moisture or oil from the hand.
9. When a weighing is completed, return the arrestment control to the full-arrest position, remove all objects from the pans, and close the balance case.

Steps in Weighing

The procedure for weighing consists of four major operations: checking the zero point to be sure the balance is properly adjusted, placing the object to be weighed on the pan, setting the weights by use of the appropriate knobs if you are using a mechanical balance, and reading the mass of the object from the appropriate dials or scales.

1. **Checking the zero point.** This must be done each time the balance is used. (If this is the first time you have used this type of balance, start this step only after instructions from the laboratory instructor.) If all students have been taking proper care of the balance, then as you begin to use a balance, the balance pan will be empty and clean, the mechanical weights will be set to zero, and the balance windows will be closed. If this is not true, remedy the situation. The balance pan may be cleaned with the brush provided. Then proceed.

    a. Slowly turn the beam arrestment control to the fully released position.
    b. When the optical scale (or digital printout) is at rest, use the zero adjustment knob to set the scale 0-line to coincide with the pointer.

2. **Placing the object on the pan.** The object to be weighed may be placed on the pan only when the balance is completely arrested. Whenever possible, use a pair of tongs or tweezers to avoid transmitting moisture and oil from the hands to the object to be weighed. After placing the object on the pan, close the window.

3. **Setting the weights.**

   a. Set the beam arrestment control in the <u>partial-release</u> <u>position</u>.

   b. Estimate the weight of the object and begin dialing the weights, using the large increments of weight first. The procedure for obtaining the final weight setting varies with the type of balance used. Obtain the specific instructions for your type of balance from your instructor.

   c. After setting the 1- and 10-g weights, return the beam to the arrest position.

   d. Fully release the beam and allow the optical scale to come to rest. Remove your hands and arms from the balance and balance table, since your mass on the table may affect the weighing.

4. **Reading the mass.**

   a. Read, making any adjustments of the micrometer or digital control that are necessary.

   b. <u>Arrest</u> <u>the</u> <u>beam</u> and remove the object, return any mechanical weight settings to zero, and then close the doors. Check to see if you have accidentally spilled any material on or in the balance; if you have had a spill, clean it up before leaving the balance area.

Since a major portion of your laboratory results will depend on your ability to make rapid and valid measurements of mass with the analytical balance, it is essential that you learn to use the instrument as soon as possible. Your instructor will show you how to use the balance during the first and second laboratory periods. You will then be asked to determine the mass of an object. If you experience difficulty in using the balance, ask your instructor for additional help.

NOTEBOOK AND REPORT

Before going to the laboratory, carefully read the steps in weighing and the rules for the care of the balance.

Prepare a data table (a sample is given on p. 41) in your laboratory notebook in which to record the results of your weighings on the two different types of balances.

On a triple-beam balance, determine the mass of crucible and its lid separately; repeat the mass determination of crucible and lid together.

On an analytical balance, determine the mass of a crucible and lid.

PROCEDURE

Before coming to the laboratory, read the section "Determination of Mass" (pp. 7-8) of the **Laboratory Techniques** of this manual. On the laboratory top-loading or triple-beam balance, determine the mass of a porcelain crucible and its lid separately and then together. Does the total weight equal the sum of the component weights? Repeat the complete weighing sequence four times and record the values. Determine the average deviations (Exp. 34) to obtain a measure of the precision of this type of balance.

Using the general rules and sequences of weighing steps listed previously and the specific operating instructions for your type of analytical balance, determine the mass of the crucible, its lid, and the combination five times on the single-pan analytical balance. From these data, calculate the average deviations, and compare the precision with that of the triple-beam balance. Ignoring all sources of error except the limitations of the balances, indicate the reliability of the determinations of mass from each of the balances.

PART B: DETERMINATION OF THE DENSITY OF A LIQUID

INTRODUCTION

Laboratory investigations in the physical sciences usually involve making measurements and observations and then interpreting them. In this part of the experiment you will measure both the volume and the mass of a sample of a liquid and then use these results to calculate the density of the liquid. Since density is defined as mass per unit volume (density = M/V), a density determination involves weighing a <u>measured volume</u> of a substance. Because only two measurements are required--the volume of a sample and its weight--this experiment provides an excellent opportunity to learn to perform these operations correctly. If an error is made, the determination can be repeated quickly. These weight and volume measurements will be used many times in this and other courses in the physical, biological, and applied sciences.

You will determine the volume of your unknown using a 10-mL pipet. If you first calibrate the pipet, the accuracy of the result will be increased. With careful work you should be confident of the volume that the pipet delivers to the nearest hundredth of a mL, or about 1 part in 1,000.

The measurement of the mass of the measured volume of a liquid raises the question of which balance to use. You need to use a balance which provides the same level of accuracy as the volume measurement. In this case the single pan analytical balance is needed. On these balances it is just as easy to weigh to the nearest 0.1 mg (0.0001 g) as to the nearest mg, but this is more accuracy than the use of the pipet for measuring the volume can justify. (See reference 2 or Experiment 3 for details.)

The density of a substance at a given temperature is a characteristic property of the substance, and it may give a valuable clue about the identity of a substance.

PROCEDURE

Read **Laboratory Techniques:** "Determination of Mass" and "Use of Volumetric Glassware," pp. 7-8 and 16-20, respectively.

Calibration of Pipets

It is necessary to determine precisely the volume of the 10-mL pipet you use in this experiment. Calibration is accomplished by weighing exactly the amount of water that the pipet delivers. The pipets used in these laboratories will deliver between 9.90 and 10.10 mL, with most delivering very close to 10.00 mL.

To calibrate your pipet, weigh a small, clean, dry Erlenmeyer flask or beaker as accurately as possible. Handle the flask with crucible tongs to avoid contaminating it with oil and moisture from your skin. Record the weight of the flask in your notebook, and later transfer that datum to the proper space on the report form. Carefully pipet 10 mL of distilled water into the weighed Erlenmeyer flask. Weigh the flask and its contents, record the weight in your notebook,

Weigh a small flask or beaker.

Carefully pipet water into container

Table 1-1. Density of Water

Temp. (°C)	Density (g/mL)	Temp. (°C)	Density (g/mL)
18	0.9986	23	0.9976
19	0.9984	24	0.9973
20	0.9982	25	0.9971
21	0.9980	26	0.9969
22	0.9978	27	0.9967

and then calculate the mass of water delivered by your pipet. Repeat the experiment at least once, and calculate to four significant figures the average mass delivered by your pipet. The density of water varies with temperature, as shown in Table 1-1. Determine the temperature of the water you used and then use the appropriate density to calculate the volume delivered by your pipet.

Determination of the Density of an Unknown Liquid

Your instructor will provide an unknown liquid. RECORD THE NUMBER OF THE UNKNOWN IN YOUR LABORATORY NOTEBOOK BEFORE YOU BEGIN WORK. The unknown solutions were prepared by dissolving NaCl in water, The densities of these solutions are between 1.000 g/mL and 1.300 g/mL.

Record the unknown number.

Weigh a small, clean, dry Erlenmeyer flask as accurately as possible. Handle the flask with crucible tongs. Record the weight of the flask in your notebook. With the same pipet you calibrated, carefully deliver 10 mL of your unknown solution into the weighed Erlenmeyer flask. If your pipet does not deliver 10.00 mL, use the actual volume of your pipet (you have just determined it) to calculate the density of your unknown solution. Weigh the flask and its contents, record the weight in your notebook, and then calculate the density of the solution.

Repeat density determination 2 times.

Repeat the density determination. Pour out the liquid that was placed in the flask for the first determination. It is not necessary to wash the flask. Dry the outside of the flask thoroughly so that no drops of water or solution adhere to it. Weigh the empty flask again (Why can't you use the first weight of the empty flask?), record its weight, pipet 10 mL of the unknown into the flask, and weigh again. Calculate the density based on this set of data. Repeat the determination a third time.

The results of three good determinations should agree within 0.1%. If necessary, refer to Experiment 34 "Treatment of Experimental Data" to decide if all three of your values should be used in calculating the average value for the density of your unknown.

REFERENCES

1. Schoonover, R. M.: "A Look at the Electronic Analytical Balance", Analytical Chemistry, **1982**, 54, 973A-979A.
2. Skoog, D. A., and West, D. M.: Fundamentals of Analytical Chemistry. 3rd edition. Holt, Rinehart, and Winston, New York, 1976, Chapter 6.
3. Day, Jr., R. A., and Underwood, A. L.: Quantitative Analysis, 4th edition, Prentice-Hall, Inc., Engelwood Cliffs, NJ, 1980, Chapter 4.

Experiment 1

**USE OF SINGLE-PAN ANALYTICAL BALANCE;
DETERMINATION OF THE DENSITY OF A LIQUID**

PRELABORATORY QUESTIONS

Name _Todd Moore_   Lab Instructor _Brian Stearns_

Student ID No. _300-68-3620_   Date _1/9/95_

1. Setting the zero point of the analytical balance is, in effect, adjusting the beam of the balance so that its pointer rests in the center of the optical scale. When a weighing is completed, the beam is returned to its zero point position. What error will be introduced if you fail to set the zero point of the balance before making a reading?

   There will be a random error in the measurement to either the positive or negative side of the true value. This is because the scale is effectively miscalibrated for the measurement

2. How will each of the following errors influence the results of your density determination, i.e., will your value be too high or too low? Why?

   a. Failure to rinse the pipet with the unknown solution after rinsing it with distilled water.

   This will cause the density of the solution to appear to be lower than it actually is, because the solution will be further diluted by the water remaining on the walls of the pipet

   b. Failure to remove the hanging drop from the tip of the pipet when the liquid is transferred into the container in which it is to be weighed.

   The result will be low because the measured mass will be slightly less than what is expected in volume.

   c. Blowing the last bit of liquid from the pipet when the liquid is transferred into the container for weighing.

   This will add to the apparent density because moisture from the mouth and lungs will condense on the inside of the pipet, and add to the mass of the measured sample

   d. Having water on the inside bottom of the container in which the liquid is to be weighed before you weigh the empty container.

   If this occurs before calibration, it will cause the apparent density to be ~~greater~~ Less, because the volume of the pipet will appear to be greater. If this occurs after calibration, there will be no effect on the results

37

3. Should the second sample of your unknown solution be pipeted into the flask which contains the first sample that was weighed? Why?

   yes, the flask will be reweighed before adding the new solution, so any thing that remains will not effect the results of the experiment.

4. How will the accuracy of your determination be affected if you pour the first sample from the flask, dry the exterior of the flask with a towel, weigh it again, and then pipet the second sample? Why?

   I will reduce the accuracy, because the old solution will remain in the pipet, an change the density of the next sample taken into the pipet

5. Would the accuracy be any better if you used a different clean, dry flask for the second and third samples? Why?

   No, because you allways reweigh the flask before each trial

6. Set-up each problem in an orderly way as you work the following problems. Show all units, and express each answer with the appropriate number of significant figures.

   a. If 50.00 mL of a liquid weighs 60.00 g, what is its density?

   $D = M/v$

   $D = 60.00g/50.00mL = 1.200 g/mL$

   b. What is the weight of 50.0 mL of a liquid of density 1.30 g/mL?

   $D = M/v$ $1.30 g/mL \cdot 50.0mL = 65.0g$

   $DV = M$

   c. If no balance is available and you need 60.0 g of carbon tetrachloride (density = 1.59 g/mL), what volume would you measure?

   $D = M/v$ $60.0g / 1.59 g/mL = 37.7 mL$
   $V = M/D$

   d. Commercial reagent-grade hydrochloric acid solution is 37.2% HCl and 62.8% H_2O by weight. The density of the solution is 1.19 g/mL. What weight of HCl is contained in 250 mL of commercial HCl solution?

   $D = m/v$

   $DV = m$

   $(1.19 g/mL \cdot 250 mL) \cdot 0.372 = 97.3 g$

Experiment 1

USE OF THE SINGLE-PAN ANALYTICAL BALANCE

REPORT SHEET

Name_____   Lab Instructor_____

Student ID No._____   Date_____

Weighings on the Platform or Triple-Beam Balance

	Trial					average value	average deviation
	1	2	3	4	5		
wt of crucible (g)	____	____	____	____	____	____	____
wt of lid (g)	____	____	____	____	____	____	____
sum of above (g)	____	____	____	____	____	____	____
wt of crucible and lid, together (g)	____	____	____	____	____	____	____

Weighings on the Analytical Balance

	Trial					average value	average deviation
	1	2	3	4	5		
wt of crucible (g)	____	____	____	____	____	____	____
wt of lid (g)	____	____	____	____	____	____	____
sum of above (g)	____	____	____	____	____	____	____
wt of crucible and lid, together (g)	____	____	____	____	____	____	____

Sample Calculation for Average Value

Sample Calculation for Average Deviation

Calibration of Pipet

	Trial		
	1	2	3
1. wt of container + water (g)	___	___	___
2. wt of empty container (g)	___	___	___
3. wt of water (g)	___	___	___
4. temp of H_2O ($^{\circ}C$)	___	___	___
5. volume of water used (mL)	___	___	___
6. volume of pipet (mL)	___	___	___

average value for volume of pipet ___ mL

Sample Calculations:

Unknown Liquid

	Trial		
	1	2	3
1. wt of container + unknown liquid (g)	___	___	___
2. wt of empty container (g)	___	___	___
3. wt of unknown (g)	___	___	___
4. volume of unknown used (mL)	___	___	___
5. density (g/mL)	___	___	___

average value for density ___ g/mL

unknown number ___

Sample Calculations:

THE SEPARATION AND QUANTITATIVE DETERMINATION

OF THE THREE COMPONENTS OF A MIXTURE

Objective

To illustrate a separation of the components of a mixture on the basis of their differences in solubility in different solvents

Equipment Needed

One 250-mL suction filter flask and trap bottle; 3-inch Büchner funnel or a long-stemmed funnel; filter paper to fit the Büchner or long-stemmed funnel; clamp and iron ring stand; stirring rod; balance (accurate to 0.001 g); aspirator; two beakers (approximately 100 mL); one 125-mL Erlenmeyer flask; medicine dropper or 3" of 8-mm glass tubing; rubber hose; flexible flat metal spatula or rubber policeman; gas burner; simple desiccator; plastic squeeze bottle

Reagents Needed

Unknown mixtures containing one organic and two inorganic components, ~6 g/student; dichloromethane; distilled water; 3 M nitric acid, HNO_3

INTRODUCTION

When two or more substances that do not react chemically with each other are present in a sample, the result is a mixture in which each component of the mixture retains its own physical and chemical properties. A chemist often faces the problem of separating a mixture and determining (qualitatively or quantitatively) the components of the mixture. For example, in chemical research, in industrial manufacturing, and in testing laboratories, separation and identification of components of mixtures on a routine basis can often mean the difference between success and failure for a new process or between life and death in hospitals.

Each component of a mixture is an element or a compound that has its own fundamental properties such as physical appearance, solubility, density, melting point, and boiling point. A pure substance will melt at a definite temperature, and if the external pressure is fixed, it will boil at a different definite temperature. The substance also has a specific solubility: a certain quantity of the pure component will dissolve in a fixed amount (e.g., 100 mL) of a given solvent at a constant temperature.

Some of the physical methods often used by a chemist in the separation of mixtures are decantation, filtration, crystallization, distillation, and sublimation. In this experiment we will use the techniques of filtration and crystallization.

We will be concerned with separating an unknown powdered solid, containing three components, into its individual components by means of solubility differences and then determining the weight percentage of each component.

Each of the components has different solubility characteristics in dichloromethane and water as follows:

Organic component: This will be a molecular organic compound with a relatively low melting point. It will be soluble in dichloromethane (and several other organic solvents).

Inorganic, water-soluble salt: This is an ionic compound which is soluble in water but not soluble in dichloromethane. It will have a relatively high melting point.

Metal carbonate or oxide: This is also an ionic, high-melting compound that is not soluble in water. It will react with acid solutions; thus, it will be at least partially soluble in aqueous acid solutions.

Each component of the mixture can be analyzed qualitatively to identify the specific ions or molecules present. Such specific tests and procedures are given in Experiment 3. If your instructor has assigned Experiment 3, be sure to save each component of your mixture in a labeled container for later use.

BACKGROUND

You should be familiar with the following terms before attempting Experiments 2 and 3:

percent	qualitative	funnel
percent carbon	quantitative	filter paper
polar compounds	cations	solute
non-polar compounds	anions	solvent
melting point	ionic	solubility
melting range	covalent	extraction
organic	filtrate	slurry
inorganic	precipitate	rubber policeman

TECHNIQUES

In this experiment, filtration and weighing are important procedures and must be be accomplished carefully. Review the procedure and operating instructions for the analytical balance given in Experiment 1 before starting this experiment.

Filtration. Separation of a solid from a slurry of solid and liquid by filtration is a frequent task in the chemistry laboratory. Filtration can often be done by gravity using a long-stemmed funnel as shown on p. 11. The process can often be speeded by applying gentle suction to draw the liquid (the filtrate) through the filtering medium (commonly porous paper, filter paper). A convenient set-up is shown on p. 10. Determine whether your laboratory locker contains the long-stemmed funnel or the Büchner funnel, and read the appropriate section (p. 9 or p. 11) on filtration techniques.

NOTEBOOK AND REPORT

Your notebook record of this experiment should include, besides the usual statement of purpose, a brief outline of procedure, i.e., which steps are to be accomplished in sequence and which are to be undertaken while waiting for filtration or other slow steps, calculations of the percentage composition, answers to the assigned questions, and a table to show the raw data collected. These data should show weights of empty and filled containers, net weights of the components, and volumes of solvents used. It is always advisable to prepare a skeleton table in your notebook before you go to the laboratory so you will have an organized manner in which to collect the data and so that your notebook record will be intelligible to you and your instructor at a later date.

CAUTION: <u>Organic solvents such as acetone and dichloromethane should be used only in well-ventilated areas. Avoid breathing vapors and contact with skin. Acetone is flammable; therefore, it must only be used inside the hoods since many people may be using their burners to heat water for another part of this experiment.</u>

PROCEDURE

A.   Before coming to the laboratory, complete the chart in the Prelaboratory Questions by referring to a Chemical Rubber Company <u>Handbook</u> <u>of</u> <u>Chemistry</u> <u>and</u> <u>Physics,</u> Lange's <u>Handbook</u> <u>of</u> <u>Chemistry,</u> or other chemistry handbooks, and your text.

Find data before lab period.

B.   Examination of Your Mixture

1.   **Physical Appearance.** Record in your notebook any aspects of your unknown sample that can be described, such as color, odor, size, and shape of the crystals and whether it looks heterogeneous or homogeneous.

Record physical properties of your unknown sample.

2.   **Solubility.** Solubility is defined as the quantity of one substance that will dissolve in another substance (usually a liquid) at a given temperature, forming a mixture that is both transparent and uniform in appearance. The resultant solution may be called a <u>homogeneous</u> <u>mixture</u>.

The separation scheme to be used is based on the fact that certain compounds are very soluble in organic solvents such as acetone or dichloromethane, whereas they may be essentially insoluble in water. Also, other compounds may be quite soluble in water but not in dichloromethane or acetone.

Carefully examine the separation scheme which follows, and prepare a stepwise outline in your notebook to be followed in the laboratory.

Scheme to Separate the Three-Component Mixture

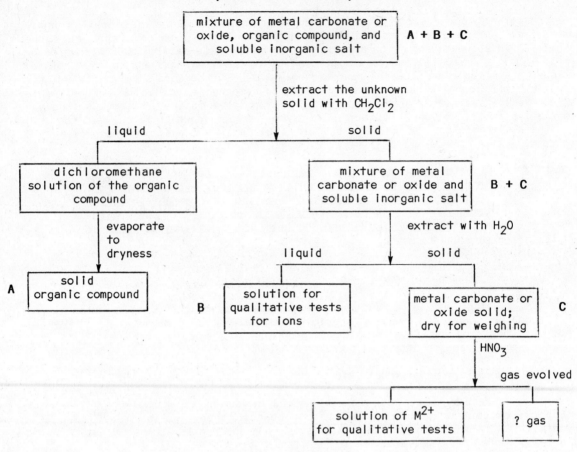

3. **Extraction with Dichloromethane.** First, look over the data sheet (p. 52) which is included with this experiment. Since all of the weights in this experiment are found by subtracting the weight of the container from that of the component(s) plus container, you must weigh the beaker or filter paper <u>before each extraction</u>. Weigh (to 0.01 g) a 100-mL beaker and a piece of filter paper that will fit the funnel you will be using (**Note 1**). (Record all weights on the data sheet in your notebook immediately!) Add approximately 6.0 g of your unknown to the 100-mL beaker, re-weigh (to 0.01 g) the beaker and sample, and record. DO NOT waste time trying to weigh exactly 6.0 g. The <u>actual</u> weight is all that is important here.) The organic component, **A**, is then extracted by adding 25 mL of CH_2Cl_2 (dichloromethane) to the beaker and stirring with a glass rod for 3 minutes, being careful not to spill or splash the solution. Allow the insoluble material (the inorganic solids) to settle.

Weigh sample and treat with CH_2Cl_2.

Use the weighed filter paper for this part of the experiment. If you are using the Büchner funnel, assemble the suction filtration apparatus as shown on p. 11. Place the filter paper flat in the funnel, and wet it with a little dichloromethane. Gently turn on the aspirator <u>just enough</u> to suck the wet filter paper snugly against the funnel. **CAUTION:** <u>If the suction is very hard, you may tear a hole in the filter paper or you may pull the finely divided solid materials into the pores of the filter paper, thereby making the filtration go abnormally slow.</u> Decant most of the liquid in the beaker onto the filter as you maintain a very gentle suction. Since some of the organic compound will remain with the wet inorganic solids, add a second 25 mL of CH_2Cl_2, and proceed as before, except this time empty the beaker with the inorganic solids (**B & C**) onto the filter paper

Filter with gentle suction.

46

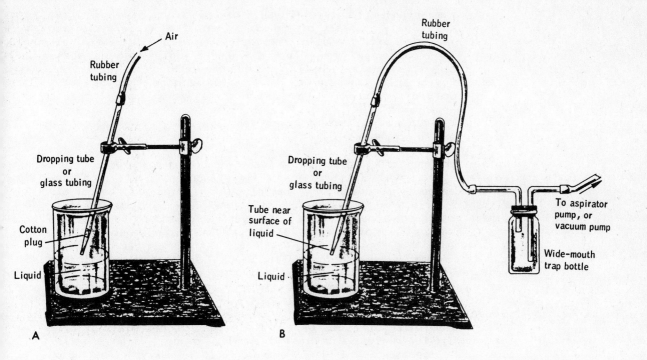

Figure 2-1. Illustration of apparatus to evaporate the dichloromethane; (A) for an air stream; (B) for a vacuum

after siphoning most of the solid. When all of the solvent has filtered through the funnel, carefully remove the filter paper, and put
it in a safe place to dry. When it is dry, weigh it, and determine
the weight of the inorganic solids (**B & C**) by subtraction. If the
mass shown on the balance is constantly changing, then it is not dry.
Wait another 5-10 minutes and try again.

Repeat the
CH₂Cl₂
extraction.

NOTE: Whenever possible, do two parts of the experiment simultaneously. For
example, if the inorganic solids are dry, you can be weighing them while
allowing the CH₂Cl₂ to evaporate from the organic component.

If you are using a long-stemmed funnel, see pp. 9-10 for a
description of filtering with it. The following additional instructions for filtering should be noted as well:

a.   Do not attempt to press the filter paper against the
funnel.

b.   Fold the filter paper several times back and forth to
form "pleats" (as demonstrated by your instructor). Be
sure to wet the filter paper with the appropriate
solvent (CH₂Cl₂) first for extracting the organic component and later H₂O. Separate the two inorganic
solids. DO NOT MIX SOLVENTS!!!

c.   Avoid clogging the filter paper by pouring too much of
the solid into the funnel at the beginning of the
filtration. Pour most of the liquid through first. To
do this, tip your beaker to a slight angle, and siphon
the clear or slightly cloudy liquid with a medicine
dropper. Put the liquid through the filter. This will
allow the filter paper to pass most of the liquid
rapidly. When the extraction is complete, stir the

remaining solids (with CH_2Cl_2, of course) to make a slurry, and quickly pour all of the slurry onto the filter. Wash the remaining bits of solid from the beaker with more solvent and use a rubber policeman (p.   , Fig. 2-3 top). Wash the medicine dropper with CH_2Cl_2, and add the washings to the filter.

d. <u>Never</u> allow the funnel to be filled more than halfway! Solvent will creep up and over the sides, carrying some solid with it.

e. Use the minimum amount of solvent possible. This speeds the entire process.

Back to the extraction.

Weigh (to 0.01 g) a 100-mL beaker, and then pour the filtrate from the filter flask into the beaker for evaporation. The dichloromethane can be evaporated fairly rapidly by directing a stream of air across the surface of the beaker as shown in Fig. 2-1. Since dichloromethane vapors are somewhat toxic, the evaporation should be <u>performed in a hood</u>. The stream of air can be a compressed air line source that is filtered with a loose cotton plug (Fig. 2-1A), or it can be created by a vacuum pump or an aspirator (Fig. 2-1B). Continue evaporation of dichloromethane while you perform the next extraction. Remove all or nearly all of the dichloromethane. Record the colors and appearances of the solid and the CH_2Cl_2 solution. At the end of the present laboratory period or at the next one, weigh the beaker that now contains the organic solid, **A**. Obtain the weight of the solid by difference. Is the residue a crystalline solid, or does it have a viscous, gummy appearance? If it is gummy or an oil, ask your instructor for some suggestions for recrystallization solvents.

Evaporate the CH_2Cl_2 filtrate.

4. Extraction with Water. Scrape the solid residue (compounds **B** and **C**) from the filter paper into a 100-mL beaker. Add 25 mL of <u>distilled</u> water, and stir the mixture moderately for 3 minutes. Assemble the filtration apparatus, <u>weigh the paper</u>, swirl or stir the mixture of solid and liquid, and pour onto the filter paper using a glass rod to guide the flow, as shown in Fig. 2-2. Collect the filtrate and transfer it to a 125-mL flask. Then transfer the remaining solid in the beaker to the filter by washing with 10-15 mL of water from the squeeze bottle as shown in Fig. 2-3. After the liquid has

Treat material insoluble in CH_2Cl_2 with H_2O.

Filter and collect the filtrate.

Save the filtrate for Experiment 3.

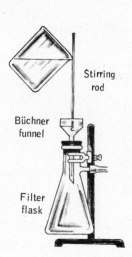

Stirring rod

Büchner funnel

Filter flask

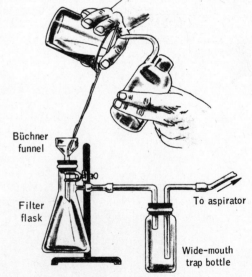

Büchner funnel

Filter flask

To aspirator

Wide-mouth trap bottle

Figure 2-2. Filtration by suction. Transfer of the liquid to the funnel

Figure 2-3. Filtration by suction. Transfer of remaining solid to the funnel by washing

drained from the solid, gently wash the solid on the filter with about 15 mL of water. When this 15-mL wash has drained from the solid (metal carbonate, **C**), remove the funnel, and take it to one of the hoods. Place the funnel into one of the large flasks (or beakers) in the hood, and rinse the solid and filter paper with 2 or 3 small amounts (5-8 mL) of acetone which is in wash bottles. Be sure to wet the entire area of the filter paper that has water on it. The purpose of the acetone wash is to displace the water with acetone which dries more rapidly than water. After most of the acetone has drained, _carefully_ remove the filter paper with a rubber policeman or a flexible metal spatula. Unfold the filter paper, and place it on a watch glass in the hood (with a filter paper cover over the solid) until it is dry. Allow at least 40 minutes of drying time. Weigh the dried solid component **C** and the filter paper as before to obtain the weight of component **C**. (How can one find the weight of the other inorganic component **B**?)

Rinse solid and filter paper with acetone in hood.

At the next laboratory period, weigh the dry filter paper containing the remaining solid metal carbonate or oxide, then carefully scrape the dry solid into a clean 100-mL beaker, and reweigh the filter paper to determine (by difference) the amount of the mixture that was not soluble in either dichloromethane or water.

Dry the solid; obtain its weight.

How can you easily obtain the weight of the substance that was soluble in water?

5. Treating the Remaining Solid (Metal Carbonate or Oxide) with Nitric Acid. After you have obtained the weight of the solid **C**, add a few mL of water to make a paste with solid **C**. Then carefully add 10 mL of 3 M nitric acid; control the addition rate so that no foam or bubbles overflow the beaker. After the nitric acid is completely added, gently heat the beaker until most of the material has dissolved and the bubbling has stopped. If the solution is not reasonably transparent, you should filter it before performing the specific ion tests in Experiment 3.

Dissolve weighed solid in HNO_3.

NOTES

Note 1. If your laboratory does not contain a top-loading or platform balance that is accurate to 0.01 g, you may use the analytical balances to obtain the weights of the sample and the three components.

Note 2. Try to plan your work so that you can allow the wet component **C** and the filter paper to dry until the next lab period.

Note 3. Save all three components for qualitative analysis (the soluble inorganic salt, **B,** is already in solution).

Experiment 3

QUALITATIVE IDENTIFICATION OF

THE COMPONENTS OF A MIXTURE

Objective

To identify the organic component of the mixture, to become familiar with qualitative analytical tests for specific ions, and to identify the inorganic ions present in a three-component mixture

Equipment Needed

250-mL beaker; thermometer; six 16 x 150 mm test tubes; 100-mL beaker; rubber bands; six capillary melting-point tubes; micro spatula; watch glass; burner; cobalt glass and platinum (or Nichrome) wire for flame tests; centrifuge

Reagents Needed

Small reagent-dropper bottles containing known solutions of simple salts in Table 3-1 and larger bottles of the reagents in Table 3-2; small bottles of each compound in Table 3-3; unknown mixture from Exp. 2

INTRODUCTION

In this experiment we will be interested in determining the identity of an organic compound and of two inorganic salts. These may be the three components from the mixture in Experiment 2 or other compounds your instructor assigns.

A pure compound has a definite melting point and boiling point (**Note 1**). Thus, an investigator can often eliminate 90-95% of the possible compounds simply by comparing the melting point or boiling point of the substance with a list of known melting points and boiling points. For solids, determination of the melting point is an easier experiment. On the basis of the experimental melting point and the fact that your compound will be one of those in Table 3-3, suppose that you were able to narrow the number of choices to two or three. Then how would you proceed to obtain a specific identification?

Chemists often resort to one or more of the following types of information: quantitative elemental analysis to obtain the percentage composition of the compound for a match with the calculated values, infrared and/or ultra-violet absorption spectroscopy to examine specific structural features of the molecule, and mixed melting point. In this experiment you are to utilize data from each of these methods to identify the organic compoment of your unknown mixture. One chemist may not perform all of these determinations him(her)self; instead he or she often does some of the measurements and then relies on another person to perform a specialized determination, e.g., the quantitative percentage of composition of the compound. As a way of illustrating this division of labor, you will determine the melting point of the unknown compound (within an acceptable range), and then your instructor will provide an experi-mental percentage of carbon and the principal infrared absorption peaks for your com-pound.

The inorganic components of the mixture will be identified by taking advantage of qualitative "wet-chemistry" tests that are specific for the ions.

PROCEDURE

1. Melting Points

For practical reasons, the organic compound to be identified in this experiment will be limited to those in Table 3-3. Conse-quently, you should be able to identify the compound with a thermometer that is accurate to one or two degrees. Depending on the time allotted for this experiment and your instructor's direction--instead of a complete calibration of your thermometer--an alternative procedure would be to determine the melting point of your compound and then to check the accuracy of your thermometer by choosing one of the known compounds in Table 3-3 that has a narrow melting-point range and that melts close to your unknown.

Determine melting point of your unknown organic compound.

Set up the apparatus shown in Fig. 23 (p. 21) or obtain a Thiele melting-point tube, and determine the melting point of your unknown organic compound, as described under **Laboratory Techniques** (pp. 21-22). Use a new capillary melting-point tube for each measurement **(Note 2)**. After you have determined the melting point, examine Table 3-3 for all of the compounds with melting points within seven degrees of your compound. After obtaining a melting range for your compound, select a number of compounds which might be likely candidates from your manual and find the % carbon for each. (Your textbook has a descrip-tion of how to determine percent carbon from the empirical or molecular formula.)

2. Analytical Data

Compare all of your data; do mixed melting point, if necessary.

Now ask your instructor for the percentage of carbon and the major infrared peaks for the organic compound in your unknown. Compare the carbon percentage with the calculated value for your compound and with calculated % C values of all the compounds that you thought were possible. You should be able to identify the organic component on the basis of the melting point, percentage of carbon, and the infrared peaks. However, if there is more than one possibility, determine the mixed melting points by mixing your unknown separately with the pos-sible compounds as discussed on p. 22. Obtain very small amounts (enough to cover the end of a small spatula) of those compounds, grind approximately an equal amount of your unknown with each of these com-pounds, and then determine the "mixed melting points" of these mix-tures. By recalling that any different compound will depress the melting point of your unknown compound, you should now have nearly a unique identification of the organic component of your original three-component mixture from Experiment 2. Is the % C consistent with your identification based on the results of the mixed melting points? On the basis of the melting point, mixed melting point, and percentage carbon, there should be only one possibility for the organic compound; thus, you have made a positive identification.

3. **Qualitative Tests on the Aqueous Filtrate,**
   i.e., the Water-Soluble Inorganic Salt,
   Component B

We shall be interested in determining the chemical species that were extracted with water, i.e., the ions that were quite soluble in water at room temperature. Take 1 mL of the filtrate obtained by extraction with water in a test tube for each of the specific tests given on pages 57 to 60. Since the unknown contains one soluble simple salt, it should be the source of only one cation and one anion. When you have identified one of each, no further tests are necessary.

4. **Qualitative Tests on the Acid Solution,**
   i.e., Prepared from the Insoluble
   Inorganic Salt, Component C

Remember that there is <u>one</u> cation and <u>one</u> anion for each of the components, **B** and **C**. Since component B is water soluble, a small amount of B may be present in your tests on compound **C**. Use a solubility chart such as that below to eliminate unlikely possibilities.

Solubility Table

	Pb^{++}	Li^+	Ni^{++}	Mg^{++}
Nitrate, NO_3^-	W	W	W	W
Oxide, O^{2-}	A	A	a	A
Chloride, Cl^-	A	W	W	W
Sulfate, SO_4^{2-}	a	W	W	W

<u>Abbreviations:</u>
W water soluble
A insoluble in water but soluble in acids
a insoluble in water but sparingly soluble in acids

Repeat the specific tests given on the following pages for identification of the cation in the nitric acid solution which was obtained from component **C** of the mixture. Use 1-mL samples of the acid solution for each test.

QUALITATIVE TESTS FOR CATIONS

Tests given below are all <u>positive</u>; i.e., they will all work as written because you are using a test compound containing the specific ion of interest. Only one cation test and one anion test should be positive for each of the inorganic components B or C. It is useful to perform the tests on the <u>known</u> <u>compounds</u> and on your <u>unknown</u> at the same time, but be <u>very</u> <u>careful</u> to do the test on the known and the test on the unknown in <u>separate</u> test tubes. Also, use the solubility data wisely. For example, it is not possible to have a nitrate (NO_3^-) compound in component C, yet many students report the presence of NO_3^- in C. Why?? We do not have a convenient test for oxide ($O^=$); therefore, oxides must be determined by the "process of elimination."

A. **Test for Cobalt(II) Ion**

Cobalt(II) salts dissolve in water to give light pink solutions of $[Co(H_2O)_6]^{2+}$. As a test for Co(II) in a <u>known</u> solution, place 1 drop of 0.1 M $Co(NO_3)_2$ in a test tube, and add 1 mL of distilled water. Add 5 drops of 1 M NH_4SCN and 1 mL of acetone to the solution and mix well. The appearance of an intense blue color, due to $[Co(NCS)_4]^{2-}$, confirms the presence of Co^{2+}.

$$Co^{2+} + 4\ NCS^- \longrightarrow [Co(NCS)_4]^{2-} \tag{1}$$

B. Test for Nickel(II) Ion

Nickel ions give light green solutions containing $[Ni(H_2O)_6]^{2+}$. A very specific test for Ni^{2+} involves the use of the organic compound dimethylglyoxime. To 1 drop of 0.1 M $Ni(NO_3)_2$, add 5 mL of water, 10 drops of 1% solution of dimethylglyoxime dissolved in alcohol, and 3 drops of concentrated ammonium hydroxide. The formation of a red precipitate is a positive test for nickel(II). If H_2D is used to represent the formula of dimethylglyoxime, the red nickel precipitate has the composition of $Ni(HD)_2$. The equation for the reaction is:

$$Ni^{2+} + 2\ H_2D \longrightarrow Ni(HD)_2 + 2\ H^+. \tag{2}$$
$$\text{red}$$
$$\text{precipitate}$$

C. Test for Magnesium Ion

Place 1 drop of 0.1 M $Mg(NO_3)_2$ in a test tube, and add 3 mL of water and 1 mL of EDTA-NaOH solution. Heat the solution in boiling water for a maximum of one minute. Add 10 drops of 0.1% thiazole yellow and divide the solution, which should be perfectly clear, into two equal parts. To one part of the solution, add 1 mL of saturated barium nitrate, $Ba(NO_3)_2$. Add 1 mL of water to the other part. If Mg(II) is present, the solution to which water is added will be yellow or light orange, and the solution to which barium nitrate is added will be red or will contain a red precipitate.

An alternative test for Mg(II) is the following. To 1 mL of the unknown solution, add 1 mL of concentrated ammonia (NH_3 or NH_4OH). Add 2 drops of ammonium phosphate solution, $(NH_4)_3PO_4$. A white precipitate indicates magnesium, Mg^{2+}.

D. Test for Lead Ion

For the confirmatory test for lead(II) ion, Pb^{2+}, add a few drops of potassium dichromate, $K_2Cr_2O_7$, solution. A yellow precipitate confirms the presence of lead. (See p. 362 for more details.) Use 0.1 M lead nitrate for your known solution.

E. Test for Sodium Ion (Note 4)

Sodium ion is usually detected directly in solution by means of a flame test. If a clean platinum or Nichrome wire is dipped into a solution containing sodium ions and then held in a burner flame, the characteristic yellow flame of sodium is observed. This test for Na^+ is very sensitive, but, unfortunately, some other ions also impart a yellowish color to the flame. Thus, it is very easy to assume the presence of Na^+ when it is actually not present. Sodium ion is also a common contaminant; a test for it should be very strong to be considered positive.

Pour 2 to 3 mL of concentrated hydrochloric acid (HCl) into a test tube, and dip the wire into the acid. Hold the wire in the hottest part of a flame until the flame shows no color except the red-hot wire. You can hasten this operation by repeating the HCl acid treatment of the wire after each 5 to 10 seconds of heating.

After the wire is clean, dip no more than 1 cm of the wire into a 0.01 M NaCl solution, and hold the wire in the hottest part of the gas flame. How many seconds does the yellow coloration persist with the known? Again, be sure the wire is clean, and dip the wire into 2 mL of your filtrate test solution. Obtain a piece of cobalt glass, and again observe the sodium flame through this glass. When the flame test shows a persistent yellow color that is completely absorbed by cobalt glass, the presence of Na^+ is indicated.

After the platinum wire is again cleaned, dip it into 0.01 M $CaCl_2$ and heat it in the flame. Be sure to observe the calcium flame through cobalt glass. Can you distinguish the color of the flame in this case from that obtained from sodium? Would calcium interfere with the detection of sodium by the flame test? or vice versa?

F. Test for Lithium Ion

The lithium test is the same as for sodium except that the flame is red. Try putting drops of your known solution (0.1 M LiCl) on the wire with an eyedropper if dipping the wire into the solution does not leave enough solution on the wire for a definite color test.

G. Test for Ammonium Ion (Note 4)

Ammonium ion in solution is easily detected since NH_4^+ is converted to NH_3 with a strong base such as NaOH [Eq. (3)].

$$NH_4^+ + OH^- \longrightarrow NH_3\uparrow + H_2O \tag{3}$$

To illustrate the test on a known solution, pick 2 watch glasses of the same size. Place a piece of red litmus paper and 1 drop of water on one watch glass. On the second watch glass, place 1 drop of 0.1 M NH_4Cl, 5 drops of water, and 1 to 2 drops of 6 M NaOH. Immediately cover the second watch glass by inverting the one with the moistened litmus paper over it. In a minute or less, the red litmus paper will turn blue if NH_4^+ is present. To increase the sensitivity of this test, place the assembled watch glasses on a beaker of hot water.

QUALITATIVE TEST FOR ANIONS

A. Test for Sulfate Ion

Barium ions cause sulfate ions to precipitate as a white solid even in strongly acidic solutions [Eq. (4)]. To observe the test, add 1 mL of 3 M HCl to 1 mL of solution to be tested for sulfate (use 0.1 M Na_2SO_4 for a known). Heat this solution in a water bath for 30 seconds. If any insoluble material is present, centrifuge the solution, and pour off the clear liquid for use in the test. If the solution is clear after heating it in the water bath, do not centrifuge. Add 0.5 mL of the 10% barium chloride solution, and wait approximately 60 seconds. The formation of a white precipitate indicates the presence of sulfate.

$$Ba^{2+} + SO_4^{2-} \longrightarrow BaSO_4\downarrow \tag{4}$$
$$\text{white precipitate}$$

B. Test for Chloride Ion

The chloride, bromide, and iodide ions all form insoluble compounds with silver ion in acidic aqueous solutions. The formation of a precipitate with silver nitrate is a specific and sensitive test for the three halides. This test will not distinguish among these three halides and, therefore, is only a general test for these three halides.

To illustrate the test on a known chloride solution, dilute 5 drops of 0.1 M NaCl to 5 mL with water. Add 10 drops of 3 M HNO_3 and then 10 drops of 0.1 M $AgNO_3$. Does a precipitate form? Describe the color and general appearance of this precipitate. Centrifuge the mixture, and discard the clear liquid. Add 1 mL of distilled water to the precipitate, centrifuge, and decant (pour off carefully) the clear liquid. Now, add 2 mL of 2 M ammonia solution to the precipitate and shake it. What do you observe? Acidify the clear solution with 3 M HNO_3, and observe the mixture. [AgCl dissolves in 2 M or stronger ammonia to form $Ag(NH_3)_2^+$ and Cl^-. Then, when the solution is acidified, the silver(I) complex, $Ag(NH_3)_2^+$, is decomposed and AgCl reprecipitates.] The reactions for formation and dissolving of the AgCl precipitate are Eqs. (5) and (6), respectively.

$$Ag^+ \; + \; Cl^- \; \longrightarrow \; AgCl\downarrow \qquad\qquad (5)$$
$$\text{white}$$

$$AgCl(s) \; + \; 2\,NH_3 \; \longrightarrow \; Ag(NH_3)_2^+ \; + \; Cl^- \qquad (6)$$

C. Test for the Carbonate Ion

Place a one-hole rubber stopper and bent delivery tube in a test tube as shown in Fig. 3-1. Add about 3 mL of the test solution to this test tube. Now insert

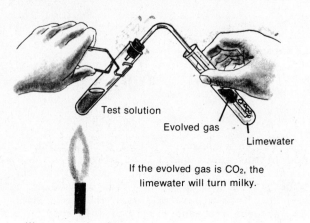

Test solution

Evolved gas

Limewater

If the evolved gas is CO_2, the limewater will turn milky.

Warm over a low flame.

Figure 3-1. Apparatus for the CO_2 Test

the delivery tube into some clear limewater, $Ca(OH)_2$, in another test tube. When you are ready, remove the stopper just enough to add a little 6 M HCl to the test solution. Immediately close the stopper again, and heat the test solution in the tube gently to boiling to drive any carbon dioxide gas into the limewater. Be careful not to let any of the boiling liquid escape through the delivery tube into the limewater. A white precipitate in the limewater indicates $CO_3^=$ or HCO_3^- in the test solution. The reactions for this test are:

$$CO_3^= \; + \; 2\,H_3O^+ \; \longrightarrow \; 3\,H_2O \; + \; CO_2\uparrow \qquad (7)$$

$$H_2O \; + \; CO_2 \; + \; Ca^{2+} \; \longrightarrow \; CaCO_3\downarrow \; + \; 2\,H^+. \qquad (8)$$
$$\text{white precipitate}$$

D. Test for Nitrate Ion

Three drops of 0.01 M nitrate test solution are placed in a test tube. Add 3 drops of the diphenylamine/sulfuric acid solution, and then add 10 drops of concentrated (18 M) H_2SO_4. Shake the test tube carefully to mix the reagents. If nitrate ion is present, the test solution will turn deep blue in color and then slowly change to a deep violet color. If the solution has a high nitrate concentration, the violet color appears immediately.

NOTEBOOK AND REPORT

Accurate and detailed records are especially important in any analysis work. Record the results of the tests on the knowns in your notebook clearly so you can refer to them for information and comparisons with the results obtained on your unknown. Report the name and the observed melting point of the organic compound and the ions found on the Report Sheet.

NOTES

Note 1.   Some compounds decompose before they reach a definite melting or boiling point; in those cases, the decomposition point is reported.

Note 2.   A wide range of melting (i.e., > 5 $^\circ$C) may indicate a _low_ value for the observed melting point of your compound. If time permits, dry the organic compound some more or get from your instructor some suggestions for a recrystallization solvent, and perform the melting-point determination again.

Note 3.   Since the accuracy of a quantitative elemental analysis depends on the skill of the investigator and the limitations of the equipment and analytical method, commerical carbon analyses are accurate to $\pm$ 1% _relative_ error; that is, a compound containing exactly 25.00% C would be expected to have reported results within the range 24.75 to 25.25% C. Your % C data conform to these relative error limits.

Note 4.   The flame test for sodium is so sensitive that a trace impurity of sodium will produce the yellow flame. A definite test for sodium should be performed for comparison. The Nichrome wire must be absolutely free of yellow flame **prior** to testing the unknown. Repeated dipping in HCl and subsequent heating is required to remove the last traces of sodium from the wire. Then if sodium ion is in the unknown, the yellow color will be very strong and persistent. It may be very difficult to remove.

Experiment 3

QUALITATIVE IDENTIFICATION OF THE COMPONENTS OF A MIXTURE

PRELABORATORY QUESTIONS

Name _Todd Moore_   Lab Instructor _Brian Stearns_

Student ID No. _300-68-3620-0_   Date _1/24/95_

1. Write formulas for the common compounds that contain only the following pairs of ions.

   a. Cd^{2+} and Cl^- _____   b. silver and nitrate ions _____

   c. Ni^{2+} and CrO_4^{2-} _____   d. calcium and carbonate ions _____

   e. barium and iodide ions _____   f. Al^{3+} and SO_4^{2-} _____

   g. sodium and sulfide ions _____   h. Cu^{2+} and NO_3^- _____

   i. ammonium and sulfate ions _____   j. K^+ and Br^- _____

   k. ammonium and nitrate ions _____   l. Ag^+ and I^- _____

2. Write correct names for the following compounds.

   a. $(NH_4)_2CrO_4$ _____   b. $CuSO_4$ _____

   c. $Al(NO_3)_3$ _____   d. Na_2CO_3 _____

   e. $CdCO_3$ _____   f. $Ca(OH)_2$ _____

   g. $BaBr_2$ _____   h. HNO_3 _____

   i. K_2S _____   j. $AgCl$ _____

3. Supply coefficients to balance the following equations.

    a. $AgNO_3$ + $NaCl$ $\longrightarrow$ $AgCl(s)$ + $NaNO_3$

    b. HNO_3 + $Ca(OH)_2$ $\longrightarrow$ $Ca(NO_3)_2$ + H_2O

    c. $Cu(OH)_2(s)$ + NH_3 $\longrightarrow$ $Cu(NH_3)_4(OH)_2$

    d. $Cu(NO_3)_2$ + Na_3PO_4 $\longrightarrow$ $Cu_3(PO_4)_2$ + $NaNO_3$

    e. $Ni(NH_3)_4(OH)_2$ + HCl $\longrightarrow$ $NiCl_2$ + NH_4Cl + H_2O

    f. K_2CO_3 + HNO_3 $\longrightarrow$ KNO_3 + $CO_2(g)$ + H_2O

4. Write balanced molecular equations for the following reactions. (You may wish to refer to your textbook.) Indicate the formation of a precipitate (a solid) with (s) following the formula of the substance. Indicate gasses with (g). If no reaction occurs, write N.R.

    a. The reaction of an aqueous solution of barium chloride with an aqueous solution of sodium sulfate

    b. The reaction of an aqueous solution of silver nitrate with an aqueous solution of sodium iodide

    c. The reaction of an aqueous solution of sodium sulfide with 6 M hydrochloric acid

    d. The reaction of an aqueous solution of nickel(II) chloride with 6 M sodium hydroxide solution

5. What is the difference between the freezing point and the melting point of pure glacial acetic acid?

Experiment 3

QUALITATIVE IDENTIFICATION OF THE COMPONENTS OF A MIXTURE

REPORT SHEET

Name_____   Lab Instructor_____

Student ID No._____   Date_____

1.   Melting point of the organic component of your unknown _____

2.   Mixed melting points

compound added to unknown	observed melting point
_____	_____
_____	_____
_____	_____
_____	_____

3.   % C in your organic compound _____

4.   Identity of organic component _____

5.   Calculated elemental composition
     of identified organic compound _____

6. Results of tests that you performed on known ion solutions

7. Results of tests on water soluble portion of the mixture, i.e., from component B

8. Results of tests on the portion that dissolved in nitric acid, i.e., component C

The reagents listed in Table 3-1 are used in Experiment 3 in DROP QUANTITIES. Each of these 18 reagents is in a 25-mL brown dropping bottle arranged in a small rack. Each bottle is labeled with the code letter following the sequence in which they appear in the procedure for Experiment 3.

Table 3-1. Test Reagents Used in DROP Quantities

Code Letter	Compound Name	Formula	Concentration
	Cation test reagents		
A	Cobalt(II) nitrate	$Co(NO_3)_2$	0.1 M
B	Ammonium thiocyanate	NH_4SCN	1.0 M
C	Nickel(II) nitrate	$Ni(NO_3)_2$	0.1 M
D	Dimethylglyoxime		solution
E	Magnesium nitrate	$Mg(NO_3)_2$	0.1 M
F	Thiazole yellow		solution
G	Lead nitrate	$Pb(NO_3)_2$	0.1 M
H	Potassium dichromate	$K_2Cr_2O_7$	0.1 M
I	Sodium chloride	NaCl	0.01 M
J	Calcium chloride	$CaCl_2$	0.01 M
K	Lithium Chloride	LiCl	0.1 M
L	Sodium hydroxide	NaOH	6.0 M
M	Ammonium chloride	NH_4Cl	0.1 M
	Anion test reagents		
N	Sodium chloride	NaCl	0.1 M
O	Nitric acid	HNO_3	3.0 M
P	Silver nitrate	$AgNO_3$	0.1 M
Q	Potassium nitrate	KNO_3	0.01 M
R	Diphenylamine-sulfuric acid		solution (in small plastic bottle)

PLEASE HELP EVERYONE BY RETURNING THESE REAGENTS IN THE CORRECT ORDER.

The reagents listed in Table 3-2 are needed in Experiment 3 in MILLILITER QUANTITIES for the individual tests.

Table 3-2. Test Reagents Used in Larger Quantities

	Compound name	Formula	
Those in large 100-mL brown glass dropping bottles (1 mL = 20 drops)			
	Barium nitrate	$Ba(NO_3)_2$	saturated
	Hydrochloric acid	HCl	3.0 M
Those in large 500-mL plastic bottles			
	Barium chloride	$BaCl_2$	10%
	Sodium sulfate	Na_2SO_4	0.1 M
	Ammonia (aqueous)	$NH_3(NH_4OH)$	2.0 M
	Lime water	$Ca(OH)_2$ aqueous	saturated
Additional reagents			
	Acetone	CH_3COCH_3	1-L glass bottle,
	EDTA-NaOH test solution		200-mL plastic squeeze bottle

PLEASE COOPERATE BY RETURNING THE REAGENTS TO THE DESIGNATED PLACE AS SOON AS YOU ARE FINISHED WITH THEM.

Table 3-3. Organic Compounds

Name	Molecular Formula	M.P.($^{\circ}$C)	Structural Formula
acetamide	C_2H_5NO	81	$CH_3\underset{\underset{O}{\parallel}}{C}-NH_2$
N-acetyl-m-toluidine (m-acetotoluidide)	$C_9H_{11}NO$	65.5	$CH_3-C_6H_4-\overset{H}{N}-\underset{\underset{O}{\parallel}}{C}-CH_3$
acetone oxime	C_3H_7NO	60-61	$(CH_3)_2C=N-O-H$
N-acetyl-N-methyl-p-toluidine	$C_{10}H_{13}NO$	80	$CH_3\underset{\underset{O}{\parallel}}{C}-\underset{\underset{CH_3}{\mid}}{N}-C_6H_4-CH_3$
allyl urea	$C_4H_8N_2O$	85	$CH_2=CHCH_2-\overset{H}{N}-\underset{\underset{O}{\parallel}}{C}-NH_2$
azobenzene	$C_{12}H_{10}O_2$	68	$C_6H_5-N=N-C_6H_5$
benzil	$C_{14}H_{10}O_2$	95	$C_6H_5-\underset{\underset{O}{\parallel}}{C}-\underset{\underset{O}{\parallel}}{C}-C_6H_5$
benzoyl acetonitrile	C_9H_7NO	80.5	$C_6H_5-\underset{\underset{O}{\parallel}}{C}-CH_2-C\equiv N$
N-benzylacetamide	$C_9H_{11}NO$	60-61	$CH_3\underset{\underset{O}{\parallel}}{C}-\underset{\underset{H}{\mid}}{N}-CH_2C_6H_5$
diphenyl	$C_{12}H_{10}$	68-70	$C_6H_5-C_6H_5$
p-bromoacetophenone	C_8H_7BrO	50-51	

Table 3-3. Organic Compounds

Name	Molecular Formula	M.P.(°C)	Structural Formula
β-bromonaphthalene (2-bromonaphthalene)	$C_{10}H_7Br$	59	
o-chloroacetanilide (2-chloroacetanilide)	C_8H_8ClNO	88	$Cl-C_6H_4-\overset{H}{N}-\underset{O}{C}-CH_3$
m-chloroacetanilide (3-chloroacetanilide)	C_8H_8ClNO	72.5	$Cl-C_6H_4-\overset{H}{N}-\underset{O}{C}CH_3$
4-chlorobenzophenone	$C_{12}H_9ClO$	77-78	$Cl-C_6H_4-\underset{O}{C}-C_6H_5$
2-chloro-4-naphthalene	$C_{10}H_7Cl$	58-60	
1-chloro-4-nitrobenzene	$C_6H_4ClNO_2$	83-84	
cyclohexanone oxime	$C_6H_{11}NO$	85-87	$CH_2 \begin{smallmatrix} CH_2CH_2 \\ \\ CH_2CH_2 \end{smallmatrix} C=NOH$
cyclooctanone	$C_8H_{14}O$	40-42	$CH_2 \begin{smallmatrix} CH_2CH_2CH_2 \\ \\ CH_2CH_2CH_2 \end{smallmatrix} C=O$
1,10-decanediol	$C_{10}H_{22}O_2$	71-73	$HO(CH_2)_{10}OH$
benzyl phenyl ketone	$C_{14}H_{12}O$	55-57	$C_6H_5-\underset{O}{C}-CH_2C_6H_5$

Table 3-3. Organic Compounds

Name	Molecular Formula	M.P.(°C)	Structural Formula
p-dibromobenzene (1,4-dibromobenzene)	$C_6H_4Br_2$	83-88	
p-dichlorobenzene	$C_6H_4Cl_2$	53-54	
o-diethoxybenzene	$C_{10}H_{14}O_2$	41-43	
p-diethoxybenzene	$C_{10}H_{14}O_2$	71-72	
N,N-diethylurea (unsymmetrical diethylurea)	$C_5H_{12}N_2O$	73-75	
p-dimethoxybenzene	$C_8H_{10}O_2$	55-57	
p-dimethylaminobenzaldehyde	$C_9H_{11}NO$	74-75	
N,N-dimethylbenzamide	$C_9H_{11}NO$	42-44	

71

Table 3-3. Organic Compounds

Name	Molecular Formula	M.P.(°C)	Structural Formula
diphenylamine	$C_{12}H_{11}N$	52.5–54.0	$(C_6H_5)_2NH$
diphenylcarbonate	$C_{13}H_{10}O_3$	79–81	$(C_6H_5O)_2CO$
1,3-diphenylpropane-1,3-dione	$C_{15}H_{12}O_2$	76–78	$C_6H_5-\overset{\displaystyle O}{\underset{}{C}}-CH_2-\overset{\displaystyle O}{\underset{}{C}}-C_6H_5$
durene	$C_{10}H_{14}$	77–81	
9-fluorenone	$C_{13}H_8O$	83–83.5	
indole	C_8H_7N	52–53	
p-iodoanisole	C_7H_7IO	52–53	
p-iodotoluene (4-iodotoluene)	C_7H_7I	34–35	
maleic anhydride	$C_4H_2O_3$	52–54	

72

Table 3-3. Organic Compounds

Name	Molecular Formula	M.P.($^\circ$C)	Structural Formula
4-methylbenzophenone	$C_{14}H_{12}O$	55-57	
2-methyl-1-nitronaphthalene	$C_{11}H_8NO_2$	79-81	
naphthalene	$C_{10}H_8$	79-80	
2-nitroacetanilide	$C_8H_8NO_3$	92-93	
phenylbenzoate	$C_{13}H_{10}O_2$	68-69	
N-phenyl-1-naphthylamine	$C_{16}H_{13}N$	59.5-60.5	
propionamide	C_3H_7NO	80-82	
salicylaldoxime	C_7H_7NO	57-59	

Table 3-3. Organic Compounds

Name	Molecular Formula	M.P.(^{O}C)	Structural Formula
m-terphenyl	$C_{18}H_{14}$	85-87	
1,1,3,3-tetramethyl-2-thiourea	$C_5H_{12}N_2S$	77-79	$(CH_3)_2N-\overset{\displaystyle \underset{\parallel}{C}}{}-N(CH_3)_2$ with S below
triphenylmethane	$C_{19}H_{16}$	93-95	$(C_6H_5)_3CH$
triphenylphosphate	$C_{18}H_{15}O_4P$	49-50	$(C_6H_5O)_3PO$

Experiment 4

DETERMINATION OF THE EMPIRICAL FORMULA OF A COMPOUND

Objective

To synthesize a compound and determine its empirical formula from the relative masses of the elements in the compound

Equipment

Two porcelain crucibles with lids; clay triangle; analytical balance; high-temperature burner; crucible tongs; simple desiccator

Reagents Needed

Two 1-g pieces of copper wire; powdered sulfur

INTRODUCTION

Concept of a Mole

Because of the extremely small size of an atom or a simple molecule, chemists must use enormous numbers of them to observe a reaction experimentally. For a convenient reference, they have chosen a very large number (6.023×10^{23}) of atoms, molecules, or ions to represent a fixed quantity called a mole. Thus, a mole is just a fixed number of a chemical species (i.e., like a dozen apples). The advantage of using the large number is that the weight of 6.023×10^{23} atoms is in the gram range, a convenient range for laboratory balances. By international agreement, the atomic weight scale is based on the carbon-12 isotope so that 1 mole of carbon atoms has a mass of 12.01 g. The gram-atomic weight of the other elements always has a fixed relationship to that of ^{12}C; thus, there are as many atoms of sulfur in one mole of sulfur (32.06 g of S) as there are atoms of carbon in one mole of carbon (12.01 g of C). This constant number of atoms contained in a mole of any element (or the number of molecules in a mole of a compound) is Avogadro's number and has the value 6.023×10^{23}.

Empirical Formula of a Compound

After a chemist has determined by a qualitative analysis which elements are present in a compound, he or she may need to know the empirical (simplest) formula of the compound, i.e., the relative number of moles of each element. Such information is determined directly from a quantitative analysis experiment.

One may calculate the empirical formula from the weights of the elements in the compound. The procedure is illustrated by the following example. Suppose it had been observed that 4.74 g of sulfur combine with chlorine to produce 10.00 g of a compound that contains only sulfur and chlorine. What is the empirical formula of this compound?

$$10.00 \text{ g of the sulfur compound}$$
$$- 4.74 \text{ g of sulfur in the compound}$$
$$5.26 \text{ g of chlorine in the compound}$$

Number of moles
of sulfur in 10.00 g $= 4.74$ g of S $\times \dfrac{1 \text{ mole of S}}{32.06 \text{ g of S}} = 0.148$ moles of S
of the sulfur chloride

(Note that the units and the substance concerned are clearly written in the arithmetical expressions and that the conversion factor relating moles and weight is written so that "grams of S" appears in the denominator of the conversion factor so that it cancels "grams of S" in the term "4.74 grams of S," leaving "moles of S" as the unit of the answer. This use of conversion factors is a characteristic of the "dimensional analysis" or the "factor-label-method" for solving problems in science.)

Number of moles
of chlorine in 10.00 g $= 5.26$ g of Cl $\times \dfrac{1 \text{ mole of Cl}}{35.45 \text{ g of Cl}} = 0.148$ moles of Cl atoms
of the sulfur chloride

Ratio of moles of sulfur
to moles of chlorine $= \dfrac{0.148 \text{ mole of S}}{0.148 \text{ mole of Cl}} = \dfrac{1 \text{ mole of S}}{1 \text{ mole of Cl}}$
in the compound

These data show that in a 10-g sample of this sulfur chloride there are 0.148 moles of sulfur atoms and 0.148 moles of chlorine atoms, i.e., there is 1 mole of sulfur atoms for every mole of chlorine atoms in the compound. Therefore, the empirical (simplest) formula is SCl.

Copper and sulfur combine under different conditions to form more than one copper sulfide, just as sulfur and chlorine form molecules whose empirical formulas are SCl_2, SCl, S_3Cl_2, and S_2Cl under different reaction conditions. The object of this experiment is to determine the weight of sulfur that will combine with a given weight of copper metal under the experimental conditions used in our laboratory. This is done by determining the increase in weight when a piece of copper is allowed to react with sulfur to form a copper sulfide under conditions such that any excess sulfur will be burned away. The reaction is performed in a porcelain crucible at high temperature.

PROCEDURE

Weighing. Since the primary object of this experiment is to determine quantitatively the relative number of copper atoms to sulfur atoms in the copper sulfide, the determination is strongly dependent upon the care and precision with which one makes the weighings on the analytical balance. Review the procedure and operating instructions for the balance in Experiment 1 before starting the present experiment.

Clean and ignite crucibles.

Igniting the Crucibles. Prior to weighing the empty crucibles, they should be heated to a dull red color to remove any absorbed dust, moisture, and oil film. It is important to note some identification mark for each crucible and to handle the crucible with crucible tongs during the weighings so that oil and moisture are not transferred from your fingers to the crucible. Place a clean, dry, covered porcelain crucible on a clay triangle in a ring stand as shown in Fig. 4-1, and heat it to redness in the hottest portion of the flame from a Meker or Fisher burner. Allow the crucible to cool somewhat, and then while it is still warm, transfer it to the desiccator to cool to room temperature.

Allow crucible to cool in the desiccator.

While the empty crucible is cooling, obtain two pieces of clean copper wire, each weighing about 1 g. Use paper or a dry cloth to wrap the wire in order to avoid transferring oil and moisture from your fingers, and turn each piece of wire into a spiral so that it will fit compactly into the bottom of a crucible. With tweezers,

While crucible is cooling, weigh the metal.

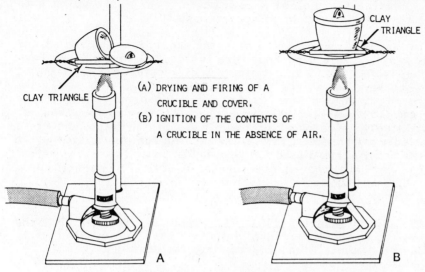

CLAY TRIANGLE

CLAY TRIANGLE

(A) DRYING AND FIRING OF A CRUCIBLE AND COVER.

(B) IGNITION OF THE CONTENTS OF A CRUCIBLE IN THE ABSENCE OF AIR.

A

B

Figure 4-1. Arrangement for heating a crucible

place a piece of metal directly on the balance pan, and weigh it to 0.0002 g. Record this weight and all subsequent data in your notebook in the form of a data table similar to the one on page 83.

Weigh a cooled crucible without the cover (use tongs; don't touch it with your fingers) to the nearest 0.0002 g on an analytical balance, and record the weight in the data table.

Weigh crucible and add metal and sulfur to it.

Add the copper spiral to the crucible, cover it with approximately 1.2 g of powdered sulfur (weigh the sulfur on a piece of paper to within 0.1 g on a triple-beam laboratory balance and then add the sulfur to the crucible), place the lid on the crucible, and support the crucible with a clay triangle on a ring stand in the hood (Fig. 4-1). Heat the bottom of the crucible slowly for 5 to 6 minutes, and then slowly increase the intensity of the flame until the bottom of the crucible becomes a dull red. The excess sulfur may be observed to burn around the edge of the crucible with a blue flame. (What is the chemical equation for the reaction producing this flame?) Continue this intense heating until no more sulfur vapor escapes around the lid, and then heat the sides and the lid of the crucible to vaporize any free sulfur present. Allow the crucible to cool until it stops glowing, remove the lid (with tongs), and inspect the crucible to see whether the excess sulfur has been driven off (as indicated by the absence of the yellow color of sulfur). If the crucible contains no free sulfur, allow it to cool in the desiccator. When the crucible has cooled to room temperature, weigh it without the lid (don't touch it with your fingers).

Heat to cause reaction.

Cool and weigh crucible and product.

If the above inspection shows the presence of free sulfur, this may mean that the flame was not hot enough to vaporize the sulfur and cause complete reaction with the copper. To insure completeness of the reaction, add approximately 0.2 g of sulfur, replace the lid, reheat the crucible to a red color for several minutes, cool it in the desiccator, and weigh it.

Add more
sulfur and
heat. Cool
and weigh.
Repeat until
weight is
constant.

All of the copper should have reacted, and the product in the crucible should now be copper sulfide. As a check on your result, add approximately 0.3 g of powdered sulfur to the crucible containing the copper sulfide, and reheat the material as before until the sulfur vapors stop escaping. Allow the crucible to cool, inspect its contents, and reweigh it. Repeat this procedure until the weights in successive weighings are constant to within 0.0004 g.

This procedure should be repeated exactly, using the second copper wire, but in this experiment use initially about 2.4 g of powdered sulfur instead of 1.2 g. Begin this duplicate experiment in the spare time you have during the first trial for the two trials. If the ratio of sulfur to copper atoms in the product does not agree within 7%, make a third trial and use the average of the two results that agree most closely in calculating the formula of the compound. Place the copper sulfide produced in all trials in a test tube, stopper it with a cork, label it, and hand it to your instructor.

Possible Alternatives

Check with your instructor for availability. The preceding directions also may be utilized to prepare a lead or iron sulfide by using strips of elemental lead or iron wire, respectively.

NOTEBOOK AND REPORT

The data for most of the quantitative experiments you will perform are most clearly recorded in tabular form. A sample data table suitable for this experiment is given on page 83. Copy this in your notebook, use it as a skeleton for filling in the blanks with your experimental data, and turn it in as a part of your report. Be sure to indicate the units of measurement for all data recorded.

The notebook should also contain statements of qualitative observations made during the experiment. (Did you smell anything during the heating? Describe the color of the flame from the crucible. Was there a yellow deposit under the lid?) Note any unclear points or questions about the experiment so that you can determine the answers in class sessions later.

The calculations and the arithmetical steps needed to obtain the empirical formula of the product should appear in your notebook, and a sample calculation must be included in your report. The number of moles of each element and the ratio should be calculated and reported to three significant figures.

REFERENCES

1. Addison, W.E. Structural Principles in Inorganic Compounds. John Wiley and Sons, New York, 1961, pp. 147-166.

2. Davis, Gailey, and Whitten, Principles of Chemistry, Saunders College Publishing, Philadelphia, PA, 1984, Chapter 3.

3. Whitten and Gailey, General Chemistry, 2nd Ed., Saunders College Publishing, Philadelphia, PA, 1984, Chapter 2.

Name_____   Lab Instructor_____

Student ID No._____   Date_____

4.   For the reaction $8 KClO_3 + C_{12}H_{22}O_{11} \longrightarrow 8 KCl + 12 CO_2 + 11 H_2O$

a.   How many moles of potassium chlorate ($KClO_3$)
     react with 1.5 moles of sucrose $C_{12}H_{22}O_{11}$? _____

b.   How many grams of potassium chlorate react
     with 1.5 moles of sucrose $C_{12}H_{22}O_{11}$? _____

c.   Two moles of $KClO_3$ will produce _____ moles of CO_2.

d.   Two moles of $KClO_3$ will produce _____ moles of H_2O.

e.   Two moles of $KClO_3$ will produce _____ g of CO_2.

f.   Two moles of $KClO_3$ will produce _____ g of H_2O.

g.   A weight of 122.5 g of $KClO_3$ will produce _____ g of KCl.

h.   A weight of 122.5 g of $KClO_3$ will produce _____ moles of CO_2.

i.   A weight of 122.5 g of $KClO_3$ will produce _____ g of H_2O.

j.   How many grams of potassium chlorate are required
     to produce 1 mole of H_2O in the preceding equation?_____

k.   _____ g of $KClO_3$ are required to form 1.0 g of H_2O.

l.   _____ g of $KClO_3$ are required to form 1.0 g of KCl.

m.   _____ g of $KClO_3$ are required to form 18 moles of CO_2.

Show three sample calculations (e.g., 4b, 4d, and 4m).

5. What is the percentage of each element in $C_{12}H_{22}O_{11}$?

6. Calculate the number of moles of carbon, hydrogen, and oxygen atoms in 100 g of $C_{12}H_{22}O_{11}$.

7. How would the mole ratios of carbon to hydrogen, carbon to oxygen, etc., obtained in Question 6 change if one calculated the number of moles of carbon, hydrogen, and oxygen atoms in 62 g of $C_{12}H_{22}O_{11}$? Explain.

8. Determine the simplest formula of a compound that has the following composition: 26.52% chromium, 42.52% sulfur, and 48.96% oxygen.

9. In the formation of an ionic compound, how many electrons would usually be gained or lost by each of the following elements? Examine a Periodic Table for the families of each element listed below.

    Cs _____   F _____   Ba _____

    Br _____   Mg _____   Al _____

    O _____   K _____   S _____

STOICHIOMETRY AND THE CHEMICAL EQUATION

(Development of an Equation)

Objective

To identify the product of a reaction and develop the chemical equation for the reaction

Equipment Needed

4-mL test tubes; medicine droppers or capillary pipets; micro spatula, centrifuge

Reagents Needed

0.10 M potassium iodide, KI; 0.10 M lead nitrate, $Pb(NO_3)_2$; 3% hydrogen peroxide, H_2O_2; 5% solution of thioacetamide, CH_3CSNH_2; solid sodium sulfite, Na_2SO_3; 3 M HNO_3; dichloromethane, CH_2Cl_2; 0.10 M potassium nitrate

INTRODUCTION

A chemical equation is a statement in chemical symbols of certain facts about a chemical reaction that have been obtained from experiments. When a chemist writes an equation, he or she is making use of these facts (which were usually discovered by others) and of generalizations derived from the results of several experiments. To write the equation for a reaction, the chemist needs to know what substances react, what is formed, and the relationship between the amounts of substances which react and the amount of substances (products) formed. This experiment illustrates the development of an equation for a simple reaction, that between lead nitrate and potassium iodide.

Since both lead nitrate and potassium iodide are water soluble ionic salts, we know that they must be present in solution as ions. In other words, a solution of lead nitrate contains lead ions and nitrate ions, and a solution of potassium iodide contains potassium ions and iodide ions. When solutions of these two salts are mixed, a yellow precipitate is formed. Since neither of the original solids, lead nitrate nor potassium iodide, is yellow, it may be presumed that the yellow solid is formed by the combination of the positive ions from one compound with the negative ions from the others, and is either lead iodide or potassium nitrate. If it is lead iodide, then potassium ions and nitrate ions must be left in the solution; if it is potassium nitrate, then lead ions and iodide ions must be left in solution. Identification of the precipitate might then be made either by examining the solid itself or by examining the supernatant solution. In the latter case, care must be taken not to confuse an excess of one of the ions (that reacted to form the precipitate and some of which remains in solution) with the ions which did not react.

In this experiment we will identify the ions in the precipitate and determine the ratio in which they occur in the precipitate. We will then have the information needed to write the equation for the reaction: we will know what reacts (lead nitrate and potassium iodide), we shall know what is formed, and we shall know the relative amounts of the two reagents required to form the product.

To carry out the identification, we need tests for two of the four ions present, one from each solution. Tests for only two are needed, since the presence or absence of the other two can be inferred. Thus, if we find lead ions in the precipitate and we know that the precipitate is either lead iodide or potassium nitrate, we will have identified the precipitate as lead iodide. If we do not find lead ion in the precipitate, then it is not lead iodide and must be potassium nitrate. A test for one of the negative ions is needed to clarify the relative amounts of ions in the precipitate after it has been identified; we will test for the iodide ion rather than the nitrate ions since the qualitative tests for iodide ion are easier. Further semi-quantitative tests then will be performed (on the supernatant liquid) to establish the relative amounts of ions in the precipitate.

PROCEDURE

A. Tests for Lead Ions and Iodide Ions

Lead Ions: To a 4-mL test tube, add 5 drops of lead nitrate solution, 2 drops of 3 M HNO_3, and 20 drops of thioacetamide solution, and place the tube in a boiling water bath for 5 minutes. The black precipitate which forms is, in the absence of cations other than those of periodic table Groups IA and IIA, a positive test for the presence of lead ion. The precipitate is lead sulfide, PbS.

Look for black precipitate in test solution.

Confirm that potassium ions do not give a black precipitate by trying the above test on 5 drops of potassium nitrate solution, instead of the lead nitrate solution.

The formation of a black precipitate with thioacetamide thus serves to distinguish material containing lead ions from material containing potassium ions.

Iodide Ions: To a 4-mL test tube, add 5 drops of potassium iodide solution, 5 drops of dichloromethane (**Note 1**), 5 drops of 3 M nitric acid, and 5 drops of 3% hydrogen peroxide. Shake the test tube vigorously. A violet color in the dichloromethane layer under the water layer indicates the presence of iodide ions. The color is due to the presence of elemental iodine in the solution which is formed by a chemical reaction in the test solution.

Look for purple color in the bottom layer.

B. Identification of the Precipitate Formed When a Lead Nitrate Solution Is Added to a Potassium Iodide Solution

Add 5 drops of lead nitrate solution to 5 drops of potassium iodide solution in a 4-mL test tube. Note the bright yellow precipitate. Insert the test tube in a centrifuge; balance the centrifuge by placing another test tube containing an equal amount of water on the exact opposite side, (see Techniques Section), and centrifuge for one minute. From the test tube that contains the yellow precipitate, remove the supernatant liquid with a medicine dropper, and add one dropper full of distilled water to the 4-mL test tube to wash the yellow precipitate. Stir the mixture with a small, clean stirring rod, centrifuge again, remove the wash water with a medicine dropper (or capillary pipet), wash again with a fresh quantity of water, centrifuge, and remove the second wash water. The precipitate is now ready to be tested to identify the ions present.

Wash yellow precipitate well.

(1) Test for Iodide Ions. Add to the yellow precipitate 5 drops of 3 M nitric acid, stir with a clean glass rod, and warm the mixture by placing the test tube in a beaker of boiling water <u>for a few minutes</u> (**Note 2**). Add 2 drops of hydrogen peroxide, stir, and again heat in boiling water. Add 3 drops of water, and allow the test tube and its contents to cool to room temperature. Add 5 drops of dichloromethane, shake, and observe the color of the dichloromethane layer. If the bottom dichloromethane layer is violet colored, iodide ion is present in the precipitate; if it remains colorless, no iodide is present.

Look for purple color of I_2 as above in A.

(2) Test for Lead Ions. Centrifuge the solution from (1) above, using a capillary pipet withdraw the water layer, and place it in a clean test tube. Discard the dichloromethane into the waste solvent can, not into the sink. Add 5 drops of dichloromethane to the water, shake, centrifuge, and again transfer the water layer to a clean tube. The purpose of this procedure is to remove any color which remains in the water layer so that the lead ion test will be more visible. Discard the dichloromethane into the waste solvent can. With a spatula, add just enough solid sodium sulfite, Na_2SO_3, to cover the bottom of the test tube, and stir to dissolve. The purpose of this addition is to destroy any excess hydrogen peroxide. Otherwise it would react with the thioacetamide which will be added next. Test for lead ion by adding 20 drops of thioacetamide solution to the water layer, stir, heat in boiling water, and centrifuge. A black precipitate of lead sulfide indicates the presence of lead ion; absence of a substantial quantity of a black precipitate indicates that the original yellow precipitate did not contain lead ion.

Look for black precipitate of PbS.

C. Determination of the Ratios in Which the Ions Combine to Form the Yellow Precipitate

In this part, the drops of solutions must be counted and measured accurately. For best results, use the same medicine dropper for both solutions and water. Be sure to rinse the dropper thoroughly between different solutions.

(1) Principle of the Method. Suppose that two ions, A and B, combine to form a precipitate of formula AB_3. If we should add A and B together in a 1:1 molar ratio, it is evident from the illustration below that precipitation of AB_3 would leave the excess quantity of A in solution since 3 moles of B are required to react with 1 mole of A, or 1 mole of B will react with only 1/3 mole of A, and (1 - 1/3), or 2/3, mole of A will remain in solution. A test of the solution above the precipitate in the 1:1 ratio experiment will thus show the presence of a large amount of A.

$$\left|\begin{array}{ccc} A & A & A \\ A & A & A \end{array}\right| \quad + \quad \left|\begin{array}{ccc} B & B & B \\ B & B & B \end{array}\right| \quad \longrightarrow \quad \left|\begin{array}{cc} A & A & A & A \\ AB_3 & & AB_3 \end{array}\right|$$

If in a second experiment we use the molar ratio 1:2, then two moles of B will react with 2/3 mole of A, and (1 - 2/3), or 1/3, mole of A will remain. A test on the liquid above the precipitate will still show the presence of A but in smaller quantity than in the first experiment. Only when the experiment is made with a molar ratio of 1:3 will the supernatant liquid show no excess A present.

If the molar ratio is further increased to 1:4, the amount of A becomes the limiting factor since 1 mole of A can react with only 3 moles of B, and (4 - 3), or 1 mole of B will be left over. Tests of the supernatant liquid will then show no A present but will show the presence of B. Continued increase of the molar ratio to 1:5 and higher will show no A present in the supernatant liquid but will show an increased amount of B.

It is possible to determine the molar ratio in which A and B combine by examining the supernatant liquid. It is necessary to make a number of experiments with different relative amounts of A and B and to find which component, and approximately how much of it, appears in excess. The ratio at which neither is present in excess is the stoi-chiometric ratio, corresponding, in our example, to AB_3.

We will now carry out such experiments and observe the forma-tion of a yellow precipitate, using the molar ratios from 3:1 to 3:9 (1:3) to cover the range of possible formulas from A_3B to AB_3: A_3B, A_2B, AB, AB_2, AB_3.

Measure quantities carefully.

(2) Procedure. Since the experiments are to be semi-quanti-tative, it is necessary to measure quantities <u>exactly</u>. Always use the same dropper for lead nitrate solution and, **after cleaning,** for potas-sium iodide solution in preparing the set of solutions described below. To get 0.5 drop, squeeze the bulb of the medicine dropper gently until a droplet appears and then touch the top of the dropper to the inside of the test tube.

Prepare five solutions with different ratios of reagents.

Prepare five marked test tubes containing the number of drops of each solution and of water shown below. The numbers of drops are chosen to make constant total volume, while varying the range of molar ratios of the reagents from 1:3 to 3:1.

	I	II	III	IV	V
Lead nitrate	9	9	9	9	9
Potassium iodide	3	4.5	9	18	27
Water	28	26.5	22	13	4

Stir the solutions and rinse.

Rinse a stirring rod, and stir each solution in turn to mix, <u>being careful to rinse and dry the stirring rod between different solutions</u>. Centrifuge each tube, being careful to counterbalance the centrifuge.

With a rinsed dropper containing no droplets of water (shake it to remove the drop which tends to remain in the tip), remove some of the supernatant liquid from Tube I and place 5 drops in each of two clean test tubes. To one of these 5-drop samples, add 2 drops of potassium iodide solution. To the second sample, add 2 drops of lead nitrate solution. (It is not necessary here to use the same medicine dropper for both solutions.) From these two results, decide which ions

Determine which ions are in excess.

were in excess in Tube I. If a precipitate forms in either test, centrifuge the tube so that you can compare the quantity of precipitate with the amount formed in later tests. Be sure the tubes are properly labeled.

Repeat these tests on 5-drop samples of supernatant liquid from each of the other precipitation tubes: II, III, IV, and V.

Use the results from all five tests, and decide upon the formula of the yellow precipitate. From the results of your experi-ments, complete and balance the equation

$$Pb(NO_3)_2 \ + \ KI \ \longrightarrow \ ? \ + \ ?$$

Use (s) after the formula of the precipitate to indicate its identity.

NOTES

<u>Note 1.</u>   For the confirmatory test for iodine, each student should obtain only slightly more than the needed amount of dichloromethane (about 10 mL per student) in a small Erlenmeyer flask, and keep it stoppered between uses.

<u>Note 2.</u>   Test for Iodide Ion--page 88: The instructions say to warm the mixture for a few minutes in a boiling water bath. Overheating can cause a purple cloud of $I_2(g)$ to form in the top of the test tube; this should be taken as a positive test for iodide. Many students ignore this valuable clue.

THE PREPARATION OF COMMON ALUM FROM SCRAP ALUMINUM

Objective

To prepare common alum, $K_2SO_4 \cdot Al_2(SO_4)_3 \cdot 24H_2O$, from a discarded aluminum beverage can or from a piece of aluminum foil

Equipment Needed

600-mL beaker (for ice bath); two 250-mL beakers or one 250-mL and one 150-mL beaker; 25-mL graduated cylinder; stirring rod; burner; ring stand with ring; wire gauze; funnel, glass wool; vacuum filtration apparatus with Büchner funnel; filter paper; heat lamp or oven; sandpaper (if aluminum beverage cans are used)

Reagents Needed

Scrap aluminum weighing $\sim$1 gram (1 in. by 2 in. piece of aluminum can or piece of aluminum foil); 6 M KOH; methyl red indicator solution; 6 M H_2SO_4, ice; 95% alcohol

TECHNIQUES

Read the sections on weighing techniques and on vacuum filtration in the **Laboratory Techniques** section of this manual.

INTRODUCTION

Aluminum is the most abundant metal in the earth's surface (7.5%). The abundance of aluminum, coupled with its attractive combination of physical and chemical properties, accounts for the fact that it is one of the world's principal industrial raw materials.

Although the weight of a single aluminum can is quite small, the large number of such containers produced each year means that a very large tonnage of the metal is used. Since the metal is not consumed rapidly by corrosion, the amount of scrap aluminum grows rapidly while the available supply of the materials for the manufacture of aluminum decreases. The ecological problems thus created are typical of those of several different metals. One obvious approach is to recycle the used fabricated aluminum cans into other useful metallic objects.

This experiment illustrates another approach in which metallic aluminum is chemically converted into an industrially important compound, hydrated potassium aluminum sulfate, $K_2SO_4 \cdot Al_2(SO_4)_3 \cdot 24H_2O$, or common alum. Presently, it is used as a mordant to harden photographic film, to prepare pickles, and for other purposes. The ancient Egyptians, Greeks, and Romans used alum as a mordant in dyeing cloth. A mordant contains metal ions that bind dyes to the fabric. **Alum** is a generic term that describes hydrated double salts of certain metals. Alums can be described by the generalized formula, $M_2SO_4 \cdot M'_2(SO_4)_3 \cdot 24H_2O$ in which M (univalent) is commonly Na, K, NH_4, or Rb, and M' (trivalent) is commonly Al, Ga, V, Cr, Mn, Fe, or Co. True alums crystallize in well-

97

defined octahedra and many are beautifully colored, particularly those containing transition metals as the M'.

Aluminum dissolves solutions of strong bases like potassium hydroxide to form hydrogen and a soluble salt containing the complex ion $[Al(OH)_4]^-$. Aluminum oxide and hydroxide are said to be amphoteric because they react with and dissolve in solutions of strong acids as well as strong bases.

$$2\ Al\ +\ 2\ KOH\ +\ 6\ H_2O\ \longrightarrow\ 2\ KAl(OH)_4\ +\ 3\ H_2$$

or

$$2\ Al\ +\ 2[K^+\ +\ OH^-]\ +\ 6\ H_2O\ \longrightarrow\ 2[K^+\ +\ Al(OH)_4^-]\ +\ 3\ H_2$$

After the aluminum has dissolved, the excess potassium hydroxide is destroyed by the addition of sulfuric acid solution. The sulfuric acid also converts the complex ion, $[Al(OH)_4]^-$, to insoluble aluminum hydroxide.

$$2\ KAl(OH)_4\ +\ H_2SO_4\ \longrightarrow\ 2\ Al(OH)_{3(s)}\ +\ K_2SO_4\ +\ 2\ H_2O$$

or

$$2[K^+\ +\ Al(OH)_4^-]\ +\ [2H^+\ +\ SO_4^{2-}]\ \longrightarrow\ 2\ Al(OH)_{3(s)}\ +\ [2K^+\ +\ SO_4^{2-}]\ +\ 2\ H_2O$$

The insoluble aluminum hydroxide is neutralized by excess sulfuric acid to form aluminum sulfate, a soluble ionic compound.

$$2\ Al(OH)_{3(s)}\ +\ 3\ H_2SO_4\ \longrightarrow\ Al_2(SO_4)_3\ +\ 6\ H_2O$$

or

$$2\ Al(OH)_3\ +\ 3[2\ H^+\ +\ SO_4^{2-}]\ \longrightarrow\ [2\ Al^{3+}\ +\ 3\ SO_4^{2-}]\ +\ 6\ H_2O$$

As the solution is cooled, the double salt, hydrated potassium aluminum sulfate, crystallizes from the solution and is collected by filtration.

$$2\ K^+\ +\ 2\ Al^{3+}\ +\ 4\ SO_4^{2-}\ +\ 24\ H_2O\ \longrightarrow\ K_2SO_4 \cdot Al_2(SO_4)_3 \cdot 24\ H_2O_{(s)}$$

PROCEDURE

Obtain piece of aluminum metal.

Add KOH solution.

Heat solution to initiate reaction.

Some beverage cans aren't aluminum but are alloys that dissolve slowly. Do not use one of that type. If you have an aluminum can, use a 1 in. by 2 in. piece for this experiment. Sandpaper it to remove as much paint and lacquer as possible before you begin. Or, your instructor may provide a piece of aluminum foil as a source of "scrap" aluminum. The scrap aluminum may be in any form, but it will dissolve more rapidly if it has a large surface area. Place approximately 1 gram (weighed to nearest 0.001 g) of aluminum in a clean, dry 250-mL beaker, and add 34 mL of water and 15 mL of 6 M potassium hydroxide, KOH, solution. EXERCISE CARE IN HANDLING THE KOH SOLUTION BECAUSE IT IS VERY CORROSIVE AND WILL DISSOLVE CLOTHING AS WELL AS HUMAN SKIN. Heat the solution on a hot plate or over a steam bath to initiate the reaction and then maintain enough heat to sustain the reaction at a moderate rate. Large amounts of hydrogen will be evolved, and it is necessary that the exhaust fans be in operation and that all doors to the laboratory be open. Since hydrogen gas is approximately 1/15 as dense as air, it rises to the top of the room as it is formed. THERE SHOULD BE NO OPEN FLAMES USED WHILE HYDROGEN IS BEING PRODUCED. Approximately 10-15 minutes should be sufficient for the aluminum to dissolve completely. Continue the reaction as long as any bubbles of gas are formed.

Filter the solution.

When the reaction has ceased (no more bubbles of gas are being formed), remove the beaker from the heat and allow it to cool to room temperature. If any solid particles remain, prepare a filter by forcing a small plug of glass wool into the bottom of a funnel. Pour the solution through the funnel; the glass wool should trap any remaining solid particles. Collect the clear liquid in a clean 150- or 250-mL beaker. Use your wash bottle to rinse all of the solution from the beaker in which the aluminum was dissolved. Direct a stream of water around the top of the beaker so that the sides are washed down. Pour the wash water (not more than 20 mL) through the plug of glass wool in the funnel so that it is added to the solution that contains the dissolved aluminum. There is no reason to filter clear, colorless solutions that contain no solid particles.

Add ten drops of methyl red indicator solution to the clear, colorless solution. Methyl red is yellow in basic solutions and red in acidic solutions. To the cool solution, add 1.5 M H_2SO_4 (**Note 1**) A FEW DROPS AT A TIME WITH CONSTANT VIGOROUS STIRRING until the _solution turns red_. The addition of sulfuric acid will cause aluminum hydroxide to precipitate as white lumps. When enough sulfuric acid has been added to turn the solution red (AVOID EXCESS H_2SO_4), heat, and stir the solution vigorously until all of the solid $Al(OH)_3$ has dissolved. The solution should be red _and_ clear (no solid suspended). If it is not red, add a few more drops of 1.5 M H_2SO_4, warm and stir until it is red.

(margin: Adjust acidity of solution.)

Cool the clear, red solution in an ice bath for 20-30 minutes, with occasional stirring. Well-defined crystals of alum should form.

(margin: Cool the solution.)

While the solution is cooling, prepare a Büchner funnel for vacuum filtration. Ask your instructor to check your apparatus before you begin the filtration.

Transfer the alum crystals onto the filter paper with your stirring rod, and let the aspirator pull air through them until they appear dry. Then wash them once by pouring 20 mL of alcohol over them. Allow the vacuum to continue for a few minutes. Dry the crystals and filter paper under a heat lamp or in an oven a few minutes before weighing them.

(margin: Collect crystals of alum product.)

Transfer the dry crystals to a dry, **previously weighed** container. Weigh the crystals and container to determine the weight of alum crystals. Show your crystals to your instructor, and ask him/her to initial your report form. Calculate the % yield of alum.

(margin: Dry the crystals.)

If time permits, an additional crop of alum crystals can be recovered by evaporating the solution from which the alum crystals were obtained. If it appears you will have time, remove the solution from the filter flask BEFORE ALCOHOL IS POURED OVER THE ALUM CRYSTALS, and evaporate it to approximately half its original volume. Cool the solution in an ice bath a second time, and collect the second crop of crystals.

NOTEBOOK AND REPORT

Prepare and submit a completed report form such as the one on page 103.

NOTES

Note 1. Prepare 1.5 M H_2SO_4 by adding 10 mL of 6 M H_2SO_4 to 30 mL of H_2O in a beaker or flask. Mix well.

REFERENCES

1. R. E. Davis, K. D. Gailey and K. W. Whitten, _Principles of Chemistry_, Saunders College Publishing/HRW, Philadelphia (1984), Sections 2-7 and 2-9 (Stoichiometry) and Section 20-4.2 (Aluminum and alums).

2. K. W. Whitten, and K. D. Gailey, _General Chemistry_, 2nd ed., Saunders College Publishing/HRW, Philadelphia (1984), Sections 2-8 and 2-10 (Stoichiometry) and Section 21-8 (Aluminum and alums).

Experiment 6

THE PREPARATION OF COMMON ALUM FROM SCRAP ALUMINUM

PRELABORATORY QUESTIONS

Name_____   Lab Instructor_____

Student ID No._____   Date_____

1. What is the weight of aluminum in 10.0 tons of the common aluminum ore bauxite if it contains 75.0% Al_2O_3 by weight?

2. Calculate the number of moles and the weight of $CuSO_4 \cdot (NH_4)_2SO_4 \cdot 6H_2O$ that can be prepared from 318 g of copper by the following reactions. Assume that all chemicals are added in sufficient quantities so that all reactions are complete and that all of the $CuSO_4 \cdot (NH_4)_2SO_4 \cdot 6H_2O$ can be isolated. The balanced equations are:

$$Cu \; + \; 2\,H_2SO_4 \; \longrightarrow \; CuSO_4 \; + \; SO_2 \; + \; 2\,H_2O$$

$$CuSO_4 \; + \; (NH_4)_2SO_4 \; + \; 6\,H_2O \; \longrightarrow \; CuSO_4 \cdot (NH_4)_2SO_4 \cdot 6\,H_2O$$

3. Answer the following questions which are based on the reactions described in this experiment.

   a. Write the molecular equation for the dissolution of aluminum in potassium hydroxide solution.

   b. How many moles of potassium hydroxide would be required to dissolve 10 g of aluminum? What weight of potassium hydroxide is this?

   c. How many moles of alum can be produced from 10 g of aluminum? What weight of alum is this? (Write the balanced equations.)

   d. Suppose 10 g of aluminum are converted completely to alum and that 75% of the alum is isolated. What weight of alum is this?

Experiment 6

THE PREPARATION OF COMMON ALUM

REPORT FORM

Name_____   Lab Instructor_____

Student ID No._____   Date_____

1. Weight of scrap aluminum used (g)   _____

2. No. of moles of aluminum atoms used (mol)   _____

3. Theoretical yield of alum in moles (mol)   _____

4. Theoretical yield of alum in grams (g)   _____

5. Actual weight of alum obtained (g)   _____

6. % yield of alum = (5)/(4) x 100% (%)   _____

SHOW YOUR CALCULATION IN DETAIL

7. Instructor's approval of crystals   _____

SOME REACTIONS OF TEN METAL IONS

Objective

To mix solutions of ten different metal ions, individually, with solutions of different anions and ammonia; to observe which combinations result in reactions; and to use this information to identify the metal ions present in unknown solutions

Equipment Needed

Ten 150-mm test tubes and test tube rack; medicine dropper; two stirring rods

Reagents Needed

If centrifuges are available, use one-half of the amounts specified in the directions and use a centrifuge to separate liquids and solids.

Dichloromethane;
0.1 M solutions of the following in dropping bottles:
$Pb(NO_3)_2$, $Mn(NO_3)_2$, $Cu(NO_3)_2$, $Fe(NO_3)_3$, $Co(NO_3)_2$, $Al(NO_3)_3$, $Zn(NO_3)_2$, $Mg(NO_3)_2$, $Ba(NO_3)_2$, KNO_3;
2 M solutions of the following in dropping bottles:
$(NH_4)_2SO_4$, NaI (KI is suitable substitute), NH_4SCN;
the following solutions in dropping bottles:
1 M $(NH_4)_2S$, 4 M NaOH, 6 M aq. NH_3;
0.1 M solutions of metal nitrates as unknowns (10 mL each)

TECHNIQUES

If centrifuges are used, read the section on their use in the **Laboratory Techniques** section of this manual.

INTRODUCTION

In this experiment, you will study the reactions of the following ten common metal ions and then use their characteristic reactions to identify cations in unknown solutions.

1. Pb^{2+}, lead(II) or plumbous ion*
2. Cu^{2+}, copper(II) or cupric ion[†]
3. Mn^{2+}, manganese(II) or manganous ion
4. Fe^{3+}, iron(III) or ferric ion
5. Co^{2+}, cobalt(II) or cobaltous ion[†]

6. Al^{3+}, aluminum(III) ion
7. Zn^{2+}, zinc(II) ion
8. Mg^{2+}, magnesium ion
9. Ba^{2+}, barium ion
10. K^+, potassium ion

You will study their reactions with a series of common anions.

1. SO_4^{2-}, sulfate ion
2. S^{2-}, sulfide ion
3. I^-, iodide ion

4. SCN^-, thiocyanate ion[‡]
5. OH^-, hydroxide ion

Additionally, you will examine the reactions of the cations with a limited amount and then with an excess of aqueous ammonia, NH_3.

It is convenient to group bases with similar properties together. We can conveniently classify bases into four classes. Refer to your text for a more detailed description and a list of common examples.

1. As the classification name implies, strong soluble bases are soluble in water and dissociate completely, or nearly completely, in dilute aqueous solutions. These include the alkali metal hydroxides, as well as the hydroxides of the heavier alkaline-earth metal ions, Ca^{2+}, Sr^{2+}, and Ba^{2+}. Thus, even dilute aqueous solutions of NaOH, the most common strong soluble base, contain large numbers of OH^- ions.

2. Weak soluble bases are soluble in water, but form relatively few ions in water. Aqueous ammonia and its derivatives, the amines, are the common weak soluble bases.

3. Insoluble bases are those that dissolve in water only very slightly. All of the common metal hydroxides other than the strong soluble bases (see 1 above) are insoluble in water.

4. Amphoteric hydroxides (bases) are insoluble hydroxides that react with and dissolve in both acids and strong soluble bases. For example, aluminum hydroxide dissolves in acids to form simple aluminum salts.

$$Al(OH)_{3(s)} \ + \ 3 H_{(aq)}^+ \ \longrightarrow \ Al_{(aq)}^{3+} \ + \ 3 H_2O$$

It also dissolves in potassium hydroxide to form a soluble compound containing a complex ion. Other amphoteric hydroxides show similar behavior.

$$Al(OH)_{3(s)} \ + \ OH^- \ \longrightarrow \ [Al(OH)_4]^-$$

You will observe several metathesis reactions and several oxidation-reduction reactions. You will also observe reactions that result in the formation of soluble compounds containing complex ions.

Many metathesis reactions involve simple ionic combinations to form insoluble compounds (precipitates) in aqueous solutions. For example, if a solution of silver nitrate, $AgNO_3$, is mixed with a solution of potassium chromate, K_2CrO_4, insoluble silver chromate precipitates from the solution, and soluble potassium nitrate remains dissolved in water as the following molecular equation indicates. (Refer to your text or to Appendix VIII to be sure you understand the distinctions among molecular, total ionic, and net ionic equations.)

---

*Because lead(II), Pb^{2+}, is the common ion of lead, its compounds are frequently named without the Roman numeral indicator of oxidation state; i.e., $Pb(NO_3)_2$ is often called lead nitrate rather than lead(II) nitrate.

[†]Ditto the comments made for Pb^{2+}.

[‡]The prefix thio- always indicates the presence of sulfur. For example, OCN^- is the cyanate ion and SCN^- is the thiocyanate ion.

$$2 \ AgNO_3 \quad + \quad K_2CrO_4 \quad \longrightarrow \quad Ag_2CrO_{4(s)} \quad + \quad 2 \ KNO_3$$

Or, as a <u>total ionic equation</u>,

$$2[Ag^+ + NO_3^-] \quad + \quad [2 \ K^+ + CrO_4^{2-}] \quad \longrightarrow \quad Ag_2CrO_{4(s)} \quad + \quad 2[K^+ + NO_3^-]$$

The K^+ and NO_3^- ions do not participate in the reaction and are called "spectator ions." Cancelling the two NO_3^- and the two K^+ ions that appear on both sides of the equation gives the <u>net ionic equation</u> which describes accurately the reaction between aqueous solutions of $AgNO_3$ and K_2CrO_4.

$$2 \ Ag_{(aq)}^+ \quad + \quad CrO_{4(aq)}^{2-} \quad \longrightarrow \quad Ag_2CrO_{4(s)}$$

All <u>oxidation-reduction</u> reactions (redox reactions) involve changes in oxidation numbers. When iron(III) ions, Fe^{3+}, are mixed with iodide ions, I^-, the colorless iodide ions are oxidized to free iodine, I_2, and iron(III) ions are reduced to iron(II) ions, Fe^{2+}. Free iodine is yellow to brown in aqueous solutions but pink to purple when dissolved in organic solvents such as methylene chloride, CH_2Cl_2.

$$2 \ Fe_{(aq)}^{3+} \quad + \quad 2 \ I_{(aq)}^- \quad \longrightarrow \quad 2 \ Fe_{(aq)}^{2+} \quad + \quad I_{2(s)}$$

In other cases, you will observe simple metathesis reactions that are also precipitation reactions, such as the combination of lead ions with hydroxide ions to form insoluble lead hydroxide,

$$Pb^{2+} \quad + \quad 2 \ OH^- \quad \longrightarrow \quad Pb(OH)_{2(s)},$$

followed by dissolution of the insoluble, amphoteric $Pb(OH)_2$ in an <u>excess</u> of the strong soluble base, NaOH, to form a soluble compound, $Na_2[Pb(OH)_4]$, containing a complex ion,

$$Pb(OH)_{2(s)} \quad + \quad 2 \ OH^- \quad \longrightarrow \quad [Pb(OH)_4]^{2-}.$$

The insoluble hydroxides of certain metal ions and several other insoluble compounds of these metal ions are soluble in an excess of aqueous ammonia. Aqueous ammonia, a weak soluble base, reacts with water only to a limited extent;

$$NH_3 \quad + \quad H_2O \quad \rightleftharpoons \quad NH_4^+ \quad + \quad OH^-$$

although solutions of aqueous ammonia contain low concentrations of OH^- ions, they contain high concentrations of nonionized ammonia molecules. When aqueous ammonia is added slowly to solutions of common metal ions whose hydroxides are insoluble bases, the metal hydroxides precipitate. Addition of <u>excess</u> aqueous ammonia dissolves the insoluble hydroxides of the metals of the cobalt, nickel, copper, and zinc families (with the exceptions of Hg_2^{2+}) by forming ammine complex ions, $[M(NH_3)_x]^{y+}$, in which x is commonly 2, 4, or 6 and y is 1, 2, or 3. For example, if aqueous ammonia is added slowly to a solution containing Cu^{2+} ions, the first reaction that occurs is the precipitation of light blue, insoluble $Cu(OH)_2$.

$$Cu^{2+} \quad + \quad 2 \ NH_3 \quad + \quad 2 \ H_2O \quad \longrightarrow \quad Cu(OH)_{2(s)} \quad + \quad 2 \ NH_4^+$$

Note that we have written the equation to show nonionized ammonia molecules and water molecules on the left side of the equation since these are the principal species present in aqueous ammonia solutions. Addition of excess aqueous ammonia dissolves $Cu(OH)_2$ and results in the formation of the deep blue to purple complex ion, $[Cu(NH_3)_4]^{2+} \quad + \quad 2OH^-$

$$Cu(OH)_{2(s)} \quad + \quad 4 \ NH_3 \quad \longrightarrow \quad [Cu(NH_3)_4]^{2+} \quad + \quad 2 \ OH^-$$

GENERAL COMMENTS ON PROCEDURES

You will observe a series of reactions of known solutions of ten common metal ions. After you have completed these reactions, you will be given two unknown solutions, each of which contains one cation. You will observe the same reactions on your unknown solutions as on the known solutions so you can identify the cations in your unknown solutions.

On the reagent shelf you will find solutions that are 0.1 molar (0.1 mol/L of solution) in the (separate) ten metal ions in the form of nitrate salts. In performing tests, place distilled water in your test tubes to a depth of approximately 0.5 in. Then add ten drops of the indicated cation, mix well, and add the indicated amount of the specifiefd reagent. As reagents are added, observe carefully for any indication of chemical reaction. ALWAYS MIX WELL1! Formation of solids (and their colors), gas evolution, color changes in solutions, and temperature changes provide evidence for chemical reactions. Record your observation on the report form

NOTEBOOK AND REPORT

Construct tabular report forms similar to those on pages 113-114. Fill them out as the reactions are performed.

PROCEDURE

Obtain solutions of ten metal ions.

Add $(NH_4)_2SO_4$ solution to each test tube.

1. Reactions of Metal Ions with Sulfate Ions, SO_4^{2-}. Place approximately 0.5 in. of distilled water in each of ten test tubes. Add ten drops of lead nitrate solution to test tube 1, ten drops of copper(II) nitrate solution to test tube 2, etc. Observe the colors of the metal ions in aqueous solution. Label the test tubes so that you do not confuse one test tube with another! To each of the ten test tubes, add ten drops of 2 M ammonium sulfate, $(NH_4)_2SO_4$, solution. Shake the test tubes to mix thoroughly, and observe carefully for any evidence of reaction. Most insoluble sulfates are slow in forming, highly crystalline, and nearly colorless. We call them "white" for want of a better term. Record your observations, and write the formulas for the insoluble sulfates in the appropriate spaces.

Repeat procedure (1) with $(NH_4)_2S$.

2. Reactions of Metal Ions with Sulfide Ions, S^{2-}. Wash your test tubes thoroughly and repeat the procedures used above exactly but add ten drops of 1 M ammonium sulfide, $(NH_4)_2S$, solution rather than ten drops of ammonium sulfate to each test tube.

Repeat procedure (1) with I^- and shake with CH_2Cl_2.

3. Reactions of Metal Ions with Iodide Ions, I^-. Wash your test tubes thoroughly, and repeat the procedures used above but add ten drops of 2 M sodium iodide, NaI, or potassium iodide, KI, solution to each metal ion. Now add 15 drops of dichloromethane, CH_2Cl_2, to each test tube in which a yellow or dark colored precipitate formed. (CAUTION: DO NOT LET DICHLOROMETHANE COME IN CONTACT WITH YOUR SKIN AND AVOID BREATHING THE VAPORS! If you do let dichloromethane touch your skin, wash immediately with soap and water.) Stir the mixture vigorously and observe the dichloromethane layer. Dichloromethane is more dense than water. Free iodine (I_2) is pink to violet in dichloromethane.

Treat the metal ions with NH_4SCN.

4. Reactions of Metal Ions with Thiocyanate Ions, SCN^-. Wash your test tubes thoroughly and repeat the above procedures but add ten drops of 2 M ammonium thiocyanate, NH_4SCN, to each metal ion. One of these reactions is different from the others. Iron(III) ions react with thiocyanate ions to form a red, complex ion, $[Fe(NCS)]^{2+}$, i.e.,

$$Fe^{3+} \;+\; SCN^- \longrightarrow [Fe(NCS)]^{2+} \quad \text{(red colored solution)}.$$

Treat the metal ions with strong base.

5. Reactions of Metal Ions with Strong Soluble Bases. Wash your test tubes thoroughly and repeat the procedures used above but add two drops of 4 M sodium hydroxide solution (a limited amount) to each ion. Record your observations. (Be careful! Some precipitates are nearly colorless.) Allow the precipitates to settle, pour off as much liquid as possible, retaining most of the solid in the test tube.* Now

*Alternatively, you may be able to withdraw most of the liquid with a medicine dropper. Discard the liquid and rinse the medicine dropper thoroughly before using it again.

add an additional ten drops of 4 M sodium hydroxide (an excess) to each precipitate. Mix well and record your second set of observations.

Treat the metal
ions with NH₃.

6. Reactions of Metal Ions with Aqueous Ammonia. Wash your test tubes thoroughly, and repeat the procedures used above but add two drops of 6 M aqueous ammonia solution (a limited amount) to each metal ion. Observe carefully to determine whether or not precipitation occurs. Record your observations. Allow the precipitates to settle; pour off as much liquid as possible while retaining most of the solid in the test tubes.* Now add an additional ten drops of 6 M aqueous ammonia (an excess) to each precipitate. Mix well and record your second set of observations.

Analysis of Unknown Solutions for Metal Ions

After you have completed your work on the known solutions and it has been approved by your laboratory instructor, s/he will issue two unknown solutions to you. Each contains one metal ion. RECORD THE UNKNOWN NUMBERS. BE ABSOLUTELY CERTAIN THAT THE RESULTS THAT YOU REPORT CORRESPOND TO THE NUMBERS ON THE UNKNOWNS.

Repeat the
tests on your
unknown
solution.

Place approximately 0.5 in. of water in each of six clean test tubes and add ten drops of one unknown to each test tube. Repeat procedures 1, 2, 3, 4, 5, and 6 above. Observe each test tube carefully for evidence of reaction. Record your observations on the unknown report form. Which metal ion does this unknown contain?

Now, determine which metal ion is present in your second unknown and complete the second part of the unknown report form.

Helpful Hints

The following "flow chart" may assist in learning to organize the information you gain from each test. When ammonium sulfate is added to solutions containing the ten metal ions, only Pb^{2+} and Ba^{2+} react to form insoluble compounds.

$$Pb^{2+} \xrightarrow{\;SO_4^{2-}\;} PbSO_4 \text{ (a white solid)}$$

Cu^{2+}	N.R.
Mn^{2+}	N.R.
Fe^{3+}	N.R.
Co^{2+}	N.R.
Al^{3+}	N.R.
Zn^{2+}	N.R.
Mg^{2+}	N.R.
Ba^{2+}	$BaSO_4$ (a white solid)
K^+	N.R.

Thus, when you add $(NH_4)_2SO_4$ to your unknown, you will observe that either (1) a white precipitate forms and you know that either Pb^{2+} or Ba^{2+} must be present **or** (2) no precipitate forms and neither Pb^{2+} nor Ba^{2+} can be present, and, therefore, one of the other eight cations must be present. From the other tests, you will gather additional information that will enable you to identify the cations present in your unknown.

---

*Alternatively, you may be able to withdraw most of the liquid with a medicine dropper. Discard the liquid and rinse the medicine dropper thoroughly before using it again.

REFERENCES

1. R. E. Davis, K. D. Gailey, and K. W. Whitten, <u>Principles of Chemistry</u>, Saunders College Publishing/HRW, Philadelphia (1984), Sections 6-13 and 6-14 (Inorganic Nomenclature), Sections 9-3 through 9-7 (Reactions in Aqueous Solutions), Section 26-2 (Ammine Complexes).

2. K. W. Whitten and K. D. Gailey, <u>General Chemistry</u>, 2nd ed., Saunders College Publishing/HRW, Philadelphia (1984), Sections 5-23 and 5-24 (Inorganic Nomenclature), Sections 7-1 through 7-7 (Chemical Reactions), Section 11-8 (Amphoterism), Section 27-2 (Ammine Complexes.)

DISCOVERING OPTIMUM REACTION CONDITIONS

USING THIN LAYER CHROMATOGRAPHY

Objective

To work as a class to discover the conditions that produce the best yield of product in a chemical reaction; to work with very small quantities of material. To learn the technique of thin layer chromatography

Equipment Needed

Four 0.5 in. x 4 in. thin layer chromatography plates coated with silica gel; two 250-mL beakers; four 6-in. and five 4-in. test tubes; hot plate, drying oven; two 3-in. capillary tubes, bore 0.25-0.75 mm

Reagents Needed

0.10 M glycine solution; 2% solution of o-phthalaldehyde in 50% acetone/water; 1% KOH in 95% ethanol; 95% ethanol; butanol; 12 M HCl; 10 M H_3PO_4; 6 M solutions of HNO_3, H_2SO_4, HBr, and HI; Kemwipes or other blotting paper

INTRODUCTION

In this experiment your class will work as a team to discover the conditions that produce the most product in a chemical reaction. The reaction will be conducted with very small quantities of material. Thin layer chromatography will be used to separate the unreacted reactants and product after the reaction is terminated.

Each student will conduct the reaction under four sets of conditions and compare his/her results with those of classmates who have used different conditions. These comparisons should make it possible to identify the most favorable conditions for yielding the product.

The Reaction. The reaction to be studied is the synthesis of a substance known as an ester--a compound formed in the reaction of an alcohol with an organic acid. The odors of many fruits--apples, bananas, pears, and oranges, for example--are due to esters found in these fruits. You will react ethyl alcohol (ethanol) with the amino acid glycine to form an ester, as illustrated by the equation below:

$$CH_2-CO_2H \ + \ CH_3CH_2OH \ \longrightarrow \ CH_2CO_2CH_2CH_3 \ + \ H_2O.$$
$$\underset{NH_2}{|} \qquad\qquad\qquad\qquad \underset{NH_2}{|}$$

glycine   ethanol   ethyl glycinate
                                  (an ester)

It is known that this reaction is favored by acid catalysts. You will try various acids and temperatures in an effort to find the best conditions for the reaction.

Thin Layer Chromatography (TLC). After conducting the reaction, this technique will be used to separate unreacted reactants from products. TLC involves (1) preparing a thin layer made of a smoothly spread layer of some absorbent material on plastic, (2) spotting the plate with small amounts of materials--dissolved in an appropriate solvent-- to be separated, (3) developing the chromatogram, that is, allowing a liquid phase to move across the stationary phase until a separation has been effected, and (4) dyeing the chromatogram, if necessary, so the separated components can be observed. The liquid on the surface of the stationary phase in most thin layer chromatography operations is water, even though the plates appear to be perfectly dry. The liquid used in the moving phase usually is a nonpolar solvent or one that is much less polar than water. The components are then partitioned (divided) between these solvents of differing polarities.

The relative rate of movement of a component across the stationary phase is characteristic of that component under the fixed conditions of solvent, stationary phase, temperature, and so forth. The relative rate of movement is symbolized by R_f:

$$R_f = \frac{\text{distance a compound moves}}{\text{distance the solvent moves}}.$$

The solid support in the stationary phase in thin layer chromatography usually is silica gel (SiO_2 and H_2O), sometimes known as silicic acid; or alumina (Al_2O_3 and H_2O). Some commonly used developing solvents are pentane, hexane, diethyl ether, acetone, and ethanol. Mixtures of these solvents also are commonly used as developing fluids. Butanol will be used as the developing solvent in this experiment.

The purity of a single developing solvent or the composition of a mixture of such solvents is an important factor in the success of chromatography. Obviously, the greater the developing power of the solvent, the more effective will be the separation. A good developing solvent should effect a satisfactory separation after it has moved approxmately 10 cm across the plate.

In order to see the glycine and ethylglycinate on your TLC plates, you will dye these substances with o-phthalaldehyde. This substance reacts with the –NH$_2$ group on both substances to give a pink to red color. Treatment with potassium hydroxide and heating in an oven facilitate the dyeing reaction.

Reaction Conditions to be Explored. A wide variety of reaction conditions can be examined for this reaction. Following are several groups, each containing four sets of reaction conditions. Your instructor will assign one of these groups to you, then you can use the procedure described below to discover how well the reaction proceeds under each set of conditions. You and your classmates will record your results on the grid designated Table 8-1. After examining the entries in Table 8-1, you should be able to identify the most favorable conditions for the reaction.

Groups of Suggested Reaction Conditions

I	II	III	IV
6 M H_2SO_4–ice$_{10}$	6 M HNO_3–ice$_{10}$	12 M HCl–ice$_{10}$	6 M HBr–ice$_{10}$
6 M H_2SO_4–room$_{10}$	6 M HNO_3–room$_{10}$	12 M HCl–room$_{10}$	6 M HBr–room$_{10}$
6 M H_2SO_4–heated	6 M HNO_3–heated	12 M HCl–heated	6 M HBr–heated
no acid, heated	no acid, heated	no acid, heated	no acid, heated

V	VI	VII	VIII
6 M H_2SO_4–heated	6 M H_2SO_4–heated	12 M HCl – heated	6 M HNO_3–heated
6 M HCl – heated	6 M H_3PO_4–heated	8 M HCl – heated	6 M HBr –heated
6 M H_3PO_4–heated	4 M H_2SO_4–heated	6 M H_3PO_4–heated	4 M HNO_3–heated
6 M HNO_3– heated	2 M H_2SO_4–heated	6 M HCl – heated	4 M HBr –heated

IX	X	XI	XII
6 M H_2SO_4-heated$_2$	12 M HCl-heated$_2$	6 M HBr-heated$_2$	6 M H_3PO_4-heated$_{20}$
6 M H_2SO_4-heated$_5$	12 M HCl-heated$_5$	6 M HBr-heated$_5$	10 M H_3PO_4-heated$_{20}$
6 M H_2SO_4-heated$_{20}$	12 M HCl-heated$_{20}$	6 M HBr-heated	6 M HI - heated
no acid, heated$_{20}$	no acid, heated$_{20}$	no acid, heated$_{20}$	6 M HI - heated$_{20}$

If not otherwise specified, heated means for 10 minutes in the water bath. Subscripts refer to the number of minutes the reaction is to remain in the water bath or other environment.

PROCEDURE

Obtain from your instructor the reaction conditions you are to examine. Then prepare the materials for the experiments as follows.

1. Start a warm (50-60 °C) water bath in a 250-mL beaker on a hot plate.

Prepare water bath, test tubes, and TLC plates.

2. Thoroughly clean four 6-in. test tubes and five 4-in. test tubes. Place the 6-in. test tubes in the oven for 10 minutes to dry.

3. Label the 4-in. test tubes as follows:
Test Tube 1: glycine, ethanol reaction mixture (GERM)
Test Tubes 2-5: reaction conditions 1, 2, 3, and 4, with each test tube having a different number (RC-1, RC-2, etc.). These test tubes will be used to conduct the four reactions.

4. Prepare four thin layer chromatography plates (TLC) as follows. Obtain four plates from the instructor. By use of a **pencil**, draw a **light** line 1 cm from the bottom on each plate. The pencil mark should not break or mar the surface of the plate. Label the plates RC-1, RC-2, RC-3, and RC-4 at the top (see Fig. 8-1). Also place your intials at the top.

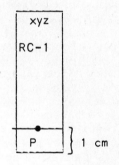

Now assemble the chemical substances needed to conduct the reaction as follows.

Figure 8-1. Sketch of the TLC plate, showing proper markings.

1. Add 2 mL of the 0.10 M glycine solution and 2 mL of ethanol to the test tube marked GERM. Stir or shake to mix thoroughly.

2. In the test tube marked RC-1, place 3 drops of the acid specified in the first of the four sets of reaction conditions assigned to you. In Test Tube RC-2, place 3 drops of the acid to be used in the second set of conditions on your list. If no acid is required, add 3 drops of distilled water to the test tube. Continue this procedure with Test Tubes RC-3 and RC-4.

Assemble and add chemicals to test tubes.

3. Now place 20 drops of the glycine ethanol mixture in each of the four test tubes (RC-1, RC-2, RC-3, RC-4), and subject each test tube and its contents to the temperature conditions indicated in your assignment. If, for example, your assignment calls for all four reactions to be heated for 10 minutes, place the four test tubes in your warm water bath for 10 minutes.

119

While the reactions are taking place, prepare the TLC materials so that when the reactions are terminated, the products can be separated from unreacted reactants and identified.

1. Pour 5 mL of butanol into each of the 6-in. test tubes (they should be at room temperature).

Add chemicals to TLC plates.

2. Observe the demonstration given by your instructor on how to spot (place samples on) the TLC plates. This is a critically important step. Learn to do it well. The spot should be as small but as intense as possible. Placement of ten or more tiny spots--one on top of the other--is much better than one larger spot.

3. When the reactions have proceeded for the specified time, remove the test tubes from the heating bath or other location. By use of a fine capillary tube, quickly spot samples of the reaction mixture from each test tube on the TLC plate marked for that mixture. Label the marked spot "P" (see Fig. 8-1). Allow the spots to dry.

Develop TLC plates.

4. Place one TLC plate (**spotted end down**) into each 6-in. test tube. Be certain that the butanol level in the test tube remains below the spot of sample on the plate. Cover the test tubes with parafilm or plastic wrap. Note the time.

5. Let the plates remain in the test tubes until the solvent front is about 1 cm from the top of the plate.

6. Remove each plate and blot on a paper towel the end that was in the solvent. Let the plates dry for a few minutes.

Treat and bake TLC plates.

7. Dip each plate into the o-phthalaldehyde development mixture, blot as before, and place them in a 250-mL beaker. Put the beaker and plates in the oven for 2 minutes.

8. Remove the plates from the oven and note any colored spots.

9. Dip each plate into the KOH development mixture, blot, and return it to the beaker. Place the beaker and plates in the oven for 10 minutes.

10. Remove the plates from the oven, and note the colored spots. Use a pencil to circle all colored spots. The colors will fade rapidly.

11. Using a ruler marked in millimeters, determine the R_f value for the product on each of the plates. Compare the R_f values found.

INTERPRETING AND RECORDING THE RESULTS

Upon removal of the TLC plates from the oven, three areas of color may be visible: one is unreacted glycine, the second is the reaction product, ethylglycinate, and the third is a yellow residue from the developing solvent. Unreacted glycine should be at the lowest point on the plate, and the yellow residue should be at the highest point. The product should appear between the two. The reason for this sequence is that unreacted glycine remains at the point at which it was spotted, and the developing solvent front (which leads to the yellow residue) moves to the highest point on the plate.

In interpreting the developed TLC plate (chromatogram), you will be primarily interested in the amount of product visible on the plate. For each of the four reaction mixtures, you must decide which of the following possibilities best describes the results:

a)   the amount of product formed was too small to produce a spot on the plate (Code 0)

b)   the amount of product formed was detectable but not substantial (Code 1)

c)   the amount of product formed was substantial (Code 2).*

When you have interpreted your chromatograms, record the results in your notebook and in Table 8-1. Use the code designation 0, 1, and 2 to record your data.

Knowing that the glycine solution you used is 0.10 M and that the 95% by weight ethanol has a density of 0.769 g/mL, and assuming that one drop of the reaction mixture is 0.05 mL, calculate the moles of glycine and the moles of ethanol you used in two of the reactions you conducted. Assuming you can get no more than 5.0×10^{-6} liters of your reaction mixture on a TLC plate, what is the maximum number of moles of glycine or ethylglycinate that could be present on the plate?

Obtain from your instructor guidance on how to acquire the results of experiments conducted by your classmates. Record these results in Table 8-1, using the 0, 1, 2 codes. Based on an examination of the data you accumulate in Table 8-1, write a short paragraph describing the most favorable and the least favorable conditions for conducting this reaction.

NOTEBOOK AND REPORT

Your notebook should be organized similar to the data sheet at the end of this experiment. It should differentiate the data you collected from that collected by your classmates. TLC plates, properly marked, should be stapled in your notebook.

QUESTIONS AND PROBLEMS

1.   The glycine/ethanol reaction mixture you used contains 0.4% glycine and 38% ethanol. Assuming one drop of this mixture weighs 45 milligrams, how many moles of each reactant are present in one drop of the reaction mixtures you used?

2.   If your yield of ethylglycinate was 40% of theoretical (40% of the maximum possible from the amounts used in the reaction), how many moles of product would be formed in one drop of the reaction mixture? Assuming you get 0.10 drops of your reaction mixture on a TLC plate, how many moles of product would you be looking at when you develop your chromatogram?

3.   One set of reaction conditions not changed in this study is the amounts and conditions of the reactants. Describe a set of two experiments you could do to see if changing the amounts and conditions of the reactants changes the yield of product. One restriction here: you cannot use more than 20 drops of total reactants. It also may be important to remember that glycine is a solid and ethanol is a liquid at room temperature.

4.   Classify the acids used in this study as strong or weak acids. Does acid strength have any influence on this reaction? Explain your answer.

5.   What role does each of the following play in this study?   a) butanol;
                                                               b) o-phthalaldehyde

6.   Are you satisfied that the conditions used in this experiment tell you the best conditions for conducting this reaction? Justify or explain your answer.

----

*See the chromatogram prepared by your instructor for an example of a substantial amount of product.

Table 8-1

Summary of Results of Running the Reaction at Different Conditions

Acid Catalysts	Reaction Conditions					
	Ice	Room Temperature	Heated$_2$	Heated$_5$	Heated$_{10}$	Heated$_{20}$
12 M HCl	_____	_____	_____	_____	_____	_____
10 M H$_3$PO$_4$	_____	_____	_____	_____	_____	_____
8 M HCl	_____	_____	_____	_____	_____	_____
6 M HCl	_____	_____	_____	_____	_____	_____
6 M H$_2$SO$_4$	_____	_____	_____	_____	_____	_____
6 M HNO$_3$	_____	_____	_____	_____	_____	_____
6 M HBr	_____	_____	_____	_____	_____	_____
6 M H$_3$PO$_4$	_____	_____	_____	_____	_____	_____
4 M H$_2$SO$_4$	_____	_____	_____	_____	_____	_____
4 M HNO$_3$	_____	_____	_____	_____	_____	_____
4 M HCl	_____	_____	_____	_____	_____	_____
4 M H$_3$PO$_4$	_____	_____	_____	_____	_____	_____
4 M HI	_____	_____	_____	_____	_____	_____
4 M HBr	_____	_____	_____	_____	_____	_____
2 M H$_2$SO$_4$	_____	_____	_____	_____	_____	_____
no catalyst	_____	_____	_____	_____	_____	_____

Meaning of entries in Table: 0 = no product observed

1 = low yield of product observed

2 = good yield of product observed

Experiment 8

DISCOVERING OPTIMUM REACTION CONDITIONS; USING TLC

PRELABORATORY QUESTIONS

Name_____   Lab Instructor_____

Student ID_____   Date_____

1.   What are you and your classmates attempting to learn by doing this experiment?

2.   Describe what you will be expected to do to achieve the goal in Question (1) above.

3.   What is TLC? How will it provide the information you seek in this situation?

4. The procedure directs you to place 10 tiny drops of your reaction mixture, one on top of the other, on the TLC plate. Why would one or two drops not be enough?

5. Why must TLC plates be marked with pencil rather than with ink?

6. What is meant by developing a TLC chromatogram? How will this be done in this experiment?

7. After spotting, developing, and dyeing a TLC plate in this experiment, what do you expect the plate to show you?

Experiment 8

DISCOVERING OPTIMUM REACTION CONDITIONS; USING TLC

REPORT SHEET

Name_____   Lab Instructor_____

Student ID_____   Date_____

	Experiments assigned to you	Reactants Used (moles)		Ethylglycinate	
		glycine	ethanol	yield (code 0,1,2)	R_f value
1.	_____	_____	_____	_____	_____
2.	_____	_____	_____	_____	_____
3.	_____	_____	_____	_____	_____
4.	_____	_____	_____	_____	_____

Results of experiments of entire class (complete Table 8-1 and attach it to your report).

Calculations

     Moles of glycine used:

     Moles of ethanol used:

     Maximum moles of glycine or ethyl glycinate that could be present on a TLC plate:

Conclusions (paragraph describing the most favorable and the least favorable conditions for conducting the reaction):

Attach answers to the assigned questions from QUESTIONS AND PROBLEMS.

SPECTROSCOPY AND COLOR

Objective

To provide experience in the experimental and interpretative aspects of emission and absorption spectroscopy; to illustrate principles of the chemical basis for color; to discover the relation between absorption and concentration; to use the technique of serial dilutions

Equipment Needed

Spectroscope; hydrogen and helium discharge tubes for atomic spectra; high-voltage transformer, or induction coil and DC power source for operating the tubes; white-light source such as a flashlight; platinum or nichrome wires; burner; spectrophotometer; matched cuvettes or cells for spectrophotometer; 10-mL pipet, two micropipets with bulbs; 250-mL beaker; 25-mL graduate; wash bottle; seven 6-in. test tubes

Reagents Needed

Solutions (0.1 M) of sodium chloride, potassium chloride, calcium chloride, strontium chloride, and barium chloride; unknown solutions containing two or more of the preceding chlorides; concentrated hydrochloric acid. Solutions: 0.20 M cobalt(II) nitrate; 0.25 M nickel nitrate; 0.005 M iron(III) chloride in 0.1 M HCl; 0.01% aluminon; a solution of 0.03 M in copper(II) nitrate, 0.12 M in ammonium hydroxide, and 2.0 M in ammonium nitrate, unknown solutions containing known concentrations of the chemicals listed in Table 9.3

INTRODUCTION

Color is said to arise from the emission or absorption of photons of visible light by chemical species. Photons are absorbed or emitted as electrons move from one energy level to another in atoms, molecules, or ions. Chemical species that have been "excited" by heat, light, electrical, or other energy sources may emit photons as excited electrons return from higher to lower energy states. Electrons in unexcited chemical species may absorb photons and move to higher energy levels.

Light emission is studied using spectroscopes; absorption is studied using spectrophotometers. In this experiment, both types of instruments will be used. You will study emission and absorption and examine some fundamental relationships among energy levels, wavelengths of photons absorbed or emitted, and the observed color of the species or chemical system.

PART A.   EMISSION SPECTROSCOPY;
CALIBRATION OF A SPECTROSCOPE

Emission spectroscopy is the study of spectra emitted by excited atoms, molecules, or ions. To observe and study such spectra, an instrument known as a spectroscope is used.

The Hydrogen Spectrum. The spectrum of an element is the light emitted or absorbed by the atoms of that element. Excited atoms emit light of particular wavelengths. This is called the emission spectrum of the element. An emission spectrum consists of discrete lines, each of a particular color. Each line corresponds to a single wavelength or to a narrow band of wavelengths of light.

In the spectroscope, light emitted from excited atoms is passed through a prism or grating and separated into its various wavelengths. This effect is very similar to the way the sun's white light is separated into its component colors by rain droplets (Fig. 9-1). The atoms may be excited by light absorption, by an electric discharge, by heating to incandescence, or by some similar means. For this experiment, excitation of atoms is accomplished by passing an electric discharge through a gaseous sample of the element. Because each element has its own unique spectrum, a listing of the wavelengths of the lines in its spectrum identifies an element just as fingerprints identify a person.

Scientists think of light as being composed of tiny packets of energy called photons. The energy carried by a photon is related to the wavelength associated with the photon by the Planck equation

$$E = hc/\lambda \tag{1}$$

in which E is the energy of the photon in joules, λ is its wavelength in meters, c is the velocity of light in a vacuum (3.0×10^8 m/sec), and h is Planck's constant (6.63×10^{-34} J-sec). The energy associated with the photons comprising each line in the spectrum of an element can be calculated from this equation.

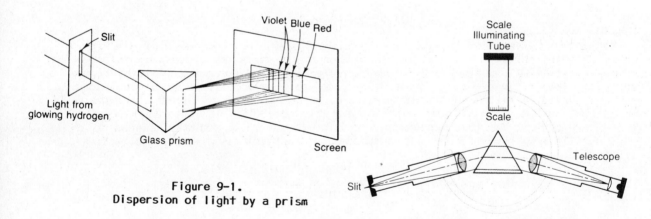

Figure 9-1.
Dispersion of light by a prism

Figure 9-2.   Spectroscope

Spectroscope. Fig. 9-2 is a diagram of the spectroscope used in this experiment.   Light from the excited atoms enters the instrument through the narrow slit, falls on the prism where it is separated into various colors, and moves along the telescope to the viewer's eye. A numerical scale is located in the third tube of the instrument. When a white light is placed at the end of this tube, the viewer can see both the spectrum of the element and the scale.

Calibration. Any study of spectra requires measurement of the wavelengths of spectra lines.   To do this, the spectroscope must contain a scale, and the operator must be able to associate each mark on the scale with a certain wavelength.   The process of finding which mark on the scale corresponds to which wavelength is known as <u>calibration</u>. With spectroscopes, the calibration is made by superimposing a set of spectral lines of known wavelength on the scale. In this way, the lines of known wavelength fall on certain marks on the scale, and the operator can now say that this certain mark corresponds to this certain wavelength. In order to save time in calibration, we obtain a wavelength fix on only about six or seven marks. Then, by plotting these six or seven points on a graph of wavelength as ordinate and scale-marking as abscissa and connecting the points with a smooth curve, we can identify any mark on the scale with a known wavelength. Such a graph is known as a calibration curve for the instrument.

Measurement of Spectral Lines. Let us now proceed to use the spectroscope by observing the spectrum of helium and obtaining the data needed to prepare a calibration curve.

PROCEDURE

Calibration of the Spectroscope. Place the helium discharge tube directly in front of the slit tube of the spectroscope. Adjust the width of the slit (on the front of the slit tube) so that you can see six or seven distinct lines of different colors.

Calibrate spectroscope with He spectrum.

Observe the spectrum of the helium discharge tube. Notice that there are distinct lines of different colors and that they are at different places on the calibration scale. In your notebook, record (to the nearest 0.1-scale division) the scale reading for at least six lines in this spectrum. Record the color of the line next to its scale reading. The first strong line should be bright red.

Observation of the Hydrogen Spectrum. Substitute the hydrogen discharge tube for the helium source, and record the scale reading for the intense red, the intense blue, and the violet line in the spectrum. Later you will use your calibration curve to determine the wavelengths of these lines.

Observe the hydrogen spectrum.

CALCULATIONS

The Calibration Curve. Table 9-1 gives the wavelengths, colors, and relative intensities of some helium lines. You may not be able to see those with relative intensities below about 50 nor those at the highest and lowest wavelengths of the spectrum. Identify the various lines with your scale readings by the colors listed, and make a plot of wavelength as ordinate against scale reading as abscissa. It should be possible to draw a smooth curve through the plotted points. If your graph does not give a smooth curve, you may have made an experimental error or you have not identified some of the lines properly. In the latter case, reassign the lines to scale readings, and replot them.

Table 9-1. The Helium Spectrum

Wavelength (nm)	Color	Relative Intensity (1 to 1000)
706.5	red	70
667.8	red	100
587.6	yellow	1000
501.6	light green	100
492.2	dark green	50
471.3	blue green	40
447.1	blue violet	100
402.6	violet	70
396.4	violet	50

Use of Calibration Curve to Obtain Wavelengths of Lines in the Hydrogen Spectrum. Using the calibration curve and the scale readings you took for the helium spectrum, determine the wavelengths for the red, blue, and violet lines in the hydrogen spectrum. Record these wavelengths.

PART B. THE ORIGIN OF ATOMIC SPECTRA

In this part of the experiment, each of the lines in the hydrogen spectrum will be related to a specific transition of the electron between energy levels inside the hydrogen atom.

Energy Emitted and Electron Transitions. According to the theory, the energy of photons emitted by excited atoms corresponds to energy differences between energy levels in the atom. For example, an electron falling from the second energy level, E_2, to the first energy level, E_1, in the hydrogen atom emits a line having a wavelength of 121.6 nm, or 1.217×10^{-7} m. This corresponds to a photon of energy

$$\Delta E = \frac{hc}{\lambda} = \frac{6.62 \times 10^{-34} \text{ J-sec} \times 3 \times 10^8 \text{ m/sec}}{1.216 \times 10^{-7} \text{ m}} = 16.3 \times 10^{-19} \text{ J.}$$

This implies that an electron in the first energy level in the hydrogen atom has 16.3×10^{-19} J less energy than an electron in the second energy level in that atom, i.e., $E_2 - E_1 = 16.3 \times 10^{-19}$ J. Measurement of the wavelengths of lines in atomic spectra thus permits the experimenter to determine energy-level differences within the atom.

Using this information, you can now calculate the energy level differences within the hydrogen atom that give rise to each of the lines you observed in the hydrogen spectrum.

To do this, you must first convert the wavelengths you determined for the red, blue, and violet lines of the hydrogen spectrum from nanometers to meters. Then, you can use the equation $E = hc/\lambda$. For example,

$$\text{Energy level difference corresponding to red line} = \frac{hc}{\lambda \text{ of red line}}.$$

Record these energy-level differences for the hydrogen lines in your notebook. Which of the three lines corresponds to the greatest energy change in the hydrogen atom?

Relation between Wavelength and Energy Levels. The equation relating energy levels in the hydrogen atom to the wavelengths of the spectral lines has the form

$$\frac{1}{\lambda} = RZ^2 \left(\frac{1}{n_x^2} - \frac{1}{n_y^2} \right) \tag{2}$$

in which R is the Rydberg constant ($10{,}967{,}772$ m^{-1}), n_x and n_y are the principal quantum numbers of the energy levels in the atom between which the electron falls (n_x is the lower and n_y is the higher quantum number), and Z is the charge on the nucleus, which is 1 for the hydrogen atom.

For the purposes of this experiment, Eq. (2) can be rearranged to give the relation

$$\frac{1}{n_x^2} - \frac{1}{n_y^2} = \frac{9.12 \times 10^{-8} \text{ m}}{\lambda}. \tag{3}$$

One line in the ultraviolet region of the hydrogen spectrum has a wavelength of 1.216×10^{-7} m. Substituting this wavelength into Eq. (3) gives

$$\frac{1}{n_x{}^2} - \frac{1}{n_y{}^2} = \frac{9.12 \times 10^{-8}\ m}{\lambda} = \frac{9.12 \times 10^{-8}\ m}{1.216 \times 10^{-7}\ m} = 0.75.$$

From this number--0.75--it is possible to calculate the exact energy levels between which the electron falls in emitting the photons that give rise to that particular spectral line. If, as in the above example,

$$\frac{1}{n_x{}^2} - \frac{1}{n_y{}^2}$$

is found to be 0.75, n_x must be 1 and n_y must be 2 since

$$\frac{1}{1^2} - \frac{1}{2^2}\ \text{is}\ \frac{1}{1} - \frac{1}{4} = \frac{3}{4},\ \text{or}\ 0.75,$$

and the line in question represents the energy emitted when the electron falls from the second quantum level to the first. If

$$\frac{1}{n_x{}^2} - \frac{1}{n_y{}^2}$$

is found to be 0.14, n_x must be 2 and n_y must be 3 since

$$\frac{1}{2^2} - \frac{1}{3^2} = \frac{1}{4} - \frac{1}{9} = 0.14,$$

and the electron falls from the third quantum level to the second.

Now use the wavelengths of the red, blue, and violet lines in the hydrogen spectrum to make the calculations just described. Record your calculations in your notebook.

Another line in the visible spectrum of hydrogen appears at 410.1 nm. Calculate n_x and n_y for this line.

Energy-Level Diagram. Once the energy levels have been identified and the energy-level differences established from the measurements, it is possible to record this information in a concise manner in an energy-level diagram. Energies of the various levels are plotted vertically--to scale--and the transitions between levels are marked as heavy lines between these levels. The wavelengths of the spectral lines may then be marked on the vertical lines representing the electron transitions, as shown in Fig. 9-3. Since only differences in energy may be determined from the wavelengths, the energy of the base or lowest level may be arbitrarily taken as zero.

Using the results of your calculations of energy levels and energy differences between levels in hydrogen atoms, construct a diagram similar to Fig. 9-3, drawn to scale. Assign the value of n_x you found for the lowest level concerned in the visible spectrum, and give the values of the higher levels in joules above this level. Indicate the values of n_y for the higher levels. Draw arrows to represent the electron transitions between levels that produce the four lines of the visible spectrum, and label them with the wavelengths of the lines, as requested in the Report Sheet. Based on the energies of the photons emitted by the hydrogen atoms and assuming a zero energy for the n = 1 energy level, assign energies in joules to each energy level from n = 2 to n = 6.

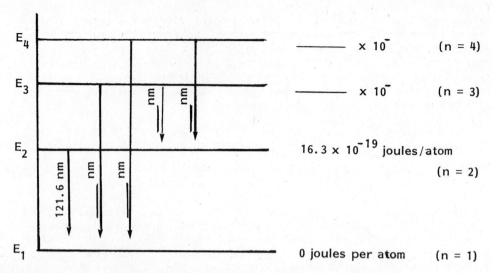

Figure 9-3. A portion of the energy-level diagram for hydrogen

NOTEBOOK AND REPORT FOR PARTS A AND B

Your notebook should contain the data and calculations referred to in the preceding paragraphs. Use the Report Sheets on pages 143 and 144 as guides in organizing your notebook and report.

PART C. QUALITATIVE ANALYSIS BY USE OF
THE SPECTROSCOPE

As discussed in Exp. 3 (on qualitative analysis procedures), chemical and physical properties of substances are used to determine the presence or absence of these substances in a sample of unknown composition. One property used frequently for this purpose is the spectrum.

Often the emission spectrum of an atom or ion is simple enough that an analyst can determine its presence or absence by examining the spectrum of the sample. Sodium, potassium, calcium, strontium, and barium ions have spectra that are simple and easy to reorganize. In fact, these ions, when excited, give characteristic colors that can be recognized visually even without a spectroscope--sodium ions appear yellow, potassium ions red-violet, calcium orange-red, strontium ions deep red, and barium ions green. If several of these ions are present in a mixture, the eye may not be able to distinguish among them, but a spectroscope can do so.

In this part of the experiment, you are asked to excite the ions of each of the five elements listed by using the flame of an ordinary burner and to observe the light emitted by using first only the naked eye and then the spectroscope. You will be asked to observe the spectrum of a solution containing two or more of these ions and, on the basis of the observation, to determine which ions are present and which are absent.

PROCEDURE

The ions to be observed can be placed in the flame on a platinum or nichrome wire (which has been sealed into one end of a piece of glass tubing), but the wire must be cleaned carefully before each new ion is introduced.

Clean wire.

To clean the wire, heat it in the hottest portion of a color- less burner flame until the color imparted to the flame by the ions adhering to the wire disappears. If this color does not disapper after the wire becomes red hot, allow it to cool for about 10 seconds, and immerse it in a small beaker containing about 2 mL of concentrated hydrochloric acid. Then return the wire to the flame. Repeat this step until the wire no longer imparts a color to the flame. The hydrochloric acid converts any salts adhering to the wire to chlorides which are volatile and sublime.

The cleaned wire can now be dipped into a solution or powder containing ions having spectra to be observed.

Place a lighted burner directly in front of the slit of the spectroscope but far enough so that the flame will not damage the instrument. Examine the spectrum of each of the ions previously discussed by dipping a clean platinum (or nichrome) wire into a solution or powder containing the ion and placing the wire in the flame. Observe the color of the flame, and record both the color and the spectroscope reading for each prominent line in the spectrum. It may be necessary to dip the wire into the solution or powder and to return it to the flame several times in order to get all of the information needed. Before you proceed to the next spectrum, the wire must be carefully cleaned.

Observe color of flame from each ion to be examined.

When all of the spectra have been viewed and the appropriate data recorded, obtain an unknown solution and, using the same procedure, view its spectrum and record both the color and the spectroscope reading for each prominent line. Use the information you have obtained to determine which ions are present and which are absent in the unknown sample.

Observe flame spectrum for unknown.

NOTEBOOK AND REPORT FOR PART C

The notebook should contain data on the color and spectroscope reading for all prominent lines in the spectra of the five ions and of the unknown solution. The report should contain a summary of the preceding information, a description of the spectrum of the unknown, and the rationale used in determining the presence or absence of each ion.

The reports for Parts A, B, and C should be combined and presented as one unit titled, "Studies in Emission Spectroscopy." The discussion section should include answers to the questions given at the end of Part C.

PART D. ABSORPTION SPECTROSCOPY

In this part of Exp. 9 you will investigate the qualitative and quantitative aspects of absorption spectroscopy by studying the absorbance properties of some ions in solution. The phenomenon of light "absorption" is essentially the opposite of light "emission." Absorption occurs when an electron accepts a photon of light and moves to a higher energy level. As with emission, only photons having the correct amount of energy to raise the electron from one energy level to another can be absorbed. Since the energy of a photon is inversely proportional to its wavelength, only certain wavelengths of light can be absorbed by a particular atom or ion. An absorption spectrum is a graph of those wavelengths (colors) of light that are absorbed by electrons in an atom, ion, or molecule.

Color and Absorption of Light. Pure white light is a mixture of photons of all visible wavelengths. When such light strikes an object, the photons can be absorbed, transmitted, or reflected. Visible photons that are transmitted or reflected can be "seen" by us as they enter our eyes. The photons absorbed by the object cannot be seen.

The color of objects that do not emit light of their own is a result of the absorption of photons of certain colors and the reflection and transmission of photons of other colors. Some examples follow. A glass of water appears clear because all visible light that strikes the water is transmitted, none is absorbed. A sheet of paper is white because all of the visible light that strikes it is being reflected, none is absorbed. The print on this page is black because all visible light that strikes it is being absorbed, none is reflected.

An important principle in vision is that if roughly equal numbers of photons of a color and its complementary color strike our eyes, we will see only white or gray. Thus, a bright red object appears red in white light because the complementary color to red is being absorbed by the object, and the other colors are being reflected. When the reflected photons reach our eyes, each color except red is accompanied by its complement; the eye perceives only brightness (white) and red.

Spectrophotometers. Instruments used to determine the amount of light absorbed at a particular wavelength are known as spectrophotometers. These are constructed so that the sample to be studied can be irradiated with light (or other radiation) of known wavelength and intensity. The wavelength can be varied continuously by the operator (or automatically) and the amount of radiation absorbed or transmitted by the sample determined for each wavelength used. In this way, it is possible to learn which wavelengths of radiation are absorbed by the sample and how effective the species in the sample are in absorbing a particular wavelength. From this information, an absorption spectrum for a species can be obtained and used to identify the species in unknown samples. For example, it is known that the $Co(NH_3)_6^{3+}$ ion absorbs wavelengths between 350 and 400 nm and between 450 and 520 nm. If this ion is present in an unknown mixture and the mixture is placed in a spectrophotometer, one would expect to see absorptions in the two wavelength regions indicated.

Spectrophotometers record the amount of light transmitted or absorbed by a sample in terms of the per cent of transmittance, %T, and/or the absorbance. The %T tells us in percentage units how much is transmitted by (passes through) the sample. Absorbance is a more complex term. It conveys information about the amount of light absorbed in logarithmic terms. If I/I_o is the ratio of the intensity of light transmitted by a sample compared with the intensity of light striking the sample:

$$\%T = I/I_o \times 100$$

$$absorbance = \log I_o/I.$$

In many cases, the amount of a substance present in a sample can be determined by spectrophotometry. Diagrams of and instructions for using simple spectrophotometers are given in Appendix II.

In this experiment, we shall use the spectrophotometer to determine the wavelengths absorbed by some simple substances in aqueous solutions and attempt to relate the color of visible light absorbed by the sample with its observed color. Then

Table 9-2. Wavelengths Associates with Various Colors of Visible Light

Color	Wavelength Range (nanometers)
red	750-610
orange	610-590
yellow	590-570
green	570-500
blue	500-450
violet	450-400

we will examine how absorption changes as concentration of the absorbing species changes.

Table 9-2 gives the wavelengths associated with various colors of visible light.

Qualitative Spectrophotometry. In this portion of the experiment, you will be asked to determine the absorption spectrum of the colored species in one of the solutions in each group below. Later you will make quantitative absorption measurements on one of these solutions.

Table 9-3. Solutions for Absorption Spectrum Determination

Solution	Colored species present
Group A	
0.20 M $Co(NO_3)_2$	$Co(H_2O)_6^{2+}$
0.03 M $Cu(NO_3)_2$ in 0.12 M NH_3 and 2.0 M NH_4NO_3	$Cu(NH_3)_4^{2+}$
0.01% aluminon	
Group B	
0.25 M $Ni(NO_3)_2$	$Ni(H_2O)_6^{2+}$
0.005 M $FeCl_3$ in 0.1 M HCl	$FeCl_4^-$

Fig. 9-4 is a color wheel showing the complementary relationship among colors. This might be useful in interpreting the information obtained from the spectrophotometer.

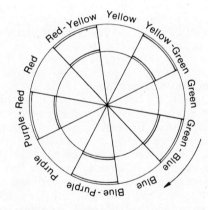

Figure 9-4. A color wheel showing the complementary relationships among colors

PROCEDURE FOR QUALITATIVE SPECTROPHOTOMETRY

The following procedure can be used to obtain the absorption spectrum of your samples and to prepare materials for the next portion of this experiment.

Thoroughly clean and rinse with distilled water all of the glassware you will need for both parts of the spectrophotometry experiment. This is:

- three 4" cuvettes (checked-out from your instructor)
- one 10-mL pipet and bulb
- one 250-mL beaker
- seven 6" test tubes
- one or more micropipets and a bulb
- a graduated cylinder
- a wash bottle

Clean glassware. Fill the wash bottle with distilled water. Label the 6" test tubes A, B, C, D, E, F, and U (for unknown), and stand them upside down in a test-tube rack to drain.

Rinse and fill test tubes with solutions. Now obtain the two solutions you wish to analyze. Your choices are given in Table 9-3. Record the names and concentrations of the solutions chosen. Rinse test tube A twice with 2 mL of one of these solutions, and then fill it to within 2 cm of the top with this solution. In the same way, rinse and fill test tube B with the second solution. Part of the solutions in the test tubes will be used in this portion of the experiment. The rest will be used in the portion on quantitative spectrophotometry.

Prepare cuvettes for absorption measurement. Now prepare the three cuvettes for the absorption measurements as follows: fill one cuvette to within 2 cm of the top with distilled water. This will be your blank or reference standard in both parts of this experiment.

Rinse a second cuvette twice with 1-mL portions of the solution from test tube A, and fill it to within 2 cm of the top with this solution. In the same way, rinse and fill a third cuvette with the solution from test tube B.

Take the filled cuvettes to the spectrophotometer, and obtain the absorption spectrum as follows.

Set for zero and 100% transmittance. Switch on the spectrophotometer, allow a 20-minute warm-up period, and turn the wavelength control to 340 nanometers (or 3400 Å), or 360 nanometers on the older models. Set the meter to zero by turning the dark current knob. Place the cuvette containing water in the sample-cell holder of the instrument and close the cover. Now set the meter at 100% transmittance by means of the percentage control (light control) knob. Replace the water-containing cuvette with the cuvette containing the solution. Close the sample-holder cover and read and record the absorbance from the appropriate scale on the meter.

Obtain absorbance data.

Obtain absorbance as a function of wavelength. Set the wavelength dial at 360 nanometers, and repeat the above procedure using both the water-filled and solution-filled cuvettes. Again, read and record the absorbance value from the meter.

In a similar manner, measure the absorbance of the solution at 20-nanometer intervals from 380 to 650 nanometers. However, in the regions of maximum absorbance, take readings at 10-nanometer inervals to achieve a smoother curve. Plot the absorbance value as a function of wavelength for both solutions. Identify the colors absorbed by the color-bearing species in the solutions, and relate this to the observed color of the solutions using Fig. 9-4.

Save all of the solutions for the quantitative portion of the experiment that follows.

Quantitative Spectrophotometry. Although you took numerical measurements in the work just completed, in fact, you observed the qualitative aspects of the absorption of light by colored species in solution. You determined the colors or wavelengths of light absorbed, not how much light was absorbed. This technique is widely used in industry and science to identify species based on their characteristic absorption spectra. But spectrophotometry can also be used as a quantitative technique. This is possible because the amount of light absorbed is related to the concentration of the absorbing species. The relationship is usually expressed as "Beer's Law." In this part of the experiment, you will discover the relationship between the amount of light absorbed and the concentration of the light-absorbing species. To do this, you will use solutions of one of the ions you examined in the section on qualitative spectrophotometry.

You can achieve this by measuring the absorbance of the ions in a series of solutions of different known concentrations and plotting the results. You can then use the plot to determine the concentration of an unknown. The solutions of known concentrations can be prepared by serial dilution. This involves a series of dilutions of a solution of known concentration with pure solvent (distilled water in this case). By carefully measuring the volumes of solutions mixed, the concentration of each new solution can be calculated. Some of the new solution can then be diluted with more pure solvent, creating another solution whose concentration can be calculated (again, if the volumes are carefully measured). You should perform four such measured dilutions which will give you five solutions of known concentration to analyze.

For a more detailed discussion of quantitative spectrophotometry, see Exp. 27.

PROCEDURE FOR QUANTITATIVE SPECTROPHOTOMETRY

For this part of the experiment, you will need the following items that were thoroughly cleaned and rinsed earlier.

* three 4" cuvettes, one containing the solution you wish to study
* seven 6" test tubes, one containing the solution
* one 10-mL pipet and bulb
* one micropipet and bulb
* a graduated cylinder
* a squeeze bottle filled with distilled water
* a 250-mL beaker. This should now be filled with distilled water. It will be used as source of water for the dilutions.

Step 1. Rinse your 10-mL pipet with a small portion (2 mL) of your test tube A solution, as demonstrated by your instructor. Pipet exactly 10 mL of this solution into test tube C. Thoroughly rinse the pipet with distilled water, and then pipet 10 mL of distilled water (from the 250-mL beaker) into test tube C. Thoroughly mix the contents of test tube C.

The serial dilutions.

Step 2. Rinse your 10-mL pipet with a small portion of your new solution in test tube C as in Step 1. Pipet 10 mL of the solution in test tube C into test tube D. Thoroughly rinse the pipet with distilled water, and pipet 10 mL of water from the 250-mL beaker into test tube D. Thoroughly mix the contents of test tube D.

Step 3. Repeat Step 2 twice more, preparing the solution for test tube E from that in test tube D and the solution for test tube F from that in test tube E. Note that each solution has a concentration half that of the solution from which it was made.

Step 4. Obtain from your instructor an unknown solution of the species you are studying. Pour your unknown solution into cleaned and dried test tube U, and compare it to your known solutions. Record your observations of which two known solutions "bracket" your unknown and which appear to be closest in appearance to your unknown.

Prepare the unknown.

Step 5. One of your cuvettes should still contain your sample solution from test tube A; the other should contain distilled water. This is your water blank.

Make the measurements.

Step 6. Inspect the absorption spectrum for your solution, and select the wavelength of maximal absorbance. (Note that this wavelength must fall between 350 and 600 nm.) If you have any doubt, consult your instructor before continuing.

Step 7. Proceed to the spectrophotometer, and adjust the wavelength dial to your chosen value. Make both zero adjustments, as you did earlier, and insert your cuvette containing the solution from test tube A. Read and record both the %T transmittance and the absorbance.

Step 8. Remove the cuvette, and discard the sample solution. Rinse the cuvette with a small portion of the solution from test tube C, discard this rinse, and fill the cuvette with more of this solution. Again, check both zero settings, insert the cuvette, and read and record both the %T and the absorbance.

Step 9. Repeat Step 8 for the remaining three known solutions and your unknown. You are now finished collecting data.

REPORT ON PART D

The report on Part D should be titled, "Studies in Absorption Spectroscopy." It should contain sections on qualitative and quantitative spectrohotometry.

Your data section should include all items on the appropriate Report Sheet along with graphs of %T vs. concentration and absorbance vs. concentration. On both graphs, you should indicate with dotted lines your interpolated unknown concentrations.

Your calculation section should include examples of your dilution calculations.

Your discussion section should address the questions given at the end of Part D.

REFERENCES

1. Day, R. H., Jr.; Underwood, A. L.; "Quantitative Analysis", 4th Edition, 1980, Prentice-Hall, Englewood Cliffs, NJ, pp. 369-382.

Experiment 9 Part D

ABSORPTION SPECTROSCOPY

PRELABORATORY QUESTIONS

Name_____   Lab Instructor_____

Student ID No._____   Date_____

1. What is the absorption spectrum of an element?

2. Compare the emission and absorption spectra of an element.

3. What causes photons to be absorbed by atoms?

4. Two roses are illuminated by the sunlight. One is red and the other is yellow.
    Account for this in terms of:

    a) colors absorbed by the flowers.

    b) colors transmitted to the eyes from the flowers.

5. What color will a green ball appear if illuminated by a red light? (Use the color wheel to help you.)

6. What is a spectrophotometer? Describe briefly how it works:

   a) as a qualitative or identification instrument.

   b) as a quantitative instrument.

7. What is meant by "serial dilution"?

8. In general, how does light absorption change as the concentration of the absorbing substance increases?

9. How are % transmission and absorbance related?

Experiment 9 Part C

REPORT SHEET

Name_____   Lab Instructor_____

Student ID No._____   Date_____

1. **Data for known solutions**

Ion	Observed color	Scale reading	Wavelength (nm) from calibration curve, Part A
Na^+	_____	_____	_____
	_____	_____	_____
	_____	_____	_____
K^+	_____	_____	_____
	_____	_____	_____
	_____	_____	_____
Ca^{2+}	_____	_____	_____
	_____	_____	_____
	_____	_____	_____
Sr^{2+}	_____	_____	_____
	_____	_____	_____
	_____	_____	_____
Ba^{2+}	_____	_____	_____
	_____	_____	_____
	_____	_____	_____

2. Data for Unknown Solutions

Observed color	Scale reading	Ion identification

Experiment 9 Part D

REPORT SHEET

Name_____   Lab Instructor_____

Student ID No._____   Date_____

Qualitative Spectrophotometry

Solution I: Colored species present _____; color of

solution_____. Maximum absorption(s),

from _____nm to _____nm; from _____nm to _____nm.

Color of maximum absorption _____   _____

Solution II: Colored species present _____; color of

solution_____. Maximum absorption(s),

from _____nm to _____nm; from _____nm to _____nm.

Color of maximum absorption _____   _____

Attach Graphs for Qualitative Spectrophotometry

Quantitative Spectrophotometry

Absorbing species _____   Concentration _____   Wavelength _____

Test Tube	Concentration	Absorbance	% Transmittance
A or B	_____	_____	_____
C	_____	_____	_____
D	_____	_____	_____
E	_____	_____	_____
F	_____	_____	_____

UNKNOWN VISUAL OBSERVATIONS: The concentration appears to lie between those of
test tube ____ and test tube ____. It is the closest to test tube ____.

147

UNKNOWN
MEASUREMENTS   Absorbance _____   Interpolated conc. _____

                 % Transmittance _____   Interpolated conc. _____

                                                         Best value for conc. _____

Attach Graphs for Quantitative Spectrophotometry

**Attach sheets with answers to the assigned question from the QUESTIONS AND PROBLEMS,
Part D**

GRAVIMETRIC DETERMINATION OF SULFATE

Objective

To study the technique of gravimetric analysis and to determine the percentage of sulfate in a soluble sulfate compound

Equipment Needed

Two 250-mL beakers; two crucibles with lids; desiccator; two Meker burners; two plastic funnels; filter support; plastic squeeze bottles containing 95% ethanol and a 50:50 ethanol/water mixture

Reagents Needed

Unknown sulfate sample (available from instructor); 10% barium chloride, $BaCl_2$, solution; 6 M hydrochloric acid, HCl; 0.1 M $AgNO_3$ test solution; plastic squeeze bottles containing 95% ethanol and a 50:50 ethanol/water mixture

INTRODUCTION

This experiment is an introduction to quantitative analytical chemistry. Because a chemist must often know precisely the composition of the materials or systems he or she studies, this area constitutes a major segment of chemistry. For example, a chemist must often know whether a given material contains 10.60% or 10.64% sulfate. Consequently, procedures have been developed for determining the amount of an element or ion that might be present in a given sample.

One of the oldest and still one of the most accurate methods for determining the composition of matter is gravimetric analysis. This procedure involves: (1) completely precipitating the desired component as a pure compound of precisely known chemical composition, (2) filtering or separating the precipitate onto filter paper that leaves no ash when burned, (3) burning the filter paper under conditions that will not alter the chemical composition of the precipitate (or will alter it in a precisely known fashion), and (4) weighing the known precipitate. From data obtained by such procedures, it is possible to calculate the percentage of the desired component in the original sample.

In this experiment you will be issued a sample containing sulfate. You will be expected to analyze the sample and to report a value for the percentage of sulfate within a certain range of the correct value. The grading scheme is based on how close your answer corresponds to the correct value. If the reported answer is outside accepted limits, you may be expected to repeat the experiment. Therefore, careful work will prove both rewarding and time-saving. It should also provide a deeper understanding of the quantitative basis of chemistry.

The method to be employed involves weighing a sample of the material to be analyzed, dissolving it in water, and adding barium chloride solution. Since barium sulfate is only very slightly soluble (about 1×10^{-5} moles of the salt will dissolve in one liter of water at 25 $^{\circ}$C), this compound immediately precipitates from the solution. The reaction may be represented by the net ionic equation

$$Ba^{2+}(aq) \quad + \quad SO_4^{2-}(aq) \quad \rightleftharpoons \quad BaSO_4(s).$$

After the precipitation has been accomplished, it is necessary to filter quantitatively the coagulated precipitate. The filter paper can then be burned in a porcelain crucible. After ignition is completed (to constant weight), the dry barium sulfate precipitate is weighed, and this weight is used to calculate the percentage of sulfate in the orginal sample.

TECHNIQUES

Sample Weight from Loss in Weight of Container

Solid materials intended for analysis are usually dried in an oven near 100 $^{\circ}$C and transferred to a small lightweight weighing bottle, which is then stored in a desiccator. When a sample is needed, the bottle is weighed, a suitable quantity is transferred to the beaker or flask in which the chemical operation is to be performed, and the bottle is reweighed and returned to the desiccator. The difference in weight before and after the transfer represents the weight of the sample taken, provided no spills occurred.

For a successful operation, the transfer must be quantitatively perfect since all material removed from the weighing bottle is presumed to have entered the chemical process. The transfer is best accomplished by tilting the weighing bottle over the beaker and tapping it gently with a pencil or spatula to pour small quantities of the solid. The amount removed may be checked periodically by a rough weighing on the balance. If the material does not absorb water rapidly, the weighing may be made with the weighing bottle uncovered; otherwise, the cover must be replaced as soon as material has been removed from the bottle.

It is also necessary that the weighing bottle not pick up additional weight during handling since this would make the apparent sample weight less than it actually is. The weighing bottle should be carefully cleaned and dried before use and, thereafter, it should not be touched with fingers which would leave perspiration salts and oils on it. It should be handled only when protected from the fingertips by a piece of clean tissue. The cover similarly should not be removed directly with the fingers, but only with tissue paper.

Filtration

A pure precipitate, once formed, must be separated from the liquid in which it is formed and washed free of any soluble components in this mother liquor. This is commonly accomplished by filtration through a filter paper, and the washing is carried out during this process also. For quantitative work, ashless filter paper, which has been treated with acids to remove inorganic materials, is employed; the type chosen should have a pore size small enough to retain particles of precipitate but not so small that it increases unnecessarily the time needed for water to flow through the filter paper.

Read about gravity filtrations in the Techniques section (pp. 9-10) before you do Exp. 10 since quantitative techniques are very important for success in this experiment.

Ignition of a Precipitate

The process of heating a crucible to incipient redness preparatory to cooling and weighing is known as ignition. It is first accomplished with the empty crucible, as in Experiment 4, so that a precise value for the empty crucible may be obtained. When a filter paper and precipitate are present, the heating should follow a definite program, as follows.

Drying and Charring the Paper. Support the covered crucible containing the wet filter paper and precipitate on a clay triangle in a slanted position. Heat it with a small flame impinging about the middle of the underside. Do not hurry the drying by using too hot a flame.

When the paper is dry, lift the cover slightly with tongs to allow access of air, and increase the heat to char the paper, moving the flame toward the bottom of the crucible. The paper must not be allowed to burst into flame, which might cause particles of precipitate to be swept out with the escaping gases. If a flame appears, close the cover immediately to smother it. Take care that the burner flame is adjusted for complete combustion so that reducing gases of CO from the flame are not swept back onto the precipitate.

Igniting the Precipitate. When the paper is completely charred, remove the cover from the crucible, and increase the heat gradually until the bottom of the crucible is a dull red. It may be necessary to rotate the crucible occasionally to remove soot and tars that may have condensed during the charring. When the dark organic material has completely burned, set the crucible upright and continue heating it for 10 minutes.

PROCEDURE

Your instructor will advise you whether to use approximately 0.5- or 1.0-g samples of the unknown (**Note 1**).

Weigh two unknown samples.

Weigh (to 0.0003 g), on the basis of loss in weight of the container, a sample of the unknown sulfate into each of two marked 250-mL beakers. Use the sample vial as the weighing bottle, and prepare it for weighing by carefully washing the outside with detergent and water, wiping it dry with a tissue and allowing it to stand in the laboratory atmosphere for 5 or 10 minutes to equilibrate it with the humidity level of the air. If there is a label on the vial, it must be removed before the vial is used; transfer any needed identification to the stopper or cap. The weighings should be made to within 0.0003 g and may be made with the vial uncovered. Record the weights of the vial before and after the samples are removed (**Note 1**).

Add H$_2$O and HCl and heat. Add BaCl$_2$ dropwise.

Add 150 mL of distilled water and 3 mL of 6 M HCl to each beaker (**Note 2**) and heat to near boiling, but do not actually boil the samples (**Note 3**). Counting the drops, add 10% BaCl$_2$ solution from a medicine dropper until precipitation appears to be complete. Test completeness of precipitation by allowing the precipitate to settle somewhat and then adding a drop of barium chloride gently so as not to disturb the precipitate. If additional cloudiness appears at the point of entry of the drop, precipitation is not complete (**Note 4**). After you have determined that precipitation is complete, add an excess of the barium chloride solution equal to one-fifth the number of drops of solution already used. Stir the sample constantly during the addition of barium chloride.

Check for complete precipitation.

Keep the solutions nearly at the boiling temperature for approximately 40 minutes (**Note 2**). Then check again for complete precipitation by adding a drop or two of barium chloride solution. If precipitation is not complete, keep adding 10% BaCl$_2$ solution until no further precipitation occurs, and then add an excess of one-fifth the total amount. The total volume of BaCl$_2$ solution should vary from 5 to 9 mL, depending on the sample. If it necessary for you to stop work at this point, cover the beakers with Paraseal or Saran Wrap, and put them away until the next laboratory period.

Set up the two plastic funnels and fit each with a piece of 11-cm ashless filter paper as illustrated in Fig. 9 (p. 9). Filter and wash the precipitate by decantation, using warm distilled water, until the filtrate shows no chloride ion present, as indicated by silver nitrate test solution. The chloride ion test is best done by placing silver nitrate test solution in a small test tube and allowing a few drops from the funnel to fall into it. A cloudy precipitate of silver chloride shows that chloride ion is still present. Use the policeman and water from the wash bottle to remove the last traces of precipitate from the beaker. Continue washing the precipitate until only a barely detectable turbidity of silver chloride appears in the wash solution. Allow the filter paper to drain in the funnel.

Filter and wash the precipitates.

Test the wash liquid for Cl^-.

During the working period, heat the empty, clean crucibles and covers over the full heat of the Meker burner, and place them in the desiccator. As always in cooling crucibles in a desiccator, wait a few minutes before covering the desiccator tightly to permit the air in the desiccator to be heated by the hot crucible and to expand safely. Then close the desiccator and allow the crucible to cool to room temperature. When the crucibles are cool, weigh them without the covers. Repeat this procedure until you get them to constant weight (within 0.0003 g).

Ignite and weigh crucibles.

Wash the precipitate with the 50:50 mixture of water/ethanol; then wash with 95% ethanol, and allow the filter paper to drain in the funnel (**Note 5**). Fold the top of the paper to encase the precipitate, and carefully transfer the paper to a marked crucible that has been ignited and weighed to constant weight as before. If you must stop work at this time, cover the crucibles and store them in a desiccator until the next laboratory period.

Wash with alcohol.

Dry and char the filter paper according to the procedure given on p. 14, and ignite the precipitate (**Note 6**). Set the crucible in a desiccator, and weigh it when cool. Repeat the ignition, cooling and weighing, until a constant weight is obtained.

Dry and char the paper; ignite and weigh the precipitates.

Much of the success in this determination depends on the ability of the analyst to obtain reliable weights of crucibles and their contents. Special precautions must be used in handling crucibles so that they are not contaminated by moisture or dust from the air, dirt or paint from the desk top, or oil from the fingers of the analyst. Therefore, crucibles should be handled with crucible tongs and should be kept in desiccators when not in use.

CALCULATIONS

From the weight of barium sulfate precipitated, calculate the weight of sulfate ion in the precipitate, using the ratio of the gram formula weight of sulfate to the gram formula weight of barium sulfate. This amount of sulfate was present in the original weight of the unknown sample. Calculate the percentage of sulfate in each sample trial.

Average the two results and calculate the average deviation in parts per thousand as follows. Find, for each trial, the difference between the measured value and the average; subtract in such a way that the difference is always positive. Add these results and divide by the number of trials. This quotient, divided by the average value and mutliplied by 1000, is the average deviation in parts per thousand.

Record the arithmetic of the calculations in your notebook and on the report sheet neatly so that you and the instructor can check them readily for errors.

NOTES

Note 1. The amount of sample to use is dependent on the range of percentage sulfate in the unknown samples. Your instructor will provide guidance on the proper sample size. Since this is a quantitative analysis, extreme care must be exercised at all times. If the sample is spilled or not <u>completely</u> transferred or if the filter paper ruptures during filtration, discard the sample and start again.

Note 2. Acid must be added to the solution to prevent precipitation of salts other than barium sulfate when the barium is added. Hydroxide ions, sulfite ions, and carbonate ions, for example, if present in the sample to be analyzed, would form slightly soluble barium salts in neutral or basic solution but would not precipitate in acid solution. A second reason for the acid is that it aids digestion of the precipitate. Digestion is the process of forming a precipitate that may be readily separated from the mother liquor by filtration; it is usually accomplished, as here, by heating the precipitate in contact with the mother liquor so that the fine particles that may be formed at first recrystallize to form larger, coarse-grained crystals.

Note 3. Barium sulfate solutions have a pronounced tendency to become supersaturated at low temperatures but not at high temperatures. The near boiling temperatures are necessary to overcome the tendency toward supersaturation.

Note 4. The excess barium ion is added to drive the reaction

$$Ba^{2+}(aq) \quad + \quad SO_4^{2-}(aq) \quad \rightleftharpoons \quad BaSO_4(s)$$

as far to the right as possible, thereby removing as many sulfate ions as possible from the solution. If excess barium ion is not added, enough sulfate ion may remain in solution to affect the final result. Because a huge excess of barium ions can also increase the solubility of barium sulfate, the 20% excess should not be greatly exceeded. The barium chloride solution is much more dense than the solution in which precipitation occurs. As a result, when precipitation is completed, you may notice a difference in the refractive index of the solution at the point of mixing as drops of barium chloride solution are added to your sulfate solution. Do not confuse this swirling or mixing behavior with precipitation.

Note 5. Ethanol will help wash out the water and speed the drying process. However, heat the crucible containing the sample slowly at first in order to dry the filter paper.

Note 6. Barium sulfate may be reduced to barium sulfide by carbon that is formed from charring of the filter paper. This reduction can be avoided by burning the paper very slowly with the lid off the crucible to allow sufficient oxygen to remain in the crucible so that the carbon is removed as carbon dioxide. When ignition is complete, the precipitate is anhydrous barium sulfate.

REFERENCE

1. Day, R.A., Jr., and Underwood, A.L.: <u>Quantitative Analysis, Laboratory Manual</u>, 4th edition. Prentice-Hall, Englewood Cliffs, NJ, 1980, Chapter 4.

GRAVIMETRIC DETERMINATION OF SULFATE

PRELABORATORY QUESTIONS

Name_____   Lab Instructor_____

Student ID No._____   Date_____

1. List the principal sources of error in this gravimetric sulfate experiment. In
    each case, state whether the error tends to make the results high or low.

2. What is digestion and how does it aid in the gravimetric determination of sulfate?

3. Describe briefly the effect of the following on the calculated value of % SO_4^{2-}:

    a) Incomplete precipitation of the sulfate ion as $BaSO_4$.

    b) Co-precipitation of some $Ba(OH)_2$ due to the omission of acid to the solution.

    c) Incomplete drying of the precipitate.

4. A 0.8262-g solid sample of an impure sulfate compound was dissolved in water, treated with HCl and aqueous $BaCl_2$ solution until precipitation was complete. The dried sample weighed 0.8240 g. Determine the percentage of sulfate in the original sample.

5. A pure compound is soluble in water and is 41.24% sulfate by weight. What weight of $BaSO_4$ would be precipitated if an excess of $BaCl_2$ were added to a solution containing 0.7816 g of the compound?

Experiment 10

GRAVIMETRIC DETERMINATION OF SULFATE

REPORT SHEET

Name_____   Lab Instructor_____

Student ID No._____   Date_____

<u>crucible mark</u>
_____

first_____   second_____

1. Weight of crucible

    a) after first heating (g)   _____   _____

    b) after second heating (g)   _____   _____

    c) after third heating (g)   _____   _____

    d) at constant weight (g)   _____   _____

2. Gross weight of sample and vial (g)   _____   _____

3. Weight of vial after removing the sample (g)   _____   _____

4. Net weight of sample (to 0.0003 g) (g)   _____   _____

5. Total weight of crucible and $BaSO_4$ precipitate

    a) after first ignition (g)   _____   _____

    b) after second ignition (g)   _____   _____

    c) after third ignition (g)   _____   _____

    d) at constant weight (g)   _____   _____

6. Net weight of $BaSO_4$ precipitate (g)   _____   _____

7. Weight of sulfate (SO_4^{2-}) in the sample (g)   _____   _____

8. Percentage sulfate in the sample (%)   _____   _____

9. Average deviation   _____

Illustrations of Calculations

Questions

1. If 0.7045 g of a soluble sulfate sample gives 0.4231 g of $BaSO_4$, what is the percentage of sulfate in the sample?

2. If an error of +1.0 mg is made in weighing the barium sulfate precipitate and the percentage of sulfate reported is 40.75, calculate the true percentage of sulfate in a 1.00-g sample.

3. If the unknown sample were to contain two different soluble sulfate compounds, how would this affect your calculation of the percentage of sulfate in the sample?

ACID-BASE TITRATIONS; VOLUMETRIC ANALYSIS

Objective

To illustrate acid-base titrations by the standardization of a sodium hydroxide solution; to use this standard solution to determine the equivalent weight of an unknown acid, to measure the neutralizing capacity of antacid tablets, or to analyze solutions for acid content

Equipment Needed

Buret; two 125-mL Erlenmeyer flasks; 400-mL beaker; burner; analytical balance

Reagents Needed

Potassium hydrogen phthalate, $KHC_8H_4O_4$; 3 M NaOH solution (carbonate free); 1% phenolphthalein indicator solution; Alconox or similar cleaning solution; samples of unknown acid or antacid tablets (from the instructor)

INTRODUCTION

One of the most important techniques for chemical analysis is titration to an equivalence-point. To illustrate this procedure, let us examine a specific problem.

Suppose that an investigator wishes to know the exact quantity of acid present in a certain mixture. He can find this value by determining the quantity of a base that must be added to the mixture just to neutralize the acid. The quantity of base needed can be measured by preparing a solution of a known concentration of the base and measuring the volume of it needed for the neutralization.

In order to find the volume of the base solution needed, he or she would add the solution from a measuring buret until an indicator in the mixture signified that the end point of the titration had been reached, that is, that he or she exactly neutralized the acid present. The volume of base solution used would then be read from the buret. In acid-base titrations, the indicator used would commonly be a dyestuff that changes color sharply at the end point. The end point can also be identified in ways other than through a color change.

For proper use, a titrating solution must be of known concentration and must contain only a single chemically active reagent. Such solutions are known as standard solutions.

A widely used procedure for preparing and standardizing solutions for titrations is to prepare a solution of approximately the desired concentration and then to titrate it against an accurately weighed quantity of a compound of known purity. The compound of known purity used in this manner is called a primary standard. Nearly all standard sodium hydroxide solutions can be standardized against a known weight of potassium hydrogen phthalate, $KHC_8H_4O_4$.

Potassium hydrogen phthalate is a monobasic acid; it contains one mole of neutralizable hydrogen per mole of substance used. This compound can be highly purified (99.97% pure material is available), it is not easily oxidized, it can be dried to constant weight, and it has a relatively high molecular weight, permitting accurate weighings to be obtained on samples as small as 0.002 mole. All of these are desirable characteristics of a primary standard. One less desirable property of potassium acid phthalate is that it is a weak acid; therefore, the end point of its titration is not so sharp as might be desired. For this reason, it is necessary to carry out the titrations in the absence of carbon dioxide; boiled water must be used to dissolve the acid, and the base to be standardized must be free of carbonate. Phenolphthalein, which is colorless in acid solutions but turns pink at the end point as base is added, is a suitable indicator in titrations of potassium hydrogen phthalate with sodium hydroxide solutions.

BACKGROUND

The reaction of an acid with a base to form a salt and water is called **neutralization.** Consider the reaction between nitric acid and calcium hydroxide. The balanced total formula equation is

$$2\ HNO_3\ +\ Ca(OH)_2\ \longrightarrow\ Ca(NO_3)_2\ +\ 2\ H_2O.$$

This equation is useful if one is given weights of one or more of these compounds and wishes to calculate the weight of other compounds involved in the reaction. However, if we examine the total ionic equation, we gain considerably more information about the reaction.

$$2[H_3O^+\ +\ NO_3^-]\ +\ [Ca^{2+}\ +\ 2\ OH^-]\ \longrightarrow\ [Ca^{2+}\ +\ 2\ NO_3^-]\ +\ 4\ H_2O$$

Since a calcium ion and two nitrate ions occur on both sides of the total ionic equation, they may be eliminated to give the **net ionic equation.**

$$2\ H_3O^+\ +\ 2\ OH^-\ \longrightarrow\ 4\ H_2O;$$

or dividing by 2 gives

$$H_3O^+\ +\ OH^-\ \longrightarrow\ 2\ H_2O.$$

As a matter of convenience, this equation is frequently written more simply as

$$H^+\ +\ OH^-\ \longrightarrow\ H_2O$$

in which H^+ is used to represent H_3O^+. This net ionic equation describes the reaction of all strong acids with all strong bases to form soluble ionic salts and water (Appendix VIII).

Concentrations of solutions may be expressed in a variety of ways. Two methods of expressing concentration which are particularly useful are molarity and normality. The molarity (M) of a solution is defined as the number of moles of solute per liter of solution, i.e.,

$$M\ =\ \frac{\text{no. of moles of solute}}{\text{liter of solution}} \quad \text{or} \quad M\ =\ \frac{\text{millimoles of solute}}{\text{milliliters of solution}}.$$

In acid-base reactions, one mole of an acid does not necessarily neutralize completely one mole of a base and vice versa. By complete neutralization, we mean that all of the hydrogen ions that an acid can produce react with hydroxide ions from a base, or all of the hydroxide ions that a base can produce react with hydrogen ions from an acid. Consider the following examples:

$$3\ NaOH\ +\ H_3PO_4\ \longrightarrow\ Na_3PO_4\ +\ 3\ H_2O$$
$$3\ mol \qquad 1\ mol$$

$$Ca(OH)_2\ +\ 2\ HCl\ \longrightarrow\ CaCl_2\ +\ 2\ H_2O.$$
$$1\ mol \qquad 2\ mol$$

In the first reaction, three moles of NaOH are required to react completely with one mole of H_3PO_4. In the second reaction, two moles of HCl are required to react with one mole of $Ca(OH)_2$. Because one mole of an acid does not necessarily react completely with one mole of a base and vice versa, concentrations of solutions are frequently expressed as normality. The normality of a solution is defined as the number of gram-equivalent weights (gew) of solute per liter of solution, i.e.,

$$\underline{N} = \frac{\text{no. of gew of solute}}{\text{liter of solution}} \quad \text{or} \quad \underline{N} = \frac{\text{no. of meq of solute}}{\text{mL of solution}}.$$

The **gram-equivalent weight (gew) of an acid** is the weight of the acid that will furnish 6.023×10^{23} of H_3O^+ in reacting with base, <u>or</u> the weight of the acid that will react with 6.023×10^{23} of OH^- ions. The **gram-equivalent weight of a base** is the weight of the base that will furnish 6.023×10^{23} of OH^- ions in reacting with an acid or the weight of the base that will react with 6.023×10^{23} of H_3O^+ ions. Thus, the term gram-equivalent weight is defined so that one gram-equivalent weight of an acid will react with <u>one</u> gram-equivalent weight of a base. Consider the following example:

H_2SO_4	$+$	$2\ OH^-$	$\longrightarrow$	$2\ H_2O$	$+$	SO_4^{2-}.
1 mol		2 mol		2 mol		1 mol
6.023×10^{23}		$2(6.023 \times 10^{23})$		$2(6.023 \times 10^{23})$		6.023×10^{23}
H_2SO_4 molecules		OH^- ions		H_2O molecules		SO_4^{2-} ions

This equation shows that one mole of H_2SO_4 can produce $2(6.023 \times 10^{23})$ of H_2O molecules; therefore, one mole of H_2SO_4 is two gram-equivalent weights. Or, one gram-equivalent weight of H_2SO_4 is one half of a mole. The **gram-equivalent weight of an acid** is obtained by dividing the formula weight of the acid (in grams) by the number of acidic hydrogen atoms in one formula unit of the acid. By similar reasoning, the **gram-equivalent weight of a base** is obtained by dividing the formula weight of the base (in grams) by the number of OH^- in one formula unit of the base. <u>Or</u>, in the case of bases like aqueous NH_3, one gram-formula weight is one gram-equivalent weight because each NH_3 molecule can combine with one H_3O^+ or one H^+ ion.

If the volume of a solution is expressed in liters and its concentration is expressed as normality, the following relationship is valid:

$$V \times \underline{N} = \text{no. of gew of solute}$$

in which V = volume of the solution in liters.

Because one gram-equivalent weight of an acid reacts with one gram-equivalent weight of a base, the following relationship is valid for <u>all</u> acid-base reactions in which neutralization is complete.

$$\text{no. of gew of acid} = \text{no. of gew of base}$$

Since volume (in liters) times normality gives the number of gew of solute, the above relationship can be represented as

$$L_{acid} \times \underline{N}_{acid} = L_{base} \times \underline{N}_{base}.$$

Both sides of this equation can be multiplied by 1000 mL/L to give

$$mL_{acid} \times \underline{N}_{acid} = mL_{base} \times \underline{N}_{base}$$

which is a more useful form of the relationship since laboratory volumes of solutions are usually measured in milliliters rather than in liters.

TECHNIQUES

Since this experiment is concerned with a quantitative result, it is important to read and understand the **Laboratory Techniques** sections on the care, cleaning, and use of volumetric glassware (pp. 16-20) before performing this experiment.

PART A.   STANDARDIZATION OF NaOH SOLUTION

In this portion of the experiment, you will standardize a sodium hydroxide solution using potassium hydrogen phthalate, $KHC_8H_4O_4$, KHP. This is achieved by titrating carefully weighed samples of KHP with an NaOH solution you have prepared for this purpose.

NOTEBOOK AND REPORT

Prepare a neat table to show your raw data, i.e., the balance readings and the buret readings before and after titration for each sample. Before going to the laboratory, design a table to contain all of the necessary data in your notebook.

Your report should include a summary of the data, sample calculations, qualitative observations made during the experiment, final conclusions, and answers to the assigned questions at the end of the experiment. Organize the report according to the outline on page 169.

PROCEDURE

Boil water to expel air.

To prepare carbon dioxide free water, pour about 200 mL of the boiling water into a flat-bottomed flask and cool the flask under the water tap, taking care not to shake the water unnecessarily which would permit carbon dioxide to dissolve in it again. When cool, add (with a graduated cylinder) to the water 40 mL of the carbonate-free 3 M NaOH solution, stopper the flask to prevent absorption of carbon dioxide, and mix it thoroughly by shaking. Keep this flask stoppered as much as possible hereafter.

Cool and add NaOH.

The diluted sodium hydroxide solution must now be standardized; i.e., its exact concentration must be determined. For this purpose we titrate the solution against a known weight of potassium hydrogen phthalate, KHP.

Clean two 125-mL Erlenmeyer flasks with detergent and water and rinse them with distilled water.

Obtain a dried sample of pure potassium hydrogen phthalate from the instructor, and prepare two samples for titration against the sodium hydroxide solution by using the following procedure. Carefully weigh the cleaned glass vial (see Exp. 10) containing the dried KHP, transfer about 1.2 g of KHP into a 125-mL Erlenmeyer flask, and reweigh the vial and its contents. Record all weighings. Dissolve the solid in about 40 mL of recently boiled water. Prepare the second sample in exactly the same way. Be sure to mark the flasks so that you will know which flask contains which sample; note that the flasks have frosted circles for easy marking with an ordinary lead pencil. Add two drops of phenolphthalein indicator to each flask.

Weigh out standard acid.

Add 2 drops of indicator.

Fill buret with NaOH.

Clean, rinse, and fill a buret with the diluted sodium hydroxide solution and record the initial buret reading.

Place one of the flasks containing the potassium hydrogen phthalate under the buret, and place a sheet of white paper under the flask to provide a suitable background for observing the color change while the base solution is being added.

Titrate the acid by allowing the sodium hydroxide solution to flow slowly into the flask. Control the flow of base solution from the buret with the left hand, and mix the solution in the flask by giving the flask an even, circular motion with the right hand, taking care not to allow liquid to splash from the flask. (Left-handed students will probably find it more convenient to reverse this procedure.) The base solution may be added in a rapid stream of drops until it is noted that the pink color begins to linger while the solution is swirling in the flask. At this stage the solution should be added at a slower rate. Near the end point, i.e., the point at which the entire solution just becomes pink, the base should be added so slowly that the color disappears between the addition of each drop and the next. When it appears that only a few more drops are needed, rinse down the walls of the titration vessel with distilled water before completing the titration (**Note 1**). Continue to add base until a barely pink color persists throughout the whole solution for at least 20 seconds (**Note 2**). If the solution is red, you may have added too much base, and the result of the trial must be regarded with suspicion. Record the final buret reading, estimating the reading to within 0.01 mL.

Titrate with NaOH until barely pink.

Repeat the titration with the second sample of potassium hydrogen phthalate.

Repeat.

CALCULATIONS

The desired quantities here are the molarity and normality of sodium hydroxide. From the equation for the reaction of NaOH with KHP, we see that

$$\text{moles of potassium hydrogen phthalate} = \text{moles of hydroxide ions used.} \tag{1}$$

Rearranging the equation for the definition of molarity, we obtain

$$\text{moles of hydroxide ions used} = \text{molarity of base solution} \times \text{liters of base solution used.} \tag{2}$$

Combining the two expressions, we get the molarity of the base solution:

$$\text{molarity of base} = \frac{\text{moles of potassium hydrogen phthalate}}{\text{liters of solution used}}. \tag{3}$$

Using this procedure, calculate M_B, the concentration of the base solution in moles per liter, for each trial. If the two trials do not agree within 0.8%, conduct a third trial, calculate M_B, and average the results of the trials. Using the relationships developed in the BACKGROUND section, determine the normality of the NaOH solution.

NOTES

Note 1.   Instead of rinsing the inside walls of the flask with distilled water near the end of the titration, you can achieve the same result by carefully tipping and rotating the flask so that the bulk of the liquid picks up any droplets adhering to the walls.

Note 2.   Volume increments smaller than a normal drop may be taken by allowing a small amount of liquid to form on the tip of the buret and then touching the tip to the wall of the flask. This droplet is then combined with the bulk of the solution by rinsing it down with distilled water from a wash bottle or by tipping and rotating the flask.

PART B.   DETERMINATION OF EQUIVALENT WEIGHT OF AN UNKNOWN ACID

The standardized NaOH solution can now be used to determine the neutralizing capacity of samples of acids or acid solutions. One such determination is to find the gram-equivalent weight, gew, or simply the equivalent weight of an unknown acid. As indicated in the BACKGROUND section, the equivalent weight of an acid is the weight of acid that can be neutralized by one mole of hydroxide ions.

For example, if titration of 0.600g of an acid requires 20.00 mL of a 0.500 molar sodium hydroxide solution, we know that 0.600 g requires

$$20.00 \text{ mL} \times \frac{0.500 \text{ mole}}{1000 \text{ mL}} = 0.01 \text{ mole}$$

of hydroxide ions for neutralization. From this we can calculate the equivalent weight of the acid from the relation

$$\text{gew} = \frac{\text{g of acid used}}{\text{mol of OH}^- \text{ needed to neutralize acid}} = \frac{0.600 \text{ g of acid}}{0.010 \text{ mol of OH}^-} = 60 \text{ g/mol.}$$

PROCEDURE

Titrate your
unknown.

Obtain a sample of an unknown acid from your instructor, and follow the same procedure used in the preparation and titration of the potassium hydrogen phthalate samples in Part A. If the two results do not agree within 0.8%, repeat with a third sample. Average the results and report the average to your instructor.

NOTEBOOK AND REPORT

Obtain approval of your results on the unknown acid, and include the calculations and results in your report. Calculate the standard deviations of your individual titrations (see Exp. 34).

Alternative Experiments

1. **Common commercial antacid tablets** containing magnesium hyroxide and aluminum hydroxide may be examined for their neutralizing capacity. Weigh a measured excess of potassium hydrogen phthalate and add to the antacid tablet in water. Titrate the excess acid with the standardized sodium hydroxide solution after adding phenolphthalein. Alternatively, a measured quantity of a standardized solution of an acid may be used to react with the tablet. Your instructor can tell your approximately how much potassium hydrogen phthalate or standard acid is needed to provide an excess. In either case the difference (moles of acid taken initially) - (moles of acid left for titration) represents the number of moles neutralized by the antacid tablet. Does Brand X neutralize "forty times its weight of stomach acid"?

2. **Unknown HCl.** Determine the normality of an unknown HCl solution by titrating two or three samples with your standard NaOH solution. DO NOT FORGET TO ADD THE INDICATOR. Use 10.0-mL samples of unknown acid measured with a pipet. The normalities that you obtain should agree within $\pm$ 0.0020. Report the average value.

3. **Unknown $HC_2H_3O_2$.** Determine the percentage of $HC_2H_3O_2$ by weight in an unknown solution of $HC_2H_3O_2$ by titrating two or three samples of the unknown acetic acid just as you performed the above titrations. DO NOT FORGET TO ADD THE INDICATOR. Use 10.0-mL samples measured with a pipet. Assume that the density of the solution is 1.000 g/mL.

REFERENCES

1. Davis, Gailey, and Whitten, <u>Principles of Chemistry</u>, Saunders College Publishing, Philadelphia, PA, 1984, Chapters 17 and 18 (Ionic Equilibria I and II: Acids, Bases, Buffers, and Acid-Base Titrations).

2. Whitten and Gailey, <u>General Chemistry</u>, 2nd Ed., Saunders College Publishing, Philadelphia, PA, 1984, Chapter 16 (Equilibria in Aqueous Solutions--I).

ACID-BASE TITRATIONS; VOLUMETRIC ANALYSIS

PRELABORATORY QUESTIONS

Name_____   Lab Instructor_____

Student ID No._____   Date_____

Write balanced (a) total formula, (b) total ionic, and (c) net ionic equations for reactions between the following acids and bases.

1. a. $HCl + Ba(OH)_2 \longrightarrow$

    b.

    c.

2. a. $HC_2H_3O_2 + KOH \longrightarrow$

    b.

    c.

3. a. $HNO_3 + Cu(OH)_2(s) \longrightarrow$

    b.

    c.

4. a. $H_2C_2O_4 + NaOH \longrightarrow$

    b.

    c.

5. a. $H_3PO_4 + Ca(OH)_2 \longrightarrow$

    b.

    c.

Set up each problem in an orderly way. Show all units and express answers with the appropriate number of significant figures.

6. What volume of 10.0 $\underline{N}$ NaOH solutions is required to prepare 40.0 liters of 0.200 $\underline{N}$ NaOH solution?

7. A 40.0-mL sample of NaOH solution reacts with exactly 0.6126 g of KHP. What is the normality of the NaOH solution?

8. If 30.0 mL of 0.200 $\underline{N}$ NaOH solution requires 20.0 mL of H_2SO_4 for complete neutralization, how many moles of H_2SO_4 were present in the acid solution?

9. What are the molarity and normality of the H_2SO_4 solution in no. 8 above?

10. What is the equivalent weight of an acid if 0.440 g of the acid requires 8.00 mL of 0.0222 M NaOH for neutralization?

11. An antacid tablet weighing 0.4800 g required 6.00 mL of 0.050 M HCl for neutralization. Assuming the tablet contained only $Mg(OH)_2$, how many moles of HCl can one tablet neutralize? How many moles of $Mg(OH)_2$ are present in one tablet?

Experiment 11, Part A

STANDARDIZATION OF NaOH

REPORT SHEET

Name_____   Lab Instructor_____

Student ID No._____   Date_____

Data   **Trial**

	1	2	3

Weight of potassium hydrogen
phthalate used   _____ _____ _____

Volume of base used   _____ _____ _____

Calculated molarity of base
(4 decimal places)   _____ _____ _____

Averaged molarity of base   _____

Average deviation   _____

Sample calculation

Observations and/or comments about any of the titrations

169

Experiment 11, Part B

DETERMINATION OF EQUIVALENT WEIGHT

REPORT SHEET

Data

	Trial		
	1	2	3
Weight of container and compound before removing sample	_____	_____	_____
Weight of container and compound after removing sample	_____	_____	_____
Net weight of sample	_____	_____	_____
Buret reading at start of titration	_____	_____	_____
Buret reading at end of titration	_____	_____	_____
Net volume of base used	_____	_____	_____
Molarity of standardized base	_____	_____	_____
Calculated equivalent weight of acid	_____	_____	_____
Averaged value of the equivalent weight	_____		
Average deviation	_____		

Sample Calculation

Observations and/or comments about any of the titrations

Attach sheets with answers to assigned QUESTIONS--PROBLEMS.

Experiment 11

QUESTIONS-PROBLEMS

1. Explain in concise statements the effect, if any, of each of the following sources
    of error upon the molarity and normality of the base as determined in the
    experiment; i.e., would the experimental value for molarity be too high or too
    low? Why?

    a. If the Erlenmeyer flask in which the titration was performed contained
        several milliliters of distilled water from the rinsing at the time the
        potassium hydrogen phthalate was weighed into it.

    b. If the tip of the buret were not filled with solution before the initial
        reading was taken.

    c. If a bubble appeared in the tip of the buret during the titration.

    d. If liquid splashed from the titration flask before the end point had been
        reached.

    e. If the buret were not rinsed with the base solution following the rinsing
        with distilled water.

2. Suppose that, instead of using sodium hydroxide, a base such as $Ba(OH)_2$ had been
    used. What changes in the calculations would then have to be made to determine
    the molar concentrations of the base? Answer this question in words, and
    illustrate your answer by calculating M_B from the following data:

    Moles of potassium hydrogen phthalate taken = 0.040

    $$Ba(OH)_2 \text{ solution}$$

Initial buret reading	0.02 mL
Final buret reading	36.70 mL

3. Calculate the equivalent weight of each of the following: H_3PO_4, HIO_4, $H_2C_2O_4$,
    KH_2PO_4, $Ca(OH)_2$, $Al(OH)_3$, NH_3, KOH.

4. How would the calculated value for the equivalent weight of the unknown acid be
    affected if:

    a. A small amount of the solid were lost in transferring it from vial to flask?

    b. The buret used were contaminated with acid solution?

    c. It was discovered after the titration that the unknown acid contained two
        titratable hydrogen atoms?

5. Can the molecular weight of an acid be calculated from its equivalent weight?
    Explain your answer.

6. How many grams of each of the following will be neutralized by 10.0 mL of 0.030 M
    NaOH?

    a) H_2SO_4 b) KHP   c) H_3PO_4 d) $H_2C_2O_4$

7. What is the molarity and the normality of an NaOH solution if 10.00 mL of the
    solution requires 0.4084 g of KHP for neutralization?

171

8. What is the equivalent weight of an acid if 0.400 g of the acid is neutralized by 12.0 mL of 0.040 M NaOH?

9. What is the equivalent weight of a base if 0.400 g of the base is neutralized by 16.0 mL of 0.040 M HCl?

10. The relatively small amounts of acids and bases involved in titrations can be described in terms of millimoles.

    a. What is the mass of one millimole of H_2SO_4, $HClO_4$, $Ca(OH)_2$, KHP?

    b. What is the molarity of a solution of an acid or base that contains 2 millimoles of acid or base per mL? 8 millimoles per mL? 0.25 millimoles per mL?

    c. What relationship exists between the molarity of a solution and the millimoles of solute present in one milliliter of the solution?

11. What is a milliequivalent, meq, of an acid or a base? How much does one meq of H_2SO_4 weigh? One meq of $Mg(OH)_2$?

12. What relationship exists between the normality of a solution and the meq present in one milliliter of the solution?

13. In the reaction $Ca(OH)_2$ + H_3PO_4 $\longrightarrow$ $Ca_3(PO_4)_2$ + H_2O (unbalanced),

    how many meq of H_3PO_4 are needed to neutralize 10 meq of $Ca(OH)_2$?

14. An antacid tablet weighing 0.3000 g required 12.00 mL of 0.500 M HCl for neutralization. The tablet contained only $Mg(OH)_2$ and NaCl [only $Mg(OH)_2$ is involved in the neutralization reaction]. How many grams of $Mg(OH)_2$ are present in one tablet? How many moles of HCl are neutralized by one tablet?

ACID-BASE EQUILIBRIA, INDICATORS, AND pH MEASUREMENT

Objective

To study chemical equilibria in solutions of acid-base indicators; to learn to use the pH meter

Equipment Needed

Three 4" test tubes; one 50-mL and two 150-mL beakers; magnetic stirrer and two stirring bars; pH meter reliable to 0.1-pH unit; plastic squeeze wash bottle; Kimwipe (or tissue paper)

Reagents Needed

6 M and 0.1 M Hydrochloric acid; 0.1 M sodium hydroxide; standard buffers, buffered at pH 4.00 and 7.00; solutions of some or all of the following indicators: alizarin, alizarin yellow R, bromocresol green, bromophenol blue, o-cresolphthalein, 2',7'-dichlorofluoroescein, methyl orange, methyl red, methyl violet, methyl yellow, methyl purple, phenolphthalein; wash bottle of distilled water

INTRODUCTION

In this experiment you will be working with acid-base indicators. There are substances that are one color in strongly acidic solutions and another color in strongly basic solutions. Each indicator changes color over a narrow pH range. Some indicators change color in slightly acid solutions, others in slightly basic solutions, and still others in a range near neutrality.

You will determine the pH range over which this color change occurs for one indicator. You will also see how color changes of indicators are related to acid-base equilibria and to the Bronsted theory of acids and bases.

As you know, pH is a measure of the acidity or basicity of a water solution. Acidic solutions--those in which the H_3O^+ concentration is greater than the OH^- concentration--have pH values less than seven. The more acidic a solution, the lower its pH. Basic solutions--those in which the OH^- concentration is greater than the H_3O^+ concentration--have pH values above seven. The more basic a solution, the higher its pH.

The pH of a solution can be estimated with indicators or determined more accurately with a pH meter. The pH meter is an electrochemical cell, similar to those in batteries. The chemical reaction that drives this cell involves H_3O^+ (or H^+aq)

ions. The cell voltage or the potential of this cell depends upon the concentration of these ions. The voltmeter in a pH meter is calculated in pH units instead of in volts.

Using the Brönsted concept of acids and bases, you have learned to consider acids as proton donors and bases as proton acceptors. You have also learned to think of an acid and its conjugate base (the acid minus its proton) or of a base and its conjugate acid (the base with an added proton). For example, the following three pairs are conjugate acid-base pairs.

HCN (acid) CN^- (its conjugate base)

NH_4^+ (acid) NH_3 (its conjugate base)

NH_3 (base) NH_4^+ (its conjugate acid)

Since all chemical reactions may be regarded as equilibrium processes if the reactants and products remain in the same environment, an acid-base reaction can be viewed in terms of the equilibrium established between the original acid and base and the new conjugate acid-base pair. The equilibrium is a typical example of an acid and

$$HCl + H_2O \rightleftharpoons H_3O^+ + Cl^-$$

acid   base   conjugate   conjugate
                               acid   base

a base reacting to give a new acid and a new base. The position of equilibrium always favors the weaker acid and weaker base since the stronger acid and stronger base have a greater reactivity than do the weaker acid and base.

Indicators, which are themselves weak acids or bases, are sometimes used in studying acid-base equilibria. The usefulness of an indicator depends upon the fact that the acid form of the indicator, HInd, has a different color than the conjugate base form of the indicator, Ind^-. Thus, for example:

Indicator	HInd Form	Ind⁻ Form
phenolphthalein	colorless	pink
litmus	pink	blue
methyl orange	pink	orange

The color of a solution containing an indicator tells us whether HInd or Ind^- is present in higher concentration. For example, if a drop of methyl orange indicator is added to a solution and the soltuion turns orange, we know that the Ind^- form of methyl orange is present in higher concentration--in mose cases ten or more times higher--than the HInd form.

Whether HInd or Ind^- is present in higher concentration depends upon:

a) the acidity or basicity of the solution, i.e., its pH, and
b) the relative strength of the acid HInd and its conjugate base Ind^-.

All of this is associated with an equilibrium that involves HInd and Ind^-.

In an acid solution, this equilibrium is:

$$Ind^- + H_3O^+ \rightleftharpoons HInd + H_2O.$$

color 1   color 2

a decrease in H_3O^+ ↓	forces the position of equilibrium to the left, favoring color 1		an increase in H_3O^+ ↑	forces the equilibrium to the right, favoring color 2

174

The position of equilibrium can be moved to the right (and the concentration and color of HInd increased) by adding acid. If base is added, the concentration of H_3O^+ will drop, and the position of equilibrium will be moved to the left. This will increase the concentration and color of Ind^-.

In a basic solution, the indicator equilibrium is

$$HInd + OH^- \rightleftharpoons Ind^- + H_2O.$$

The position of this equilibrium can be moved to the right by adding base or to the left by adding acid.

The color of the solution at any given pH depends upon the relative strengths of HInd as an acid and Ind^- as a base. If HInd is a relatively strong acid, the color of the solution will be that of the weak base Ind^- until the solution becomes quite acidic (reaches a low pH). If HInd is a relatively weak acid, the solution will be the color of HInd until it becomes quite basic. Here is the reason.

If HInd is a relatively strong acid, the equilibrium

$$Ind^- + H_3O^+ \rightleftharpoons HInd + H_2O$$

will lie to the left (in favor of the weak base Ind^-) unless H_3O^+ becomes high enough to push it to the right.

As long as Ind^- is present in much larger amounts than HInd, the solution will be the color of Ind^-. The weaker a base Ind^- is, the more acidic the solution must become before the equilibrium will be pushed far enough to the right to cause a color change.

The reverse argument holds if HInd is a relatively weak acid. As a very weak acid, HInd will predominate in solution until the solution becomes quite basic and equilibrium

$$HInd + OH^- \rightleftharpoons Ind^- + H_2O$$

can move far to the right.

If you understand the preceding reasoning, you also can appreciate why an indicator changes color at a certain pH or over a narrow pH range. This is the pH at which the H_3O^+ or OH^- concentration is just high enough to move the position of equilibrium from one side of the arrows to the other.

Although all indicators are weak acids, those that are the strongest acids change colors at low pH values. The weakest indicator acids change color at the highest pH values.

After you have determined the pH range over which the indicator assigned to you changes color, you will be asked to compare your color-change range with that found by other students who used different indicators. With this information, you can arrange the indicators in order of the acid strength of their HInd form.

Plan of the Experiment. The major activities you will perform in this experiment include:

1. Determining the colors of HInd and Ind^- for your assigned indicator and deciding whether it changes color at acidic or basic pH values;

2. Discovering with the acid or a pH meter the pH range over which it changes color;

3. Comparing the color-change range of your indicator with that of four other students, arranging the five indicators in order of the acid strength of their HInd forms;

4. Exchanging your indicator for that of a neighbor and finding if you obtain the same color-change range for this indicator as he/she did.

Find the color of your indicator in acid, base, and water.

Assemble three clean 4" test tubes. Fill half of one of them with 0.1 M HCl. Fill half of a second with 0.1 M NaOH. Fill half of the third with water. Add two drops of your indicator to each test tube. Stir the solutions; observe and record the colors in each test tube.

Is the color of your indicator in water the same as its color in acid or in base? On the basis of your answer, you should be able to decide whether the indicator changes color on the acid or on the basic side of neutrality.

Determine the color change range of your indicator.

Place about 50 mL of distilled water and 5-7 drops of your indicator in each of two clean 150-mL beakers. If your indicator changes color in acid, add to one beaker dropwise and with stirring 0.1 M HCl until the solution just begins to change color. To the second beaker, add 0.1 M HCl dropwise and with stirring until the color change has occurred and the second color is clearly dominant. If your indicator changes color in base, follow the preceding procedure using 0.1 M NaOH instead of 0.1 M HCl.

Carefully place a clean, dry magnetic stirring bar in each beaker. Take the two beakers and an empty 50-mL beaker to the pH meter and measure the pH of each solution using the following procedure.

Using the pH Meter

Measure the pH of your solutions.

1. Read the general directions for operating pH meters in Appendix IV.

2. At the pH meter, carefully remove the protective cap from the electrode and set it where you won't lose it. Place your empty 50-mL beaker beneath the electrode, and wash the electrode with a stream of distilled water from your wash bottle. BLOT the electrode dry with a Kimwipe (or tissue paper). BLOT rather than wipe the electrode to avoid scratching the glass tip.

3. Replace the 50-mL beaker with one of those containing a solution whose pH is to be measured. Set the magnetic stirrer control knob so that the magnetic stirrer rotates smoothly. Lower the electrode into the solution, making sure that its sensing bulb is fully immersed yet remains clear of the stirring bar.

4. Switch the mode control of the pH meter from "standby" to "pH". After the meter has stabilized, read and record the pH of the solution. Turn the mode control back to "standby".

5. Raise the electrode from the solution. Replace the beaker containing the solution with the 50-mL beaker containing rinse water. Again wash the electrode with distilled water from a squeeze bottle, and blot it dry with a Kimwipe. Again, BLOT rather than wipe the electrode to avoid scratching the tip.

6. Repeat steps 3 through 5 with the second solution whose pH is to be determined. After performing step 5 for the last time, replace the protective cap on the electrode.

Collecting Data from Other Students. Obtain the names and pH color-change ranges of four other indicators from your neighbors. Record this information in the data table. Compare the pH-change interval—the number of pH units over which the indicator changes color—for the five indicators. Can you make a generalization about this interval?

Exchanging Indicators. Exchange your indicator with that of a neighbor, and determine the color-change range of this indicator using the same procedure as before.

Compare the pH range you found with that by your neighbor. Account for inconsistencies.

TREATMENT OF DATA

Record the following in the data table:

1. The color of your assigned indicator in acid, base, and neutral solutions
2. The pH at the beginning and at the end of the color-change range of your indicator
3. The color-change range for indicators assigned to four other students
4. The color-change range you found and your neighbor found for your indicator and for his/her indicator

REFERENCES

1. Davis, Gailey, and Whitten, Principles of Chemistry, Saunders College Publishing, Philadelphia, PA, 1984, Chapters 17 and 18 (Ionic Equilibria I and II: Acids, Bases, Buffers, and Acid-Base Titrations).

2. Whitten and Gailey, General Chemistry, 2nd Ed., Saunders College Publishing, Philadelphia, PA, 1984, Chapter 16 (Equilibria in Aqueous Solutions--I).

QUESTIONS--PROBLEMS

1. Write an equation that describes the indicator equilibrium for your indicator in pure water. On the basis of your observations, describe the position of this equilibrium. Describe also the reasoning that led you to select the position of the equilibrium.

2. If an indicator were blue in base, red in acid, and red in water,

   a) What color is HInd?   What color is Ind$^-$?

   b) Will the indicator change color in acid or in basic solution?

   Describe in terms of the indicator equilibrium how you arrived at the answers to a) and b).

3. On the basis of your work on this experiment, offer an explanation for the observation that indicators changing color at relatively low pH cannot be used in titrations involving weak acids.

4. You wish to determine the pH of vinegar, but you have no pH meter and must use indicators. When you added methyl orange indicator, the vinegar became red. When malachite green was added, the vinegar turned green. Methyl orange is red at low pH and orange at higher pH. It changes color between pH 3.1 and 4.4. Malachite green is yellow at low pH and green at higher pH. Its color-change range is pH 0.2 to 2.0. On the basis of this information, estimate the pH of vinegar.

5. Apples have a pH of 3.1. What color would you expect to see if you placed a drop of each of the five indicators in your data table at different points on a slice of apple? How did your arrive at these answers?

Experiment 12

ACID-BASE EQUILIBRIA

PRELABORATORY QUESTIONS

Name______________________________ Lab Instructor____________________

Student ID No_____________________ Date______________________________

1. What is meant by each of the following?

   Brönsted theory of acids and bases

   conjugate acid

   conjugate base

   acid-base equilibrium

   position of equilibrium

   pH

2. Write an equation for the reaction of:

   a) HNO_3 with water

   b) an indicator HInd with water

3. What causes an acid-base indicator

   a) to exhibit two or more different colors?

   b) to change from one color to another?

4. Do all indicators change colors at the same pH? Why or why not?

5. What precautions must be taken to protect the electrode of the pH meter?

Experiment 12

ACID–BASE EQUILIBRIA, INDICATORS, AND pH MEASUREMENT

REPORT SHEET

Name_____ Lab Instructor_____

Student ID No_____ Date_____

Data Table

		Assigned Indicator			
Name	Color in acid	Color in base	Color in water	Color of HInd	Color of Ind$^-$

Color-Change Range	
pH of first observable color change	pH when second color dominates

Comparison of Color–Change Ranges of Five Indicators

	Color Change		
Name of Indicator	HInd	Ind$^-$	Color-Change Range
I. _____ (your indicator)	_____	_____	_____
II. _____	_____	_____	_____
III. _____	_____	_____	_____
VI. _____	_____	_____	_____
V. _____	_____	_____	_____

Order of Acid Strengths of Five Indicators

_____ _____ _____ _____ _____

(strongest acid)   (weakest acid)

Comparison of Observations on Same Indicator

	Color-Change Range	
	Your Observations	Neighbor's Observations
Your Indicator	_____	_____
Neighbor's Indicator	_____	_____

VAPOR DENSITY AND THE GAS LAWS

Objective

To study some fundamental properties of gases and to determine the molar volume, molecular weight, and the constants **a** and **b** of the van der Waals equation for an unknown volatile compound

Equipment Needed

250-mL flask modified as shown in Fig. 13-1; hot plate; water trough or a 600- or 800-mL beaker; barometer; thermometer; 1-mm glass capillary tubing; Tygon or other inert plastic tubing; platform balance accurate to 0.001 g; burner

Reagents Needed

Liquids that boil between 55 and 90 $^\circ$C to be used as unknowns; elemental analysis and density of liquids at room temperature need to be provided

INTRODUCTION

From Avogadro's hypothesis, which states that equal volumes of different gases at the same temperature and pressure contain the same number of molecules, many important experimental and mathematical approaches for studying the behavior of gases have been undertaken. In this experiment we shall make use of facets of both of these approaches to illustrate their power and scope.

Two inferences can be made directly from Avogadro's hypothesis. (1) The molar volume of a gas should be a constant for all gases at a given temperature and pressure. At standard temperature and pressure (0 $^\circ$C and 1 atm), this volume is 22.414 liters. (2) The molar gas constant, R, in the perfect gas law $PV = nRT$ is a universal constant. In the perfect gas law expression, P, V, n, and T represent the pressure, volume, number of moles, and temperature ($^\circ$K) of the gas, respectively.

Real gases show perfect gas behavior only at low pressures and relatively high temperatures, and the deviations from ideal behavior have led us to important ideas about attractive forces between molecules and about molecular sizes. Students often are confused as to when they can assume that a gas or vapor behaves according to the perfect gas law and when they must assume that it deviates from ideal behavior. Perhaps the simplest resolution of this dilemma is to assume that although no gas is ideal, deviations from ideal behavior are seldom large enough to change the general pattern of gas behavior. As a consequence, the perfect gas law can be used for real gases with the exception that the numerical values obtained from calculation are, in many cases, reliable approximations to actual values.

To illustrate the above point, we shall use the data obtained in this experiment in parallel calculations. In one application--estimation of molecular weight--we use the data in conjunction with the perfect gas law. In a second application, we use the same data to estimate the extent of deviation from ideal behavior.

183

The experiment involves determining the density of the vapor of a volatile liquid. In this experiment, the mass of a known volume of volatilized liquid at a known pressure and at the temperature of boiling water is measured. From this information, the vapor density (mass/volume) of the liquid is obtained. Then, the molecular weight of the liquid can be approximated, and the deviation of the vapor from perfect gas behavior can be estimated.

If we assume that the vapor approximates perfect gas behavior and if we recall that the number of moles of vapor, n, is equal to the mass of vapor divided by its gram-molecular weight, the perfect gas law becomes

$$PV = nRT = \frac{g}{M}RT$$

in which g is the mass of the vapor and M is its gram-molecular weight. Solving this equation for the molecular or molar weight, we get

$$M = \frac{gRT}{PV}.$$

All of the data needed to evaluate the molecular weight, except the molar gas constant, R, are obtained in measuring the vapor density. In assuming that the vapor behaves ideally, we also are assuming that R is a constant of known value. The value for the molar weight thus obtained is approximate, but it should be within 10 to 15 percent of the actual value. The error is not entirely attributable to the assumption that the gas is ideal. What other factors might introduce errors in the molar weight thus calculated?

The value for the molar weight should be reliable enough to be used to calculate the molecular formula of the substance if an elemental analysis is provided. For the purposes of this experiment, you will be given an unknown liquid and its elemental analysis. Hence, you should be able to report not only the approximate molar weight and the molecular formula but also a more exact molecular weight.

Now let us set aside considerations of molar weight and use the experimental data to estimate the deviation of the assigned unknown vapor from ideal behavior. A ready measure of this deviation is in the value for the molar gas constant, R. If the gas were ideal, the value for R would be 0.082054 atm $\times$ L $\times$ mol^{-1} $\times$ K^{-1}. From our data we can calculate a value for R, assuming

$$R = \frac{PV}{nT}.$$

We know the values for P, V, and T directly from our data, and we also know the mass of the vapor. To determine the number of moles of vapor present, we need to know the exact molar weight of the vapor. This is obtainable from the molecular formula which we have determined previously. Once the value for R is calculated from the data, we can compare it with that of an ideal gas; the difference should give some indication of the non-ideality of the liquid vapor. However, such a comparison may not greatly increase our understanding of non-ideality. Is it possible to use the information we have collected to estimate the magnitude of the major causes of non-ideality in gases, i.e., the attractive forces between molecules and the sizes of the molecules? We should at least try to do so.

The van der Waals equation adds the parameters **a** (a measure of attractive forces between molecules) and **b** (a measure of the volume occupied by individual molecules) to the parameters of the perfect gas law to give

$$\left(P + \frac{an^2}{V^2}\right) \times \left(V - nb\right) = nRT.$$

If the vapor behaves according to this equation, we see that we have values available for all parameters except **a** and **b**. If we can get the value for either **a** or **b** from another source, we can determine the other constant from the van der Waals equation. The value for **b** (the volume occupied by 1 mole of molecules when they are packed so close that they can be said to be touching) might be estimated from data on the liquid. If it is assumed that in the liquid state at room temperature the distance between molecules is very small, the volume of 1 mole of the liquid at this temperature can be used as an approximation for **b**. To determine the molar volume of liquid, we use the density of the liquid and its molar weight. Once a value for **b** has been estimated, we can then use this, the

184

accept value for R, and our measured values for P, V, T, and n to calculate a value for **a**. These values for **a** and **b**, when compared with corresponding values for other gases, should provide a greater appreciation for the causes of the magnitude of deviations of gases and vapors from ideal behavior.

There are many sources of error in this experiment. One of the most serious errors appears in the calculation of **a** because this value is obtained as a small difference by subtracting two large numbers. All of the errors and approximations inherent in the values for the other parameters in the equation finally appear in **a**. Although this should discourage calculation of **a** in this manner, no scientist would refuse to make such a calculation if there were no other way to estimate the value of an important parameter.

TECHNIQUE

A small volume of a volatile liquid is added to a 250-mL flask, the orifice of which has been modified as shown in Fig. 13-1. The flask is **immersed in** (not floated on) a pneumatic trough or a beaker of water that is heated to boiling. As soon as all of the liquid in the flask has vaporized, the flask is removed from the boiling water and

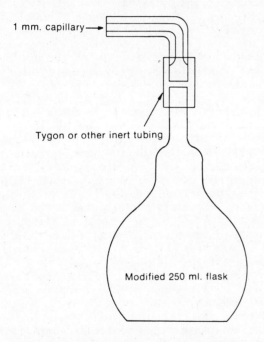

1 mm. capillary —→

Tygon or other inert tubing

Modified 250 ml. flask

Figure 13-1

Flask for determination of vapor density. Care must be taken to avoid trapping liquid in the junction between the capillary tube and the orifice of the flask.

allowed to cool. The vaporized liquid remaining in the flask condenses to a liquid. The mass of the liquid is determined by comparing the weight of the empty flask with that of the flask containing the condensed liquid. The volume of the vapor is the volume of the flask; the temperature is the boiling point of water, which is not necessarily 100.0 $^{\circ}$C; the pressure is the atmospheric pressure at the time of the experiment.

PROCEDURE

Weigh the **clean, dry** flask (without the capillary tip) to the nearest milligram. Add 5 mL of the unknown liquid to the flask. Dry the orifice of the flask, and replace the capillary tip, being sure to get the junction of the capillary tubing and the end of the flask as snug as possible to avoid trapping liquid at this junction.

Weigh the flask and add the unknown liquid.

Clamp the flask with a clamp which will serve as a handle, and place the flask and its contents in a water trough or a beaker of mildly boiling water (**Note 1**). Heat the flask and its contents until the schlieren jet of vaporizing liquid disappears from the capillary tip of the flask (**Note 2**). Immediately remove the flask from the hot water

Heat to vaporize the liquid.

bath, note the temperature of the bath, and allow the flask to cool by clamping it on a ring stand or by setting it on a **clean** surface. Meanwhile, determine the atmospheric pressure from the laboratory barometer. When the flask is cool, wipe it dry, remove the capillary tip, wipe the top of the flask dry, and weigh the flask again (to 0.001 g) to obtain (by difference) the weight of vapor in the flask. Determine the vapor density of your sample two more times by adding 5 mL of sample and repeating the heating and cooling steps outlined above.

Determine the volume of the flask by disconnecting the capillary tip, drying and weighing the dry flask (**Note 3**), filling the flask level-full with water, and weighing the filled flask on the triple-beam or platform balance. Calculate the volume of the flask from the mass of water contained and its density at room temperature. Repeat the volume determination to check your first result; average the two values (**Note 4**).

CALCULATIONS

Calculate the gram-molecular (molar) weight by using the equation

$$M = \frac{gRT}{PV}$$

as indicated earlier. Be sure to use a value for R consistent with the units used for pressure and volume. Using the elemental analysis data provided with your unknown, determine its simplest and molecular formulas and its exact molar weight.

Using your experimental data and the exact molar weight, calculate an experimental value for R. Compare this with the literature value, and calculate the percent deviation of the experimental from the literature value. Compare your results with those of several other students, and comment on these comparisons in your report.

Estimate the value for **b** in the van der Waals equation for your liquid, using its molar weight and density. The value for the density will be provided by the instructor. Finally, calculate a value for **a** in the van der Waals equation as described earlier. Compare your values for **a** and **b** with values in the literature (if possible) and with those obtained by several other students. Comment in your report on the differences in **a** and **b** for different liquids, and discuss briefly how the values for **a** and **b** are reflected in the bulk properties of the vapor and the liquid.

NOTEBOOK AND REPORT

In addition to the data and calculations already discussed, both the notebook and report should include statements on sources of errors. Whenever possible, the magnitude of the error introduced by a given procedure should be estimated.

NOTES

Note 1.   You should be very careful with flames while working on this experiment. If hot plates are unavailable, use a burner to heat to boiling 500 mL of water in an 800-mL beaker secured to a ring stand; then reduce the size of the flame to a size just sufficient to fit under the beaker and to maintain a gentle boiling action.

Note 2.   If you are unable to see the schlieren vapor stream clearly, obtain a small piece of tissue paper, and hold this in front of the capillary to determine when the liquid stops vaporizing rapidly.

Note 3.   Dry the flask by removing the capillary tip, rinsing the inside with 5 mL of acetone to remove the organic unknown, and drying a few minutes in an 80-100 $^{\circ}$C oven. If an oven is unavailable, insert a long capillary tube to near the bottom of the flask, and attach the capillary to an aspirator (via tubing) to circulate air in the flask (see Fig. 13-2).

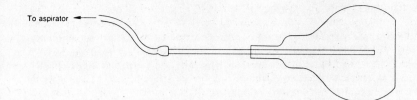

Figure 13-2

Drying a flask by sucking
air through it.

<u>Note 4</u>.   Both the mass of the EMPTY flask and that of the flask containing the condensed
liquid should be determined with the **same** analytical balance.   Use a **triple-
beam or a platform balance** to determine the mass of the **flask** when **filled with
water.**

REFERENCES

1.   Davenport, D.A. <u>J. Chem. Educ.</u> (1962) <u>39</u>, 253.
2.   Davenport, D.A.; Saba, A.N. <u>J. Chem. Educ.</u> (1962) <u>39</u>, 617.
3.   Davis, Gailey, and Whitten, <u>Principles of Chemistry</u>, Saunders College Publishing,
Philadelphia, PA, 1984, Chapter 11 (Gases and the Kinetic-Molecular Theory).
4.   Whitten and Gailey, <u>General Chemistry</u>, 2nd Ed., Saunders College Publishing,
Philadelphia, PA, 1984, Chapter 8 (Gases and the Kinetic-Molecular Theory).

1. What error is introduced by not removing the flask from the boiling water as soon as the schlieren jet disappears from the tip of the flask? What error is introduced if we remove the flask too soon? You may wish to examine the results of the experiment given in Table 13-1, which records the final weight of the flask and liquid as a function of the time after the schlieren jet disappeared.

Table 13-1. Weight of Flask and Liquid as a Function of Time

Time after Disappearance of Jet (sec)	Final Weight of Bulb and Unknown (g, ± 0.0002 g)	
	cis-1,2- dichloroethylene	1,1,1- trichloroethane
5	67.2731	67.5890
30	67.2720	67.5870
60	67.2715	67.5863
90	67.2712	67.5859
120	67.2703	67.5854
180	67.2689	67.5850
240	67.2534	67.5837

Use these data to decide the optimum time to leave the flask in the boiling water. Note that these two compounds have different vapor pressures.

2. Upon what factors measurable or determinable in this experiment does the density of a vapor depend? State this in mathematical terms based on the perfect gas law.

3. Is it reasonable for the constant **a** in the van der Waals equation to have a negative value? Why or why not?

4. Let us suppose that the only error you make in the entire experiment is that you read the volume of the flask as 5% less than it actually is. Estimate the error in each of the following:

   a. The molecular weight

   b. The calculated value for R

   c. The value for **b**

   d. The value for **a**

5. Is the value you calculated for R likely to be a constant for the substance you used at all temperatures and pressures at which it is a gas or vapor? Why or why not?

6. Calculate the pressure exerted by 0.6 mol of ammonia at 25 °C when confined to a volume of 0.5 L, assuming ideality. Repeat the calculation, using the van der Waals equation (van der Waals constants for ammonia are: $a = 4.17$ $L^2 \cdot atm/mol^2$; $b = 0.0371$ L/mol.

7. According to Charles' Law, when the absolute temperature of a gas is doubled, the volume doubles. However, in the case of hydrogen fluoride gas, the volume may increase by more than two times. Explain.

188

Experiment 13

VAPOR DENSITY AND THE GAS LAWS

PRELABORATORY QUESTIONS

Name _____   Lab Instructor_____

Student ID No _____   Date_____

1. Why are we justified in using atmospheric pressure as the pressure exerted by the vapor in the flask? What error, if any, is introduced by this?

2. How would the weight of vapor remaining in the flask after the heat treatment be affected if you added 10 mL of the unknown liquid into the flask in Fig. 13-1 instead of the recommended 5 mL?

3. What two features of real gases are being considered when the van der Waals constants **a** and **b** are introduced into the equation PV = nRT?

4. Explain how, if at all, each of the following affects the vapor density of a gas:

    surface area of the container for the gas

    volume of the liquid

    temperature of the gas

    presence of other gases in the vapor

5. Calculate the volume occupied at 87 $^\circ$C and 950 torr (950 mm Hg pressure) by a quantity of gas that occupied 20 L at 27 $^\circ$C and 570 torr.

6. The density of a gas is 3.54 g/L at 25 $^\circ$C and 1520 torr.

    (a) Find the density of the gas (g/L) at standard conditions of temperature and pressure.

    (b) Find the molecular (molar) weight of the gas.

ATTRACTIVE FORCES BETWEEN MOLECULES;

VAPOR PRESSURE AND ENTHALPY OF VAPORIZATION OF LIQUIDS

Objective

To measure the vapor pressure of a volatile liquid at several temperatures and to use the values obtained to calculate the enthalpy of vaporization of the liquid; to compare the enthalpies of vaporization of several liquids as a measure of the attractive forces between the molecules of each compound

Equipment Needed

5 mm x 9 mm Serum stopper, 30-mL glass syringe with Luer-Lok fitting, syringe (1-5 mL), ring stand, iron ring, iron gauze, buret clamp, gas burner, thermometer (0-100 °C), beaker (600 mL), #22 or #24 gauge hypodermic needle, rubber bands, melting-point capillary tubes

Reagents Needed

Hexane, heptane, octane, nonane, methanol, ethanol, 1-butanol, 1-propanol, acetone, tissue paper, unknown compounds

INTRODUCTION

The magnitude of the forces of attraction between molecules can be determined by measuring the amount of energy required to separate them. One process by which molecules are separated is vaporization. During vaporization, closely spaced molecules in a liquid are transformed into a gas in which the same molecules are widely separated. The energy required for vaporization is thus a measure of the energy required to separate molecules from each other and represents the work done against the attractive forces between the molecules. If the energy required for the vaporization of several liquids is measured, a comparison of the values obtained represents a comparison of the attractive forces between the molecules in each liquid. If the vaporization is done at constant pressure, the energy measured is the enthalpy change in the process. Vaporization at constant pressure also requires that work be done in pushing back the atmosphere, and the corresponding energy is included in the enthalpy of vaporization. (This is a small amount of energy compared to the energy needed to separate the molecules. It does not differ greatly from one liquid to another if the measurements are based upon the vaporization of 1 mole of the substance since the volumes occupied by 1 mole of different gases are nearly the same at pressures near that of the atmosphere.) Hence, a comparison of the molar enthalpies of vaporization of different liquids is a valid comparison of the relative magnitudes of the attractive forces between their molecules.

Although the enthalpy of vaporization can be determined directly by measuring the quantity of heat energy necessary to vaporize a given quantity of liquid at constant pressure, the experiment is not easy to perform, mainly because heat tends to

193

leak from the apparatus, making the measured heat input greater than the amount actually used for vaporization. It is much easier to measure the <u>vapor pressure</u> of the liquid at several temperatures and to <u>calculate</u> the enthalpy of vaporization from those measurements. A frequent practice in science is to choose a sequence of measurements that are easy to make with precision in order to arrive at a desired quantity that may not be easy to measure. Although the route to determining this quantity may seem at first glance to be unnecessarily complicated, a consideration of the experimental difficulties and likelihood of error in the direct route shows that it is not.

The relation between vapor pressure and enthalpy of vaporization of a liquid is:

$$\log P = -\left(\frac{\Delta H_v}{2.3\ R}\right)\frac{1}{T}\ +\ C \tag{1}$$

Here P is the vapor pressure, ΔH_v is the molar enthalpy of vaporization, R is the gas constant in joules (or calories) per degree per mole, T is the Kelvin temperature at which the vapor pressure is measured, and C is a constant, the value of which depends upon the liquid being studied. Eq. (1) is one form of the Clausius-Clapeyron equation which relates equilibrium constants for a reaction to the enthalpy change in the reaction.

Comparing the Clausius-Clapeyron equation to the general equation for a straight line, y = mx + b, we can identify y with log P and x with 1/T. Using measurements, P_1, P_2, P_3, ..., of the vapor pressures of the liquid at the corresponding absolute temperatures, T_1, T_2, T_3, ..., we can construct a graph. For this graph the ordinate (y axis) is log P and the abscissa (x axis) is 1/T. The enthalpy of vaporization is calculated from the slope of the best straight line drawn through these points:

$$-\frac{\Delta H_v}{2.3\ R} = \text{SLOPE} = m \tag{2}$$

or

$$\Delta H_v = -(\text{SLOPE}) \times 2.3\ R \tag{3}$$

See pages 28-30 on how to determine the slope of a line.

A. Determination of the Vapor Pressure at Several Temperatures

In this experiment, each student will be asked to obtain data for the determination of the heats of vaporization of both an unknown and of a known liquid. For the known compound, the class will be divided into teams of four students. Each team member will obtain data for the vapor pressure of one compound from either Set 1 or Set 2 from the list below and provide his data to the three other members of his team. Each student is asked to calculate and report independently the results for each compound in his or her set.

<u>Set 1</u>	<u>Set 2</u>
n-Hexane	Methanol
n-Heptane	Ethanol
n-Octane	1-Propanol
n-Nonane	1-Butanol

The results of the team experiment should be analyzed independently with regard to any trend observed in the heats of vaporization. The trend should be discussed in terms of the relative magnitudes of the forces of attraction between (among) molecules. Finally, the trend in the forces of attraction should be related in terms of the structures of the four compounds in the set.

The technique used for measuring the vapor pressure of a liquid is to determine the volume of a mixture consisting of a known amount of air and of a small amount of the volatile liquid. This liquid is assumed to be in equilibrium with its vapor at each measured temperature. All volume measurements are made at a constant (atmospheric) pressure. The volume of the air-vapor mixture is measured in a 30-mL glass hypodermic syringe. When this mixture is heated, the known amount of air expands, and, more significantly, an additional portion of the liquid vaporizes until a new liquid-vapor equilibrium is established at the higher temperature. This procedure can be repeated at higher temperatures until the capacity of the syringe is exceeded or until the normal boiling temperature of the liquid is reached. Using Dalton's law of partial pressures and accounting for the expansion of the known amount of air as the temperature increases, the vapor pressure of the liquid may be calculated.

> **CAUTION:** Acetone, some of the unknowns, and some of the knowns are flammable. Keep them away from flames.

PROCEDURE

Preparation of the Syringe

Remove the old red rubber serum stopper if it is still attached. CAUTION, do not allow the glass plunger to drop and break. Wipe the plunger with a piece of tissue, and place it in a clean 400-mL beaker. Rinse the barrel twice with 5-mL portions of acetone. Thoroughly dry the barrel by drawing air through it, using an aspirator. Place the small end of the serum stopper (see Fig. 14-1) around the outside of the inner metal tube of the Luer-Lok fitting.

Clean the syringe and dry it.

Bend the larger outer end of the serum stopper around the outside of the Luer-Lok fitting (see Fig. 14-2). Avoid stretching the serum stopper too tightly.

Attach stopper; insert and then remove needle.

Gently insert a loose hypodermic needle into the center of the newly attached serum stopper and leave it there. This allows the air to escape through the needle when the plunger is replaced. Replace the plunger, push it until about 5 mL of air remain in the syringe, and remove the needle.

Figure 14-1. Enlarged cross section of the rubber serum stopper prior to attachment of syringe

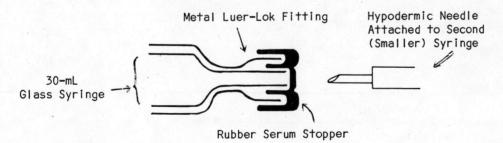

Metal Luer-Lok Fitting

Hypodermic Needle Attached to Second (Smaller) Syringe

30-mL Glass Syringe

Rubber Serum Stopper

Figure 14-2. Syringe with rubber serum stopper attached

Volume and Temperature Measurements

Attach the previously prepared 30-mL syringe to a ring stand at a height so that a beaker and burner can later be placed under it.

Test for
leaks.
The plunger should point upward. Gently rotate the plunger to be sure it moves freely in the barrel. If the plunger moves down, there is a leak. Replace the serum stopper and check again for leakage. If leakage still occurs, the problem may be with the syringe itself. Obtain a different one.

Measure volume
and
temperature.
Measure and record the volume of air in the syringe to the nearest 0.1 mL. Place a thermometer near the syringe and record the temperature reading.

Inject sample.
Clean a small syringe and then rinse it with your sample. Inject 0.20 mL of sample into the 30-mL syringe through the serum stopper. Take care that no additional air is also injected. Remove the small syringe. Immerse the 30-mL syringe, now containing the sample plus air, in a 600-mL beaker filled with water. Heat the water until the volume increases to about 6 mL. Stir the water to insure a uniform temperature, and wait a minute or two until the syringe and water are at the same temperature. Rotate the plunger; then read and record the volume in the syringe and the temperature of the water.

Measure volume
and
temperature.
Repeat the measurements of volume and temperature after heating the water until the volume is approximately 11, 16, 21, and 26 mL. Rotate the plunger each time before reading the volume.

In compounds of high molecular weight, the volume may not exceed 15 mL even at the boiling point of water. Do not attempt to heat the sample to a temperature greater than 100 °C.

Don't forget
to record
pressure.
Record the barometric pressure.

CALCULATIONS

The total pressure of a mixture of gases is the sum of the partial pressures of these gases. This is a statement of Dalton's Law of Partial Pressures. For use in this experiment, Dalton's Law can be written as:

$$P_A + P_S = P_B \tag{4}$$

in which

P_A is the pressure of air in the syringe
P_S is the vapor pressure of sample in the syringe
P_B is the barometric, and hence the total,
pressure on the syringe.

The pressure of air is related to the number of moles of air, n_A, at any temperature, T, and volume, V, by the general gas law

$$P_A = n_A \frac{RT}{V} \tag{5}$$

so that [from (4)]

$$n_A \frac{RT}{V} + P_S = P_B \tag{6}$$

in which

T is the absolute temperature of the mixture
V is the volume of the mixture in liters.

But we know n_A from the initial measurement of the volume of air (V_R) at room temperature (T_R) before the sample was injected. In that measurement also, the pressure exerted on the piston was the atmospheric pressure (P_B).

$$P_S = P_B - \frac{T}{T_R}\frac{V_R}{V}P_B$$

where
$$n_A = \frac{V_R}{RT_R}P_B \qquad\qquad (7)$$

Substitution of Eq. (7) into Eq. (6) permits the calculation of the vapor pressure of the sample, P_S, for each temperature T, at which the volume of the mixture, V, is measured.

Use your expression to calculate the vapor pressure at each temperature for each liquid studied. Look up the logarithms of the vapor pressures, calculate the reciprocals of the Kelvin temperatures, and plot the data according to Eq. (1). Draw the best straight line through the points, determine the slope of the line, and calculate the enthalpy of vaporization from Eq. (3). Use 1.987 calories per degree per mole as the value for R. Record your value of ΔH_v. Using the conversion factor from calories to joules, record it also in kilojoules per mole.

B. Determination of the Boiling Point of a Liquid

In the procedure used in Part A, the temperature is fixed by the experimenter, and the vapor pressure corresponding to that temperature is determined. The apparatus shown in Fig. 14-3 reverses the process. Here the pressure is fixed at atmospheric pressure, and the temperature at which the vapor pressure reaches this value, i.e., the boiling point, is measured. A small amount of the liquid under examination is placed in the 10 x 75 mm test tube fastened to the thermometer, and a capillary melting-point tube is dropped into it with the open end of the capillary tube below the surface of the liquid. As the temperature of the bath is increased, air bubbles emerge from the capillary tube, slowly at first and then in a rapid stream as the liquid boils. The boiling is continued for a few seconds to remove nearly all of the air from the

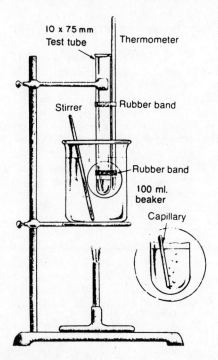

Figure 14-3. Determination of the boiling point of a liquid in the capillary

197

capillary tube and fill it with vapor. The bath is then allowed to cool slowly. It is stirred constantly, and the open end of the capillary tube is watched carefully. When the liquid begins to re-enter the capillary tube, the pressure inside is equal to the atmospheric pressure on the surface of the liquid, and the temperature read on the thermometer is the boiling point. In this measurement it is presumed that the pressure exerted by any residual air in the capillary tube is negligible, and the infinitesimal effect of the hydrostatic pressure exerted because the capillary opening is below the surface of the liquid is ignored.

PROCEDURE

Assemble apparatus.

Set up the apparatus shown in Fig. 14-3. The test tube is clamped to the ring stand, and the thermometer is attached to it with rubber bands so that the thermometer bulb is opposite the bottom of the test tube. The capillary tube is about 2-cm long and is made by scratching a melting-point tube with a file (gently) 2 cm from the closed end and breaking it off at that point. Put 1 mL of the liquid for vapor-pressure determination into the test tube and heat the water in the beaker, with stirring, looking for the phenomena described above. Record the boiling temperature and the barometric pressure.

Determine boiling point.

For some liquids, the boiling point may be higher than 100 °C. In these cases, the boiling point cannot be determined in a water bath. Do not attempt to substitute another bath liquid.

CALCULATIONS

Look up log P_B, calculate 1/T, and place the result on the graph you made for Part A. Mark the point clearly as the measured boiling point.

If your liquid was one of those boiling above 100 °C, extrapolate your curve of Part A to the point at which log P_B is reached, and evaluate the boiling point as the corresponding value of 1/T, that is, of T. Record the boiling point thus evaluated.

NOTEBOOK AND REPORT

Each student should maintain in his or her notebook the records needed to enable a reader to reconstruct his or her experiments. Each student should draw the graph and make the calculations indicated. The report of the second portion of the experiment should be a team effort. It should include the graphs for each of the four compounds examined by the team and the calculated values of the enthalpies of vaporization. The report should include a discussion of the information gained about trends in attractive forces as a result of comparing the enthalpies of vaporization of the four compounds in the set. This discussion might relate, for example, to the effect on the enthalpy of vaporization with changing molecular weights of compounds of the same chemical nature; of changing the shape, polarity, hydrogen bonding possibilities, or other structural features of the compounds without changing the molecular weight; of changing the chemical nature of the compounds; etc.

REFERENCES

1. Davenport, D.A. J. Chem. Educ. (1962) 39, 253.
2. Davenport, D.A.; Saba, A.N. J. Chem. Educ. (1962) 39, 617.
3. Whitten, K.W.; Gailey, K.D. General Chemistry 2nd Ed., Saunders College Publishing, Philadelphia, 1984, Chapter 12, pp. 303-307.
4. Davis, Gailey, Whitten, Principles of Chemistry, Saunders College Publishing, Philadelphia, 1984, pp 539-540.

Experiment 14

Prelaboratory Questions and Problems

Name_____   Lab Instructor_____

Student ID No._____   Date_____

1. Define (or describe the significance of) the following terms clearly and concisely:

    a. torr (or mm Hg)

    b. one atmosphere

    c. standard conditions

    d. Avogadro's number in relation to a gas

2. State the following in your own words and with equations:

    a. Charles' law

    b. Boyle's law

    c. Dalton's law

3. a. A sample of helium occupies 300 mL at 27 $^\circ$C under a pressure of 730 torr. What volume would it occupy at standard conditions?

    b. At what temperature ($^\circ$C) would the helium occupy 600 mL under a pressure of 740 torr?

4. A 3.00-g sample of gas occupies 1.12 liters at standard conditions. What is the molecular weight of the gas?

5. a. What volume would 3.2 g of CH_4 occupy at 27 $^\circ$C under a pressure of 760 torr?

    b. What volume would 3.2 g of CH_4 occupy if it were collected over water at 27 $^\circ$C under a pressure of 760 torr?

Experiment 14

VAPOR PRESSURE AND ENTHALPY OF VAPORIZATION OF LIQUIDS

REPORT SHEET

Name_____   Lab Instructor_____

Student ID No._____   Date_____

1. Volume of air in the 30-mL syringe _____ mL

    Room temperature   _____ °C

    Barometric pressure   _____ torr (or mm Hg)

2. Vapor-Volume Measurements

	Temperature	Total Volume	Vapor Pressure of Liquid (calculated)
a.	_____	_____	_____
b.	_____	_____	_____
c.	_____	_____	_____
d.	_____	_____	_____
e.	_____	_____	_____

3. Calculated values of ΔH_v: _____ kcal/mol   _____ kJ/mol

4. Boiling point: Experimental _____ or from graph _____

5. Attach sheets showing:

    a. the calculations of the vapor pressure of the liquid
    b. the graph of the vapor-pressure data
    c. the calculation of ΔH_v from this graph
    d. the answers to the assigned questions from the next page
    e. the data, graphs, calculations, and discussion of the team experiments

Questions--Problems

1. Calculate the pressure (in atmospheres) exerted by the plunger if it has a mass of 40 g and a diameter of 23 mm. Is this pressure small compared to one atmosphere? Explain why this contribution to the pressure can be omitted in the calculation of the vapor pressure.

2. Discuss the magnitude of the error introduced by neglecting the small volume of liquid in the 30-mL syringe.

3. The internationally accepted standard unit of pressure is the newton per square meter (N/m^2), 1 mm Hg = 133 N/m^2. Suppose that you already have constructed a graph of log P (in mm Hg or in torr) vs. 1/T for your unknown. How would the value for the enthalpy of vaporization of your unknown be affected if you had used log P (in N/m^2) instead of log P (in mm Hg or in torr) for this graph?

4. Air is a mixture containing very nearly 78% nitrogen, 21% oxygen, and 1% argon, by volume. We have not used this information in calculating the number of moles of air nor the vapor pressures of the sample. Outline the reasons why the fact that air is not a single pure substance can be ignored in making these calculations.

5. How would you use the procedure of Part B to measure the boiling point of a liquid which boils above 100 $^{\circ}C$?

6. The vapor pressure of a solution of a nonvolatile solid in a liquid is less than the vapor pressure of the pure liquid. How can this be explained?

7. When the vapor pressure of a mixture of 1 mole of liquid A and 1 mole of liquid B is measured at some fixed temperature, it is sometimes (though rarely) found to be halfway between the vapor pressures of pure A and pure B at that temperature; for some liquid pairs it is above this value, and for others is is below. The first case is said to represent an ideal solution and indicates that the attractive forces between molecules A and B are no different from the attractive forces between molecules of A and A or between molecules of B and B. What can you suggest about the relative magnitudes of the A-B forces, compared to the A-A and B-B forces, in the other two cases?

Experiment 15

SOLUBILITY OF SALTS

THE VARIATION OF SOLUBILITY WITH TEMPERATURE

Objective

>To study the solubilities of inorganic salts and saturation equilibria as
functions of temperature and solvent

Equipment Needed

>Large test tube solubility apparatus; buret or 10-mL pipet

Reagents Needed

>Potassium dichromate, $K_2Cr_2O_7$; oxalic acid dihydrate, $H_2C_2O_4 \cdot 2\ H_2O$; ice; 70:30
water/dioxane mixture

INTRODUCTION

In this experiment we shall study some of the factors that determine the amount
of substance that can be dissolved in a given amount of liquid. The substances chosen for
investigation are a salt or an acid, and the liquid chosen is water because solutions of
salts and acids in water are among the most common type of solutions observed.

The generalization that systems tend to change from an ordered state to one of
less order suggests that there is a natural tendency for all solids to dissolve. The
dissolved state is a more disordered arrangement, with the molecules or ions distributed
at random through the solution, in contrast to their ordered arrangement in the solid
state. During the dissolution process, this tendency to become disordered is opposed by
the forces holding the molecules or ions to each other in fixed positions in the solid.
Work must be done against these forces--i.e., energy must be expended--to separate the
particles (molecules or ions) of the solid from each other.

In the dissolved state there are also forces of interaction between the molecules or ions of the solute and the molecules of the solvent. These forces bring the
particles of solute and solvent (initially separated before dissolution occurs) together
in the solution; the solute-solvent interactions release energy which is known as solvation energy. In the specific case of water solutions, the energy released when a salt
dissolves and interacts with the water molecules is known as the hydration energy.

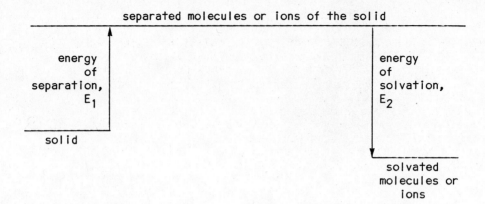

Figure 15-1. Energy considerations in dissolving solids

When a solid dissolves in a liquid, the net energy change is the sum of two opposing energy effects*: (1) the energy needed to separate the particles of solid from each other and (2) the energy released when molecules or ions of the solid are solvated by molecules of the solvent. We may sketch these effects in an energy diagram (Fig. 15-1). If the energy of separation, E_1, is less than the energy of solvation, E_2, energy will be released in the overall solution process. The opposite case—E_1 greater than E_2—is more usual for dissolution of salts, and energy (heat) is commonly absorbed when salts dissolve. Solubility represents a compromise between the tendency toward randomness (entropy) and the favorability of absorption of heat energy (enthalpy change).

In accordance with LeChatelier's principle, the change in solubility with temperature usually depends upon the overall heat change in the solution process. If heat is absorbed; i. e.,

$$\text{heat} + \text{salt} + \text{solvent} \rightleftharpoons \text{solution}$$

an increase in temperature will increase the solubility. (Addition of heat causes the position of equilibrium to shift to the right so that heat is used up.) For the few ionic substances for which heat is evolved when the solid salt dissolves, i.e.,

$$\text{solute} + \text{solvent} \rightleftharpoons \text{solution} + \text{heat},$$

the solubility usually decreases with an increase in temperature, again in accord with LeChatelier's principle.

In this experiment we shall investigate how the solubility of a salt changes with both temperature and solvent. Solubility changes with a change in temperature for different salts can be exploited to provide a method of separating one salt from another in a mixture of the two.

NOTEBOOK

Before going to the laboratory, prepare a data table in your notebook to record all of the experimental information needed, e.g., the weights of solute used, the volumes of solvent used, and the temperatures of the solutions.

A. The Variation of Solubility with Temperature

The variation of solubility with temperature may be determined experimentally by either of two methods: (1) by analyzing solutions saturated at various fixed temperatures to determine the concentration of dissolved solute or (2) by preparing solutions of various known concentrations and observing the temperature at which each solution becomes saturated. The second method is more convenient for a general chemistry class; thus, it will be employed in this experiment.

---

*A third, but much smaller endothermic energy change occurs when the solvent molecules are separated from each other.

PROCEDURE

Weigh salt.

A-1. Weigh accurately 7 to 8 g of potassium dichromate, $K_2Cr_2O_7$, or 5 to 5.5 g of oxalic acid dihydrate, $H_2C_2O_4 \cdot 2 H_2O$, on an analytical balance and carefully place it in a large test tube equipped with a rubber stopper, through which a stirrer and a thermometer are inserted. (Ask your instructor for the location of this apparatus; do not use a copper stirrer if you are using oxalic acid.) From a buret or pipet, add an accurately measured volume (approximately 10.0 mL) of water to the test tube. Put the test tube and its contents into a beaker of boiling water and stir it as the temperature increases and until all of the solid has dissolved, but not much longer.

Add H_2O, stir, and heat to dissolve salt.

After the solid has dissolved, remove the test tube from the hot water bath, and allow it to cool in the air while stirring the contents constantly. Note and record the temperature at which the <u>first</u> crystals are observed. If a considerable mass of crystals has been allowed to form before the temperature is noted, the concentration of the solution has changed to such an extent that the observed temperature is not the point of saturation of the original solution. Consequently, you must observe as nearly as possible the temperature at which crystallization first begins. If uncertainty exists regarding an observed temperature, the solution may be warmed again, and a second set of observations may be made. In any case, it is suggested that each point be confirmed at least once.

Stir while cooling and record temperature at which the first crystals appear.

After a satisfactory value has been obtained, dilute the original solution by adding another accurately measured volume (approximately 10.0 mL) of distilled water and observe, in the same manner as before, the temperature at which the new solution is saturated. Repeat this procedure until the saturation temperatures of four different concentrations of solution have been observed.

Dilute, and repeat.

A-2. Repeat the above experiment with <u>accurately weighed portions</u> of about 2 g of $K_2Cr_2O_7$ or 1.8 g of $H_2C_2O_4 \cdot 2 H_2O$ and 10.0, 20.0, and 30.0 mL of water as before. In the most dilute solutions, it may be necessary to cool the solutions in ice water to cause the salt to crystallize. While stirring the solution, note carefully the temperature at which crystals first appear.

Repeat with a smaller quantity of the same salt.

CALCULATIONS

Calculate the concentration of each solution observed in this experiment, assuming the density of water to be 1.00 g/mL and expressing the concentration in terms of grams of solute per 100 g of H_2O. Plot the solubility (in grams per 100 g of H_2O) as the ordinate and the temperature as the abscissa on a piece of graph paper, and draw a smooth curve through the points (Graph 15-I).

Many deductions in chemistry show that the properties of two-component systems are dependent upon the relative number of moles of the two substances present. Transform the solubility in grams per 100 g, as recorded in your data table, into the quantity known as the <u>mole fraction</u>, defined for a solute and solvent system as:

$$\text{mole fraction of solute} = \frac{\text{moles of solute}}{\text{moles of solute} + \text{moles of solvent}}.$$

The mole fraction for a sample of 5.030 g of $K_2Cr_2O_7$ dissolved in 10.0 g of H_2O would be:

mole fraction of potassium dichromate =

$$\frac{5.030 \text{ g} \times \frac{1 \text{ mol}}{294.2 \text{ g}}}{5.030 \text{ g} \times \frac{1 \text{ mol}}{294.2 \text{ g}} + 10.0 \text{ g} \times \frac{1 \text{ mol}}{18.0 \text{ g}}} = \frac{0.0171}{0.0171 + 0.555} = 0.0299.$$

205

Plot your experimental results on a second graph (Graph 15-II), this time using the temperature as the ordinate and the mole fraction of solute as the abscissa.

Examine the graph. You know that pure water freezes at 0 °C. Can the temperature at which the solution freezes be less than 0 °C? Does it appear that your temperature-mole fraction curve will go through the point (0,0)? How do you explain the curve? Record the answers to these questions in your notebook and report.

B. Effect of Change of Solvent on Solubility

Having examined the solubility of a substance in water, one may now raise the question of whether the solubility-temperature behavior will be the same in solvents other than water or in a liquid which is composed of water and some other substance. Since one of the criteria for distinguishing between ionic and covalent compounds is that many ionic compounds are soluble in water but not in nonpolar liquids, we may conclude that addition of a nonpolar liquid to water will change the solubilities of the two classes of compounds differently. To test this conclusion, repeat the solubility experiments in Part A using a 70:30 (by weight) water/dioxane mixture. Use an accurately weighed quantity of approximately 3.5 g of potassium dichromate or of 5.5 g of oxalic acid. Use 10.0 mL of the mixed solvent initially, and dilute with successive 10.0-mL portions of the same mixture. Record the temperature readings as before.

Taking the density of the water/dioxane mixture as 1.023 g/mL, calculate the solubility per 100 g of solvent as in part A, and plot the data on Graph 15-I. Draw a smooth curve through the points. Examine the graph and report the difference in solubility between pure water and the mixed solvent at 30 °C. Suggest a reason for the difference.

REFERENCES

1. Whitten and Gailey, General Chemistry and General Chemistry with Qualitative Analysis, Saunders College Publishing, Philadelphia, 1984, Chapter 13.
2. Whitten and Gailey, General Chemistry and General Chemistry with Qualitative Analysis, 2nd Ed., Saunders College Publishing, Philadelphia, 1984, Chapter 10.
3. Pimentel and Spratley, Understanding Chemical Thermodynamics, Holden Day, San Francisco, 1969, Section 6-2.

SOLUTIONS OF SALTS

PRELABORATORY QUESTIONS

Name_____   Lab Instructor_____

Student ID No._____   Date_____

1. What error in the observed solubility (Part A) would be introduced if:

    a. Some water were lost through excessive heating?

    b. Some of the solute were spilled before being transferred to the test tube?

    c. The solute tended to give supersaturated solutions?

2. Suppose you forget to stir one of the four salt solutions as it cools; what effect would this have on the solubility data and the resulting curve on Graph 15-1?

3. Do you expect the potassium dichromate (or the oxalic acid) to be more or less soluble in the mixed water/dioxane solvent?

Experiment 15

SOLUBILITY OF SALTS

REPORT SHEET

Name_____   Lab Instructor_____

Student ID No._____   Date_____

Part A-1

1.   Weight of sample of _____

    a.   Weight of container + sample (g) _____

    b.   Weight of empty container (g)   _____

    c.   Net weight of sample (g)   _____

		Temperature at which first crystals formed ($^\circ$C)
2. **Volume of H_2O**		
a. First volume of H_2O _____ mL		_____
b. Second volume of H_2O _____ mL		_____
c. Third volume of H_2O _____ mL		_____
d. Fourth volume of H_2O _____ mL		_____
e. Total volume of H_2O _____ mL		_____

Sample calculations

Part A-2

1. Weight of sample of _____

    a. Weight of container + sample (g) _____

    b. Weight of empty container (g) _____

    c. Net weight of sample (g)   _____

		Temperature at which first crystals formed (^{O}C)
2. Volume of H_2O		

    a. First volume of H_2O _____ mL   _____

    b. Second volume of H_2O _____ mL   _____

    c. Third volume of H_2O _____ mL   _____

    d. Fourth volume of H_2O_____ mL   _____

    e. Total volume of H_2O _____ mL   _____

Sample calculations

210

Name_____   Lab Instructor_____

Student ID No._____   Date_____

Part B-1

1. **Weight of sample of** _____

    a.   Weight of container + sample (g) _____

    b.   Weight of empty container (g)   _____

    c.   Net weight of sample (g)   _____

<table>
<tr><td></td><td></td><td></td><td>Temperature
at which first
crystals formed ($^{\circ}$C)</td></tr>
<tr><td>2.</td><td colspan="2">**Volume of 70:30 water/dioxane**</td><td></td></tr>
<tr><td></td><td>a.</td><td>First volume of
70:30 water/dioxane (mL) _____</td><td>_____</td></tr>
<tr><td></td><td>b.</td><td>Second volume of
70:30 water/dioxane (mL) _____</td><td>_____</td></tr>
<tr><td></td><td>c.</td><td>Third volume of
70:30 water/dioxane (mL) _____</td><td>_____</td></tr>
<tr><td></td><td>d.</td><td>Fourth volume of
70:30 water/dioxane (mL) _____</td><td>_____</td></tr>
<tr><td></td><td>e.</td><td>Total volume of
70:30 water/dioxane (mL) _____</td><td>_____</td></tr>
</table>

Sample calculations

Experiment 15

SOLUBILITY OF SALTS

QUESTIONS--PROBLEMS

Name_____   Lab Instructor_____

Student ID No._____   Date_____

1. According to the solubility curve obtained in this experiment, what is the solubility of the solute you studied at 55 $^{\circ}$C and 75 $^{\circ}$C?

2. Explain the phenomena observed near the origin of Graph 15-II.

3. What is the solubility difference of your sample in water and 70:30 water/dioxane at 30 $^{\circ}$C? Reason for the difference in solubility?

4. Suppose you had a saturated water solution of your solute at 30 $^{\circ}$C in an amount sufficient to contain 100 g of water. If you added dioxane (also at 30 $^{\circ}$C) until the ratio of water to dioxane was 70:30, would solid crystallize? If so, how much?

5. Suppose it was possible to remove dioxane from a solution containing solute, dioxane, and water so that only solute and water were left. If this were accomplished with a saturated solution of your solute in 70:30 water/dioxane, using an amount of solution which contained 100 g of solvent, would solid crystallize? If so, how much?

6. Answer the questions raised in the text at the end of Part A.

ATTACH GRAPHS 15-I AND 15-II TO YOUR REPORT SHEETS.

FREEZING-POINT DEPRESSION

Objective

To determine the molecular weight of a soluble unknown compound by measuring the depression of the freezing point of a solvent when a known weight of the compound is dissolved in a known weight of the solvent; to compare the freezing point depressions for solutions of equal molal concentrations of covalent nonelectrolytes and ionic compounds

Equipment Needed

Freezing-point apparatus, including a special thermometer, buret, 600-mL beaker

Reagents Needed

Ice; water; salt; cyclohexane; unknowns; 0.5 molal solutions of the electrolytes listed in Part B

INTRODUCTION

In the "mixed melting points" portion of Experiment 3, we observed that the melting point of one pure compound was lowered when it was mixed with a second compound. In a similar manner, the freezing point of a mixture (solution) of solute and solvent is below the freezing point of the pure solvent. This effect may be understood from the following considerations.

As the temperature of a liquid is lowered, the average kinetic energy of the molecules decreases and collisions among them become less vigorous until, at the freezing point, the attractive forces are able to overcome the dispersion effect of their kinetic motion, and the molecules stick together. In a solution, the solute molecules interfere with the organizing of the solvent molecules to form a solid, and the kinetic motion must be reduced by a further lowering of the temperature in order for the solvent molecules to form crystals. Thus, the temperature at which the solvent crystallizes--the freezing point of the solution--is lower than that of the pure solvent.

The extent of the freezing-point depression depends on the number of interfering solute particles (molecules or ions) in a given amount of solvent, that is, on the concentration of the solution. Raoult found that the freezing point depression is directly proportional to the molal concentration of the solution. This law is exact for ideal solutions, i.e., solutions in which the forces between molecules are not altered when molecules of more than one kind are mixed, and it is nearly exact for covalent nonelectrolytes in water solution. Table 16-1 gives the data for sucrose solutions as an example.

Table 16-1. Freezing-Point Depressions of Sucrose Solutions in Water

Molal Concentration m	Freezing-Point Depression ΔT_f (°C)	Proportionality Constant $K_f = \Delta T_f / m$
0.005	0.0093	1.86
0.010	0.0186	1.86
0.020	0.0372	1.86
0.050	0.0935	1.87
0.100	0.188	1.88
0.200	0.380	1.90

In addition, the depression, ΔT_f, for a fixed concentration is the same for most covalent solutes in the same solvent, but the value for ΔT_f changes from one solvent to another, as shown in Table 16-2. Each solvent exhibits a specific value for the change in temperature per mole of solute per kilogram of solvent.

Table 16-2. Freezing-Point Depression for the Same Solutes in Various Solvents

Solute	Solvent	Density of Solvent at Room Temperature (grams per millimeter)	ΔT_f, Lowering Produced by Adding 1 Mole of Solute to 1000 g of solvent
methyl alcohol	water	1.00	1.86 °C
dextrose (sugar)	water	1.00	1.86 °C
urea	water	1.00	1.86 °C
methyl alcohol	benzene	0.879	5.12 °C
urea	benzene	0.879	5.12 °C
methyl alcohol	cyclohexane	0.779	20.00 °C
urea	cyclohexane	0.779	20.00 °C

Because the freezing-point depression is nearly proportional to the number of solute molecules in solution, determination of the depression is one of the simplest and most accurate means of estimating the apparent molecular weight of a nondissociating covalent solute. The equation that relates the freezing point depression to the concentration of solution is

$$\Delta T_f = K_f \times m \tag{1}$$

where

ΔT_f is the experimental freezing point depression
m is the molality of the solution
K_f is the freezing-point constant of the solvent.

For a 1 molal solution that approximates ideal behavior, K_f is found to be 1.86 °C for water, 5.12 °C for benzene, 2.00 °C for nitrobenzene, and 20.00 °C for cyclohexane. In solutions of moderate concentration, Eq. (1) can be used for practical molecular weight determinations. From the measured value of the freezing-point depression and the known value of K_f, the molality of the solution can be calculated. The mass of solute in a given mass of solvent is determined by weighing the solute, by measuring the volume of solvent used and calculating the mass of solvent from its known density. We calculate the mass of solute that would be present in 1000 g of solvent in a solution of the same concentration. This corresponds to the calculated molality, which is defined as the number of moles of solute in 1000 g of solvent. Thus, the relationship between moles and mass--the molecular weight--is obtained.

For example, if 9.00 g (0.050 mol) of glucose is dissolved in 500 mL of water, we can calculate the molality and the change in the freezing point of water as follows:

$$m = \frac{\text{moles of solute}}{\text{kg of solvent}}; \text{ moles of solute} = 0.050$$

$$\text{g of solvent} = 500 \text{ mL} \times \text{density}$$
$$= 500 \text{ mL} \times 0.996 \text{ g/mL}$$
$$= 498 \text{ g, or } 0.498 \text{ kg}$$

$$m = 0.050/0.498 = 0.1004 \text{ or } 0.100 \text{ to 3 significant figures}$$

$$\Delta T_f = 1.85\ ^\circ\text{C/molal} \times 0.100 \text{ molal} = 0.186\ ^\circ\text{C}$$

A. Molecular Weight by Freezing-Point Depression

In this part of the experiment, you are to determine the molecular weight of a solute by measuring the freezing point of cyclohexane and the depression of that freezing point when the solute is dissolved in the cyclohexane. For pure cyclohexane, the precise freezing point is 6.55 $^\circ$C, and the density at room temperature is 0.779 g/mL. The mass of the solvent can be calculated from its volume.

PROCEDURE

Obtain the freezing-point apparatus and assemble it in the manner shown in Fig. 16-1. The apparatus consists essentially of a 600-mL beaker which serves as a cooling bath, covered with a metal lid. Through a hole in the center of the lid passes a large test tube, held in place by a tightly fitting cork. Held inside the test tube is a smaller test tube containing the freezing mixture, a special thermometer, and a small stirrer. The freezing tube, therefore, is surrounded by an insulating layer of air through which heat must be transferred, thereby insuring a slow and uniform rate of cooling (or heating) of the solution in the inner test tube.

Assemble freezing-point apparatus.

Experience with cyclohexane as a solvent has shown that more reproducible freezing points (melting points) are obtained if one cools the solution to form crystals, allows the solution to warm slowly, and observes the disappearance of the last crystals of cyclohexane. Thus, for the prodecure in Part A, after the solution is cooled to form crystals, only the central part of Fig. 16-1 (consisting of two large test tubes and the special thermometer) is used. That is, the central part of the apparatus is not maintained in the cooling bath as pictured in Fig. 16-1; instead, it is removed from the cooling bath and allowed to warm slowly, while stirring the solution in the inside test tube.

Using the buret, measure to 0.02 mL about 20 mL of dry cyclohexane into the clean dry inner test tube. Put the thermometer in place, and immerse the test tube containing the thermometer and stirrer in the cooling liquid--an ice/water mixture that should contain several pieces of ice at all times. Use enough cooling liquid to cover the level of the solvent in the test tube. (**Note 1**).

Obtain an accurately measured quantity of pure cyclohexane.

With the lid removed from the cooling bath, place the test tube containing the pure solvent directly into the ice bath, and hold it there until the solvent partially freezes (**Note 2**). Take out the test tube and dry the outside thoroughly. Place the tube in the air jacket, as illustrated in Fig. 16-1. Stir gently until the last crystal of solid melts. Record this temperature (to the nearest 0.01 degree) as the freezing point. Repeat the freezing point determination until a consistent value is obtained. (The first two or three determinations should be used for practice and ignored.) Do not be overly concerned if the experimental freezing point for cyclohexane is not the exact literature value. Deviations are due to small impurities and to the calibration of the thermometers. Since the same

Determine freezing point of pure cyclohexane.

errors will occur when the freezing point of the solution is taken, the
net error in the temperature _difference_ will be negligible.

Transfer the unknown compound to a small labeled vial or
weighing bottle. Weigh to the nearest 0.0001 g the vial containing the
unknown compound, lid and all. Carefully introduce about 0.3 to 0.5 g
(weighed to the nearest 0.0001 g) of the compound directly from the

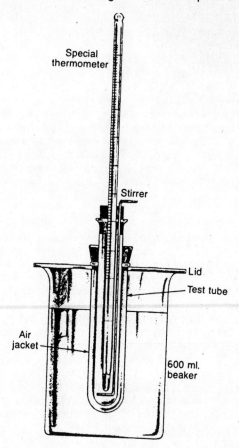

Figure 16-1. Freezing point apparatus

Weigh unknown
accurately and
dissolve it in
cyclohexane
solution.

vial into the cyclohexane in the small test tube. Try to deposit all
of the sample directly into the bottom of the test tube without
allowing any to adhere to the walls at the top. The entire sample
should dissolve in the cyclohexane. Reweigh the vial with the lid to
the nearest 0.0001 g. The difference is the weight of sample taken.

Eq. (1) relates T_f to m, i.e., the change in the freezing
point to the concentration of the solution. The freezing point is
defined as the temperature at which solid and liquid are in equilibrium; solid solvent must be present for its determination. But if
some solvent has crystallized, the concentration of the solution is
greater than that calculated from the known weight of solute and of
cyclohexane added to the test tube. Since the concentration of the
solution does not change rapidly with slight changes in the amount of
solvent present, we shall, as an approximation, measure the equilibrium
temperature when only a small quantity of solvent has solidified and
use that value as the freezing point of the solution of calculated
concentration m. It is easy to measure this temperature on a warming
cycle as follows.

Stir the contents of the test tube until all of the solid has
dissolved. As before, cool the test tube (without the outer jacket)
until freezing begins. Remove the tube from the ice-water bath, wipe it

dry, and place it into the outer jacket. Note carefully the temperature, to the nearest 0.01 degree, at which the last trace of solid melts. Repeat the melting-point determination for the solution until a consistent value is obtained. (Again, the first two or three determinations are used for practice and should be ignored.)

Determine
freezing point
of solution.

Repeat the
measurement as
necessary.

Determine a second freezing point by adding an additional 0.2-0.3 g of the unknown and determine the new melting point. For this calibration, use the total of the two weights of the unknown. Calculate the molecular weight for both samples of the unknown organic compound.

CALCULATIONS

Using the density data in Table 16-2, calculate the weight of cyclohexane used as solvent and the proportional weight of solute that would be present if 1000 g of cyclohexane had been used. From the measured freezing-point depression, calculate the molality of the solution, using the value 20.00 for K_f of cyclohexane in Eq. (1). Then calculate the weight of 1 mole of solute; this is the molecular weight that was to be determined. For the second solution, use the total of the two weights of the unknown added to the cyclohexane. Calculate the molecular weight of your unknown for both solutions.

NOTES

Note 1. Cyclohexane is flammable; thus, extinguish all fires close to your work area and dispose of the cyclohexane solution in the waste solvent can when you have finished this experiment.

Note 2. This is to cool the solvent rapidly to its freezing point.

Note 3. This is to make sure the mercury column of the thermometer is not stuck to the walls of the capillary tube. If it is stuck, a gentle tap will release it so that an accurate reading can be made.

Note 4. If the mercury column in the thermometer becomes separated, immerse the bulb slowly in a slush of dry ice and acetone (or isopropyl alcohol) until the column is reconnected.

B. Relation of Freezing-Point Depression to Chemical Composition of Solute

Many solutes, when dissolved in water, give values for the freezing-point depression that are larger than those predicted by Eq. (1) for the concentration of the solution. These are called abnormal freezing-point depressions. The magnitude of the abnormality is frequently recorded as the value of a quantity i known as the van't Hoff i factor, which may be defined as the ratio of the observed freezing-point depression $\Delta T_f'$ to the freezing-point depression calculated from Eq. (1) for the molality of the solution.

$$i = \frac{\Delta T_f'}{\Delta T_f} = \frac{\Delta T_f'}{1.86 \times m} \tag{2}$$

For common solutes, i factors from 1 (sometimes less than 1) to about 5 have been observed.

The reason for abnormality of freezing-point depressions was recognized by Arrhenius as (usually) the result of a dissociation of solutes into ions.

In this part of the experiment, students will operate as teams of three. Each student will determine the freezing-point depression for an aqueous solution having an accurately determined concentration near 0.5 molal of one of the solutes in the set assigned to his or her team. The results of each member of the team are then to be compared, and any trends in the data are to be noted, discussed, and interpreted in the team report prepared for the instructor.

Set 1

Sodium chloride
Magnesium chloride
Aluminum chloride

Set 2

Potassium nitrate
Calcium nitrate
Aluminum nitrate

Set 3

Lithium sulfate
Magnesium sulfate
Aluminum sulfate

Set 4

Cadmium chloride
Cadmium bromide
Cadmium iodide

Set 5

Hydrochloric acid
Sulfuric acid
Phosphoric acid

PROCEDURE

Determine freezing point of water and aqueous solutions.

Use the entire apparatus shown in Fig. 16-1 for this part of the experiment (i.e., support the inner test tube and air jacket in the 600-mL beaker that contains the ice water. You can save time by pre-cooling the contents of the inner test tube nearly to the freezing point before inserting it into the air jacket. Determine the freezing point of distilled water and of 10 mL of your solution. Use a mixture of ice and salt to lower the temperature of the cooling bath below 0 °C, so you can obtain the freezing point of water and of the 0.5 molal solution.

CALCULATIONS

Calculate the i value from Eq. (2).

NOTEBOOK AND REPORT

Your team should prepare a table of i values for the solutions investigated, describe any trends, and interpret them in terms of dissociation or ionization of the solutes. Some of the values, although abnormal for a (covalent) nonelectrolyte substance, may yet be less than expected for a completely dissociated ionic substance; your discussion should include comment on the latter aspect of the data as well as on the former.

REFERENCES

1. Davis, Gailey, Whitten, *Principles of Chemistry*, Saunders College Publishing, Philadelphia, 1984, pp. 430-435.
2. Whitten, K.W.; Gailey, K.D. *General Chemistry 2nd Ed.*, Saunders College Publishing, Philadelphia, 1984, pp. 356-360.

Experiment 16

PRELABORATORY QUESTIONS

Name_____   Lab Instructor_____

Student ID No._____   Date_____

1. In your own words, define the following terms clearly and concisely:

    a. solvent

    b. solute

    c. solution

    d. molarity

    e. molality

    f. freezing point

    g. melting point

2. What are some of the advantages that may have encouraged the choice of cyclohexane rather than water as a solvent for this experiment?

3. Calculate the freezing point of solutions that contain:

   a. 6.4 g of CH_3OH in 100 g of H_2O [CH_3OH does not ionize in H_2O. K_f for H_2O is 1.86 $^\circ$C/m.]

   b. 6.4 g of CH_3OH in 100 g of benzene, C_6H_6 [CH_3OH does not ionize. K_f for benzene is 5.12 $^\circ$C/m. The freezing point of benzene is 5.48 $^\circ$C.]

4. If a 4.0-g sample of a nonelectrolyte dissolved in 100 g of H_2O gives a solution that freezes at −0.93 $^\circ$C, what is the molecular weight of the compound?

Experiment 16

FREEZING-POINT DEPRESSION

REPORT SHEET FOR 16A

Name_____   Lab Instructor_____

Student ID No._____   Date_____

		Trial		
		I	II	III
1.	Volume of cyclohexane taken (mL)	_____	_____	_____
2.	Mass of cyclohexane (g)	_____	_____	_____
3.	Freezing point of pure cyclohexane (^{O}C)	_____	_____	_____
4.	Mass of the vial and unknown (g)	_____	_____	_____
5.	Mass of the vial after removing sample (g)	_____	_____	_____
6.	Mass of the sample (g)	_____	_____	_____
7.	Mass of solute in 1 kg of solvent	_____	_____	_____
8.	Freezing point of cyclohexane solution of the unknown solute (^{O}C)	_____	_____	_____
9.	Freezing-point depression (^{O}C)	_____	_____	_____
10.	Molality of the solute (m)	_____	_____	_____
11.	Molecular weight of the solute (g/mol)	_____	_____	_____
12.	Average molecular weight		_____ g/mol	

REPORT SHEET FOR 16B

1. Freezing point of distilled or de-ionized water_____°C

2. Freezing point of your 0.5-m solution_____°C

   _____°C

   _____°C

3. Identity of salt_____

4. ΔT_f = _____°C

5. What ΔT_f value would you expect if your salt were 100% dissociated?

   _____

   Write the dissociation equation and show your logic or method of calculation.

6. i value_____

7. i values for the other solutions by your team_____for_____

   _____for_____

8. Attach graphs showing temperature-time plots

Experiment 16

QUESTIONS--PROBLEMS

1. In Part A, if you spill a little of your unknown compound as you transfer it into the test tube containing cyclohexane:

   a. will the reported freezing point be too high or too low? Why?

   b. will the molecular weight that you calculate for your unknown be too high or too low? Why?

2. If a small amount of your unknown fails to dissolve in cyclohexane will the molecular weight that you calculate for your unknown be too high or too low? Why?

3. If a liquid cools to a temperature below its freezing point and then starts to freeze, the temperature increases to the freezing point, even though no heat is added from outside the system. What is the source of the heat that causes the increase in temperature?

4. In Part A, which one of the measurements contributes the largest error to the calculated molecular weight? Explain why.

5. 1,2-Dibromoethane ($BrCH_2CH_2Br$) can be used as a solvent for freezing-point experiments. It has a freezing point of 9.79 $^{\circ}$C and a molal freezing-point depression constant of 11.8 $^{\circ}$C/molal unit. Calculate the molecular weight if a solution of 2.5969 g of the unknown dissolved in 100.00 g of 1,2-dibromoethane had a freezing point of 7.92 $^{\circ}$C.

6. From the data gathered by your team, calculate the apparent percentage of ionization of the three electrolytes examined, in the (approximately) 0.5-m solutions used.

7. Cobalt(III) forms a large number of compounds containing other ions and/or molecules which are often called ligands. These molecules or ions retain their identity to some degree in the Co(III) compound. Table 16-Q-1 lists some of these compounds, giving, for each kind of ligand, the ratio of each ligand to the cobalt ion in the compound, as found by analysis. Table 16-Q-2 gives freezing-point depression data for solutions of these compounds in water. In this table, the symbol m represents the number of moles of cobalt ions, each with its accompanying ligand groups, dissolved in 1000 g of H_2O.

Calculate the van't Hoff i factors for each solution in Table 16-Q-2 and, using the data of Table 16-Q-1, determine the formula of each compound. Show by an equation how the solid compound dissociates in solution. It will be helpful to consider that the ammonia molecule, NH_3, and the nitrite ion, NO_2^-, remain intact in the Co(III) complex. Also, each ammonia and each nitrite functions as one ligand. Cobalt(III) compounds are uniformly six-coordinate, i.e., they bind to six ligands. Chloride, potassium, and sodium ions exhibit their usual ionic charges in these compounds.

Table 16-Q-1. Composition of Some Cobalt(III) Compounds

Compound	Cobalt Ions	Ammonia Molecules	Nitrite Ions	Chloride Ions	Sodium Ions	Potassium Ions
I	1	6	-	3	-	-
II	1	2	4	-	-	1
III	1	3	3	-	-	-
IV	1	4	2	1	-	-
V	1	-	6	-	3	-
VI	1	5	-	3	-	-

Table 16-Q-2. Freezing-Point Depressions for Aqueous Solutions of Cobalt(III) Compounds

Compound	m	ΔT_f (°C)
I	0.0050	0.031
II	0.0052	0.019
III	0.0021	0.0039
IV	0.0066	0.024
V	0.016	0.110
VI	0.0046	0.024

226

EQUILIBRIA IN CHEMICAL REACTIONS

--THE PRINCIPLE OF LE CHATELIER

Objective

To study several factors that affect the position of chemical equilibria and the completeness of chemical reactions

Equipment Needed

Test tubes; 25 x 200 mm test tube; 10-mL graduated cylinder; 25- or 50-mL buret; 100-mL beaker; 125-mL Erlenmeyer flask; bunsen burner; medicine droppers

Reagents Needed

Antimony trichloride, 0.5 M in 6.0 M HCl; 6 M and concentrated (12 M) HCl; 0.4 M $CoCl_2$; 0.4 M $Co(NO_3)_2$; 0.4 M $Co(NO_3)_2$ in absolute ethyl alcohol; solid cobalt(II) chloride, $CoCl_2 \cdot 6 H_2O$; solid cobalt(II) nitrate hexahydrate, $Co(NO_3)_2 \cdot 6 H_2O$; acetone; absolute ethyl alcohol; ice; 1 M $Pb(NO_3)_2$; 1 M NaCl; 1 M Na_2CO_3; 0.1 M Na_2S; 6 M HNO_3; solution of methyl orange indicator; 0.1 M HCl; 0.1 M CH_3COOH; solution of 0.1 M CH_3COOH and 0.1 M $NaCH_3CO_2$; solid $NaCH_3CO_2$

INTRODUCTION

Often a chemist finds that he does not isolate 100% of the product(s) from a chemical reaction, perhaps because his experimental technique does not allow quantitative isolation of the product or because the reaction actually does not proceed to completion to yield the theoretical quantity of product(s). In this experiment we are interested in the latter aspect--the manner in which conditions affect the position of equilibrium. In pursuing this we first ask the question, how far does a reaction proceed before reaching equilibrium? For example, does it proceed almost completely to products, proceed about 50% to completion, or proceed only slightly to products? What factors affect this?

Almost every chemical reaction may be considered to be reversible. For example, in the generalized reaction

$$A_2 + B_2 \rightleftharpoons 2 AB + heat, \tag{1}$$

it is observed that not only do A_2 and B_2 react to form 2 AB, but 2 AB also react to form A_2 and B_2. This observation is the basis for describing the reaction as reversible and for using the double arrow in the chemical equation.

Experiment shows that if A_2 and B_2 are brought together under suitable conditions for reaction, the conversion to product AB is incomplete even if the reactants are left in contact with each other for a very long time. At some point a condition is reached in which the concentration of the product and the concentrations of the reactants are not changing. This is the condition of chemical equilibrium. A system at equilibrium may appear to be undergoing no change, but it actually is undergoing product formation and decomposition at the same rate.

If both the forward and reverse reactions of Eq. (1) are simple one-step reactions, we can, according to the law of mass action, represent the rate of formation of the product, AB, by $R_f = k_f[A_2][B_2]$, in which k_f is a proportionality constant and $[A_2]$ and $[B_2]$ are the effective concentrations of the reactants in moles per liter. The rate of the reverse reaction, that of decomposition of the product, is expressed by $R_r = k_r[AB]^2$. Under equilibrium conditions, the rate of the forward reaction, R_f is equal to the rate of the reverse reaction, R_r, and the reactants and products are at their equilibrium concentrations. Therefore,

$$R_f = R_r = k_f[A_2][B_2]_{eq} = k_r[AB]^2_{eq}.$$

Since k_f and k_r are both constants at room temperature, they may be combined into a single constant, K, which is commonly known as the equilibrium constant. The value of K changes only with a change in temperature, i.e., it does not change with different concentrations of A_2, B_2, or AB so long as $R_f = R_r$.

$$K = \frac{k_f}{k_r} = \frac{[AB]^2_{eq}}{[A_2]_{eq}[B_2]_{eq}}.$$

A generalization known as Le Chatelier's principle governs systems at equilibrium. According to this principle, **when a change is made in a system at equilibrium, the position of equilibrium shifts in such a direction as to minimize the effect of the change.** The following examples should help to clarify this principle.

Suppose the system represented by Eq. (1) **had attained equilibrium,** and then you added more reagent A_2 to the system. What would happen? Le Chatelier's principle suggests that some B_2 would react with some of the excess A_2 to reduce the concentration of the added reagent. This reaction would increase the concentration of AB and reduce the concentration of B_2 and A_2 so that equilibrium would again be established, and the ratio $\frac{[AB]^2}{[A_2][B_2]}$ would be equal to the original value. In the new equilibrium mixture, $[AB]'_{eq}$ would be greater than the $[AB]_{eq}$ in the original equilibrium mixture; $[A_2]'_{eq}$ would be greater than $[A_2]_{eq}$, and $[B_2]'_{eq}$ would be less than $[B_2]_{eq}$.

By similar reasoning, we can see that addition of the compound AB to the system would shift the position of equilibrium to the left until the ratio of the concentrations of the three species again attained the equilibrium constant value, K.

If we add heat to a system that is at equilibrium, the system shifts in the direction that absorbs heat, i.e., in the direction of the endothermic reaction. In the case of the reaction represented by Eq. (1), heating the system would shift the position of equilibrium to the left since this reaction absorbs heat and tends to minimize the effect of the added heat.

PART A. EFFECT OF CONCENTRATION ON EQUILIBRIUM; CALCULATING K

In this part of the experiment, you will observe the effect of changing the concentration of reactants or products on an equilibrium and calculate a value for K.

Antimony trichloride undergoes hydrolysis (reaction with water) in aqueous solutions, forming a heavy white precipitate of antimony oxychloride:

$$SbCl_3 + H_2O \rightleftharpoons SbOCl(s) + 2\ HCl. \tag{2}$$

Eq. (2) shows that an equilibrium is established in which hydrochloric acid is a product of the hydrolysis reaction. By increasing the concentration of hydrochloric acid, one would cause some of the solid antimony oxychloride to dissolve, and a new position of equilibrium would be established in which the concentrations of the reactants and products would be different from those under the original conditions.

The solution of antimony trichloride (labeled "for Expt. 17") is prepared by dissolving 0.5 mole of solid antimony trichloride in enough 6 M HCl to make 1 liter of solution. At this acid concentration, the position of equilibrium is so far to the left that the concentration of antimony oxychloride is negligible, and no precipitate can be observed.

PROCEDURE

Dilution of an Acidic Antimony Trichloride Solution in Water

Carefully measure 5.0 mL of the antimony trichloride solution (0.5 M SbCl$_3$ in 6 M HCl) into a 25 x 200 mm test tube. Carefully add 5.0 mL of distilled water from a graduated cylinder; then shake the test tube to mix the solution thoroughly (or stir the mixture with a clean glass stirring rod). Record your observations in the notebook, and calculate the resulting hydrochloric acid concentration in the total volume of 10 mL, assuming that the amount of hydrochloric acid formed via Eq. (2) is negligible. Why did the solid that formed as water was added disappear on shaking or stirring?

Carefully mix SbCl$_3$ and H$_2$O.

Now add an additional 3 mL of distilled water to the solution. Note and explain your observations, taking into account the new hydrochloric acid concentration **(Note 1)**.

Continue to add increments of H$_2$O.

Add 2 mL more of distilled water to the solution. Record your observations. Recall the total volume of sample at this point and calculate the hydrochloric acid concentration, again assuming that the amount formed according to Eq. (2) is negligible compared to the amount in the original 6 M solution.

Add 5 mL more of distilled water to the solution. Compare in your record book the result with that when a total of 10 mL of water had been added.

In calculating the concentrations of hydrochloric acid in each of the four solutions, as a first approximation, you may neglect the amount formed from Eq. (2). However, does the hydrochloric acid concentration increase or decrease as a result of the hydrolysis reaction represented by Eq. (2)? As a check on the assumption that you can neglect the amount of hydrochloric acid that is formed via Eq. (2), after you have added 15 mL of water, make the assumption that 50% of the antimony trichloride in the test tube hydrolyzed according to Eq. (2). Consider that your original 5 mL of solution was 0.5 M in antimony trichloride, and calculate the amount of hydrochloric acid produced via Eq. (2). Is this value small compared with the amount of hydrochloric acid that is present at every dilution from the 6.0 M solution? Was it reasonable to neglect the amount of hydrochloric acid formed by the hydrolysis reaction in the first two or three dilutions?

Calculate HCl concentrations.

Addition of Hydrochloric Acid to Antimony Oxychloride (Demonstration of Equilibrium Reversibility)

Add 2 mL of 6 M HCl to the test tube containing the 5 mL of antimony chloride solution and 15 mL of water. Mix thoroughly. Record and explain your observation in your notebook. Add 3 mL of 6 M HCl to the solution, and again mix the contents thoroughly. Record your results and explain the observations in terms of Eq. (2).

Add HCl to the suspension.

Determination of the Equilibrium Constant for Eq. (2)

Two additional factors must be considered in calculating an equilibrium constant for the reaction given in Eq. (2). The first is the concentration of water in the expression for the equilibrium constant; the second is the concentration of antimony oxychloride in the solid phase.

Since this equilibrium is studied in dilute aqueous solution, water is present in tremendous excess. Moreover, its concentration is virtually unaffected when small amounts of other reagents are added to the equilibrium mixture. Therefore, the concentration of water to be substituted into an expression for the equilibrium constant of Eq. (2) is a large and (very nearly) constant number. To avoid carrying this large and constant number in the calculation of the equilibrium constant, chemists have agreed, merely as a convenience, to define a new equilibrium constant expression that includes only the concentrations of the reactants and products having concentrations that may change appreciably in the reaction under consideration. In accord with this agreement, the concentration of water is <u>not</u> included in the equilibrium constant expression for those reactions performed in aqueous solutions.

A similar situation arises in connection with solid reactants or products. The concentration of a solid in the reaction mixture is the <u>number of moles of solid per liter of the solid</u>; it is a measure of the concentration of the solid in its own solid phase and not the concentration of the solid in the reaction solution. Of course, the packing of units in a pure crystalline solid is the same throughout any one crystal and among all crystals of a given solid. Therefore, the concentration of a solid component is a constant; for this reason, concentrations of solids are not included in equilibrium constant expressions.

The equilibrium constant expression used to calculate K for Eq. (2) includes neither the water nor the antimony oxychloride concentrations because the concentrations of these compounds are not changed by the experimenter (unless he/she works with concentrated solutions). It does include the concentration of hydrochloric acid and antimony trichloride because these concentrations change relatively rapidly by adding more water or more of either reagent. Thus, the complete equilibrium constant expression for Eq. (2)

$$K = \frac{[HCl]^2[SbOCl]}{[SbCl_3][H_2O]}$$

is conventionally written as

$$K' = \frac{[HCl]^2_{eq}}{[SbCl_3]_{eq}}.$$

PROCEDURE

Determine (as accurately as possible) the concentration of hydrochloric acid required to give a permanent precipitate of antimony oxychloride by obtaining another 5-mL sample of the antimony trichloride solution and carefully (very slowly) adding distilled water from a buret just to the point at which a slightly milky color persists after thorough mixing.

Determine concentration of HCl needed for SbOCl to first remain as a solid.

From the previous experiments you should be able to estimate approximately how much water is required. When you have added almost enough water to cause precipitation of antimony oxychloride, add the water a drop at a time. Assume that an equilibrium is established between the solid antimony oxychloride and antimony trichloride in solution when the slightly milky color first remains after thoroughly mixing the solution. Record the total amount of water used and then calculate the concentrations of both antimony trichloride and hydrochloric acid in the final volume.

At the point at which the solution has a permanent slightly milky appearance, you may assume that very little antimony oxychloride or hydrochloric acid has been formed, and consequently very little antimony trichloride has reacted. This assumption permits you to calculate the antimony trichloride and hydrochloric acid concentrations from the original concentrations, taking into account the dilution. These concentrations can be used in determining the equilibrium constant. Record in your notebook all of the arithmetic steps necessary to calculate the equilibrium constant K' for Eq. (2).

PART B. EFFECT OF CONCENTRATION ON AN EQUILIBRIUM INVOLVING A GEOMETRIC STRUCTURAL CHANGE

Cobalt has oxidation states of II and III in its compounds. Unlike the iron(II) ion, the cobalt(II) ion is quite stable to oxidation, and aqueous solutions of cobalt(II) salts can be exposed indefinitely to air. The pink aqueous solutions of cobalt(II) salts show the characteristics of the complex ion $[Co(H_2O)_6]^{2+}$, in which the cobalt(II) ion is bonded with six water molecules in a symmetrical arrangement, that of an octahedron. The pink cobalt(II) salts may be crystallized from solution and give solids of formula $CoX_2 \cdot 6H_2O$, in which X is the nitrate, acetate, or chloride ion. Both solutions and solids exhibit properties of $[Co(H_2O)_6]^{2+}$ ion.

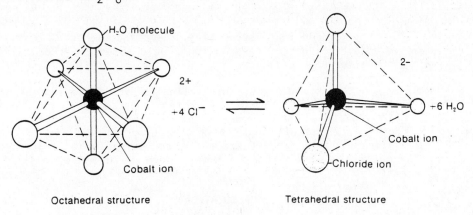

Figure 17-1

In this part of the experiment, we shall study the manner in which the concentration of a reagent affects the equilibrium and the way in which this may change the structure and color of the complex ions in solution. Divalent cobalt commonly assumes a coordination number of either 4 or 6 in its molecules from $[Co(H_2O)_6]^{2+}$ to form the $[CoCl_4]^{2-}$ anion. The concentration of water in dilute aqueous solutions is approximately 55 M and, according to the law of mass action, the water molecules effectively compete with chloride for bonding to the cobalt(II) ion. We may express this equilibrium by Eq. (3) and Fig. 17-1 (**Note 2**):

$$[Co(H_2O)_6]^{2+} + 4 Cl^- \rightleftharpoons [CoCl_4]^{2-} + 6 H_2O. \qquad (3)$$

Small concentrations of $[CoCl_4]^{2-}$ are detected easily since this tetrahedral ion is deep blue color and is approximately 100 times as intensely colored as the pink $[Co(H_2O)_6]^{2+}$ ion. In the following sections we shall investigate the effect of chloride concentration, solvent, and temperature on the equilibrium represented by Eq. (3). In addition to changing the number of ligands bonded to cobalt, this reaction involves a change in the geometry of the complex ion from octahedral, $[Co(H_2O)_6]^{2+}$, to tetrahedral, $[CoCl_4]^{2-}$.

In alcohol and acetone solutions some of the water molecules in $[Co(H_2O)_6]^{2+}$ are replaced by the alcohol or acetone molecules as a result of the very large relative concentrations of these solvent molecules, i.e., the mass law favors bonding an alcohol or acetone molecule rather than water. Also, chloride ion can displace the alcohol or acetone molecules even more readily than water. Consequently, the blue color characteristic of the tetrahedral $CoCl_4^{2-}$ ion appears at much lower concentrations of chloride ion in the organic solvents.

231

PROCEDURE

Determine the colors of Co(II) salts in different solvents.

Obtain about 0.5 g of each of the cobalt(II) salts, $CoCl_2 \cdot 6 H_2O$ and $Co(NO_3)_2 \cdot 6 H_2O$, and record their colors as solids. Add two or three small crystals to each salt to separate dry test tubes, and dissolve the crystals in 5 mL of water. Record your observations. Repeat this procedure, using absolute ethyl alcohol and then acetone. What differences are noted between the chloride and nitrate salt in each of the solvents, water, alcohol, and acetone? Do the colors of each salt in the three solvents produce trends? How are your data explained in terms of the equilibrium represented by Eq. (3)? For example, which solvent tends to give the deepest blue color with the chloride salt? Consider the huge difference in the number of moles of water present in the aqueous solution compared with the ethyl alcohol and acetone solutions. On this basis, do the relative colors make sense if the equilibrium represented by Eq. (3) is appropriate?

Add increments of HCl.

Add 5.0 mL of 0.4 M $Co(NO_3)_2$ solution to a 6-in. test tube. Now add concentrated hydrochloric acid to the solution in eight successive 2.0-mL increments, and shake the solution thoroughly (or stir) after each addition. Record the color of the solution after each addition, and explain the trend observed.

Now add _three_ successive 5.0-mL increments of distilled water to the cobalt(II) nitrate/hydrochloric acid solution. Record your observations after each dilution.

Use mixed solvent of ethyl alcohol and water.

It should now be interesting for you to repeat the procedure in a mixture of ethyl alcohol and water. To do this, add 5.0 mL of 0.4 M $Co(NO_3)_2$ dissolved in ethyl alcohol to a 5-in. test tube, and then add dropwise concentrated hydrochloric acid to the solution until you obtain a distinct blue color. Compare the concentration of chloride required to produce the blue color in the alcohol solution with that required in water.

CALCULATIONS

Calculate the molarity of concentrated hydrochloric acid. This acid solution contains 37% hydrochloric acid by weight and has a specific gravity of 1.185 grams per milliliter. Use this concentration to calculate the concentration of chloride ion in your cobalt solution after each addition, assuming solution volumes are additive. Also calculate the concentration of chloride ion in the solution after each addition of distilled water. Then calculate the approximate concentration of chloride required to give a visually perceptible blue color in water and in the ethyl alcohol/water mixture.

PART C. EFFECT OF TEMPERATURE ON THE POSITION OF EQUILIBRIUM

PROCEDURE

In the introduction we stated that the value of the equilibrium constant, K, is specific for a given temperature. This part of the experiment demonstrates the effect of temperature on the position of equilibrium (3).

Add HCl to make violet solution.

Carefully measure 10.0 mL of 0.4 M $CoCl_2$ solution into a small Erlenmeyer flask. Add 6.0 mL of concentrated hydrochloric acid, and swirl the flask to mix thoroughly. The resulting solution should be violet (between the original pink-red and bright blue). If it is not violet, adjust the solution color by carefully adding, a drop at a time, distilled water or concentrated hydrochloric acid, depending upon the color of the solution. Divide the violet solution about equally into three test tubes. Place one test tube in ice, heat one gently to 80 °C to 90 °C, and allow the third one to remain at room temperature. Record the colors of each solution. Determine whether the color changes are reversible.

What can you conclude about the effect of temperature changes on the position of equilibrium for this reaction? Rewrite Eq. (3) to include the word <u>heat</u> on the proper side of the equation.

PART D. EFFECT OF SOLUBILITY ON COMPLETENESS OF CHEMICAL REACTIONS

PROCEDURE

Mix 10 mL of 1 M $Pb(NO_3)_2$ and 10 mL of 1 M NaCl in a 50-mL beaker. Account for your observation by writing total and net ionic equations for this chemical reaction in your notebook. Filter and wash the solid lead chloride with 25 mL of distilled water. Discard the wash solution, add the solid lead chloride plus 25 mL of water to a small Erlenmeyer flask, and agitate it for three minutes. Allow the precipitate to settle, decant 10 mL of the clear supernatant liquid into a test tube, and add 5 mL of 1 M Na_2CO_3. Again explain your observations with words and a balanced equation.

Combine Pb^{2+} with Cl^-.

Repeat with CO_3^{2-}.

Shake the test tube to which sodium carbonate has been added, pour half of the suspension into a second test tube, and add 3 mL of 0.1 M Na_2S solution. Results? Add 6 or 7 drops of dilute nitric acid to the test tube containing the black solid. Results?

Treat suspension with Na_2S.

To the remainder of the suspension in the first test tube, add 6 or 7 drops of 6 M HNO_3. What happens to the solid?

Treat suspension with HNO_3.

For each of the above reactions, consider that some Pb^{2+} ion is present in solution; that is, the solids may be considered to be partially soluble. Formation of each successive precipitate results from the fact that the new solid is less soluble than the preceding one. Thus, each successive reaction proceeds further to completion and removes more of the Pb^{2+} ion from solution. As an example, the lead chloride precipitate is partially soluble and can be represented by Eq. (4).*

$$PbCl_2(s) \rightleftharpoons Pb^{2+} + 2 Cl^- \qquad (4)$$

You should then be able to write equations for each reaction and to decide which lead compounds are less soluble, i.e., which reactions go further toward completion. Arrange the following compounds in order of decreasing solubility: lead nitrate, lead carbonate, lead sulfide, and lead chloride.

PART E. EFFECT OF BUFFERS ON ACID–BASE EQUILIBRIA

In this part of the experiment, you will determine the predominant form of the indicator methyl orange present in solution under several different conditions. Also, you will determine the effect of adding small amounts of acid or base to aqueous solutions of methyl orange in the presence and in the absence of a buffer and to interpret the observations in terms of the equilibria present in the solutions. **Read the introduction to Exp. 12 to review the chemistry of indicators.**

---

*This is a grossly simplified representation of the $PbCl_2$ equilibrium. $PbCl_2$ is primarily covalent and the equilibrium is more accurately represented as

$$PbCl_{2(s)} \rightleftharpoons PbCl_{2(aq)} \rightleftharpoons Cl^- + PbCl^+ \rightleftharpoons Pb^+ + Cl^-.$$

Because equilibrium is concerned with **equilibrium concentration**, the important point is made by the simplified representation of Eq. (4).

A buffer solution of a weak acid can be prepared by dissolving the acid and a soluble salt of the acid in water. For example, acetic acid ionizes according to the following equation:

$$CH_3COOH + H_2O \rightleftharpoons H_3O^+ + CH_3COO^-. \tag{5}$$

Its K_a is 1.8×10^{-5} at 25 °C. Introduction of added acetate ion would repress the amount of ionization (predicted by Le Chatelier's Principle) compared to the situation with only acetic acid in the same concentration. If a relatively large concentration of acetate ions is present in solution, the acetate ion can readily react with any added proton source to form more CH_3COOH and minimize the effect of adding the strong protonic species. Thus, the buffer resists marked changes in hydronium ion concentration (or pH) with introduction of small amounts of strong acids or bases such as HCl or NaOH, respectively.

PROCEDURE

Determine Colors of HInd and Ind⁻.

First, determine the colors of the acid and base forms of the indicator methyl orange by placing 1 drop of indicator solution in 2 mL of 0.1 M HCl and 1 drop in 2 mL of 0.1 M NaOH. Record the colors of HInd and Ind⁻ for the indicator. Assume the colors of HInd and Ind⁻ are the colors you see when the indicator is placed in solutions that are 0.1 M H_3O^+ and 0.1 M OH⁻, respectively.

Determine the color of the indicator in 0.1 M acetic acid solution by adding 1 drop of methyl orange solution to 2 mL of 0.1 M acetic acid in a test tube. Add (one crystal at a time) 4 or 5 small crystals of solid sodium acetate. What do you observe?

Determine form of indicator present in buffer.

Determine the color of the indicator in a solution that is 0.1 M in CH_3COOH and 0.1 M in $NaCH_3COO$ by adding 2 drops of indicator to 4 mL of the solution (from the reagent shelf). Add dropwise 0.1 M HCl to the above solution. What do you observe? Repeat this experiment with 0.1 M NaOH solution using a new solution of methyl orange in the 0.1 M CH_3COOH/0.1 M $NaCH_3COO$ solution. How do your observations compare with the above HCl case? Also, how do these experiments compare or contrast with the first determinations of the colors of methyl orange in 0.1 M HCl and 0.1 M NaOH solutions?

Account for the colors of methyl orange in the CH_3COOH/$NaCH_3COO$ solution (and when a strong acid or base was added) in terms of the equilibrium expressed by Eq. (5) and the predominant form (HInd or Ind⁻) of the indicator present in the solutions.

NOTEBOOK AND REPORT

Before going to the laboratory, prepare data tables in your notebook in which to record the volumes of water and acid and concentrations of reagents in Parts A and B and the temperatures, concentration of chloride, and observations in Part C. Give all necessary data in your report that are useful in obtaining the chloride concentrations in Parts A and B, the equilibrium constant for Eq. (2), the effect of solvent on equilibrium shown in Eq. (3), and the effect of temperature on this equilibrium. Include detailed calculations for one example of each type of calculation used in your studies. Give your equations for the tests in Part D and discuss step by step the significance of each precipitate in terms of the appropriate equilibrium. For Part E, your notebook should show a careful record of your observations and the relative amounts (i.e., the number of drops) of the HCl or NaOH solutions needed to convert the indicator from one form to the other.

234

NOTES

<u>Note 1.</u>   You will need to calculate the concentration of HCl and $SbCl_3$ several times during this experiment. Recall that for <u>dilution</u>, $mL_1 \times M_1 = mL_2 \times M_2$. For example, when the initial 5 mL of antimony trichloride solution which is 6 M in HCl is diluted to 10 mL by the addition of 5 mL of water,

$$5 \text{ mL} \times 6 \text{ M} = 10 \text{ mL} \times M_2.$$

Thus, M_2 = the concentration of HCl in the diluted solution, i.e., 3 M; on further dilution to 13 mL, M_2 becomes 2.3 M; etc.

<u>Note 2.</u>   The blue tetrahedral cobalt anion is described as $[CoCl_4]^{2-}$ in Eq. (3) even though some spectrophotometric studies indicate that an appreciable concentration of $[Co(H_2O)Cl_3]^-$ exists in aqueous solutions that are less than 12 M in chloride.

REFERENCES

1.   David, Gailey, and Whitten, <u>Principles of Chemistry</u>, Saunders College Publishing, Philadelphia, 1984, Chapters 15, 16, and 17 (Chemical Equilibrium and Ionic Equilibria).
2.   Whitten and Gailey, <u>General Chemistry</u>, Saunders College Publishing, Philadelphia, 1984, Chapter 15, 16, 17, and 18 (Chemical Equilibrium and Equilibria in Aqueous Solution-I).

QUESTIONS--PROBLEMS

1. In Part A of the experiment, why does a precipitate form when water is added to the antimony trichloride solution and then disappear when the test tube is shaken? How does this behavior relate to differences in local concentrations?

2. Is the position of equilibrium, as shown in Eq. (3), further to the right in acetone or ethyl alcohol than in water? How is the observation explained?

3. For your observations in this experiment, could you say that water, alcohol, or acetone competes most effectively with the chloride ion for coordination with the cobaltous ion? Why?

4. For a quantitative determination of the heat term involved in the equilibrium of Eq. (3), what additional data would you need?

5. It has been observed that an indicator gives a different color in a solution of a strong acid than that in a solution of a strong base. Write equations for the reaction of the indicator with H_3O^+ and with OH^-.

6. Explain why the indicator color changes at the equivalence or neutralization point in the titration of a strong acid with a strong base.

7. Explain why buffered solutions should be used for comparing the acid strengths of the indicators or weak acids in general.

8. Write the expression for the ionization constant of acetic acid in terms of the equilibrium concentrations of reactants and products in the reaction of acetic acid and water. In terms of this equation, what is the value of the hydronium ion concentration in a solution 0.1 M in acetic acid and 0.1 M in the conjugate base?

9. Suppose you were titrating a weak acid, such as acetic acid, into a beaker of sodium hydroxide solution containing methyl orange indicator.

   a. Write the equation for the reaction between HInd and OH^-. (This reaction occurs while OH^- is in excess.) What species gives the color?

   b. Now, write the equation for the reaction of acetic acid with Ind^-. (This presumably should occur when acetic acid is in excess.) From what you know about the relative strength of the acid form of methyl orange compared with acetic acid, where is the position of equilibrium in this reaction? What color will methyl orange be in excess acetic acid?

   c. Would methyl orange be a good indicator in the titration of acetic acid with sodium hydroxide? Explain your answer.

Experiment 17

EQUILIBRIA IN CHEMICAL REACTIONS

PRELABORATORY QUESTIONS

Name_____   Lab Instructor_____

Student ID No_____   Date_____

1. Starting with the reaction $SbCl_3(aq) + H_2O \rightleftharpoons SbOCl(s) + 2\ HCl(aq)$ in equilibrium, what will happen to the equilibrium concentrations of $SbCl_3$ and HCl and the equilibrium constant K if

    a) water is added to the reaction mixture?

    b) SbOCl is removed from the reaction mixture?

2. What is the Cl^- concentration if 5 mL of 6 M HCl is added to 10 mL of water?

3. Is the K' value you will calculate for the reaction in question 1 expected to

    a) depend upon the concentration of the reactants and products?

    b) depend upon the temperature?

    Why or why not?

4. If a solution containing $CoCl_2$ and HCl is blue, what does this tell us about the position of equilibrium in reaction (3) of this experiment?

5. If heating the mixture of $CoCl_2$ and HCl in question 4 causes the solution to become violet and then pink, is reaction (3) exo- or endo-thermic? Explain your answer.

6. Offer an explanation for the observation that adding a Na_2S solution to a test tube containing water and a precipitate of $PbCl_2$ produces a black precipitate on top of the white $PbCl_2$?

7. Explain in terms of chemical equilibrium why acid-base indicators change color as the pH of the solution changes?

8. What are buffered solutions? Explain their chemical behavior.

Experiment 17

EQUILIBRIA IN CHEMICAL REACTIONS

REPORT SHEET, PART A

Name_____   Lab Instructor_____

Student ID No_____   Date_____

1. **Dilution of acidic antimony trichloride solution with water**

    a) What do you see when 5 mL of water is added?

        Resulting hydrochloric acid concentration:_____
        Why did the solid disappear upon shaking?

    b) After adding 3 mL of water, what do you see?

        Hydrochloric acid concentration:_____
    c) After adding 2 mL of water, what do you see?

        Hydrochloric acid concentration:_____
    d) After adding 5 mL of water:
        Observations and comparison

e) Assuming 50% hydrolysis of $SbCl_3$, how much HCl is produced?_____

f) Is the value small by comparison with the amount originally present?

g) Was it reasonable to neglect the amount of HCl formed via Eq. (2)?

2. **Determination of the value of K' for the $SbCl_3$ hydrolysis**

   a) Amount of water added:_____

   b) Concentration of antimony trichloride in the final volume:_____

   c) Concentration of hydrochloric acid in the final volume:_____

   d) Calculation of K'

Experiment 17

EQUILIBRIA IN CHEMICAL REACTIONS

REPORT SHEET, PART B

Name_____   Lab Instructor_____

Student ID No_____   Date_____

Colors

	$CoCl_2 \cdot 6 H_2O$	$Co(NO_3)_2 \cdot 6 H_2O$
solid	_____	_____
in acetone	_____	_____
in ethyl alcohol	_____	_____
in water	_____	_____

What differences, similarities, and trends do you notice from the above table?

How do you explain these data in terms of Eq. (3)?

Upon adding 2-mL increments of hydrochloric acid to the aqueous solution of $Co(NO_3)_2 \cdot 6 H_2O$:

a)   Complete the table, giving the color observed after each added increment:

0 mL_____   6 mL_____   12 mL_____

2 mL_____   8 mL_____   14 mL_____

4 mL_____   10 mL_____   16 mL_____

241

b) Explain the trend.

c) Concentration of chloride ion at each step in this solution. (Make a table.)

Upon adding 5-mL increments of water to the above solution, what do you see after each dilution? (Make a table.)

Comparison of the chloride ion concentration required to produce the blue color in ethyl alcohol with the concentration required in aqueous solution.

EQUILIBRIA IN CHEMICAL REACTIONS

REPORT SHEET, PARTS C AND D

Name_____   Lab Instructor_____

Student ID No_____   Date_____

PART C

What are the colors at the three temperatures?

Are the color changes reversible?

What is the effect of temperature on the position of equilibrium?

Write Eq. (3) including <u>heat</u> on the appropriate side of the arrows. How do you justify this choice?

PART D

Explain what happens when you mix solutions of $Pb(NO_3)_2$ and NaCl.

What do you see after adding Na_2CO_3?

What do you see after adding Na_2S?

What do you see after adding nitric acid?

What do you see after adding nitric acid to the second test tube?

What happened to the precipitate?

What are the pertinent equations for each precipitate?

List the compounds in order of decreasing solubility.

REPORT SHEET, PART E

Name_____   Lab Instructor_____

Student ID No_____   Date_____

Data

Interpretations of Your Observations in Terms of Equilibrium (5).

ACID-BASE EQUILIBRIA DURING TITRATIONS, DETERMINATION OF K_a (Use of a pH Meter)

Objective

To use a pH meter to follow the pH during the titration of a weak acid with a strong base. To determine the K_a of the acid being titrated

Equipment Needed

Buret; two 50-mL and one 100-mL beakers; one 10-mL pipet; magnetic stirrer and stirring bar; pH meter reliable to 0.1 pH units; plastic squeeze wash bottle; Kimwipe or tissue paper

Reagents Needed

Standard buffers, buffered at pH 4.00 and 7.00; standardized 0.10 M NaOH; solutions of some or all of the following acids: glycolic, acetic, formic, lactic, propionic, mandelic, potassium hydrogen phthalate

INTRODUCTION

In this experiment you will use a pH meter to follow the pH changes during an acid-base titration. From the data obtained you will determine the K_a of the weak acid being titrated.

In water solutions, weak acids react with water to establish the equilibrium:

$$HA + H_2O \rightleftharpoons H_3O^+ + A^-.$$

This equilibrium is represented by the **acid dissociation constant**, K_a, in which

$$K_a = \frac{[H_3O^+]_{eq} \times [A^-]_{eq}}{[HA]_{eq}}$$

$[\ ]_{eq}$ is the equilibrium concentration in mol/L.

K_a is a constant for a given acid at a given temperature. Its value can be determined by several experimental methods. Two of these that will be used in the experiment are:

1. measurement of the pH of a solution containing a known concentration of a weak acid and

2. measurement of the pH at the half-neutralization point in the titration of the weak acid with a strong base.

By following the pH during the titration of a weak acid with a strong base, you can obtain data that will enable you to calculate the K_a of the acid by both methods.

You also can see why only some indicators are reliable in the titration of a given weak acid with a base.

BACKGROUND

Titration Curves. In the titration of a weak acid, HA (having an ionization constant, K_a) with a strong base, a plot of pH against milliliters of base added will look like that in Fig. 18-1.

That the graph should have this appearance is readily shown by the following reasoning. After each addition of base, the equilibrium between the weak acid and its ion is re-established, according to the relation:

$$K_a = \frac{[H_3O^+]_{eq}[A^-]_{eq}}{[HA]_{eq}}.$$

Rearranging this K_a expression gives

$$[H_3O^+]_{eq} = K_a \frac{[HA]_{eq}}{[A^-]_{eq}}.$$

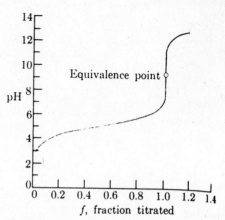

Figure 18-1

Titration curve for the titration of a weak monoprotic acid with a strong base

Taking the logarithm of both sides of the expression and mutiplying by −1, we get

$$-\log [H_3O^+]_{eq} = -\log K_a + \log \frac{[A^-]_{eq}}{[HA]_{eq}}$$

or, in terms of pH and pK_a (in which $pK_a = -\log K_a$),

$$pH = pK_a + \log \frac{[A^-]_{eq}}{[HA]_{eq}}. \tag{1}$$

This equation gives the pH at any $[A^-]/[HA]$ ratio. However, this ratio changes as base is added to the acid. The reason is that the reaction

$$HA + OH^- \rightleftharpoons H_2O + A^-$$

is pushed farther toward the right with each addition of base.

At the beginning of the titration, only the acid HA and the small concentrations of H_3O^+ and A^- from its ionization are present. As base is added, the acid is neutralized, thus decreasing the concentration of HA. At the same time, salt formation increases $[A^-]$. Throughout the titration, [HA] drops, and $[A^-]$ increases until all HA is neutralized. Eq. (1) tells us that as this happens and the ratio $[A^-]:[HA]$ increases from a low to a high value, the pH of the solution should change as shown in Fig. 18-1.

It is easy to calculate the concentrations of HA and A^- at various stages during a titration. If these concentrations and the pK_a of the acid are substituted into Eq. (1), the pH at each stage also can be calculated. The results of such calculations for one titration are given in the table below.

pH CHANGES DURING THE TITRATION OF 50 mL OF
0.1 M HA($K_a = 1 \times 10^{-5}$) WITH 0.1 M NaOH

NaOH Added (mL)	Total Volume (mL)	pH	NaOH Added (mL)	Total Volume (mL)	pH
0.00	50.0	3.0	49.95	95.95	8.00
5.00	55.0	4.05	50.00*	100.0*	8.85*
10.00	60.0	4.40	50.05	100.05	9.70
20.00	70.0	4.82	50.10	100.1	10.00
30.00	80.0	5.18	50.50	100.5	10.70
40.00	90.0	5.60	51.00	101.0	11.00
45.00	95.0	5.95	55.00	105.00	11.68
49.00	99.0	6.69	60.00	110.0	11.96
49.50	99.5	7.00	70.00	120.0	12.23
49.90	99.9	7.70			

*Equivalence point

Note that the first addition of base produces a significant rise in pH. This is followed by a region in which the pH changes only slightly. In this region, the solution is buffered by the presence of both weak acid and its salt. As addition of base continues, the acid concentration drops so much that the solution is no longer buffered. Now the pH rises rapidly through the neutralization or **equivalence point** and slightly beyond. Beyond this region, the acid has been neutralized and the pH of the solution changes only slightly as more base is added. The rise of pH beyond the equivalence point is due to the addition of base to a relatively large volume of solution.

The rapid change in pH near the equivalence point makes a quantitative titration of acid by base a feasible experiment. Note that 2 drops of base solution near the equivalence point (from 49.95 mL of base to 50.05 mL) causes a change in pH of 1.70 units in this solution. Such a change in pH is sufficient to change the color of an indicator from its acid to its basic color, so that we can easily measure to 0.05 mL in a 50 mL addition, a precision of 1 part in 1000.

The rapid change near the equivalence point is the reason titrant must be added in smaller and smaller amounts as the equivalence point is approached.

Although the data in the table were obtained by calculation using Eq. (1), similar data can be obtained by measuring the pH of the solution during any similar titration. When plotted, it gives a curve similar to that in Fig. 18-1.

In this experiment, you will collect such data as you titrate a weak acid with a strong base. You will use the data to determine K_a for the acid and to select a suitable indicator for titrations involving this acid.

Calculation of K_a. Because the equilibrium

$$HA + H_2O \rightleftharpoons H_3O^+ + A^-$$

is re-established after each addition of base during a titration, a value of K_a could be obtained from the data corresponding to any point before the equivalence point on the titration curve. Using the data from two particular points--the first point on the curve and that at the half-neutralization point--makes the calculations easier.

The first point on the curve is the pH of the acid solution before any base is added. Knowing the concentration of the acid in the solution and the pH, you should be able to calculate K_a. If necessary, review the text for the course to see how this calculation is made.

When the acid is exactly half neutralized, the pH of the solution is equal to the pK_a of the acid. Eq. (1)

$$pH = pK_a + \log \frac{[A^-]}{[HA]} \qquad (1)$$

shows why this is so. When half of the acid is neutralized (and present as A^-) and the other half is not neutralized (and present largely as HA), the concentrations $[A^-]$ and $[HA]$ are equal. At this point the $\log \frac{[A^-]}{[HA]}$ term in Eq. (1) becomes zero. (Remember that $\log 1 = 0$.) Eq. (1) then becomes

$$pH_{1/2} = pK_a.$$

There are several ways to identify the half-neutralization point. The easiest way is to select the point on the curve that corresponds to one half the number of milliliters of base needed to reach the equivalence point. The K_a of the acid can be obtained from the pH corresponding to this point by taking the antilog of $-pH$ (the negative of the pH). Here is an example:

Suppose the pH at the half-equivalence point is 5.2.

Then
$$pH_{1/2} = pK_a = -\log K_a = 5.2.$$

From this,
$$K_a = 10^{-5.2} = 10^{-6} \times 10^{0.8} = 10^{-6} \times 6.3,$$

or,
$$K_a = 6.3 \times 10^{-6}.$$

NOTEBOOK AND REPORT

Your notebook should contain the data you obtained, organized according to the outline on page 257. Your report should include a summary of the data, sample calculations, a plot of pH vs. mL base added, calculated values of K_a for your acid, the name and rationale for an indicator that could be used in the titration you performed.

PROCEDURE

Plan of Experiment. Your instructor will give you a solution containing a weak acid. You will obtain a titration curve for this acid by titrating it with a standard NaOH solution and observing the pH after each addition of titrant. From the titration curve you will obtain the equivalence point in the titration, the original concentration of acid in the solution, the K_a of the acid, and the color change range for an indicator that could be used in titrations of this acid.

Following the pH during a Titration

Prepare your acid solution for titration.

1. Obtain the unknown acid solution from your instructor; pour about 10 mL of this solution into a 50-mL beaker. Use this solution to rinse a 10 mL pipet; discard the rinse solution.

2. Now add about 30 mL more of your unknown solution to the 50-mL beaker. Pipet exactly 10 mL of this from the 50-mL beaker into a **clean, dry** 100-mL beaker. Rinse the pipet several times with distilled water. Pipet exactly 10 mL of distilled water into the 100-mL beaker containing the acid solution. Carefully place a clean, dry magnetic stirring bar in the beaker with the acid solution.

3. Proceed to the pH meter. (Read Appendix IV for details and precautions for using the pH meter.) Fill a 25-mL or 50-mL buret with

the standard NaOH solution provided. Record the initial buret reading.

Fill the buret and prepare the pH meter.

Remove the protective cap from the electrode, and place it where you will not lose it. Rinse the electrode with distilled water from your wash bottle, and **blot (do not rub)** it with a Kimwipe or tissue.

Center the beaker containing your acid over the magnetic stirrer. Lower the pH electrode into the solution, making sure that its sensing bulb is fully immersed yet remains clear of the stirring bar. Adjust the magnetic stirrer so that the bar rotates at a steady, moderate rate that does not splash the solution from the beaker.

4.   Switch the mode control of the pH meter from "standby" to "pH". After the meter has stabilized (1 min), record the pH of your acid solution opposite "0 mL of titrant" in the data table.

5.   Titrate the sample. This is done by adding an increment of NaOH, waiting for equilibrium (15 to 30 seconds), then reading and recording the pH of the solution. The size of the increment to be added will change during the course of the titration. Initially, rather large (3- to 4-mL) increments of base can be added. Near the equivalence point, rather small increments (3 to 5 drops) will be used. For each increment, the amount of base added should be that amount which will cause a change in pH of approximately 0.2 pH units. The recommended procedure is to add base slowly, while observing the pH meter. When the pH has changed by about 0.15 pH units, stop adding base, and allow equilibrium to be established. Read and record the volume of base added and the pH of the solution. Since the concentration of base is within 20% of the original concentration of your unknown acid, you can expect to reach the equivalence point between the addition of 14 to 22 mL of base. You will observe sharp increases in pH as you approach this point. After the equivalence point, continue adding base, but in 3- to 4-mL increments, until a pH reading of 12 is obtained.

Titrate the sample, recording the pH after each addition of titrant.

6.   Return the mode control switch to "standby," and remove the pH electrode from solution. Rinse the electrode with distilled water from your wash bottle, blot it dry with a Kimwipe or tissue, and recap it with a protective cap.

Return the pH meter to its original condition.

TREATMENT OF DATA

Record in the data table the volume of unknown acid used, the molarity of standard base used, and the buret reading and the pH after each addition of base.

1.   Complete the data table by calculating for each increment from the buret readings the **total volume** of base added to that point in the titration. For example, if 3 mL of base were added, then 3 more and then 3 more, the numbers in the second column would be 3 mL, 6 mL, and 9 mL.

2.   Prepare a graph with pH on the vertical axis (ordinate) and mL of base added to the horizontal axis (abscissa).

3.   Identify the equivalence point in the titration. This point can be approximated as the mid-point of the sharply increasing, nearly vertical, portion of the titration curve.

More precisely, the equivalence point is the point at which the moles of base added equal the moles of acid originally present. On your titration curve, it is the point at which the slope changes from increasing to decreasing values. This point

Here is a magnification of the curve near the equivalence point.

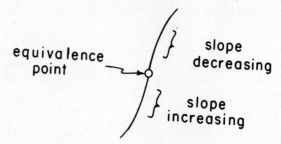

equivalence point → slope decreasing

slope increasing

4. Knowing the equivalence point, determine from your data the number of milliliters of base added to reach this point. This is the equivalence volume.

Equivalence volume _____

5. Using the equivalence volume and molarity of base used, calculate the concentration of acid in your unknown. Show your calculations.

[HA] original _____

6. Determine K_a by the two methods described in the background section. Show your calculations.

K_a from pH of original solution

K_a _____

K_a from pH of half-neutralization point

K_a _____

7. From your curve, select the pH color change range of indicators suitable for use in titrations of your unknown acid. From the table of indicators provided, select two or more indicators that could be used in titrating your unknown acid.

pH color change range
of suitable indicators _____

suitable indicators _____

_____

REFERENCES

1. Whitten and Gailey, _General Chemistry_, Saunders College Publishing, Philadelphia, 1984, pp. 554-565, 587-590, 640-642.
2. Davis, Gailey, and Whitten, _Principles of Chemistry_, Saunders College Publishing, Philadelphia, 1984, pp. 594-598, 643-645.

ACID-BASE INDICATORS

Name	Range	Color of Acidic Form	Color of Basic Form
Methyl Violet	0.0 - 1.6	yellow	blue
Crystal Violet	0.0 - 1.6	yellow	blue
Malachite Green	0.2 - 1.8	yellow	blue-green
Cresol Red[a]	0.4 - 1.8	red	yellow
Thymol Blue[a]	1.2 - 2.8	red	yellow
Methyl Yellow	2.8 - 4.0	red	yellow
Bromphenol Blue	3.0 - 4.6	yellow	purple
Methyl Orange	3.1 - 4.4	red	yellow
Bromcresol Green	3.8 - 5.4	yellow	blue
Methyl Red	4.4 - 6.2	red	yellow
Chlorophenol Red	4.8 - 6.4	yellow	red
Bromcresol Purple	5.2 - 6.8	yellow	purple
Alizarin	5.5 - 6.8	colorless	yellow
Bromthymol Blue	6.0 - 7.6	yellow	blue
Phenol Red	6.6 - 8.0	yellow	red
Neutral Red	6.8 - 8.0	red	yellow-brown
Cresol Red[b]	7.2 - 8.8	yellow	red
Cresol Purple	7.4 - 9.0	yellow	purple
Thymol Blue[b]	8.0 - 9.6	yellow	blue
Phenolphthalein	8.0 - 9.8	colorless	pink
o-Cresolphthalein	8.2 - 9.8	colorless	red
Thymolphthalein	9.3 - 10.5	colorless	blue
Alizarin Yellow R	10.2 - 12.0	yellow	violet

[a]The acid range of this diprotic indicator.
[b]The basic range of this diprotic indicator.

Experiment 18

ACID–BASE EQUILIBRIA DURING TITRATIONS; DETERMINATION OF K_a

PRELABORATORY QUESTIONS

Name _____   Lab Instructor _____

Student ID _____   Date _____

1. Sketch a titration curve for an acid-base titration, label all important points, and describe how such a curve is obtained in the laboratory.

2. How would the curve in Question 1 change in each of the following situations:

    a. If twice as much acid were present in the acid solution?

    b. If the concentration of base were doubled?

    c. If the acid were exchanged for a weaker acid?

3. Describe the two kinds of data that must be obtained from the curve in Question 1 in order to calculate the K_a value of the acid being titrated.

4. Describe how you would use the curve in Question 1 and the table of indicators to select suitable inidicators for titrations involving weak acids.

5. Select one indicator from the table that would be unsuitable in the titration represented by the curve in Question 1, and show why this indicator is unsuitable.

Experiment 18

ACID–BASE EQUILIBRIA DURING TITRATIONS; DETERMINATION OF K_a

REPORT SHEET

Name _____   Lab Instructor _____

Student ID _____   Date _____

DATA TABLE   Unknown # _____

Volume of unknown acid used _____

Molarity of NaOH solution _____

Buret Reading	Volume of Base Added	pH		Buret Reading	Volume of Base Added	pH
	00.00 mL					
_____	_____	_____		_____	_____	_____
_____	_____	_____		_____	_____	_____
_____	_____	_____		_____	_____	_____
_____	_____	_____		_____	_____	_____
_____	_____	_____		_____	_____	_____
_____	_____	_____		_____	_____	_____

Equivalence volume _____

[HA] in original solution _____

K_a from original solution _____

K_a from half-neutralization point _____

pH range of suitable indicators _____

Suitable indicators _____ _____ _____

Please attach sheets to answer the assigned QUESTIONS AND PROBLEMS from the next page.

1. Which method for determining K_a would you expect to be more reliable. Why?

2. Is it reasonable to expect K_a for your acid to remain constant during the neutralization process? Why or why not?

3. Calculate the pH of a 1.0×10^{-3} M solution of your unknown acid.

4. Assume that a student used a pipet that contained some water and failed to rinse the pipet with the acid solution before making the transfer to the 100-mL beaker (procedure step 4). How would this affect the following:

    a. the determination of acid concentration?

    b. the determination of K_a by Method 1?

    c. the determination of K_a by Method 2?

5. Why is it necessary to use smaller increments of base as you approach the equivalence point of the titration?

6. A student performed two titrations on an unknown acid solution. He obtained pK_a values of 5.4 and 5.6. Calculate the average K_a value. Show your work.

ELECTROLYTIC CELLS

Objective

To study the relationships between the number of electrons, as represented by a flow of electricity, and the oxidation and reduction half-reactions that occur at the anode and the cathode, respectively, in electrolytic cells

Equipment Needed

Electrolytic apparatus (Fig. 19-1) or the simple components shown in Fig. 19-2; emery cloth or fine sand paper; copper, zinc, or lead electrodes; 100-mL beaker; clock or watch with a second hand; source of direct current; wash bottle of water; porous cup; wash bottle of acetone

Reagents Needed

1 M solutions of zinc sulfate, copper(II) sulfate, and lead nitrate; acetone

INTRODUCTION

Electrochemistry is the area of chemistry that deals with the phenomena associated with the interaction of electricity with matter. Two broad areas of electrochemistry are: (1) that related to electrolytic cells (cells in which electrical energy is used to promote an oxidation-reduction reaction and (2) that related to galvanic or voltaic cells (cells in which an oxidation-reduction reaction takes place in such a way that electrical energy is generated).

In this and the following experiment, some fundamental laws of the two branches of electrochemistry will be developed. In this experiment an attempt is made to establish a connection between the quantity of electricity passed through the electrolytic cell and the amount of chemical change occurring therein. In the next experiment some factors that determine the voltage of a cell will be investigated, and these factors will be related to the driving force of chemical reactions in general.

Electrolytic Cells. When an electric current is passed through a solution of a salt of a metal such as copper, lead, zinc, or cadmium, the weight of the metal deposited by a given current passing for a measured period of time can be determined. From such observations, it is possible to discover the laws relating the quantity of electricity passing and the amount of metal deposited. It has been found that these laws apply to all kinds of electrolytic cells and not only to those in which metals are deposited.

The weight of metal plated by (deposited in) an electrolytic cell may be determined by measuring the increase in weight of a cathode made of that metal. The quantity of electricity that passes through the cell can be measured by multiplying the current (in amperes = coulombs per second) by the time (in seconds) during which the current flows through the cell. The quantity of electricity is expressed in coulombs.

Another way of considering the quantity of electricity passing is to ask the question: How many electrons have passed through the cell? This can be calculated from the number of coulombs passing by recalling that the charge on the electron is 1.602×10^{-19} coulombs. Thus, the number of electrons passing through the cell is the number of coulombs times this conversion factor.

$$\text{No. of electrons passing} \ = \ \text{no of coulombs passing} \ \times \ \frac{1 \text{ electron}}{1.602 \ \times \ 10^{-19} \text{ coulombs}}$$

For convenience, the number of electrons passing through the cell may be expressed as the number of moles of electrons passing. This number of moles is obtained by using Avogadro's number:

$$\text{Moles of electrons passing} \ = \ \text{no. of electrons passing} \ \times \ \frac{1 \text{ mole}}{6.022 \ \times \ 10^{23} \text{ electrons}} .$$

Electrode Reactions. Parts of chemical reactions, called half-reactions, occur at both electrodes during electrolysis. At the cathode (the electrode at which reduction occurs), electrons enter the solution and react with substances that can accept electrons such as metal ions. In the electrolysis of copper(II) sulfate solutions, for example, the reduction half-reaction at the cathode is

$$Cu^{2+} \ + \ 2e^- \ \longrightarrow \ Cu. \tag{1}$$

At the anode (the electrode at which oxidation occurs), electrons leave the solution. Several reactions are possible and several may occur simultaneously. Three possible anode reactions are:

(a) Oxidation of a negative ion, as illustrated by iodide ion

$$2I^- \ \longrightarrow \ I_2 \ + \ 2e^- \tag{2}$$

(b) Decomposition of water

$$2 \ H_2O \ \longrightarrow \ O_2 \ + \ 4H^+ \ + \ 4e^- \tag{3}$$

(c) Dissolution of the metal of the anode, as illustrated by the process that occurs at a copper anode

$$Cu \ \longrightarrow \ Cu^{2+} \ + \ 2e^- \tag{4}$$

The particular half-reaction that occur at an anode depends upon the chemical species present, their concentrations in the solution, and the voltage of the cell. However, dissolution of metal anodes is one of the more common anode reactions.

Electron Transfer. Electrons, of course, are not directly observable reactants and products in chemical reactions, and the _overall_ reaction in an electrochemical cell is the sum of the _half-reactions_ taking place at the anode and cathode, representing a _transfer_ of electrons. Thus, the sum of Eqs. (1) and (2) represents the reaction that occurs when a copper(II) iodide solution is electrolyzed,

$$Cu^{2+} \ + \ 2 \ I^- \ \longrightarrow \ Cu \ + \ I_2.$$

Electrons are transferred from the iodide ions to the copper ions through the external circuit.

It has been stated that a relation between the quantity of electricity passed and the quantity of material plated from solution can be obtained by measuring the increase in mass of the cathode as a result of an electrolysis. Since a chemical half-reaction occurs at both electrodes, it is important to ascertain whether a similar relation also applies to the anode half-reaction.

Quantitative Electrolysis. In this experiment, we will measure the quantity of material that reacts at each electrode by conducting the electrolysis in such a way that the increase in weight of the cathode and the decrease in weight of the anode can serve as measures of the amount of reaction at each electrode.

From the weight gain or loss of the electrodes, the number of moles of material reacting can be calculated. These values may then be compared with the number of moles of electrons passing through the cell. The most accurate measurements of this kind are made at very low electric currents over long periods of time. In order to avoid making the experiment too time-consuming, the current suggested will be higher than required for the most accurate results. However, the conditions are suitable for obtaining results within 10% of accepted values.

This experiment may be performed with a variety of cathodes and anodes. The solution should contain a salt of the metal to be plated at the cathode. Examples of typical cells are:

Cell	Anode Metal	Anode Solution	Cathode Solution	Cathode Metal
1	copper	1 M $CuSO_4$	1 M $CuSO_4$	copper
2	zinc	1 M $ZnSO_4$	1 M $ZnSO_4$	zinc
3	lead	1 M $Pb(NO_3)_2$	1 M $Pb(NO_3)_2$	lead
4	copper	1 M $CuSO_4$	1 M $Pb(NO_3)_2$	lead

PROCEDURE

Obtain from your instructor an electrolytic apparatus* as shown in Fig. 19-1, or assemble the apparatus from components (e.g., an ammeter and a power supply) as shown in Fig. 19-2. In either case, assemble an electrical circuit as shown in Fig. 19-4. In a 100-mL beaker set up the electrolytic cell assigned by your instructor from the table above.

Obtain electrolytic apparatus and select electrodes.

Use a piece of emery cloth (or fine sand paper) to polish the two metallic electrodes. After polishing, touch the electrode only on the edge. About 2 cm from the top (Fig 19-3), bend the electrodes, and weigh each one on an analytical balance. Record both weights to the nearest milligram in your laboratory notebook. Assemble the electrolytic cell as shown in Fig 19-3, with the bend hooked over the top of the beaker or cup for support. Be sure to place about 70 mL of one assigned solution in the beaker and about 20 mL of the other assigned solution in the unglazed ceramic cup. The ceramic cup is porous and allows ions to pass through it. The cup barrier is needed to keep the electrodes from touching and to reduce the diffusion of the solution from one electrode to the other. The long arm of one electrode should extend into the solution and the long arm of the second electrode should extend into the porous cup. Assemble the rest of the circuit as shown in Fig. 19-5. The electrolysis cell, power supply, adjustable resistor, fuse, switch, and ammeter are connected in series. **Be sure the cathode is connected to the negative terminal on the power supply.** The negative terminal is the

Polish and weigh electrodes.

Assemble cell. Connect cell to power supply.

*This particular electrolytic apparatus can be readily constructed by the stockroom personnel from available components; detailed drawings and instructions will be provided gladly by DWM at Ohio State.

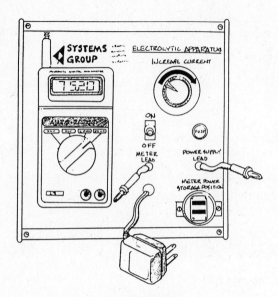

Figure 19-1.

Pre-assembled electrolysis apparatus

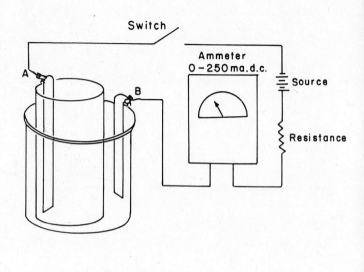

Figure 19-2.

Electrolysis apparatus to be assembled from simple components

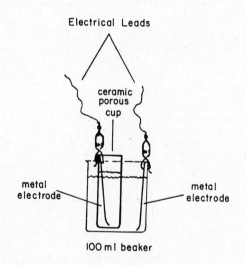

Figure 19-3.

Cell for electrolysis (Exp. 19) or for voltage measurements (Exp. 20)

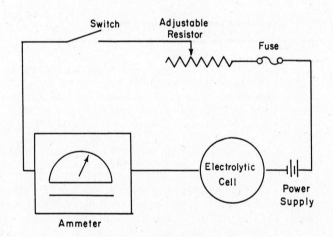

Figure 19-4.

Circuit diagram for electrolysis

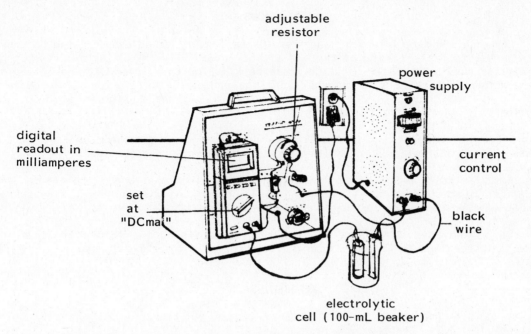

adjustable resistor

power supply

digital readout in milliamperes

current control

set at "DCma"

black wire

electrolytic cell (100-mL beaker)

Figure 19-5. Electrolysis experiment

source of electrons which flow from the power supply into the cathode of the electrolytic cell.

The **negative** terminal on the power supply is **black,** and the **positive** terminal is **red,** i.e., usually, red is + and black is −.

Rotate the adjustable resistor to the zero current position (full left or counter-clockwise). Adjust the current control (if any) on the power supply to zero also. Ask your instructor to inspect your apparatus before proceeding. After instructor's inspection, start current.

Carefully turn on the ammeter and power supply. Then rotate the current control (if any) on the power supply about half way. Now quickly rotate the adjustable resistor until the ammeter reads between 65 and 85 milliamperes (ma). Quickly note the starting time on the clock. The electrolysis should be conducted for about 30 minutes. During this time take the current reading every two minutes. If at any time the current is found to be outside the 65-85 ma range, adjust the resistor until a proper current is re-established. Maintain current at steady rate.

After about 30 minutes, turn off the power supply, and record this exact time in your laboratory notebook. Carefully dismantle the electrolysis cell, and prepare each electrode for weighing as follows. Carefully remove the electrodes from the cell, and wash them in distilled water from a wash bottle. Aim the stream of water **above** the deposit, and allow the water to run down gently. If the stream is aimed directly onto the deposit, some of it may be dislodged. Then wash both electrodes with acetone in the same way (use the special bottle marked for this experiment). Acetone evaporates more rapidly than water and helps dry the electrodes. Wait about 10 minutes for the acetone to dry, and then weigh each electrode. Wash, dry, and weigh electrodes.

CALCULATIONS

For each 2-minute interval, add the current flowing as adjusted at the beginning of the interval to that flowing at the end of the interval, and divide by 2 to get the average current during the interval. Add these results for each interval, and divide the sum by the number of intervals to get the overall average. Calculate the total number of moles of electrons that passed through the cell, using the equations given in the **Introduction.**

From the changes in weight of the anode and cathode and the atomic weights of the metals, calculate the number of moles of metal dissolved and deposited.

Find the ratio of moles of metal to moles of electrons, and calculate for each electrode the number of moles of metal that would be dissolved or deposited by the passage of one mole of electrons.

Using the chemical equations for the reactions as the theoretical result, calculate the percentage deviation of your results from the theoretical result.

REFERENCES

1. Davis, Gailey, And Whitten, <u>Principles</u> <u>of</u> <u>Chemistry</u>, Saunders College Publishing, Philadelphia, 1984, Chapter 19 (Electrochemistry).
2. Whitten and Gailey, <u>General</u> <u>Chemistry</u>, Saunders College Publishing, Philadelphia, 1984, Chapter 19 (Electrochemistry).

QUESTIONS--PROBLEMS

1. Write a balanced equation for the reaction at each electrode.

2. What error would result if some of the deposit were to break off the cathode during the electrolysis?

3. What error would result if the ammeter reading were 100 milliamperes when only 90 milliamperes were actually flowing through the cell?

4. If the average amount of current flowing in your experiment had flowed for the same length of time through a cell that had a cathode and an anode of metallic silver and silver nitrate solution as the electrolyte, what weight of silver would have deposited on the cathode? What would have been the loss in weight of the anode? Write equations for the reactions occurring at the cathode and anode.

Experiment 19

ELECTROLYTIC CELLS

PRELABORATORY QUESTIONS

Name_____   Lab Instructor_____

Student ID No._____   Date_____

1. Why are all electrochemical reactions necessarily oxidation-reduction reactions?

2. Define each and distinguish between the following:

    a. Anode and cathode

    b. Electrolytic cell and voltaic cell

    c. Positive electrode in an electrolytic cell and in a voltaic cell

3. State the error that would result if a portion of the total anode reaction were the decomposition of water to give oxygen, i.e.,

$$2 H_2O \longrightarrow O_2 + 4H^+ + 4e^-.$$

4. How many coulombs constitute 1 mole of electrons? Show your calculations.

Experiment 19

ELECTROLYTIC CELLS

REPORT SHEET

Name_____   Lab Instructor_____

Student ID No._____   Date_____

Data

	Anode	Cathode
Metal used	_____	_____
Electrolyte used	_____	_____
Weight **before** electrolysis (g)	_____	_____
Weight **after** electrolysis (g)	_____	_____
Change in weight (g)	_____	_____

Current	Time	Coulombs
_____	_____	
_____	_____	_____
_____	_____	_____
_____	_____	_____
_____	_____	_____
_____	_____	_____
_____	_____	_____
_____	_____	_____
_____	_____	_____
_____	_____	_____

Current	Time	Coulombs
_____	_____	
		_____
_____	_____	
		_____
_____	_____	
		_____
_____	_____	
		_____
_____	_____	
		_____
_____	_____	
		_____

1. Total number of coulombs passed through the electrolysis cell?_____

2. Total number of moles of electrons passed through the electrolysis cell?_____

3. Number of moles of metallic _____ dissolved at the anode?_____

4. Number of moles of metallic _____ deposited at the cathode?_____

5. Calculate atomic weight of the anode metal?   _____
   (Assume that 2 moles of electrons are required
   to dissolve one mole of the anode metal.)

6. Theoretical value?   _____

7. Percentage deviation?   _____

8. Calculated atomic weight of the cathode metal?   _____
   (Assume that two moles of electrons are required
   to deposit one mole of the cathode metal.)

9. Theoretical value?   _____

10. Percentage deviation?   _____

VOLTAIC CELLS

Objective

To determine the cell potentials of several voltaic cells and to examine the effect of concentration changes and complex ion formation on the potential

Equipment Needed

Porous cup; power supply and voltmeter (can be the same as used for Exp. 19); lead, iron, cadmium, nickel, magnesium, tin, zinc, and copper metal strips for electrodes; 100-mL beaker; flexible copper connecting wires; battery clips; fine sand paper or emery cloth; graduated cylinder

Reagents Needed

1.0 M solutions of iron(II) sulfate, zinc sulfate, copper(II) sulfate, lead nitrate, cadmium nitrate, magnesium sulfate; tin(II) chloride, and nickel nitrate; 6 M ammonia

INTRODUCTION

Electrochemical cells that produce electricity are called voltaic or galvanic cells. Sometimes they are called batteries, although this term properly refers to groups of voltaic cells connected together.

In a voltaic cell a chemical reaction is carried out so that it produces an electric current that is conducted through an external wire that connects the two parts of the cell. The chemical reactions used in voltaic cells are oxidation-reduction processes and involve the transfer of electrons from one part of the cell to the other part. A typical example of such a reaction is:

$$Zn^0 + Cu^{2+} \longrightarrow Zn^{2+} + Cu^0. \tag{1}$$

In this process electrons are transferred from metallic zinc to copper(II) ions, resulting in the formation of metallic copper and zinc(II) ions. If a zinc strip is placed in a copper sulfate solution, the transfer of electrons takes place directly at the metal-solution boundary, and metallic copper will begin to plate the zinc strip. This same reaction can be carried out so that the electrons are transferred from the metallic zinc to the copper ions through an external wire connecting the two reactants. This is illustrated in Fig. 20-1. Metallic zinc, in the beaker on the left, transfers electrons to copper(II) ions present in the beaker on the right by means of the metal conductor connecting the two beakers through the voltmeter.

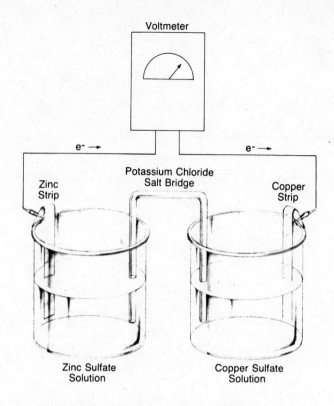

Figure 20-1. A zinc-copper voltaic cell

The complete voltaic cell assembly for this reaction is illustrated in Fig. 20-1 and includes: (1) a zinc strip immersed in a solution containing zinc ions, (2) a copper strip immersed in a solution containing copper(II) ions, (3) wires connecting the zinc and copper electrodes to the voltmeter, (4) a salt bridge* or a porous cup used, as in Exp. 19, to allow ions to migrate from one compartment to the other, and (5) a voltmeter in the external circuit to indicate the cell potential.

The reading on the voltmeter is a measure of the tendency for the electron-transfer process to occur. By measuring the potentials or voltages of cells containing a variety of metals and their ions at the same concentrations, it is possible to learn just which electron-transfer processes occur readily and which occur with difficulty.

As in electrolysis, cell reactions are often viewed in terms of the individual processes occurring at the two electrodes. For the reaction in Eq. (1), the two <u>half-reactions</u> are:

$$Zn^0 \longrightarrow Zn^{2+} + 2e^- \text{ (oxidation at the anode)} \qquad (2)$$

$$Cu^{2+} + 2e^- \longrightarrow Cu^0 \text{ (reduction at the cathode)}. \qquad (3)$$

The overall cell reaction is the sum of the two half-reactions. In this case the sum of the reactions in Eqs. (2) and (3) is the reaction in Eq. (1).

The notion that the voltaic cell reaction is the sum of two half-reactions has two implications:

---

*A salt bridge may be prepared by filling a U-tube with a 1 M solution of potassium chloride, tightly plugging the ends with cotton, and inverting the tube so that one arm rests in each compartment of the cell. No air bubbles should appear in the bend of the U-tube.

1. That a variety of cells can be made simply by changing the cathode components (the metal and its ions) and leaving the anode component the same or by changing the anode components and leaving the cathode components the same. For example, if the beaker containing the copper strip and copper sulfate solution (Fig. 20-1) is replaced by one containing a strip of silver and silver nitrate solution, a new cell would be obtained. Presumably, any metal and a solution of its ions may be used in preparing a cell. Even if the metal reacts with the water of the solution, it may often be dissolved in mercury and the resulting mercury amalgam used as an electrode.

2. That the cell voltage may be regarded as the sum of the contributions from each half-reaction, i.e., from each electrode compartment. If these contributions could be measured for each electrode system, we could have a quantitative indication of the tendency of a particular metal to be oxidized or of its ion to be reduced.

In this experiment a number of voltaic cells will be prepared and their voltages measured. You will devise a scheme for determining the potentials of a number of electrodes. You will also examine some factors that affect the cell potential.

PROCEDURE

Assemble the voltaic cell as shown in Fig. 19-3. Place about 40 mL of 1.0 M copper(II) sulfate solution in a 100-mL beaker. In the porous cup, place enough (approximately 15 mL) of 1.0 M zinc sulfate solution to fill it within 5 mm of the top. With emery paper (or fine sand paper), clean the zinc and copper metal strips. Place the copper strip in the copper(II) sulfate solution and the zinc strip in the zinc sulfate solution. Now put the entire porous cup assembly into the 100-mL beaker containing the copper(II) sulfate solution.

Assemble the zinc/copper voltaic cell.

Attach the red voltmeter lead from the electrolytic apparatus to the zinc strip and the black lead to the copper strip (Fig. 20-2). Record the initial voltage in your laboratory notebook.

Read initial voltage.

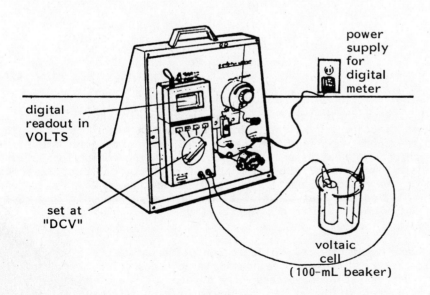

Figure 20-2. Apparatus and cell for voltmeter experiments

Note the algebraic sign of the recorded voltage.

a)* What does this mean in terms of the flow of electrons from the voltaic cell to the voltmeter? Reverse the leads, and now the voltage should be the same value as before, but opposite in sign. Whenever the sign of the voltage is positive, the metal electrode connected to the negative voltmeter lead is the metal at which electrons are produced. This corresponds to an anodic or oxidation half-reaction, i.e.,

$$(M^0 \longrightarrow M^{n+} + ne^-).$$

Change exposed surface area of electrode.

b)* What type of half-reaction occurs at the other electrode?

Now lift the copper electrode slowly from the solution.

c)* Does the voltage change appreciably upon decreasing the area of the electrode exposed to the solution?

For each of the following parts of the experiment, do not leave the voltmeter connected longer than necessary to read it; disconnect it as soon as you have read the voltage.

Determination of the Direction of Electron Flow. It is important for the next set of experiments that you are able to use the voltmeter to determine the <u>direction</u> of electron flow. Try to recall whether reaction occurs when a zinc strip is placed in copper sulfate solution or when a copper strip is placed in zinc sulfate solution. In other words, which of the following reactions is spontaneous?

$$Zn + Cu^{2+} \longrightarrow Zn^{2+} + Cu \qquad (4)$$

$$Cu + Zn^{2+} \longrightarrow Cu^{2+} + Zn \qquad (5)$$

Eqs. (4) and (5) correspond to the individual electrode half-reactions

$$Zn \longrightarrow Zn^{2+} + 2e^-$$
$$Cu^{2+} + 2e^- \longrightarrow Cu \qquad (4')$$

and

$$Cu \longrightarrow Cu^{2+} + 2e^-$$
$$Zn^{2+} + 2e^- \longrightarrow Zn. \qquad (5')$$

Determine direction of electron flow.

Find whether the voltmeter operates properly when the negative (−) terminal is connected to the electrode at which electrons leave the solution (the anode) or the electrode at which electrons enter the solution (the cathode). What happens when you reverse the connections at the two voltmeter terminals? Do not proceed until you can associate the direction of the voltmeter deflection to the electrode at which electrons enter the solution and that at which electrons leave the solution. Describe your experiments and record the results in your notebook.

Measurement of Cell Voltages for Different Cells. Now measure the voltage for cells that contain other electrodes. The zinc/zinc sulfate electrode is replaced successively by each of the other metal/metal ion systems listed in Table 20-1. The copper/copper(II) sulfate systems is not changed; it is your reference electrode system.

_____

*The lower case letter refers to questions which are to be answered in the report.

Table 20-1. Electrode Systems

Metal	Solution
cadmium	cadmium nitrate
copper	copper(II) sulfate
iron	iron(II) sulfate (ferrous sulfate)
lead	lead nitrate
magnesium	magnesium sulfate
nickel	nickel nitrate
tin	tin(II) chloride (stannous chloride)
zinc	zinc sulfate

Quickly remove the porous cup containing the zinc strip and zinc sulfate solution, thereby preventing the zinc sulfate solution from draining into the 100-mL beaker of copper sulfate solution. Discard the zinc sulfate solution, wash the porous cup, and place about 15 mL of the next solution (e.g., 1.0 M cadmium nitrate) in the porous cup. Place a cleaned electrode of the proper metal (e.g., cadmium) into the porous cup, and place the cup assembly back into the beaker containing the copper sulfate solution. Connect the cell to the voltmeter, and record the voltage in your notebook. Also record which electrode has to be connected to the negative (-) terminal on the voltmeter in order to obtain a positive value for the voltage. Repeat this procedure until the voltage of each metal/metal ion combination listed in Table 20-1 has been determined against the copper/copper(II) sulfate electrode.

Determine voltages of other cells.

Effect of Concentration on Cell Voltage. To investigate the effect of concentration, both of the 1.0 M solutions in one of the previous cells will be diluted.

Prepare one of the cells as before. Use a copper/copper(II) sulfate electrode and one of the following which may be assigned by your instructor: cadmium/cadmium nitrate, nickel/nickel nitrate, or copper/copper(II) sulfate. Start with 1.0 M solutions for both electrodes, and dilute one by a factor of 10. After recording the new voltage, dilute the same solution again by a factor of 10. Dilute the other solution in the same manner, recording the voltage after each dilution. After two dilutions each, both solutions are 0.010 M.

Change concentration of ions.

d)* How does the voltage of the 0.010 M cell compare with that when both solutions were 1.0 M?

e)* In your report explain each change in the cell voltage after diluting the anode solution and after diluting the cathode solution.

Effect of a Complex Ion on Cell Voltage. In the above experiments, you have examined the potentials of several cells at 1.0 M concentration of metal ion and the effect of varying the concentration of the salt solution. We may now be curious whether other factors affect the cell potential. For example, suppose the metal ion is present in some form other than the hexa-aqua ions $[M(H_2O)_6]^{2+}$ that exist in aqueous solutions of the Fe^{2+}, Ni^{2+}, and Cu^{2+} salts. The Cd^{2+}, Mg^{2+}, Pb^{2+}, and Sn^{2+} ions exist probably as tetra-aqua complex ions in water, i.e., $[M(H_2O)_4]^{2+}$.

---

*The lower case letter refers to questions which are to be answered in the report.

With the ions Cd^{2+}, Cu^{2+}, and Ni^{2+}, ammonia forms the corresponding complex ions of ammonia: $[Cd(NH_3)_4]^{2+}$, $[Cu(NH_3)_4]^{2+}$, and $[Ni(NH_3)_6]^{2+}$. The ammonia molecules in these complex ions are bound more strongly to the metal ions than are the water molecules. Solutions containing these ammonia complexes (called ammine complexes) will be studied to determine the effects of the complex ions on the cell voltages, using a 0.10 M lead/lead nitrate reference electrode to complete the cell.

Prepare ammonia solutions of 0.10 M $Cd(NO_3)_2$, $CuSO_4$, and $Ni(NO_3)_2$ by mixing the following solutions:

	1 M solution	6 M NH$_3$	H$_2$O
$Cd(NO_3)_2$	4.0 mL	28 mL	8.0 mL
$CuSO_4$	4.0 mL	28 mL	8.0 mL
$Ni(NO_3)_2$	4.0 mL	5.0 mL	31 mL

Determine voltages of cells containing different complex ions.

Use these solutions to measure the voltages of the cells in which the solution contains a 0.10 M NH_3 complex.

Prepare 0.10 M aqueous solutions by dilution of 1 M aqueous solutions with distilled water, and use them to measure the voltages of the cells in which the solution contains 0.10 M aqueous salt. The same reference electrode system consisting of a lead strip and a 1.0 M lead nitrate solution is used to complete each of these six cells.

f)* Compare the voltage of each cell containing the 0.10 M ammonia complex with the cell containing the same 0.10 M salt without ammonia.

g)* In your report, explain the changes in the cell voltages after adding the ammonia to an anode solution and after adding ammonia to the cathode solution.

CALCULATION OF ELECTRODE POTENTIALS

It has been suggested that the cell potential is the sum of contributions from the two individual electrode reactions. However, no reliable method for determining the potential of only one half-reaction is available; our measured voltages are only the potential of the overall reaction. Situations of this type in science are often solved by agreeing to a convention by which an arbitrary value is assigned to one quantity, and all other values are referred to this "standard." Suppose we adopt the convention that the potential is zero for both of the half-reactions.

$$Cu(s) \longrightarrow Cu^{2+} \text{ (1 M)} + 2e^-$$

$$Cu^{2+} \text{ (1 M)} + 2e^- \longrightarrow Cu(s)$$

Then the measured cell voltages for cells having such a copper electrode would indicate directly the potential for the half-reaction involving the other metal and its ions. Let us further adopt the convention that the potential for the other half-reaction will be negative when copper acts as the anode and positive when copper acts as the cathode. The sign of the potential then tells us the direction of electron flow.

For example, the measured voltage of the cell

$$Co|CoSO_4 \text{ (1.0 M)} ||CuSO_4 \text{ (1.0 M)}|Cu$$

is 0.62 volt. The connections to the voltmeter show that the direction of electron flow corresponds to the two half-reactions:

---

*The lower case letter refers to questions which are to be answered in the report.

$$Co(s) \longrightarrow Co^{2+} (1.0 \text{ M}) + 2e^- \text{ (the anode = cobalt)}$$

$$Cu^{2+} (1.0 \text{ M}) + 2e^- \longrightarrow Cu(s) \text{ (the cathode = copper)}.$$

If the second half-reaction is given a potential of zero, the total cell voltage of 0.62 volt may be taken as the contribution from the cobalt electrode. According to the convention, it is given a positive sign.

$$E_{cell} = E_{Co \to Co^{2+}} + E_{Cu^{2+} \to Cu} = 0.62 \text{ volt} + 0 \text{ volt} = 0.62 \text{ volt}$$

In a similar way, relative half-reaction or electrode potentials may be obtained for a variety of metal/metal ion systems.

REFERENCES

1. Davis, Gaily, and Whitten, Principles of Chemistry, Saunders College Publishing, Philadelphia, 1984, Chapter 19 (Electrochemistry)
2. Whitten and Gailey, General Chemistry 2nd Ed., Saunders College Publishing, Philadelphia, 1984, Chapter 19 (Electrochemistry)

1. Considering what you have learned in this experiment, what difficulty would you expect to encounter if an electrolysis cell were constructed using both a copper electrode and a zinc electrode immersed in a 1.0 M copper sulfate solution?

2. The discussion and the experimental examples in this experiment have been concerned with metal/metal ion systems. Is it possible to use nonmetals and their ions as one or both electrodes? Why or why not?

3. The dissolution of metal in aqueous solution may be considered the result of three steps as follows:

    a) Separation of the atoms of the solid into separated gaseous atoms

    $$M(s) \longrightarrow M(g)$$

    b) Ionization of the separated gaseous atoms

    $$M(g) \longrightarrow M^{2+}(g) + 2e^-$$

    c) Solution of the gaseous ions to a given concentration in water

    $$M^{2+}(g) + n\ H_2O \longrightarrow M(H_2O)_n^{2+} \ (1.0\ M)$$

    The energies involved for these steps are:

    for zinc

    a) 31.2 kcal/mol (131 kJ/mol)

    b) 630.8 kcal/mol (2639 kJ/mol)

    c) −491 kcal/mol (−2054 kJ/mol)

    for copper

    a) 81.1 kcal/mol (339 kJ/mol)

    b) 646.0 kcal/mol (2703 kJ/mol)

    c) −507 kcal/mol (−2121 kJ/mol)

    Calculate the total energies per mole of metal in the two processes

    $$Zn(s) \longrightarrow Zn^{2+} \ (1.0\ M) + 2e^-$$

    $$Cu(s) \longrightarrow Cu^{2+} \ (1.0\ M) + 2e^-$$

    and suggest which of the a, b, c steps is responsible for metallic zinc being more readily oxidized to ions in solution than is metallic copper.

4. Using your data, calculate the free energy change that would occur if 1 mole of zinc were oxidized to zinc ion in the cell

    $$Zn(s) | ZnSO_4 \ (1.0\ M) \| CuSO_4 \ (1.0\ M) | Cu(s)$$

    under conditions that would maintain the 1.0 M concentrations throughout the oxidation half-reaction.

5. It is useful to assign a separate voltage contribution to each of the two electrode systems which comprise a voltaic cell. The problem is that the experimental measurement of the voltage of a **single** electrode is not possible. Therefore, a system based on an assumed value for one electrode system must be used. The assumption that the standard hydrogen electrode system has a voltage of zero is commonly found in textbooks. For this experiment, no measurements were taken for cells containing a standard hydrogen electrode system, so we will use the copper electrode system as our standard. ($E_{Cu} = 0.00$ V)

Furthermore, assume that any electrode system which acts as an anode in a cell with copper has a **negative** electrode potential. Likewise, any electrode system which acts as a cathode in a cell with copper would have a **positive** electrode potential. The sign of the potential tells us the direction of electron flow. Using these assumptions, construct a table of electrode potentials from your data for the voltages of different cells. Place the electrode systems in numerical order with the most positive value at the top of the list and the most negative at the bottom. Write for each electrode system a reduction half-reaction (electrons as reactants). Finally, consult your textbook or other suitable reference, write the literature value for each half-reaction, and calculate the difference between your value (based on $E_{Cu} = 0.00$ V) and the literature value (based on $E_H = 0.00$ V). What do you conclude from this difference?

Reduction Half-Reaction	Observed Voltage	Literature Value	Difference of Literature Value Minus Observed Voltage
_____	_____	_____	_____

Experiment 20

VOLTAIC CELLS

PRELABORATORY QUESTIONS

Name_____   Lab Instructor_____

Student ID No._____   Date_____

1. Explain why the porous cup is necessary in the design of a copper/zinc voltaic cell.

2. How is the chemical reaction that occurs at the negative (-) terminal of an electro-
    lytic cell (Exp. 19) related to that which occurs at the zinc terminal in the
    zinc/copper voltaic cell?

3. How can you rationalize the fact that the voltage of a voltaic cell changes if
    the concentration of one of the electrode solutions is changed?

4. Discuss the validity of assigning values to the electrode potentials, based on the assumption that the copper/copper ion half-reaction has a zero value.

5. What is the standard half-reaction on which the accepted electrode potentials are based, and what value is assigned to it? Can you suggest reasons why this might be a better choice than the copper/copper ion reaction?

6. The voltage of the cell

$$Pt|Pt^{2+} (1.0 \text{ M}) ||Cu^{2+} (1.0 \text{ M})|Cu$$

is 0.88 volt, and the cell reaction is

$$Cu(s) + Pt^{2+} (1.0 \text{ M}) \longrightarrow Pt(s) + Cu^{2+} (1.0 \text{ M}).$$

Write the half-reactions, and calculate the oxidation potential for the half-reaction of platinum.

Experiment 20

VOLTAIC CELLS

REPORT SHEET

Name_____   Lab Instructor_____

Student ID No._____   Date_____

CELL VOLTAGES

	Anode Metal	Cathode Metal	Observed Voltage
1.	_____	_____	_____
2.	_____	_____	_____
3.	_____	_____	_____
4.	_____	_____	_____
5.	_____	_____	_____
6.	_____	_____	_____
7.	_____	_____	_____

VOLTAIC CELL REACTIONS

	Anode Half-Reaction	Cathode Half-Reaction	Total Voltage of Reaction
1.	_____	_____	_____
2.	_____	_____	_____
3.	_____	_____	_____
4.	_____	_____	_____
5.	_____	_____	_____
6.	_____	_____	_____
7.	_____	_____	_____

Answers to the questions posed in the procedure.

a)

b)

c)

EFFECT OF CONCENTRATION ON CELL VOLTAGE

Metal used_____

Solution used___ _____

	CONCENTRATIONS	OBSERVED VOLTAGE
Both solutions at 1.0 M		
_____solution 0.10 M,	_____solution 1.0 M	_____
_____solution 0.010 M,	_____solution 1.0 M	_____
_____solution 0.010 M,	_____solution 0.10 M	_____
_____solution 0.010 M,	_____solution 0.010 M	_____

Answers to the questions posed in the procedure

d)

e)

VOLTAIC CELLS (continued)

REPORT SHEET

Name_____   Lab Instructor_____

Student ID No._____   Date_____

EFFECT OF AMMONIA ON THE CELL VOLTAGE

	OBSERVED VOLTAGE		OBSERVED VOLTAGE

$Cd(NO_3)_2$ 0.10 M aqueous _____   0.10 M ammonia _____

$CuSO_4$ 0.10 M aqueous _____   0.10 M ammonia _____

$Ni(NO_3)_2$ 0.10 M aqueous _____   0.10 M ammonia _____

Answers to the questions posed in the procedure.

f)

g)

POTENTIOMETRIC DETERMINATION OF IRON IN A SOLUBLE

IRON SALT--AN OXIDATION-REDUCTION TITRATION

Objective

To learn how to perform potentiometric titrations and to analyze an unknown sample for its iron content

Equipment Needed

Three 250-mL beakers; 250-mL volumetric flask; 100-mL graduated cylinder; stirring rod; buret; pH meter with glass and platinum electrodes; magnetic stirrer and stirring bars

Reagents Needed

Solid reagent-grade potassium dichromate; 6M H_2SO_4; unknown solid containing iron(II) ammonium sulfate

INTRODUCTION

Iron may exist in solution in either the +II or the +III oxidation state. The quantity of dissolved iron can be determined if it can first be reduced to Fe(II) and then oxidized to Fe(III) by titrating with a standard solution of an oxidizing agent until the equivalence point is reached, that is, until an amount of oxidating agent exactly sufficient to react with the amount of Fe(II) present has been added. If, for example, we used Ce(IV) as the oxidizing agent, the equivalence point would be reached when exactly 1 mole

$$Fe^{2+} + Ce^{4+} \longrightarrow Fe^{3+} + Ce^{3+} \tag{1}$$

of Ce^{4+} had been added for each mole of Fe^{2+} originally present. This is an example of a general procedure known as an oxidation/ reduction titration.

Obviously, we need some means of identifying the equivalence point when we reach it during the titration. One method is to measure the voltage of a cell in which the oxidation/reduction (electron-transfer) reaction is taking place. A titration conducted by measuring the voltage or potential of an electrochemical cell is called a **potentiometric titration.**

The cell which we might consider is one such as that in Fig. 21-1, showing a reference electrode connected through a salt

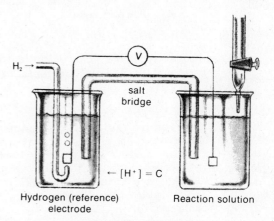

Figure 21-1

Apparatus for potentiometric titration

bridge to a reaction solution. The potential difference between the hydrogen electrode and the inert metal conductor in the reaction solution is measured on the voltmeter or potentiometer, V.

During the early stages of the titration, Fe^{2+} is the reactant present in highest concentration, and the cell voltage can be associated with the reaction

$$Fe^{3+} + 0.5 H_2 \longrightarrow Fe^{2+} + H^+_{aq}. \tag{2}$$

As the titration proceeds, the concentration of Fe^{2+} drops and that of Fe^{3+} rises. During this period the cell voltage is given by the Nernst equation:*

$$E = E^O - \frac{RT}{nF} \ln \frac{[Fe^{2+}]}{[Fe^{3+}]} = 0.77 + 0.059 \log \frac{[Fe^{3+}]}{[Fe^{2+}]}. \tag{3}$$

This equation shows that the cell voltage will rise as Fe^{2+} is oxidized to Fe^{3+}.

After the equivalence point in the titration, the cell voltage is associated with the reaction

$$Ce^{4+} + 0.5 H_2 \longrightarrow Ce^{3+} + H^+, \tag{4}$$

and the cell voltage is given by the equation

$$E = E^O - \frac{RT}{nF} \ln \frac{[Ce^{3+}]}{[Ce^{4+}]} = 1.44 + 0.059 \log \frac{[Ce^{4+}]}{[Ce^{3+}]}. \tag{5}$$

This equation shows that addition of Ce^{4+} after the equivalence point results in a rise in cell voltage.

The net result of the phenomena described by Eqs. (3) and (5) above is that a plot of cell voltage and milliliters of Ce^{4+} added takes the form shown in Fig. 21-2. As this figure indicates, the equivalence point of the titration occurs along the steep vertical position of the curve.

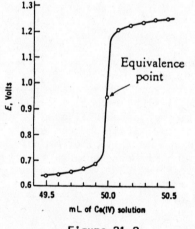

Figure 21-2

Potentiometric titration of 50 mL of 0.100M iron(II) with 0.100M cerium(IV) solution.

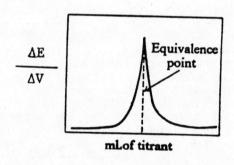

Figure 21-3

Plot of $\Delta E/\Delta V$ with mL of titrant added. The equivalence point is at the peak of the curve.

In practice, it is not always easy to locate the equivalence point along the vertical portion of the curve. A more accurate method of doing this is by means of a differential plot. In this plot, the differences in adjacent voltage reading per unit volume of titrant added, $\Delta E/\Delta V$, are plotted with the volume of titrant added. The equivalence point corresponds to the highest point of this curve, as illustrated in Fig. 21-3. Values for $\Delta E/\Delta V$ are obtained by taking the difference in adjacent voltage measurements and dividing this by the difference in milliliters of titrant corresponding to the two voltage measurements.

*See Exp. 20 or your text for more detail about this equation.

Oxidation/Reduction Titrations Using Dichromate Ion as the Oxidizing Agent.
Although the previous discussion has concerned the simple reaction of oxidation of ceric
ion, the use of dichromate ion is in some ways more convenient. Dichromate ion, as
potassium dichromate, is readily obtained pure; also, it is inexpensive. Standard solutions may be prepared directly by weighing an appropriate quantity of the pure solid
substance. No special precautions must be observed in dissolving the solid; the solutions
are stable. From the theoretical view, the use of dichromate ion is not so satisfactory
because, although the electronic partial equation for the reduction of dichromate ion has
the form

$$Cr_2O_7^{2-} + 14 H^+_{aq} + 6 e^- \longrightarrow 2 Cr^{3+} + 7 H_2O, \tag{6}$$

the voltage of a cell in which this reaction is presumably taking place does not show the
dependence on $[H^+]$ or on $[Cr^{3+}]$ predicted by this equation. It appears that the reduction
occurs in several steps in several reactions before finally reaching Cr^{3+}. In spite of
this difficulty, the formal potential (Appendix V) for the dichromate reduction has been
measured and combined with that for iron(II) ion oxidation to give a potential at the
equivalence point close to 0.9 V.

Analysis for Iron by Oxidation/Reduction Titration Using Dichromate. A weighed
quantity of the substance containing iron(II) ions is brought into solution. For reliable
results, Fe^{2+} must be prevented from oxidizing to Fe^{3+} by air. This is achieved by
forming the hexammine iron(II) ion, $Fe(NH_3)_6^{2+}$. The reaction is performed in the presence
of an excess of acid.

The titration reaction is

$$6 Fe^{2+} + Cr_2O_7^{2-} + 14 H^+_{aq} \longrightarrow 6 Fe^{3+} + 2 Cr^{3+} + 7 H_2O. \tag{7}$$

In Eq. (7), each mole of potassium dichromate contains 2 moles of Cr(VI) which
are reduced to Cr(III). One-sixth of a mole of potassium dichromate gains 1 mole of
electrons in the analytical reaction, and 1 mole of Fe^{2+} loses 1 mole of electrons.

Potentiometric Method for Oxidation of Iron(II) by Dichromate Ion. The potentiometric method you will follow in this experiment is, in principle, the same as that
described above, with two modifidations. The first is that the hydrogen reference electrode is replaced with the hydrogen ion selective (glass) electrode used to measure pH.
Since the pH is constant throughout this titration--due to the excess of acid present--
this electrode can serve as a reliable reference electrode. The second modification is
the use of dichromate ion instead of cerium(IV) ion as the oxidizing agent.

NOTEBOOK AND REPORT

In your notebook you should record the weights, molarities, and volumes of
reagents used, the buret and millivoltmeter readings after each addition of titrant, the
calculations for the analysis of the unknown, and the answers to the problems at the end
of the experiment. Do not forget to record the code number of the unknown, if given.

PROCEDURE

Preparation of Standard Potassium Dichromate Solution. Weigh
accurately on a weighed piece of clean paper about 1.2 g of pure dry
potassium dichromate. Transfer all of it, brushing the paper, to a 250-
mL beaker, add about 50 mL of distilled H_2O, and stir to dissolve the
dichromate. Transfer the solution to a clean, though not necessarily
dry, 250-mL volumetric flask without losing a drop, and rinse the beaker
with three additonal 50-mL portions of water. Add the rinsings to the
volumetric flask without spilling any. Shake the liquid in the volumetric flask to mix it thoroughly, and add water little by little to
bring the level of liquid carefully to the mark. Mix the contents for
not less than five minutes by shaking and inverting the flask (with the
stopper on) to insure homogeneity. Calculate the molarity of the solution from the weight of salt taken, and record this on the label.

Weigh out $K_2Cr_2O_7$.

Dissolve and transfer to volumetric flask.

Mix thoroughly, dilute to the mark, and mix.

Analysis of the Unknown. Weigh accurately two samples (about 0.50 g each) of the iron unknown into marked 250-mL beakers.

Dissolve each of the weighed samples by adding 100 mL of 3.0M H_2SO_4 to each beaker.

Using a proper technique, fill a buret with the standard potassium dichromate solution.

Prepare the pH meter for making measurements as follows:

1. Turn on the pH meter, set it at the standby position, and allow it to warm.

2. Place a platinum or other inert electrode and a glass (or other) reference electrode in electrode holders, and rinse water to run into a small beaker. Blot the electrodes dry with a Kemwipe or other tissue. (BLOT, DO NOT WIPE THE ELECTRODES, TO AVOID SCRATCHING THEM.)

3. **Carefully** add a magnetic stiring bar to the beaker containing one of the samples to be analyzed, and place the beaker on a magnetic stirrer. Lower the electrodes into the solution, making sure that their sensing elements are fully immersed but clear of the stirring bar. Adjust the magnetic stirrer so that the bar operates at a steady, moderate rate.

4. Place the buret containing the standard dichromate solution in titrating position above the beaker.

5. Attach the electrical leads from the electrodes to the pH meter. Turn the function mode knob of the pH meter from standby to mV (millivolts). **Do not make any other adjustments** on the pH meter.

6. Titrate the sample by adding a volume of $K_2Cr_2O_7$ solution, waiting for equilibrium (15-30 seconds), then reading and recording the millivolts and the volume of titrant added. The size of the quantity of titrant added will change during the titration. Initially, rather large (0.25-0.50 mL) increments of titrants will be needed. Near the equivalence point, small increments (3-5 drops) should be added. For each addition, the quantity of titrant added should be that amount needed to cause a change of about 2 mV. After the equivalence point, keep adding titrant until a nearly constant millivolt reading is obtained.

7. Following the titration, return the pH meter to the standby position, and remove the electrodes from the solution. Wash them with distilled water as before, and blot them dry.

8. Titrate the second sample, following steps 3 through 6, as appropriate.

9. Following this titration, return the pH meter and electrodes to their original condition.

TREATMENT OF DATA

Your data table should contain the weights of the samples taken, the molarity of the $K_2Cr_2O_7$ solution used, and the buret and millivolt meter readings after each addition of titrant. Complete the data table by calculating $\Delta E/\Delta V$ for each adjacent set of millivolt/volume of titrant readings, beginning at a volume of titrant just before the large rise in voltage.

Prepare two graphs for each titration. On the first, plot millivolt reading with mL of titrant added. On the second, plot $\Delta E/\Delta V$ with mL of titrant added. Identify the equivalence points, using each plot. To identify the equivalence point on the first plot, follow the procedure described in Exp 18. Use Fig. 21-3 as a guide in determining it by the second method. Write a short paragraph, critically comparing the equivalence points found by the two methods.

Using your data, calculate the percent of iron in your sample. Results for duplicate samples should agree within 0.1%.

REFERENCES

1. Skoog, D. A.; West, D. M.: "Fundamentals of Analytical Chemistry," 3rd Ed., Holt, Rinehart and Winston, New York, NY, 1976, Chapter 5.

2. Day, R. A., Jr.; Underwood, A. L.: "Quantitative Analysis," 4th Ed., Prentice-Hall, Inc., Englewood Cliffs, NJ, Chapters 10 and 11.

3. Davis, Gailey, and Whitten, Principles of Chemistry, Saunders College Publishing, Philadelphia, 1984, section 9-7.

4. Whitten and Gailey, General Chemistry, Saunders College Publishing, Philadelphia, 1984, pp. 235-236 and Chapter 12.

QUESTIONS--PROBLEMS

1. If your unknown were pure $Fe(NH_4)_2(SO_4)_2 \cdot 6 H_2O$, how many milliliters of your standard $K_2Cr_2O_7$ solution would be required to titrate a sample that weighed the same as that you used in the first titration in this experiment?

2. Assuming that you can determine the equivalence point in this titration with a reliability of ± 0.1 drop or 5×10^{-3} mL, what is the smallest number of moles of Fe^{2+} you can detect by this method? To do this, calculate the moles of Fe^{2+} that can be oxidized by the $Cr_2O_7^{2-}$ in 0.1 drop.

3. Write the equation for the reaction of dichromate ion with Sn(II) [being oxidized to Sn(IV)], and calculate the volume of your $K_2Cr_2O_7$ solution required to titrate a sample containing 0.458 g of $SnCl_2$.

4. What volume of a 0.020M $Ce(SO_4)_2$ solution would be needed to oxidize the Fe(II) ion in the sample you used in your first titration?

5. How would your plot of millivolts with mL titrant be changed if you used:

   a) reference electrode with a smaller E^O value than the glass electrode?

   b) a $K_2Cr_2O_7$ solution having twice the molarity of the solution you used?

6. Using Eq. (3), calculate the voltage of the cell when the concentrations of Fe^{2+} and Fe^{3+} are:

   a) 0.020M Fe^{2+}, 0.0020M Fe^{3+}

   b) 0.020M Fe^{2+}, 0.020M Fe^{3+}

   c) 0.0020M Fe^{2+}, 0.020M Fe^{3+}

7. Cite the major advantages and disadvantages of determining the equivalence point by each of the two methods used in this experiment.

POTENTIOMETRIC DETERMINATION OF IRON;
AN OXIDATION/REDUCTION TITRATION

PRELABORATORY QUESTIONS

Name_____   Lab Instructor_____

Student ID No_____   Date_____

1. Write a chemical equation for the reaction involved in the titration you will do in
    this experiment. Identify the oxidizing and reducing agents and the molar relations
    between them.

2. What is meant by a potentiometric titration? How is the equivalence point determined
    in such titrations?

3. How is the standard solution of titrant prepared for this experiment? How is its
    molarity determined? What does this tell you about the care you must exercise in
    preparing this solution?

4. List three sources of error in this experiment, and describe what you can do to minimize each of them.

5. Using Eqs. (2) and (3), show why the voltage of the electrochemical cell used to monitor the titration increases as more titrant is added to the sample.

6. What is $\Delta E/\Delta V$ in this experiment? Describe how values of $\Delta E/\Delta V$ are calculated and how they are used.

Experiment 21

AN OXIDATION/REDUCTION TITRATION

REPORT SHEET

Name_____   Lab Instructor_____

Student ID No_____   Date_____

Unknown No_____

Data	Trial 1	Trial 2	Trial 3
Weight of unknown iron sample (g)	_____	_____	_____
Molarity of $Cr_2O_7^{2-}$ solution (mol/L)	_____	_____	_____

Titration of Sample 1			Titration of Sample 2		
Buret Reading (mL)	Millivolt Meter Reading (mV)	$\dfrac{\Delta E}{\Delta V}$	Buret Reading (mL)	Millivolt Meter Reading (mV)	$\dfrac{\Delta E}{\Delta V}$
_____	_____		_____	_____	
		_____			_____
_____	_____		_____	_____	
		_____			_____
_____	_____		_____	_____	
		_____			_____
_____	_____		_____	_____	
		_____			_____
_____	_____		_____	_____	
		_____			_____
_____	_____		_____	_____	
		_____			_____
_____	_____		_____	_____	
		_____			_____
_____	_____		_____	_____	
		_____			_____
_____	_____		_____	_____	

Equivalence Point: Plot 1   _____   _____

                    Plot 2   _____   _____

Moles of iron in sample   _____   _____

Percent iron in sample   _____   _____

Average percent iron in sample   _____   _____

Sample Calculations

Attach sheets with your observations and answers to the assigned QUESTIONS--PROBLEMS.

RATES OF CHEMICAL REACTIONS

Objective

(1) To determine the relationship between the concentration of a reactant and the rate of a reaction at constant temperature; (2) to determine the concentration of an unknown solution of that reactant by observing the rates at which it undergoes the same reaction at the same temperature with the same concentrations of the other reactant as used in (1); (3) to determine the effect of raising the temperature on the rate of the same reaction

Equipment Needed

Seven beakers or flasks (at least 150 mL); 100-mL graduated cylinder; two 50-mL or 25-mL burets; buret clamps; ring stand; watch with second hand; 10-mL pipet with bulb; sheet of white paper; 250-mL Erlenmeyer flask; thermometer (0-100 $^\circ$C); buret reading card (optional)

Reagents Needed

0.0400 M KIO_3 solution, 0.0200 M H_2SO_3 solution (actually $NaHSO_3/H_2SO_4$) with starch; ice; unknown solutions of KIO_3

TECHNIQUES

Read the sections on the use of burets and pipets and on graphing in the **Laboratory Techniques** section of this manual.

INTRODUCTION

Chemical kinetics is the study of the rates of chemical reactions and the mechanisms by which they occur. The rate of a reaction describes how rapidly a chemical change occurs. The mechanism describes the pathway by which the reaction occurs.

Some reactions, such as the explosive reaction of a mixture of hydrogen and oxygen, occur so rapidly that their rates are extremely difficult to determine accurately. Others, such as the rusting of iron, occur so slowly that accurate rate determinations are difficult. Between these two extremes we find many rections that proceed at easily measurable rates. It is difficult to determine when many reactions have achieved equilibrium or gone to completion. Thus, we usually study the initial rate of the reaction which is the average rate over the first few seconds or minutes.

On the submicroscopic level, a necessary condition for chemical reaction is actual contact between the reacting species. Therefore, the frequency with which atoms, ions, or molecules collide is an important factor in reaction rates. Not all collisions produce chemical reactions. In order for two particles to react, they must possess a certain minimum energy known as the activation energy. Additionally, in many reactions, the individual particles must be properly aligned before reaction can occur. Thus, many collisions do not result in reaction, and the particles simply rebound after collision.

However, any change that increases the frequency of collisions should increase the rate of a particular reaction.

Increases in concentrations of reactant increase reaction rates because there are more particles in a given volume, and, of necessity, collisions occur more frequently. An exception is an increase in the concentration of a reactant that is not involved in the rate-determining step of a reaction. An increase in temperature increases velocities of molecules which in turn increase collision frequency. Also, at higher temperatures more molecules possess sufficient energy to react (the activation energy).

Consider a hypothetical reaction such as

$$A_{2(g)} \quad + \quad B_{2(g)} \quad \longrightarrow \quad 2 \; AB_{(g)}.$$

The rate expression for this reaction can be written as

$$rate \quad = \quad k[A_2]^x[B_2]^y$$

in which values for the specific rate constant, k, and the exponents, x and y, <u>must be determined experimentally</u>. Values for x and y are commonly 0, 1, 2, or 3, though they may be fractional. Consider the following reaction.

$$S_2O_8^{2-} \quad + \quad 2 \; I^- \quad \longrightarrow \quad 2 \; SO_4^{2-} \quad + \quad I_2$$

In order to determine the effect of varying a particular factor on the rate of a given reaction, it is necessary to hold all of the other factors constant. Experiments have shown that if the concentration of I^- is held constant while the initial concentration of $S_2O_8^{2-}$ is doubled, the rate of the reaction increases by a factor of two. Thus, we can deduce that the concentration of $S_2O_8^{2-}$ is raised to the first power in the rate expression. Additional experiments have shown that doubling the concentration of I^- while holding the concentration of $S_2O_8^{2-}$ constant doubles the rate of reaction. We conclude that the concentration of I^- is raised to the first power in the rate expression. Therefore, we can write

$$rate \quad = \quad k[S_2O_8^{2-}][I^-],$$

and we describe the reaction as being first order in both $S_2O_8^{2-}$ and I^- and second order overall.

The reaction you will study is known as the "iodine clock" reaction which is, in fact, a series of reactions believed to be the following.

$$IO_3^- \quad + \quad 3 \; H_2SO_3 \quad \longrightarrow \quad I^- \quad + \quad 3 \; SO_4^{2-} \quad + \quad 6 \; H^+ \tag{1}$$

$$IO_3^- \quad + \quad 6 \; H^+ \quad + \quad 5 \; I^- \quad \longrightarrow \quad 3 \; I_{2(s)} \quad + \quad 3 \; H_2O \tag{2}$$

$$I_2 \quad + \quad starch \quad \longrightarrow \quad starch \cdot I_2 \; complex \quad (dark \; blue \; colored) \tag{3}$$

Reactions (2) and (3) are known to be instantaneous; i.e., both reactions occur in a fraction of a second. However, H_2SO_3 is a stronger reducing agent than I^-, and as long as any H_2SO_3 remains in the solution, reaction (2) cannot occur. As soon as the H_2SO_3 has been used up in reaction (1), reaction (2) begins. Even tiny traces of I_2 turn starch solutions blue; thus, the appearance of a blue coloration in the solution signals the beginning of reaction (2). In summary, the variation in the rate of reaction (1) using different concentrations of KIO_3 is easily followed by measuring the time required for appearance of the deep blue coloration in the colorless solutions. You will derive a rate expression of the form

$$rate \quad = \quad k'[IO_3^-]^x$$

in which

$$k' = k[H_2SO_3] = constant$$

and x will be determined from experimental observations.

The rate of a chemical reaction varies inversely with time; i.e., the faster the reaction, the less time required; the slower the reaction, the more time required. Thus, we can write

$$rate = \frac{1}{t}$$

in which t is the time in seconds required for the reaction to occur. To determine the relationship between concentration of IO_3^- and rate of reaction, a plot of concentrations of IO_3^- versus the reciprocal of time (1/t) will be made. This graph will then be used to determine the concentration of an unknown KIO_3 solution.

Finally, you will determine the relationship between rate of reaction and temperature by using identical concentrations of all reactants at three different temperatures.

NOTEBOOK AND REPORT

Construct tabular report forms such as those on pages 99-100. Fill in the data as you perform the experiment, do the necessary calculations, make the appropriate plots, and answer the questions included.

PROCEDURES

Relationship between Concentration and Rate of Reaction

Two students may share burets for measuring the solutions. Each student, however, is expected to mix and time each reaction mixture independently. Label one buret H_2SO_3 and the other KIO_3.

Place 120 mL of 0.0400 M KIO_3 solution (no more) in a clean, dry beaker or flask. Label it. Place 85 mL of the $NaHSO_3/H_2SO_4$/starch solution (called H_2SO_3 solution, **Note 1**) in a clean, dry beaker or flask. Label it. Rinse one buret with three 5-mL portions (no more) of KIO_3 solution, and then fill the buret with KIO_3 solution. Rinse the other buret with three 5-mL portions (no more) of $NaHSO_3/H_2SO_4$/starch solution, and then fill the buret with this solution. This solution is 0.0200 M in H_2SO_3.

Rinse burets with solutions.

Place the amounts of H_2SO_3 solution and distilled water indicated on the report form in five beakers. Measure both carefully. Label the beakers H_2SO_3–**a, b, c, d, e.** Place the indicated amounts of KIO_3 soluiton in five other beakers. Label these beakers KIO_3–**a, b, c, d, e.**

Measure solutions into five beakers.

Use a watch with a second hand to measure time. Pour the contents of beaker H_2SO_3–**a** _into_ beaker KIO_3–**a,** place the beaker over a piece of white paper, and stir until the solution turns blue. Record the time elapsed from the instant of mixing until the solution turns blue. Record the final temperature of the solution. It is important to pour the H_2SO_3 solution into the KIO_3 solution! (Can you suggest a reason?) Repeat the experiment, using your other solutions, and complete the report form.

Mix the two solutions.

Plot the data obtained from these five experiments on the graph paper (see the sample report form). Plot concentrations of IO_3^- on the abscissa (x axis) and rate of reaction (1/t) on the ordinate (y axis). The KIO_3 solutions were diluted by mixing. Calculate the concentration of KIO_3 in each solution _after mixing_, before plotting the data.

Plot the results.

Determination of Concentration of an Unknown KIO_3 Solution

Repeat the experiment twice using 5.0 mL of H_2SO_3 solution, 85 mL of water, and 10 mL (pipet) of your unknown KIO_3 solution each time. Record the data on the report form. Use the graph that you plotted earlier to estimate the concentration of your unknown KIO_3 solution. Locate its reciprocal time (use the average value) on the vertical axis, go horizontally across to the line you drew on the graph, and then drop straight down to the horizontal (concentration) axis. The concentration of your unknown corresponds to the point at which the vertical line intersects the concentration axis. Recall that 10.0 mL of unknown KIO_3 solution was diluted to 100 mL. Calculate and record the <u>original</u> concentration of your unknown KIO_3 solution.

Determine the KIO_3 concentration.

Effect of Temperature on Rate of Reaction

Fill a 250-mL beaker approximately two-thirds full of clean ice cubes and then with distilled water to cover the ice cubes. Stir several minutes until the temperature drops to near 0 °C. At the same time, put 100 mL of distilled water in a 250-mL Erlenmeyer flask and heat to approximately 60 °C.

Run the experiment once, using cold water and once using hot water. Use 5.0 mL of H_2SO_3 solution, 85 mL of water, and 10 mL of KIO_3 solution each time. Measure the time required for the blue coloration to appear. Note the final temperature in both cases. Record the data on the report form together with the data obtained in (b) above for 10 mL of KIO_3 solution. What do you observe about temperature and the rate of this reaction?

Repeat the experiments at different temperature.

NOTES

<u>Note 1.</u> The following reaction occurs in solutions containing $NaHSO_3$ and H_2SO_4.

$$H_{(aq)}^+ \ + \ HSO_{3(aq)}^- \ \longrightarrow \ H_2SO_{3(aq)}$$
(from H_2SO_4)

REFERENCES

1. R. E. Davis, K. D. Gailey, K. W. Whitten, <u>Principles of Chemistry</u>, Saunders College Publishing/HRW, Philadelphia (1984), Chapter 15 (Chemical Kinetics).

2. K. W. Whitten and K. D. Gailey, <u>General Chemistry</u>, 2nd ed., Saunders College Publishing, RHW, Philadelphia (1984), Chapter 14 (Chemical Kinetics).

Experiment 22

RATES OF CHEMICAL REACTIONS

PRELABORATORY QUESTIONS

Name_____   Lab Instructor_____

Student ID No._____   Date_____

1.   The following rate data were obtained at 25 $^{\circ}$C for the following reaction.   What is the rate law expression for this reaction? $2A + B \longrightarrow 3C$

Experiment	$[A][\frac{mol}{L}]$	$[B][\frac{mol}{L}]$	Initial Rate of Formation of C (M/min)
1	0.10	0.10	4.0×10^{-4}
2	0.30	0.30	1.2×10^{-3}
3	0.10	0.30	4.0×10^{-4}
4	0.20	0.40	8.0×10^{-4}

_____
Answer

2.   The following data were obtained for the following reaction at 25 $^{\circ}$C.   What is the rate law expression for the reaction? $2A + B + 2C \longrightarrow 3D$

Experiment	Initial [A] (M)	Initial [B] (M)	Initial [C] (M)	Initial Rate of Formation of C (M/min)
1	0.40	0.20	0.20	4.0×10^{-4}
2	0.40	0.60	0.40	1.2×10^{-3}
3	0.40	0.20	0.60	4.0×10^{-4}
4	1.2	0.60	0.80	3.6×10^{-3}

_____
Answer

3.   The following data were collected for the indicated reaction at a particular temperature. $A + B \longrightarrow C$.   What is the rate law expression for this reaction?

Experiment	Initial [A] (M)	Initial [B] (M)	Initial Rate of Formation of C (M/min)
1	0.20	0.20	4.0×10^{-4}
2	0.40	0.40	3.2×10^{-3}
3	0.20	0.40	1.6×10^{-3}

_____
Answer

4. Given that the rate expression for the following reaction at a certain temperature is rate = $k[NO]^2[O_2]$. If two experiments involving this reaction are performed at the same temperature, but in the second experiment the initial concentration of NO is tripled while the initial concentration of O_2 is halved, the initial rate in the second experiment will be _____ times that in the first.

$$2\ NO\ +\ O_2\ \longrightarrow\ 2\ NO_2$$

5. a. The following data were obtained from experiments just like the ones you will do. Calculate the speed of the reaction in reciprocal seconds (1/t), and then plot the concentration of substance XYZ on the x axis versus the speed of reaction (1/t) on the y axis.

Experiment	Molarity XYZ	Time (s)	Speed (s^{-1})
A	0.0050	20	_____
B	0.0040	22	_____
C	0.0030	29	_____
D	0.0020	38	_____
E	0.0010	55	_____

Reaction Speed versus Molarity of XYZ

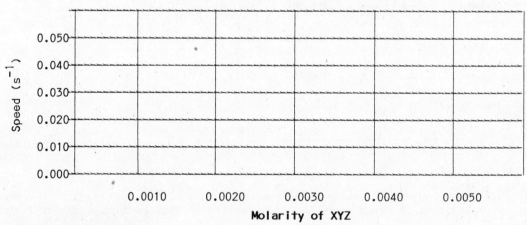

b. Suppose an unknown solution of XYZ required 45 seconds to react. What is the molarity of XYZ in the solution? Draw lines on the graph to show how you obtain an answer.

XYZ (M) _____

Answer

Experiment 22

RATES OF CHEMICAL REACTIONS

REPORT FORM

Name_____   Lab Instructor_____

Student ID No._____   Date_____

1. Relationship between concentration of KIO_3 and rate of reaction.

Run	H_2SO_3 (mL)	H_2O (mL)	KIO_3 (mL)	Molarity* H_2SO_3	Molarity* KIO_3	Time (seconds)	Speed $(1/t = s^{-1})$	Final Temperature
a	5.0	83	12					
b	5.0	85	10					
c	5.0	87	8.0					
d	5.0	89	6.0					
e	5.0	91	4.0					

Based on these five observations, the rate expression is:

rate = $k'[IO_3^-]^x$ and x = _____.

2. Determination of concentration of unknown KIO_3 solution.

Run	H_2SO_3 (mL)	H_2O (mL)	KIO_3 (mL)	Molarity* H_2SO_3	Molarity* KIO_3	Time (seconds)	Speed $(1/t = s^{-1})$	Final Temperature
a	5.0	85	10					
b	5.0	85	10					

Unknown KIO_3 number _____

Average value for speed (s^{-1}) _____

Concentration of unknown KIO_3 _____

*After mixing

301

3. Effect of temperature on speed of reaction.

Run	H_2SO_3 (mL)	H_2O (mL)	KIO_3 (mL)	Molarity* H_2SO_3	Molarity* KIO_3	Time (seconds)	Speed $(1/t = s^{-1})$	Final Temperature
(cold) a	5.0	85	10					
b	5.0	85	10					
(hot) c	5.0	85	10					

Consider runs (a) and (b). What is the ratio of difference in the speeds of these reactions to the difference in temperature, i.e.,

$$\frac{\text{speed (b) - speed (a)}}{\text{temp (b) - temp (a)}} = \underline{\hspace{3cm}} = \underline{\hspace{3cm}} = \underline{\hspace{3cm}}$$

Consider runs (b) and (c). What is the ratio of difference in the speeds of these reactions to the difference in temperature, i.e.,

$$\frac{\text{speed (c) - speed (b)}}{\text{temp (c) - temp (b)}} = \underline{\hspace{3cm}} = \underline{\hspace{3cm}} = \underline{\hspace{3cm}}$$

*After mixing

CALORIMETRY

Objective

To measure the enthalpy of neutralization in an acid/base reaction and to use these values to calculate enthalpy changes in other reactions

Equipment Needed

1500-mL beaker or plastic container; 5-mL and 10-mL pipets; medicine dropper; 3 styrofoam coffee cups; -15 $^\circ$C to +15 $^\circ$C thermometer graduated in tenths of degree; 3 tubes; 16 x 150 mm tubes; spatula; regular -10 $^\circ$C to +100 $^\circ$C thermometer; 2 copper cylinders about 1.2-cm diameter and 3.1-cm long

Reagents Needed

Magnesium turnings; 6 M HCl; standardized solutions of 3.0 M HCl and 3.0 M NaOH; crushed ice

INTRODUCTION

The change in enthalpy accompanying a chemical or physical change can often be measured in a calorimeter--an instrument that measures heat changes in a system. A calorimeter usually is used to measure the heat liberated in exothermic processes. Several types of calorimeters are in common use. In most calorimeters the amount of heat evolved is calculated by multiplying the heat capacity of the calorimeter and its contents by the observed increase in temperature. The heat capacity is the amount of heat necessary to increase the temperature of the calorimeter and its contents 1.00 $^\circ$C. A calorimeter of this type will be used in this experiment.

In this experiment the enthalpy changes associated with two different reactions will be measured to determine the enthalpy change for a third reaction which is not measured directly.

In the first determination, the enthalpy change accompanying the displacement of hydrogen from an acid solution by a divalent metal is obtained by observing the heat liberated in the reaction*:

$$M(s) + 2 H_3O^+ \rightleftharpoons M^{2+}(aq) + H_2 + 2 H_2O \qquad \Delta H_{(1)}. \qquad (1)$$

Any of several metals, such as zinc, magnesium, iron, or cadmium, added to a hydrochloric acid solution will satisfy this equation.

In the second determination, the enthalpy of neutralization is obtained by adding a solution of a base such as sodium hydroxide to a hydrochloric acid solution. The reaction is*:

_____

*See the Discussion section for a more precise explanation of enthalpy changes accompanying reactions (1) and (2) and their relation to the data obtained in this experiment.

$$H_3O^+ \; + \; OH^- \; \rightleftharpoons \; 2\,H_2O \qquad \Delta H_{(2)}. \qquad\qquad (2)$$

By use of Hess' law of heat summation and the ΔH values obtained by these determinations, we can calculate the enthalpy change for a reaction having an equation that is the sum of or difference between Eq. (1) and (2). For example, multiplying Eq. (2) by two and subtracting it from Eq. (1) gives:

$$M(s) \; + \; 2\,H_2O \; \rightleftharpoons \; M^{2+}(aq) \; + \; 2\,OH^-(aq) \; + \; H_2 \qquad\qquad (3)$$

The ΔH for this reaction is $\Delta H_{(1)} - 2\,\Delta H_{(2)}$.

Similarly, the enthalpy change in the reaction

$$Mg^{2+}(aq) \; + \; 2\,OH^-(aq) \; \longrightarrow \; Mg(OH)_2(s) \qquad\qquad (4)$$

can be calculated by making use of the measured enthalpy changes and tabulated values of the enthalpies of formation of $Mg(OH)_2(s)$ and $H_2O(\ell)$: -924.7 kJ (221.0 kcal) and -285.8 kJ (-68.32 kcal), respectively.

The Coffee–Cup Calorimeter

Measurement of the enthalpy change in a reaction can be made in a calorimeter; one measures the temperature rise (or fall) produced by the reaction in an insulated vessel containing a mass of known heat capacity. For the insulated vessel in this experiment, we shall use a styrofoam coffee cup. To take advantage of the greater precision of the $-15\ ^{\circ}C$ to $+15\ ^{\circ}C$ special thermometers used in Experiment 16, we will operate in a temperature range below 15 $^{\circ}C$.

In a calorimeter, which itself warms during a reaction, some of the heat of the reaction is consumed in heating the calorimeter, and some may be transferred to the environment, but most of the heat warms the solution. You may assume that the escape of heat to the environment is small during the time required to do the experiment. In order to take into account the absorption of heat by the calorimeter, we need to determine the heat capacity of the calorimeter; i.e., we need to calibrate the calorimeter to determine its constant (in J/$^{\circ}$C or cal/$^{\circ}$C) In precise work, the calibration is accomplished by introducing heat from an electric current which can be measured precisely. In a simpler procedure, we shall calibrate the styrofoam coffee cup by measuring the heat absorbed by the cooling of hot copper metal, taking the specific heat of copper as a known constant. The calibration procedure will be to heat a measured weight of copper to a measured temperature, add the hot copper metal to a measured quantity of water, and measure the temperature rise of the water (and the calorimeter). If we know the specific heats and weights of copper and water and the temperature change, the only unknown quantity is the amount of heat used to warm the calorimeter vessel. The determination of this unknown quantity is the purpose of the calibration procedure.

PROCEDURE

Preliminary for Part B. Before starting Part A, prepare for Part B by placing a 15-mL sample of 3.0 M NaOH in a clean test tube in some ice in a styrofoam cup. Put a second 15-mL sample of 3.0 M NaOH in another test tube (referred to later as test tube no. 2).

Cool NaOH solution.

A. Calibration Procedure. On a balance, weigh two copper cylinders, obtained from your instructor, to the nearest 0.01 g. Do not take the time needed to get the weight more precisely. (Observe, however, proper procedure, particularly if you are using an analytical balance; remember to support the balance pan and beam when adding or removing something from the pan.) Place the weighed cylinders in a dry test tube and set the test tube into a beaker of boiling water. The level of water in the beaker must be well above the height reached by the

Weigh Cu cylinders; heat in boiling H_2O.

Measure boiling temperature with regular thermometer.

---

*See the Discussion section for a more precise explanation of enthalpy changes accompanying reactions (1) and (2) and their relation to the data obtained in this experiment.

cylinders in the test tube. Use an ordinary -10 °C to 110 °C thermometer (not the -15 °C to +15 °C thermometer) to measure the temperature of the boiling water, estimating to the nearest 0.1 °C. Record the value.

Weigh to the nearest 0.01 g a clean, dry styrofoam coffee cup of about 200-mL capacity. Add to the weighed cup 60 mL of distilled or de-ionized water and a few pieces of clean ice to cool the water to 3 °C to 5 °C as read on the thermometer. Remove any excess ice with a clean spatula, and reweigh the cup and water to the nearest 0.01 g.

Determine weight of cooled H$_2$O in cup.

Using the special thermometer with 0.1 °C gradations, read and record the temperature of the cooled water every 30 seconds for 5 minutes. At the next 30-second mark, remove the test tube from the boiling water (use a test-tube holder), immediately wipe the outside with tissue or a towel, and drop the copper cylinders into the water in the styrofoam cup. Record the time of addition and continue to read the time and temperature at 30-second intervals until the temperature change within the interval is about what it was before adding the copper metal and for 5 minutes longer. Stir the water occasionally during the period.

Take temperature readings at measured time intervals; add hot Cu, and continue readings.

B. Enthalpy of Neutralization. Remove the copper cylinders from the water, and add 10 mL of 3.0 M HCl to the water, using a pipet. Add ice, and cool the solution to below 5 °C. Remove excess ice, and weigh the cup and solution to the nearest 0.01 g.

Determine weight of cooled HCl solution in cup.

Rinse the pipet with water and with 3.0 M NaOH solution from test tube no. 2 prepared before you started Part A. Rinse and wipe the thermometer, take the temperature of the cold sodium hydroxide solution, and record the value. Rinse and wipe the thermometer again, and place it in the hydrochloric acid solution in the plastic cup. Observe and record the temperature of the solution at 30-second intervals for 5 minutes. Rinse the pipet with water and then the 3.0 M NaOH solution, and then pipet 10 mL of the cold 3.0 M NaOH solution into the acid in the styrofoam cup, noting the time of addition. Stir. Observe and record the temperature at 30-second intervals for 5 minutes.

Take temperature readings at intervals; add NaOH, and continue readings.

C. Enthalpy of Dissolution of Mg in HCl(aq). Weigh on clean paper or a watch glass 2.5 x 10^{-3} mole of magnesium turnings.

Discard the salt solution in the styrofoam cup, rinse it with distilled or de-ionized water, and, using a graduated cylinder, add 20 mL of 6 M HCl, 40 mL of H$_2$O, and sufficient ice to cool the solution below 5 °C. Remove the excess ice, and weigh the hydrochloric acid solution to 0.01 g. Observe and record the temperature of the solution at 30-second intervals for 5 minutes. Add the magnesium, noting the time of addition. Stir and record the temperature at 30-second intervals until all of the magnesium has disappeared; continue for 5 minutes longer.

Measure temperature rise for known weight of acid; add weighed Mg, and continue to measure temperature rise.

D. Since both Parts B and C depend upon the calibration results of Part A, if you have laboratory time available, repeat Part A, and average the calculated results with those of the first set.

CALCULATIONS

Plot the data of Parts A, B, and C on three (separate) graphs, using temperature as the vertical axis. On each graph, draw a vertical line at the time at which the copper, sodium hydroxide, or magnesium was added, and extrapolate the nearly horizontal portions of the curves to intersect it. Determine the temperature difference, ΔT, and resulting from the additions and the corrected final temperature of the calorimeter and its contents, ΔT_F. The latter is the temperature corresponding to the intersection of the upper extrapolated curve and the vertical line drawn as above.

If T_B is the temperature of the boiling water in which the copper was heated, then in Part A we have:

(a) $\begin{array}{c}\text{Joules lost}\\\text{by copper}\end{array}$ = (grams of copper) $\times$ (0.385 $J\cdot g^{-1}\cdot {}^{\circ}C^{-1}$) $\times$ ($T_B - T_F$)

(b) $\begin{array}{c}\text{Joules gained}\\\text{by water}\end{array}$ = (grams of water) $\times$ (4.192 $J\cdot g^{-1}\cdot {}^{\circ}C^{-1}$) $\times \Delta T$

(c) Joules gained by the calorimeter vessel = $X \times \Delta T$.

Here, 0.385 $J\cdot g^{-1}\cdot {}^{\circ}C^{-1}$ is the heat capacity of one gram of copper near room temperature, and 4.192 $J\cdot g^{-1}\cdot {}^{\circ}C^{-1}$ is the heat capacity of one gram of water in the region near 10 $^{\circ}C$; the unknown, X, is the amount of heat in joules needed to change the temperature of the calorimeter vessel by 1.00 $^{\circ}C$ when it holds about 65 g of H_2O.

Since the amount of heat loss by copper equals the amount of heat gained by the water and the calorimeter, then

$$(a) = (b) + (c)$$

$$X = \frac{(a) - (b)}{\Delta T}.$$

For Part B we have, letting T_F represent the final temperature of the calorimeter, ΔT the temperature change, and T_N the temperature of the sodium hydroxide solution,

(a) Joules produced in the neutralization reaction = Y

(b) $\begin{pmatrix}\text{Joules to warm}\\\text{the solution}\\\text{in the calorimeter}\end{pmatrix}$ = $\begin{pmatrix}\text{mass of}\\\text{HCl solution} \quad g\\\textit{with water}\end{pmatrix}$ $\times$ (4.192 $J\cdot g^{-1}\cdot {}^{\circ}C^{-1}$) $\times \Delta T$

(c) Joules to warm the calorimeter = $X \times \Delta T$

(d) $\begin{pmatrix}\text{Joules to warm}\\\text{the sodium}\\\text{hydroxide solution}\end{pmatrix}$ = $\begin{pmatrix}\text{mass of}\\\text{NaOH}\\\text{solution}\end{pmatrix}$ (4.205 $J\cdot g^{-1}\cdot {}^{\circ}C^{-1}$) $\times$ ($T_F - T_N$)

In (b) and (d) we have assumed that the specific heats of the dilute solutions do not differ significantly from that of pure water, and in (d) we have used 4.205 $J\cdot g^{-1}\cdot {}^{\circ}C^{-1}$ as the heat capacity of one gram of water near 3 $^{\circ}C$. Also, as before, heat loss equals heat gain, and

$$Y = (a) = (b) + (c) + (d).$$

Use 1.083 $g\cdot mL^{-1}$ as the density of the sodium hydroxide solution to calculate its mass.

The calculated value of Y represents the number of joules evolved on reaction of (10/1000) $\times$ 3.0 moles of HCl and an equal number of moles of sodium hydroxide. From these data, calculate the enthalpy of neutralization for one mole of each, at the dilution represented in your experiment.

All of the heat liberated by the reaction of Part C goes to heating the calorimeter and contents.

(a) Joules evolved in forming magnesium ion in solution = Z

(b) Joules to warm the calorimeter = $X \times \Delta T$

(c) $\begin{pmatrix}\text{Joules to warm}\\\text{the hydrochloric}\\\text{acid solution}\end{pmatrix}$ = $\begin{pmatrix}\text{mass of}\\\text{HCl}\\\text{solution}\end{pmatrix}$ (3.73 $J\cdot g^{-1}\cdot {}^{\circ}C^{-1}$) $\times \Delta T$

Here, 3.73 $J\cdot g^{-1}\cdot {}^{\circ}C^{-1}$ is the heat capacity for 2 M HCl in the region near 8 $^{\circ}C$.

Also, Z = (b) + (c) for the quantity of magnesium used. Calculate the enthalpy change for the dissolution of one mole of magnesium in acid solution.

Use the results for Parts B and C and the data give on p. 302 to calculate the enthalpy changes in reactions (3) and (4).

DISCUSSION

Strictly speaking, the change in enthalpy measured in the reaction of the metal with acid is not the enthalpy of formation of the metal ion M^{2+}(aq). However, we should like to evalue it. In addition to the measured quantity, the changes in enthalpy for at least two other processes must be taken into account if the enthalpy of formation of the metal ion is to be calculated accurately. Fortunately, the contribution of these additional reactions to the enthalpy of formation is very small--at the most, a few tenths of 1%--and well within the experimental error of our measurement. However, because it is important to understand the principles involved in the concept of the enthalpy of formation of ions and to appreciate the approximations made in determining it as we do in this experiment, the following explanation is provided.

For the reaction of metal with acid, the quantity measured in Part C is the change in enthalpy for the reaction

$$Mg(s) \ + \ 2 \ H_3O^+ \ (2.0 \ M) \ \longrightarrow \ Mg^{2+} \ (0.042 \ M) \ + \ H_2 \ (2 \ atm) \ 2 \ H_2O. \qquad (5)$$

Since only 2.5×10^{-3} moles of metal are used in the experiment, the heat liberated in the calorimeter must be multiplied by 4.0×10^2 to get the H value for reaction (5) in which one mole of metal is specified.

The enthalpy of formation of a hydrated divalent metal ion corresponds to the energy change for the equation:

$$M(s) \ \longrightarrow \ M^{2+}(aq) \ + \ 2e^-(aq). \qquad (6)$$

By convention, this is measured in the reaction

$$M(s) \ + \ 2 \ H_3O^+(aq) \ \longrightarrow \ M^{2+}(aq) \ + \ H_2 \ (1 \ atm) \ + \ 2 \ H_2O \qquad (7)$$

in which the enthalpy change for the process

$$2e^-(aq) \ + \ 2 \ H_3O^+(aq) \ \longrightarrow \ H_2 \ (2 \ atm) \ + \ 2 \ H_2O \qquad (8)$$

is taken as zero.

The difference between Eq. (7)--the equation defining the approximate enthalpy of formation of the ion--and Eq. (5)--for which the enthalpy change is measured in this experiment--appears in the different concentrations of the ions H_3O^+(aq) and M^{2+}(aq). The symbolism in Eq. (7) implies that these ions are present in the solution at infinite dilution; in Eq. (5) they are present at the concentrations specified. In taking these ions from the concentrations specified to infinite dilution, the following processes can be imagined to occur:

$$2 \ H_3O^+ \ (2.0 \ M) \ \longrightarrow \ 2 \ H_3O^+(aq) \qquad (9)$$

$$Mg^{2+} \ (0.42 \ M \ or \ 0.042 \ M) \ \longrightarrow \ Mg^{2+}(aq). \qquad (10)$$

Because the heats of dilution of ions are small-often much less than $0.2 \ kJ \cdot mol^{-1}$-- reliable enthalpies of formation of metal ions can be obtained by measuring the change in enthalpy for the reaction of the metal with acid as described in this experiment.

By similar reasoning, it can be shown that the change in enthalpy measured in Part B is not actually the enthalpy of neutralization. Here, again, the difference between the measured and defined values is small and is associated with the heats of dilution of the ions. This is illustrated by the following equations:

$$H_3O^+ \ (3.0 \ M) \ + \ OH^- \ (3.0 \ M) \ \longrightarrow \ 2 \ H_2O \qquad (11)$$

$$H_3O^+(aq) \ + \ OH^-(aq) \ \longrightarrow \ 2 \ H_2O. \qquad (12)$$

Eq. (11) represents the reaction in which the change in enthalpy is measured; Eq. (12) is the equation defining the enthalpy of neutralization.

The enthalpies of dilution of the ions not involved in the reactions--sodium and chloride ions--should be included in the calculations, but these enthalpies also are very small and can be neglected in the calculations.

Sample Calculation of Heat Released in Neutralization

Suppose 50.0 mL of a solution of an acid is mixed with 50.0 mL of a solution of a base, both initially at 21.7 $^{\circ}$C, in a coffee-cup calorimeter with a constant of 27 $J \cdot {}^{\circ}C^{-1}$. The temperature rises to 27.8 $^{\circ}$C. Calculate the heat of the neutralization reaction.

We first calculate the amount of heat absorbed by the solution. We assume that the solution has essentially the same specific heat as pure water, 4.18 $J \cdot g^{-1} \cdot {}^{\circ}C^{-1}$, and the same density, 1.00 g/mL.

Heat absorbed by solution

$$? \ J = 4.18 \ J \cdot g^{-1} \cdot {}^{\circ}C^{-1} \times (27.8 \ {}^{\circ}C - 21.7 \ {}^{\circ}C) = 2.55 \times 10^3 \ J.$$

Now, we add to this the
heat absorbed by the calorimeter.

$$? \ J = 2.55 \times 10^3 \ J + (27.8 \ {}^{\circ}C - 21.7 \ {}^{\circ}C) \times 27 \ J \cdot {}^{\circ}C^{-1}$$

Total heat absorbed

$$= 2.55 \times 10^3 \ J \ + \ 1.6 \times 10^2 \ = \ \underline{2.71 \times 10^3 \ J.}$$
$$\text{(by} \qquad\qquad \text{(by}$$
$$\text{solution)} \qquad \text{calorimeter)}$$

The amount of heat absorbed by the calorimeter and its contents and released by the neutralization reaction is equal to the heat absorbed. Therefore, the heat released is $\underline{2.71 \ kJ}$.

REFERENCES

1. Shoemaker, D. P., and Garland, C. W.: Experiments in Physical Chemistrty. 2nd edition, McGraw-Hill, New York, 1967, Chapter 5

2. Mahan, B.: J. Chem. Educ. (1960) 37, 634.

3. Davis, Gailey, and Whitten, Principles of Chemistry, Saunders College Publishing, Philadelphia, 1984, pp. 98-107, 454-456.

4. Whitten and Gailey, General Chemistry 2nd Ed., Saunders College Publishing, Philadelphia, 1984, pp. 444-453.

Experiment 23

PRELABORATORY QUESTIONS

Name_____   Lab Instructor_____

Student ID No._____   Date_____

1. Consider the reaction of 50.0 mL of 1.06 M HCl with 50.0 mL of 0.93 M NaOH.

   (a) How many moles of HCl and of NaOH are initially present?

   (b) How many moles of HCl and of NaOH are actually neutralized?

2. (a) Why is it necessary to use graphical methods to determine the maximum temperature rise due to an <u>exothermic</u> reaction in solution in a calorimeter?

(b) Predict and sketch the shape of a plot of temperature versus time for an
<u>endothermic</u> reaction. Show ΔT.

3. The complete neutralization of 0.59 mole of a monoprotic acid with excess NaOH
evolves 31.2 kilocalories. What is the heat of neutralization of the acid
with NaOH per mole of acid?

4. How many grams of magnesium are equal to 2.5×10^{-3} moles of magnesium?

Name_____   Lab Instructor_____

Student ID No._____   Date_____

Part A. Weight of water in cup (g)   _____

Weight of copper added (g)   _____

$T_B - T_F$ ($^{\circ}$C)   _____

Calculated value of X   _____

Part B. Weight of HCl solution (g)   _____   Concentration
                                                                       of acid used   _____

Weight of NaOH solution (g)   _____   Concentration
                                                                       of base used   _____

ΔT for the reaction ($^{\circ}$C)   _____

$T_F - T_N$ ($^{\circ}$C)   _____

Molar enthalpy of neutralization   _____

Part C. Weight of HCl solution (g)   _____

Weight of magnesium added (g)   _____

ΔT for the reaction ($^{\circ}$C)   _____

ΔH_f for Mg^{2+} _____

Enthalpy changes for reactions (3) and (4) from your data: (3) ΔH = _____

(4) ΔH = _____

Attach graphs of temperature against time.

Questions

1. In each of Parts A, B, and C, the quantity of liquid in the styrofoam cup has been kept nearly the same. What scientific reason is there for this, other than the practical one that this gives a convenient depth for covering the thermometer bulb with liquid?

2. Was there an increase or a decrease in temperature in Part B when the hydrochloric acid solution was added to the water? To what do you attribute this change in temperature?

PREPARATIONS OF PHOSPHORUS AND SULFUR OXYANIONS

Objective

To prepare representative oxygen anions of elements in Groups VA and VIA of the periodic table

Equipment Needed

A 6-inch porcelain casserole; suction filter and trap bottle; filter paper to fit 3-inch Büchner funnel; 4-inch crystallizing dish; 3-inch Büchner funnel; 400-mL beaker; iron ring and ring stand; burner; two 125-mL Erlenmeyer flasks; 100-mL beaker; hydrogen sulfide source and generator in hoods; rubber policeman; watch glass; buret; 250-mL Erlenmeyer flask

Reagents Needed

30 g of bone ash, 80% $Ca_3(PO_4)_2$, or tribasic calcium phosphate, $Ca_{10}(OH)_2(PO_4)_6$; concentrated (18 M) sulfuric acid, H_2SO_4; solid anhydrous sodium carbonate, Na_2CO_3; phosphoric acid wash solution; 0.2 M ammonium molybdate solution; 0.1 M KH_2PO_4; 0.1 M Na_2HPO_4; 0.1 M Na_3PO_4; Kodak D-72 developer; calcium chloride hexahydrate, $CaCl_2 \cdot 6H_2O$; absolute ethanol, C_2H_5OH; methyl orange and phenolphthalein indicators; solid potassium sulfite dihydrate, $K_2SO_3 \cdot 2H_2O$; powdered sulfur; ice; iodine; 95% and 50% ethanol; crystallized barium hydroxide octahydrate, $Ba(OH)_2 \cdot 8H_2O$; Aich-Two-Es, solid source of hydrogen sulfide; dilute hydrochloric acid; carbon disulfide; 8 M nitric acid; 0.4 M cobalt(II) chloride, $CoCl_2$; tetrachloroethylene, C_2Cl_4; 3% hydrogen peroxide, H_2O_2; ammonium sulfide, $(NH_4)_2S$, 22.6%; 0.1 M $AgNO_3$; sodium thiosulfate pentahydrate, $Na_2S_2O_3 \cdot 5H_2O$; potassium iodide, KI

INTRODUCTION

All of the elements of Groups VA, VIA, and VIIA form strong bonds with oxygen. In all compounds containing nonmetal-oxygen bonds except that containing fluorine (OF_2), the element other than oxygen is assigned a positive oxidation number. This experiment illustrates some of the chemical reactions and preparative routes to oxygen compounds of the nonmetallic elements. The experiment is divided into two subsections, one concerning phosphorus and one concerning sulfur. A separate experiment (No. 25) will explore some of the chemical reactions of the oxy-halogen compounds. You may be asked to prepare one or more compounds for a given element, or you may prepare one compound of each element. Read the entire experiment to obtain experience with the general preparative chemistry, but follow your instructor's directions regarding the assignment and preparation of specific compounds.

A. Group VA--Phosphorus

Each of the Group VA elements has an outer-shell electronic configuration of ns^2np^3. Since each p orbital is half filled and may be involved in the formation of a covalent bond, a common molecular formula in this family is EX_3 (in which E represents either N, P, As, Sb, or Bi). In addition to forming compounds utilizing the three p electrons, the elements of Group VA also form molecules or ions in which they exhibit formal oxidation states of +3 and +5 (for example, NO_3^-, N_2O_5, P_4O_{10}, Sb_2O_5, PO_4^{3-}, and AsO_4^{3-}).

Orthophosphoric acid, H_3PO_4, a hydrolysis product of its anhydride, P_4O_{10}, can be represented by the Lewis electron dot representation or by the structural formula below. All structures of orthophosphoric acid, the condensed phosphoric acids, and their normal salts are based upon the tetrahedral PO_4^{3-} unit illustrated in H_3PO_4.

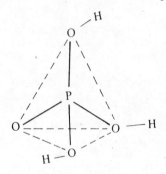

In dilute aqueous solution, orthophosphoric acid is a weak triprotic acid; the three protons do not show equal acid strengths, but they exhibit successive ionization constants which decrease by a factor of $\sim10^{-5}$. The values for the three ionization steps at 25 °C are:

$$H_3PO_4 + H_2O \rightleftharpoons H_3O^+ + H_2PO_4^- \qquad K_{a_1} = 7.5 \times 10^{-3}$$

$$H_2PO_4^- + H_2O \rightleftharpoons H_3O^+ + HPO_4^{2-} \qquad K_{a_2} = 6.2 \times 10^{-8}$$

$$HPO_4^{2-} + H_2O \rightleftharpoons H_3O^+ + PO_4^{3-} \qquad K_{a_3} = 3.6 \times 10^{-13}$$

Note that the value for the third ionization constant is so low that appreciable concentrations of PO_4^{3-} can exist only in very basic solutions. As a result, normal orthophosphate salts (salts containing PO_4^{3-} ions) are difficult to obtain. The normal orthophosphate compounds which may be obtained pure are those that exhibit only a slight solubility in water (for example, $NH_4MgPO_4 \cdot 6H_2O$, Ag_3PO_4, and $FePO_4 \cdot 4H_2O$). The hydrogen orthophosphate, HPO_4^{2-}, and dihydrogen orthophosphate, $H_2PO_4^-$, anions appear in well characterized series of salts, especially those of the alkali metals.

The species present in solution are strongly dependent on the pH as illustrated by the following equilibria:

$$H_3PO_4 \rightleftharpoons H_2PO_4^- \rightleftharpoons HPO_4^{2-} \rightleftharpoons PO_4^{3-}$$

increasing pH,
<u>decreasing acidity</u> →

decreasing pH,
← <u>increasing acidity</u>

In the present experiment, we will (1) extract orthophosphate from a natural source, bone ash, or from a chemical source, tribasic calcium phosphate, $Ca_{10}(OH)_2(PO_4)_6$; (2) isolate the hydrogen orthophosphate compound $Na_2HPO_4 \cdot 12H_2O$; and (3) use the phosphate to prepare a complex anion of phosphorus. The extraction of the HPO_4^{2-} ion provides a pure reagent to use in the subsequent synthesis. Thus, this experiment should illustrate some of the steps often followed by a synthetic chemist: (1) preparation of an intermediate compound,

(2) analysis or characterization of a product, and (3) utilization of the intermediate compound for tests or for preparation of another compound.

B. Group VIA--Sulfur

Oxygen and sulfur belong to the same family (VIA) of the periodic table. Consequently, each element has an outer-electron configuration of ns^2np^4, and the chemistry of the two elements is sometimes quite similar. However, in some cases the chemistry of oxygen is quite different from that of sulfur. In this experiment some similarities in oxygen and sulfur are illustrated by the chemical bonding and structures that are formed. However, part of the experiment is chosen to illustrate an important difference (the tendency for catenation) because sulfur forms stable -S-S-S-S- chains, but a chain containing more than three oxygen-oxygen linkages is <u>unknown</u>.

One of the objectives of this portion of the experiment is to prepare sulfur analogs of the familiar sulfate and carbonate anions. As a possible extension of this experiment, you may determine the purity of your potassium thiosulfate sample by an iodine titration of the thiosulfate ion.

The term **thio** is used in the name of a compound when an oxygen atom in a chemical species is replaced by a sulfur atom. The thio analogs to be prepared in this experiment are the thiosulfate and the trithiocarbonate ions. These species and their oxygen analogs may be represented by the following Lewis structures in which each dash (-) represents a pair of electrons:

| Sulfate ion | Thiosulfate ion | Carbonate ion | Trithiocarbonate ion |

For each of the ions, only one of the resonance structures is pictured. The two carbonate ions are planar (using sp^2 hybridization at carbon) whereas the two sulfate ions are tetrahedral.

The thiosulfate ion can be synthesized by a reaction between the sulfite ion and sulfur [Eq. (1)].

$$8 \, \text{sulfite} + S_8 \rightarrow 8 \, \text{thiosulfate}^{2-} \tag{1}$$

Sulfite ion + elemental sulfur ⟶ thiosulfate ion

The trithiocarbonate ion can be synthesized by a combination of sulfide ion with carbon disulfide as:

$$|\overline{\underline{S}}|^{2-} + |\overline{S}=C=\overline{S}| \rightarrow |\overline{S}=C \underset{|\underline{S}|}{\overset{|\overline{S}|^{2-}}{\diagup}} \tag{2}$$

Sulfide ion + carbon disulfide ⟶ trithiocarbonate ion

The thiosulfate ion can be converted into the tetrathionate ion $S_4O_6^{2-}$ (part 2) by oxidation with iodine [Eq. (3)].

$$2 \, \text{thiosulfate} + I_2 \rightarrow \text{tetrathionate}^{2-} + 2I^- \tag{3}$$

A. Syntheses of Phosphorus Compounds

1. Disodium Hydrogen Phosphate·Dodecahydrate, $Na_2HPO_4 \cdot 12H_2O$

The raw material from which phosphorus and its compounds are prepared industrially is calcium phosphate, either as natural phosphate rock or as bone ash. For laboratory preparations, bone ash is preferable because it is nearly free of fluorides and iron compounds. The bone ash may be assumed to be 80% $Ca_3(PO_4)_2$, 10% $CaCO_3$, and 10% inert material. When bone ash is dissolved in sulfuric acid, the following reactions may occur:

$$CaCO_3 + H_2SO_4 \longrightarrow CaSO_4\downarrow + CO_2\uparrow + H_2O \tag{4}$$

$$Ca_3(PO_4)_2 + 3 H_2SO_4 \longrightarrow 3 CaSO_4\downarrow + 2 H_3PO_4 \text{ (soluble)} \tag{5}$$

$$Ca_3(PO_4)_2 + 2 H_2SO_4 \longrightarrow 2 CaSO_4\downarrow + Ca(H_2PO_4)_2 \text{ (soluble)} \tag{6}$$

$$Ca_3(PO_4)_2 + H_2SO_4 \longrightarrow CaSO_4\downarrow + 2 CaHPO_4\downarrow \tag{7}$$

The inert material does not react with the acid and can be separated by filtration with the insoluble calcium salts.

It can be seen from Eqs. (4) and (7) that if all of the phosphate is to be dissolved, a sufficient amount of sulfuric acid must be used to react with all of the calcium carbonate and to provide more than 2 moles of sulfuric acid per mole of calcium phosphate. However, there must not be more than 3 moles of sulfuric acid per mole of calcium phosphate, as shown in Eq. (5) because the excess acid would remain in solution and cause the product to be contaminated with calcium sulfate after neutralization. A quantity of sulfuric acid is chosen, therefore, that is more than sufficient to complete Eq. (6) but insufficient to exceed Eq. (5).

After removal of the insoluble calcium sulfate, the filtrate is neutralized with sodium carbonate which reacts according to Eqs. (8) and (9).

$$H_3PO_4 + Na_2CO_3 \longrightarrow Na_2HPO_4 + CO_2\uparrow + H_2O \tag{8}$$

$$Ca(H_2PO_4)_2 + 2 Na_2CO_3 \longrightarrow 2 Na_2HPO_4 + CaCO_3\downarrow + CO_2\uparrow + H_2O \tag{9}$$

An excess of sodium carbonate does not convert disodium hydrogen phosphate into trisodium orthophosphate because the orthophosphate ion, PO_4^{3-}, is a stronger base than the carbonate ion, CO_3^{2-}. The ionization constants K_a (or K_2) of the conjugate acids, HCO_3^- and HPO_4^{2-} are 4.8×10^{-11} and 3.6×10^{-13}, respectively. Because the position of equilibrium lies always toward the weaker acid, the reaction represented by Eq. (10) is favored instead of the reverse reaction.

$$NaHCO_3 + Na_3PO_4 \longrightarrow Na_2HPO_4 + Na_2CO_3 \tag{10}$$

PROCEDURE

Place 30 g of bone ash [~80% $Ca_3(PO_4)_2$, labeled "for Exp. 24"] in a 6-inch porcelain evaporating dish, add 30 mL of distilled or de-ionized water, and stir the mixture until a thick paste is obtained. Stir it with a porcelain spatula or a glass stirring rod, and add 14.1 mL of concentrated (18 M) H_2SO_4 as rapidly as is possible without causing excessive heating. CAUTION! 18 M H_2SO_4 IS VERY CORROSIVE! Continue to stir the mixture vigorously until it begins to stiffen. This usually requires 10 to 15 minutes. Slowly add 150 mL of cold distilled or de-ionized water, and stir the mixture until a thin paste, free from lumps, is obtained. Filter the cold mixture on a Büchner funnel, using a gentle suction (Techniques Section, p. 11). Wash the solid in the funnel with 15 mL of cold water, and then discard the precipitate. Combine the filtrates, and add to them solid anhydrous sodium carbonate, Na_2CO_3, in small portions, with stirring, until effervescence no longer takes place and a

Treat bone ash with H_2SO_4.

Filter and evaporate solution.

drop of the solution turns the phenolphthalein indicator solution pink (**Note 1**). This should require 16.5 to 18 g of Na_2CO_3. Filter and evaporate the solution to about 80 mL. Transfer the clear liquid (filter while hot, if necessary) to a 4-inch crystallizing dish, cover it so that dust cannot fall into the dish, and allow it to stand until the next laboratory period so that a satisfactory crop of crystals is obtained. Decant the liquid from the crystals, and rinse them with 5 to 10 mL of cold distilled or de-ionized water.

Disodium hydrogen phosphate, $Na_2HPO_4 \cdot 12H_2O$, is effluorescent (**Note 2**). Such crystals should be dried as quickly as possible and protected from the carbon dioxide of the air. To do this, quicky press the disodium hydrogen phosphate crystals between large pieces of filter paper until as much of the liquid as possible is absorbed. Then enclose the crysals in a tightly folded package of three or four layers of fresh filter paper, and leave it in the desk for not more than 48 hours (**Note 3**). The layers of filter paper permit the water to be soaked and minimize diffusion of air through the paper with consequent contamination of the crystals by carbon dioxide absorption. When the product is dry, place it in a closed bottle until needed for the second part of this experiment.

Isolate crystals of product.

Test 0.1 M KH_2PO_4, 0.1 M Na_2HPO_4, and 0.1 M Na_3PO_4 solutions with litmus paper. Explain and write equations for your observations. How can a compound be an acid salt and give an alkaline test to litmus? Check the pH of each solution with pH paper. Which is more basic? Why?

Test known phosphate solutions.

2. Synthesis of a Heteropoly Anion of Phosphorus

As the pH is lowered, the oxyanions of elements in Subgroups VB and VIB undergo self-condensation to form condensed (or _isopoly_) anions. For example, ammonium molybdate, the chief source of molybdenum compounds in the laboratory, has the composition $(NH_4)_6Mo_7O_{24}$. The highly symmetric anion has a central molybdenum atom in an octahedral hole of a "cage" formed by condensation of six molybdate ions so that each molybdenum atom has an octahedral MoO_6 unit sharing edges (Fig. 24-1). The central molybdenum atom, but apparently no others, may be replaced by other elements such as iodine, iron, chromium, or cobalt, which can sustain the six-coordination with oxygen. The latter condensed species are referred to as _heteropoly_ anions since they contain two different types of anions.

Just as it is possible to copolymerize organic compounds, e.g., 1,3-butadiene and styrene in synthetic rubber, one can also copolymerize some inorganic oxyanions. For example, condensed anions (and acids) having characteristic yellow colors are formed by the condensation of simple anions such as AsO_4^{3-}, PO_4^{3-}, and SiO_4^{4-} with a large but definite amount of molybdenum(VI), MoO_3 oxide. Analogous heteropoly anions based on vanadium and tungsten are also known.

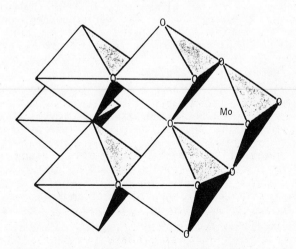

Figure 24-1. Arrangement of MoO$_6$ octahedra in a 6-acid

The heteropoly anions (and acids) are usually described in terms of the number of molybdenum (or tungsten or vanadium) atoms associated with the other anionic atom, such as phosphorus, in the empirical formula. Three main classes of heteropoly species are now recognized: the 6-, the 9-, and the 12-polyacids. The large polyanions are important as (1) good precipitating agents for high molecular weight cations such as in proteins, (2) agents for producing intense and excellent quality color toners for the printing industry, (3) catalysts for hydrocarbon reactions, and (4) analytical reagents. X-ray crystallography has recently provided a basis for systematically classifying the different series of isopoly and heteropoly compounds. Fig. 24-2 shows the structure of 12-phosphotungstic acid. The hetero-atom phosphorus occupies a tetrahedral hole in a "cage" formed by 12 WO_6-bridged octahedra. Fig. 24-3 depicts how each oxygen atom of the PO_4^{3-} ion is bridged equally to three tungsten atoms. The $[PMo_{12}O_{40}]^{3-}$ salts have analogous structures.

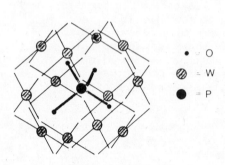

Figure 24-2

The structure of the $[PW_{12}O_{40}]^{3-}$ anion in the 12-polyacids. The PO_4 tetrahedron is shown with heavy black lines whereas the WO_6 or MoO_6 octahedra are drawn with thin lines.

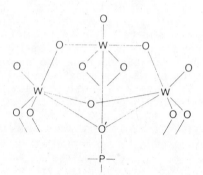

Figure 24-3

Illustration of how each oxygen of PO_4^{3-} is bridged to three WO_6 octahedra. (MoO_6 is analogous.)

In this experiment we will prepare a yellow crystalline 12-phosphomolybdate salt, using the sodium dihydrogen orthophosphate. We will also qualitatively test the effect of reducing agents on the color of the $[PMo_{12}O_{40}]^{3-}$ ion.

PROCEDURE

Dissolve $Na_2HPO_4 \cdot 12H_2O$.

Dissolve 2.0 g of $Na_2HPO_4 \cdot 12H_2O$ or 1.5 g of $Na_2HPO_4 \cdot 7H_2O$ in 30 mL of 8 M nitric acid contained in a 150-mL Erlenmeyer flask, and cool the solution to room temperature, if necessary. Add 60 mL of 0.2 M ammonium molybdate solution (**Note 4**) an eyedropperful at a time, while stirring with a glass rod. A deep yellow, microcrystalline salt should precipitate immediately. Collect the compound on a Büchner funnel (Techniques Section, p. 11), and then wash it twice with 10-mL portions of hot water to which a few drops of concentrated nitric acid have been added. Dry the crystals in air for 5 minutes, and then dry them in the desiccator until the next laboratory period. Transfer the dry materials to a weighed sample vial, and determine the yield.

Add molybdate solution.

Collect and dry the yellow compound.

Label the bottle, and give it to your instructor, along with the remainder of your sample from Part 1 of this experiment.

Test of phosphate.

Qualitative Test for Phosphate. Dissolve a small crystal of your disodium hydrogen phosphate in 0.5 mL of H_2O, make it acidic with 1 drop of nitric acid, and place 2 or 3 drops of the solution on a piece of filter paper. Add 1 drop each of ammonium molybdate and D-72 developer. A blue stain, with the intensity depending on the phosphate content, indicates the presence of phosphate.

The reduction of the simple and heteropoly anions of molybdenum and tungsten leads to bright blue colors which have intense electronic absorption bands in the spectral region 700 to 800 nm. It is thought that the color results from reduction of approximately 4 of the 12 molybdenum atoms in the heteropoly anion, permitting some electronic charge transfer to occur in which an electron on a Mo(V) atom jumps to a Mo(VI) atom within the "cage" structure of the heteropoly anion. Reducing agents include salts of Cu(I), Sn(II), Sb(III), Fe(II), Hg(I), and Tl(I).

Possible Research Extensions. If you are interested and have laboratory time available, several interesting additional studies could be undertaken with these materials.

1. You could investigate other reducing agents to obtain the "molybdenum blue" color.

2. You could construct an absorbance (at the wavelength of maximum absorbance) vs. concentration curve by using different volumes of a carefully prepared standard solution of $Na_2HPO_4 \cdot 2H_2O$ with a spectrophotometer after developing the blue color.

Other possible reactions.

3. You may wish to obtain the free acid $H_3[PMo_{12}O_{40}]$ by ion-exchange of the ammonium salt (see Ref. 2, p. 321).

4. You may wish to prepare the nearly colorless phosphotungstate ion $[PW_{12}O_{40}]^{3-}$ (see Ref. 2, p. 321].

Check with your instructor before undertaking any of these suggested extensions.

B. Syntheses of Sulfur Compounds

1. Preparation of Potassium Thiosulfate, $3 K_2S_2O_3 \cdot 5H_2O$

The sulfite ion, which contains sulfur with an oxidation number of +4, can be oxidized easily by oxygen or sulfur to form the sulfate ion, SO_4^{2-}, or the thiosulfate ion, $S_2O_3^{2-}$, respectively, in which the (formal) oxidation number of the <u>central</u> sulfur atom is +6. The two sulfur atoms in $S_2O_3^{2-}$ are quite different chemically.

PROCEDURE

Prepare a slurry of 3 g of sulfur in 5 to 6 mL of 22% ammonium sulfide, $(NH_4)_2S$, contained in a 125-mL Erlenmeyer flask. Prepare a solution by dissolving 15 g of potassium sulfite dihydrate, $K_2SO_3 \cdot 2H_2O$, in 40 mL of water. Add 1.0 mL of the sulfite solution to the slurry of sulfur in ammonium sulfide. Swirl the flask for 1 minute to mix the reagents. Continue adding the sulfite solution in 1.0-mL increments, swirling the flask for one minute after each addition.

Combine the reagents.

Remove any undissolved or suspended material by gravity filtration through a long-stemmed funnel (Techniques Section, p. 9). Boil the filtrate in a 125-mL Erlenmeyer flask in the hood for 10 minutes to drive out the ammonium sulfide as gaseous NH_3 and H_2S. Then concentrate the filtrate to a volume of 15 mL (**Note 13**).

Filter the mixture, heat to boiling, and evaporate the filtrate.

Cool the beaker in ice to induce crystallization. Potassium thiosulfate often forms supersaturated solutions; hence, scratching the bottom of the beaker with a glass rod or adding a small seed crystal of potassium thiosulfate may be necessary to obtain crystals. Collect the cold crystals by suction filtration* as rapidly as possible to prevent redissolving the crystals (**Note 5**). Concentrate the filtrate to 5 mL, and cool it in an ice bath to obtain an additional batch of crystals. The total sample should be 10 to 12 g (**Note 13**).

Collect the resultant crystals.

*The Büchner funnels must be washed <u>very</u> thoroughly if any work was done previously with PO_4^{3-} solutions.

Dry the crystals.   Remove the absorbed water from the crystals by pressing them between two pieces of filter paper; then dry the crystals on a watch glass in your desiccator until the next laboratory period.

Determine % yield.   Determine the total weight of crystals, and place each batch in a separate, labeled bottle. Use the first batch for determination of purity. Calculate the percentage yield in the preparation on the basis of the amount of potassium sulfite used.

Test the compound in HCl.   Dissolve about 0.5 g of the product in 5 mL of water, and add 2 mL of dilute hydrochloric acid. Carefully observe the odor of the gas and the color of the precipitate. What is the free acid that corresponds to the salt, potassium thiosulfate? What may you conclude about the stability of this acid? Write equations in your laboratory notebook to represent the reaction of the thiosulfate ion with hydrochloric acid.

Test the product for SO_3^{2-}.   Test your product for the presence of unreacted potassium sulfite by the following method. Dissolve about 0.1 g of your product in 10 drops of distilled water in a 4-mL test tube. Add 10 drops of 0.4 M cobalt(II) chloride solution. A red (or carmine) precipitate of $CoSO_3$ indicates the presence of unreacted sulfite ions.

2. Preparation of Potassium Tetrathionate, $K_2S_4O_6$

PROCEDURE

In a 100-mL beaker, dissolve 8.9 g of sodium thiosulfate pentahydrate, $Na_2S_2O_3 \cdot 5H_2O$ and 12.8 g of potassium iodide, KI, in 10 mL of distilled water (**Note 6**). After the KI is dissolved, cool the solution in ice while you do the next step. Using the <u>triple-beam balance</u>, weigh 5.2 g of iodine, I_2 (**Note 7**), and dissolve it in 30 mL of <u>absolute</u> ethyl

Dissolve the reagents and combine dropwise.   alcohol, C_2H_5OH, in a 125-mL Erlenmeyer flask. Plug the flask with a rubber stopper, and shake it briskly until all of the iodine has dissolved. Add the iodine solution drop by drop, with stirring, to the cold thiosulfate solution. <u>Very vigorous stirring is needed during the addition</u>. The reaction is instantaneous. Potassium tetrathionate, which is insoluble in ethyl alcohol, separates as small crystals or a lumpy solid. When the addition is complete, collect the solid on a Büchner funnel, and wash it with 5-mL portions of alcohol until the wash solution is free of iodine and iodide. Collect a few drops of the wash solution, and then test for iodide ion, I^-, using the procedure described on p.328. (How can you detect the absence of iodine?)

Collect and dry the crystals.   To purify the salt, redissolve it in a minimum amount of water at room temperature, and reprecipitate it by stirring in 3 volumes of absolute ethyl alcohol. The precipitate of small, shiny crystals should be pure anhydrous potassium tetrathionate. Dry the crystals by pressing them between filter paper, and then place them on a watch glass in the desiccator until the next laboratory period (**Note 8**).

Weigh the potassium tetrathionate crystals, and calculate the percentage yield on the basis of the amount of sodium thiosulfate used. Place the sample in a labeled bottle, and give it to your instructor.

3. Preparation of Barium Trithiocarbonate, $BaCS_3$

PROCEDURE

Dissolve barium hydroxide.   Dissolve 15 g of barium hydroxide in approximately 75 mL (or less) of warm water in the following manner: add the barium hydroxide to 10 mL of H_2O and heat slightly with stirring; add another 10 mL of H_2O, heat, and stir; repeat this process until all (or nearly all) of the barium hydroxide dissolves. Divide this solution into two equal parts.

Hydrogen sulfide generators, like that shown in Fig. 24-4, are in the hood, and they are to be used in the hood (**Note 9**). Warm the tube gently to liberate the hydrogen sulfide gas. Saturate one portion of the barium hydroxide solution with hydrogen sulfide (be sure the generator tube extends nearly to the bottom of the flask), and then add to it the other portion of the barium hydroxide solution. This gives a solution of barium sulfide.

Add H$_2$S to one half of the barium hydroxide.

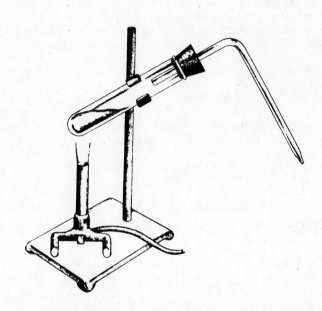

Figure 24-4. Apparatus for generating hydrogen sulfide

Filter the solution, using suction filtration, to remove undissolved barium hydroxide, barium carbonate (**Note 10**), and any elemental sulfur that may have formed. Wash the residue with a little distilled water until it is nearly colorless; let the washings run into the filtrate. Discard the residue.

Filter the solution.

At the hood, add 3 mL of carbon disulfide, CS$_2$ (**Note 11**), to the barium sulfide solution, stopper the flask, and shake vigorously (at the hood) for about 10 minutes. **CAUTION:** the flask must be unstoppered frequently to prevent the build-up of pressure from vaporized carbon disulfide. During this process, barium trithiocarbonate will precipitate as a yellow crystalline powder. All of the carbon disulfide should react.

Carefully add CS$_2$.

Collect the product by filtration, and return the filtrate to the flask. A second crop of crystals may be obtained by adding absolute alcohol to the filtrate (**Note 12**). Add approximately 10 mL at a time until no more precipitate appears to form. Add these crystals to the first batch on the filter, wash them first with a few mL of cold distilled or de-ionized water, then with 50% alcohol, and finally with absolute alcohol. The first washing removes unreacted barium sulfide; the alcohol wash removes water so the product can be dried more easily. Dry the yellow crystals between filter paper until the next lab period. Turn in the product in a labeled bottle.

Collect, wash, and dry the compound.

NOTEBOOK AND REPORT

Record in your notebook the quantities of reagents used for each synthesis and any observations that differed from the procedure described in this manual. Prepare a

321

report on the experiment that includes a brief statement of the purpose and procedure, complete and balanced quations for all reactions, a statement about any difficulties encountered, and any modifications that you made in the procedure.

For <u>one</u> of the three syntheses, explain in terms of sound chemical principles and procedures why it was necessary to do each of the things specified in the procedure. For example, in the preparation of potassium thiosulfate: Why were potassium sulfite crystals dissolved in water? Why was the mixture boiled? Was the length of heating chosen the proper length of time? Why could sulfur separate from the solution? Why is the solution evaporated to 15 mL? There are several other points to consider.

If you are not able to answer these questions, try to find the answers by thinking carefully about each step of the reaction, by going to the library (books on inorganic preparations may be useful), and finally by asking your instructor. Your instructor should not be expected to supply answers to the questions when you can collect enough information to arrive at a satisfactory answer without help.

CALCULATIONS

Indicate in your notebook and report the data used and the arithmetic steps needed to determine the number of moles of reagents and products and the percentage yield of the product.

NOTES

Note 1.   A 0.5 to 1% phenolphthalein indicator solution is used. Students should not add phenolphthalein to the entire solution; use one drop of your solution as instructed.

Note 2.   An effluorescent substance is subject to changing to a powdery substance throughout or on the surface upon exposure to air, as a crystalline substance changing through loss of water of crystallization.

Note 3.   If you do not intend to return to the laboratory within two days, store the solid in your desiccator.

Note 4.   Commercial ammonium molybdate is generally $(NH_4)_6Mo_7O_{24} \cdot 4H_2O$. The 0.2 M solution is to contain 250 g of $(NH_4)_6Mo_7O_{24} \cdot 4H_2O$ and 1.5 moles of NH_3 per liter.

Note 5.   Potassium thiosulfate is very soluble in water at room temperature; thus, the filtration must be done while the mixture is cold and as rapidly as possible.

Note 6.   At room temperature, a long mixing time will be required to dissolve all of the KI, so warm the solution gently.

Note 7.   An aluminum weighing dish cannot be used to weigh the I_2. Iodine and aluminum react.

Note 8.   The potassium tetrathionate crystals are colorless and platelike or prismatic in shape; the pure dry material is stable for a very long time without change, but it decomposes if potassium thiosulfate or occluded mother liquor is present, producing a characteristic odor. When strongly heated, potassium tetrathionate decomposes to potassium sulfate, sulfur dioxide, and sulfur.

The compound potassium tetrathionate is readily soluble in water: 12.60 g per 100 g of H_2O at 0 $^{\circ}C$; it is insoluble in ethyl alcohol. An aqueous solution of potassium tetrathionate undergoes disproportionation slowly to potassium tri-thionate, $K_2S_3O_6$, and potassium pentathionate, $K_2S_5O_6$.

Note 9.   Hydrogen sulfide is toxic. The reaction and the shaking should be performed in the hood.

Note 10.   Barium carbonate may be formed (due to carbon dioxide, CO_2, from the air). This must be removed by filtration before continuing.

Note 11.   CARBON DISULFIDE IS EXTREMELY FLAMMABLE; be sure there are no flames near where carbon disulfide is being poured or near your work space.

Note 12.   Beware of careless technique when C_2H_5OH and flames are not far apart. The alcohol has been denatured--it is poisonous (and it cannot be made fit for human consumption).

Note 13.   The experimental set-up for the apparatus for directing a stream of air across the surface is given on p. 47.

REFERENCES

1.   Schlessinger, G. G.: _Inorganic Laboratory Preparations_. Chemical Publishing Co., New York, 1962, pp. 40, 50, and 66-68.

2.   Brauer, G.: _Handbook of Preparative Inorganic Chemistry_. Academic Press, New York, 1963, pp. 399-400, 543-552, and 1698-1735.

3.   Davis, Gailey, and Whitten, _Principles of Chemistry_, Saunders College Publishing, Philadelphia, 1984, pp. 566-568, 716-719, and 737-739.

4.   Whitten and Gailey, _General Chemistry_, Saunders College Publishing, Philadelphia, 1984, pp. 568-570, 728-730, and 751-754.

Experiment 24

PREPARATIONS OF PHOSPHORUS AND SULFUR OXYANIONS

QUESTIONS

1. What type of experiment could one do to prove that the central sulfur atom in $S_2O_3^{2-}$ did not come from the elemental sulfur used in the synthesis?

2. How do you explain the yellow color of barium trithiocarbonate whereas barium carbonate, potassium thiosulfate, and potassium tetrathionate are white crystals?

3. Balance the following equation that represents the reaction for the formation of the molybdenum heteropoly anion. Show the steps in your method for balancing the equation.

$$\underline{}HNO_3 \ + \ \underline{}Na_2HPO_4 \ + \ \underline{}(NH_4)_6Mo_7O_{24}\cdot4H_2O \ \longrightarrow$$

$$\underline{}(NH_4)_3PMo_{12}O_{40} \ + \ \underline{}NaNO_3 \ + \ \underline{}NH_4NO_3 \ + \ \underline{}H_2O$$

4. Acid decomposes barium trithiocarbonate to give an unstable oily substance, trithiocarbonic acid (H_2CS_3), which dissociates into carbon disulfide and hydrogen sulfide. Write the equations.

PREPARATIONS OF PHOSPHORUS AND SULFUR OXYANIONS

PRELABORATORY QUESTIONS

Name_____   Lab Instructor_____

Student ID No._____   Date_____

1. Using the preparative conditions of the experiment, what controls the pH of the solution so that you can isolate the $Na_2HPO_4 \cdot 12H_2O$ compound rather than compounds containing the $H_2PO_4^-$ or PO_4^{3-} ions in Part A-1?

2. If the reduced heteropoly anion of molybdenum absorbs in the 600- to 800-nm region, why is it blue?

3. What can you deduce about the absorption region in the yellow heteropoly anions? Is the energy of the absorption higher or lower than for the blue form? Why?

4. What is the average oxidation number of sulfur in each of the following ions: the sulfite ion, thiosulfate ion, tetrathionate ion, and trithiocarbonate ion?

5. From a practical consideration, why is it preferable to use a slight excess of
    polysulfide, S_x^{2-}, rather than an excess of potassium sulfite in the synthesis of
    potassium thiosulfate?

Experiment 24

PREPARATIONS OF PHOSPHORUS AND SULFUR OXYANIONS

REPORT SHEET

Name_____   Lab Instructor_____

Student ID No._____   Date_____

Synthesis of _____

A. State concisely what each step in the procedure accomplished in terms of physical
    transformations or chemical reactions.

B. Balanced equation(s) for all of the important reactions of the synthesis

C.   **Properties of the product (color, crystal shape, etc.)**

D.   **Calculation of yield(s)**

 1.   Theoretical yield (show calculations) _____

 2.   Weight obtained (g) _____

 3.   Percentage yield obtained _____

CHEMISTRY OF THE HALOGEN ELEMENTS AND THEIR COMPOUNDS

Objective

To explore the chemistry of the halogen (Group VIIA) elements in different oxidation states in compounds

Equipment

Burner; 16 x 150-mm test tubes; 4-mL test tubes; medicine droppers; filter paper (Whatman No. 1 or equivalent); 6-, 7.5, or 9-V battery; microspatula; Petri dish

Reagents Needed

Solid sodium chloride, NaCl; solid sodium bromide, NaBr; solid sodium bromate, $NaBrO_3$ (or potassium bromate, $KBrO_3$); solid potassium iodide, KI; solid potassium iodate, KIO_3; solid manganese dioxide, MnO_2; 0.1 M $AgNO_3$; 0.1 M NaCl; 0.1 M KBr; saturated NaBr; 0.1 M KI; 6 M HNO_3; 2 M NH_3; concentrated (18 M) sulfuric acid; chlorine water; 1,2-dichloroethane; 6 M NaOH; phenolphthalein indicator solution

INTRODUCTION

The common halogens--fluorine, chlorine, bromine, and iodine--comprise a group of elements that exhibit similar chemical properties. Fluorine reacts with other elements to form compounds in which the oxidation number (state) of fluorine is always -1. The other halogen elements show, in addition to -1 oxidation number, a number of positive oxidation numbers, +1 and +5 being common.

This experiment suggests some procedures for identifying the presence of chlorine, bromine, and iodine in compounds and illustrates some oxidation/reduction reactions that can occur among the halogen compounds. Also, the halogens in the -1 state are treated with three non-halogen oxidizing agents: manganese dioxide, MnO_2 (in the presence of acid); sulfuric acid, H_2SO_4 (concentrated); and an electrical potential supplied by a lantern battery. Manganese dioxide, acting as an oxidizing agent under the conditions of this experiment, is reduced to the manganese(II) ion, Mn^{2+}.

Oxidation state of S	Compound	Properties
-2	H_2S	Colorless gas, smelling like rotten eggs
0	S_8	Yellow powdery solid which becomes brown liquid when heated to 100 °C
+4	SO_2	Colorless gas with a choking odor; recall the odor when elemental sulfur was burned in Experiment 4

Sulfuric acid, H_2SO_4, is used for two purposes in this experiment. **In dilute solutions, it is added simply to make the solution acidic;** in concentrated form, it is a good oxidizing agent. In sulfuric acid, sulfur has an oxidation number of +6. Thus, when concentrated sulfuric acid is reduced, the products could be any of the compounds containing sulfur with an oxidation number lower than +6. Other compounds are also possible but are outside the scope of this experiment.

PROCEDURE

PART A.   REACTIONS OF CHLORIDE, BROMIDE, AND IODIDE IONS

1.   Tests for the Ions

A.   Chloride Ion. Recall your tests for chloride ion, in Experiment 3 (pp. 59-60 of this laboratory manual). If your notebook record of that test is not clear, repeat it, paying particular attention to the observations needed to answer the questions at the end of this experiment.

B.   Test of Bromide Ion. Dilute 5 drops of 0.1 M KBr to 5 mL with water. Add 10 drops of 3 M HNO_3 and 10 drops of 0.1 M $AgNO_3$. Is the precipitate formed in this case the same color as that from chloride? Centrifuge the solution and discard the clear liquid. Add 1 mL of distilled water, and shake the test tube to wash the precipitate, centrifuge, and decant the clear liquid. Treat the washed precipitate with 2 mL of 2 M ammonia solution, and, if the precipitate does not dissolve completely, centrifuge the mixture. Decant the clear liquid into a clean test tube, and acidify the liquid with 3 M HNO_3. What do you observe? From this experiment, is silver bromide very soluble in 2 M ammonia? Is there enough difference in the solubility of silver chloride and silver bromide in 2 M ammonia so that you could make a good separation of these two substances? How would you perform this separation if both were present? The reaction for the bromide precipitation is:

$$Ag^+ \ + \ Br^- \ \longrightarrow \ AgBr\downarrow$$
$$\text{cream}$$
$$\text{color}$$

C.   Test for Iodide Ion. Repeat all of the steps given above for the bromide ion using 5 drops of 0.1 M KI instead of KBr. Is the solubility difference between silver chloride and silver iodide in 2 M ammonia sufficient for you to separate silver chloride from silver iodide if both of these substances were present in the mixture? The reaction for formation of the iodide precipitate is:

$$Ag^+ \ + \ I^- \ \longrightarrow \ AgI\downarrow$$
$$\text{yellow}$$

2.   Oxidation of a Bromide or Iodide Salt with Chlorine.

In a clean (but not necessarily dry) 16 x 150-mm test tube, put a microspatula full of solid sodium bromide; in a second 16 ×150-mm test tube, place a like quantity of solid potassium iodide. Add 3 mL of water to each tube to dissolve the solids; then add chlorine water, dropwise, until a color change is noted. Now add 3 mL of 1,2-dichloroethane to each. Close the test tube with a stopper, and shake it vigorously. Release the stopper cautiously to avoid spattering, and wipe the stopper dry. Set the test tubes aside until the liquid layers separate, and record your observations in your notebook.

Repeat Procedure 2 with a small quantity (about enough to cover one-eighth of the spoon of a small spatula) of each of sodium bromide and potassium iodide in the same test tube. Add 2 mL of water, then add 1 mL of 1,2-dichloroethane, and then add 10 drops of chlorine water. Shake the tube, allow the liquid layers to separate, and remove the 1,2-dichloroethane layer (the bottom layer) and add it to a 4-mL test tube using a medicine dropper. To the water layer, add a second quantity of 1,2-dichloroethane (1 mL) and 5 drops of chlorine water, shake it, allow the liquid layers to separate, and remove the 1,2-dichloroethane layer into a second 4-mL test tube. Repeat this procedure 3 times, adding fresh 1,2-dichloroethane and fresh chlorine water each time. Compare the colors of the 5 samples of 1,2-dichloroethane removed, and record the results in your notebook. If all 5 samples look the same, then continue the extraction process until a color change becomes apparent.

3. Oxidation of Halogen Compounds in the -1 State.

Set 3 clean, dry 16 x 150-mm test tubes in your test-tube rack, and put a microspatula full of manganese dioxide into each. Now place a similar amount of sodium chloride into the first test tube, of sodium bromide into the second, and of potassium iodide into the third. Twist the spatula (clean between the stirrings) in each of the solids to mix the black and white materials. With a medicine dropper, add 4 or 5 drops of 9 M sulfuric acid to each tube in turn. Record your observations in your notebook.

4. Reduction of Sulfuric Acid by Halide Ions.

Repeat the above experiment, using dry 16 x 150-mm test tubes with sodium chloride, sodium bromide, and potassium iodide; however, this time, do NOT add manganese dioxide; i.e., add only concentrated sulfuric acid, and warm gently. Remove the test tube from the flame, fan the fumes CAUTIOUSLY toward you, and then gently blow your breath across the top of each tube in turn. Record all observations in your notebook.

5. Oxidation by Electrolysis.
Put 5-10 mL of 0.1 M KI solution into a 16 x 150-mm test tube, and add 10 drops of phenolphthalein solution. Shake to mix the solutions. Place a piece of filter paper on a Petri dish, and, using a medicine dropper, saturate the filter paper with the KI/phenolphthalein solution. Touch the two wires from a battery to the wet paper, holding the ends of the wires about 1 cm apart. Leave the wires touching the paper for an instant, and then lift and touch, still 1 cm apart, another place on the paper for a longer time. Record your observations.

Repeat Procedure 5, using a saturated solution of sodium bromide and phenolphthalein and then using a solution of sodium chloride and phenolphthalein. Clean the wires with distilled or de-ionized water after each experiment. Record your observations in each case.

PART B. REACTIONS OF BROMATES AND IODATES

1. Reaction of a Bromide with a Bromate.

In each of two test tubes, place small quantities of both sodium bromide and sodium bromate.* Add 3 mL of water to each test tube, and shake it. After each mixture has dissolved, add 1 mL of 1,2-dichloroethane, and shake it. To one of the test tubes, add a few drops of concentrated sulfuric acid, and shake it. Record your observations. Use a medicine dropper to remove the 1,2-dichloroethane layer from the test tube containing the sulfuric acid, and place it into a 4-mL test tube. Add several drops of 6 M sodium hydroxide to the 1,2-dichloroethane layer, and shake it. Record your observations.

---

*Potassium bromate may be substituted for sodium bromate.

2. Reaction of an Iodide with an Iodate.

Repeat the experiment described in B1 using two test tubes with mixtures containing potassium iodide and potassium iodate. Record your observations.

3. Distinguishing between Iodate and Bromate.

Place a small quantity of sodium bromate in a test tube. Put a similar quantity of potassium iodate in another. To each tube add 5-6 drops of concentrated sulfuric acid. Heat each tube gently, and record the results.

PART C. IDENTIFICATION OF THE ANION IN AN UNKNOWN

Your instructor will assign you an unknown compound. The unknown will be either a sodium salt or a potassium salt containing one of the following anions: IO_3^-, BrO_3^-, I^-, Br^-, Cl^-. Perform tests described in Parts A and B on your unknown. Choose the tests wisely; some tests are more definitive than others. From these tests, determine the identity of the anion in your assigned salt.

REFERENCES

1. Jolly, W. L.: <u>Chemistry of the Non-metals</u> Prentice-Hall, Englewood Cliffs, NJ, 1966, Chapter 4.
2. Johnson, R. C.: <u>Introductory Descriptive Chemistry</u>, W.A. Benjamin, Inc., New York, NY, 1966, Chapter 6.
3. Davis, Gailey, and Whitten, <u>Principles of Chemistry</u>, Saunders College Publishing, Philadelphia, 1984, pp. 700-711.
4. Whitten and Gailey, <u>General Chemistry</u>, Saunders College Publishing, Philadelphia, 1984, pp. 699-709.

Experiment 25

CHEMISTRY OF THE HALOGEN ELEMENTS

PRELABORATORY QUESTIONS

Name_____   Lab Instructor_____

Student ID No._____   Date_____

1. Compare the electron configuration of atoms of chlorine, bromine, and iodine; also, for each, compare the electron configuration of the atoms with their ions in the -1 oxidation state.

2. What would you need to know about bromine and potassium iodide in order to predict what would happen if you added bromine water to potassium iodide solution? Look up this information in your textbook and make the prediction.

3. List all substances present in a solution of chlorine and water. If sodium hydroxide is added to cold chlorine water, what substances will be present in the resulting solution? Check your textbook in the halogen chapter.

4. Write electron-dot formulas for chloric acid and for perchloric acid. Which would you predict to be the stronger acid? Give your reasons.

Experiment 25

CHEMISTRY OF THE HALOGEN ELEMENTS

REPORT SHEET

Name_____   Lab Instructor_____

Student ID No._____   Date_____

Part A

1. What did you observe when:

    a) You added silver nitrate to a bromide salt?

    b) You added ammonia to the solid obtained in a)?

    c) You added nitric acid to the solution from b)?

    d) Write balanced equations for the reactions that occurred to produce the observations of a), b), and c).

e)   Compare the results of the tests on potassium iodide with the results
     with potassium bromide.

2.   a)   Write equations for all reactions that occurred in Part A2 of the
          experiment.

     b)   What purpose does the 1,2-dichloroethane serve?

3.   What conclusions can you draw from this series of experiments?

CHEMISTRY OF THE HALOGEN ELEMENTS

REPORT SHEET
(continued)

Name_____   Lab Instructor_____

Student ID No._____   Date_____

PART A

4. a)   What did you observe when you treated a chloride, a bromide, and an iodide
         salt with a combination of manganese dioxide and sulfuric acid?

    b)   Write a complete and balanced equation for the reaction of each of the
         three substances.

    c)   What substances were oxidized in the reactions of question 4a? Which
         substances were reduced?

    d)   If an oxidation-reduction reaction occurs, there must have been a transfer
         of electrons from one reactant to another. Write the two half-reactions
         for the reaction of a chloride with manganese dioxide in sulfuric acid,
         showing the gain of electrons by one reagent and the loss by another.

e) Write the two half-reactions of d) as if they were both reduction half-reactions.

f) If the chemical reagents on the left side of the half-reactions of d) are imagined to be competing for electrons, which reagent wins the competition, as shown by your experiments?

g) What do you conclude about the relative oxidizing power of manganese dioxide and chlorine in an acid medium? Does this conclusion apply also to the other halogens?

5. a) What did you observe when concentrated sulfuric acid was added to:

    i)   a chloride salt?

    i)   a bromide salt?

    iii) an iodide salt?

    b) Write equations for the reactions in each case in question 5a.

CHEMISTRY OF THE HALOGEN ELEMENTS

REPORT SHEET
(continued)

Name_____   Lab Instructor_____

Student ID No._____   Date_____

PART A

6.   What did you observe when a current was passed through a solution of phenol-
     phthalein and

   a)   potassium iodide?

   b)   sodium bromide?

   c)   sodium chloride?

   d)   Write equations for the reactions in each of the cases a), b), and c).

PART B

1.   What observations did you make concerning the behavior of the bromide/bromate
     mixture:

   a)   in water with 1,2-dichloroethane?

   b)   in water, sulfuric acid, and 1,2-dichloroethane?

c)   Write equations for all reactions that occurred.

d)   How does the equation suggest a reason for the difference in the observa-
     tions in a) and b) below?

e)   What observations did you record when sodium hydroxide was added to the
     1,2-dichloroethane layer?

f)   Write a balanced equation for the reaction that occurred.

2.   a)   What observations did you record about the behavior of the iodide/iodate
          mixture?

     b)   Write equations for all reactions that occurred for the tests in PART B.

3.   Describe the results when sulfuric acid was added to a solution of:

     a) $KBrO_3$

     b) KIO_3

340

CHEMISTRY OF HALOGEN ELEMENTS

REPORT SHEET
(continued)

Name_____   Lab Instructor_____

Student ID No._____   Date_____

Part C

Description of the sequence of tests developed for determining the identity of the anion in the unknown.

Results of the tests.

Identification of the anion in the unknown.

SYNTHESES OF THREE TRANSITION METAL COMPOUNDS

Objective

To prepare three transition metal compounds, a double salt, and two coordination compounds. These syntheses illustrate some of the common procedures used to prepare and isolate inorganic compounds.

Equipment Needed

Vacuum filtration apparatus (see Fig. 11 on p. 11 of the **Laboratory Techniques** section); Büchner funnel; 250-mL filter flask; filter vac; 250-mL bottle (for trap); two-hole rubber stopper, heavy walled tubing; 6-mm glass tubing; short piece of thread (6 in.)

Reagents Needed

$CuSO_4 \cdot 5 H_2O$, solid; $(NH_4)_2SO_4$, solid; 15M aqueous NH_3; 95% ethyl alcohol (ethanol); acetone; $Fe(NH_4)_2(SO_4)_2 \cdot 6 H_2O$, solid; 6M H_2SO_4 in dropping bottles; 1M oxalic acid, $H_2C_2O_4$; saturated aqueous $K_2C_2O_4$; 3% aqueous H_2O_2

TECHNIQUES

Study the description of vacuum filtration on p. 11 of the **Laboratory Techniques** section.

INTRODUCTION

Double salts consist of two simple salts crystallized together in simple stoichiometric proportions. For example, if equimolar quantities of the simple salts copper(II) sulfate pentahydrate, $CuSO_4 \cdot 5 H_2O$, and ammonium sulfate, $(NH_4)_2SO_4$, are dissolved in the minimum amount of hot water, cooling the solution results in the formation of crystals having the composition $CuSO_4 \cdot (NH_4)_2SO_4 \cdot 6 H_2O$. Dissolution of solid $CuSO_4 \cdot (NH_4)_2SO_4 \cdot 6 H_2O$ in water gives a solution containing the ions Cu^{2+} plus 2 NH_4^+ plus 2 SO_4^{2-}. Double salts are a phenomenon of the solid state, i.e., double salts exist **only** in the solid state.

Many **coordination compounds** (complex compounds) are salts. Most contain a simple ion and a complex ion. Complex salts contain groups (usually neutral molecules or anions) coordinated to one of the elements (usually the metal) of the salt. When an excess of aqueous ammonia is added to sky-blue aqueous copper(II) sulfate solutions, the solutions turn deep blue. The deep blue coloration is due to the presence of a complex cation that contains four neutral ammonia molecules coordinated to a copper(II) ion, i.e., $[Cu(NH_3)_4]^{2+}$. Formulas for complex species, i.e., the metal and molecules or anions contained in the coordination spheres, are enclosed in brackets. The deep blue-colored compound, $[Cu(NH_3)_4]SO_4 \cdot H_2O$ is a typical coordination compound. Its dissolution in water gives a solution that contains $[Cu(NH_3)_4]^{2+}$ and hydrated SO_4^{2-} ions in equal concentrations. Because $[Cu(NH_3)_4]SO_4 \cdot H_2O$ is quite soluble in water, it is usually isolated by adding a liquid such as ethyl alcohol to decrease the polarity of the solvent. If alcohol is poured carefully onto the surface of the aqueous solution of the complex compound, the slow diffusion of alcohol into the water results in the formation of long needle-like crystals of $[Cu(NH_3)_4]SO_4 \cdot H_2O$.

Another common coordination compound is $K_3[Fe(C_2O_4)_3] \cdot 3 H_2O$. Historically, this compound has been called potassium ferric oxalate. More properly, it is called potassium tris(oxalato)ferrate(III) trihydrate. This complex compound is not very soluble in cold water. Thus, allowing hot saturated solutions of the compound to cool slowly results in the formation of well-defined crystals. When the pure compound $K_3[Fe(C_2O_4)_3] \cdot 3 H_2O$ is placed in water, it does dissolve to some extent to produce solutions containing hydrated ions in the ratio three K^+ to one $[Fe(C_2O_4)_3]^{3-}$.

PROCEDURE

Preparation of a Double Salt: $CuSO_4 \cdot (NH_4)_2SO_4 \cdot 6 H_2O$

Weigh, mix, and heat reagents.

Place 40 mL of water in a 100-mL beaker, and then add 25 g of copper(II) sulfate pentahydrate, $CuSO_4 \cdot 5 H_2O$, and 13.2 g of ammonium sulfate, $(NH_4)_2SO_4$. Heat the mixture, with constant stirring, until the solids dissolved completely. Remove the burner, and place the beaker containing the hot solution on a towel. Allow the beaker to cool to room temperature, and then place it in an ice bath for 10 to 15 minutes. Collect the crystals that form on a Büchner funnel. Dry them by pressing the crystals between two or three pieces of filter paper. Place the crystals in a small, dry, previously weighed beaker or flask, and allow them to stand in your locker exposed to the open air until the next laboratory period. At that time, weigh the container and crystals, and calculate the percent yield. If requested, hand in the crystals to your laboratory instructor in a labelled container; in any case, show the crystals to your instructor and ask him/her to initial your data form.

Allow solution to cool; collect crystals.

Dry crystals.

The formation of $CuSO_4 \cdot (NH_4)_2SO_4 \cdot 6 H_2O$ can be represented by Eq. (1).

$$Cu^{2+} + 2 NH_4^+ + 2 SO_4^{2-} + 6 H_2O \longrightarrow CuSO_4 \cdot (NH_4)_2SO_4 \cdot 6 H_2O \text{ (s)} \quad (1)$$

Preparation of a Coordination Compound: $[Cu(NH_3)_4SO_4] \cdot H_2O$

Combine reagents, and stir.

Place 12 mL of distilled water and 12.5 g of $CuSO_4 \cdot 5 H_2O$ in a small beaker, and stir for five minutes. Now add 20 mL of concentrated aqueous ammonia and mix well. Note the color of this solution. How does it compare with the color of the copper(II) sulfate solution before aqueous ammonia was added?

Add ethyl alcohol.

To precipitate the complex salt from its aqueous solution, VERY CAREFULLY pour 20 mL of ethyl alcohol down the side of the beaker so that the alcohol runs over the top of the solution, and CAREFULLY set it inside your desk until the next laboratory period. **Avoid agitating the solution any more than absolutely necessary.** As the alcohol slowly diffuses into the aqueous solution, long needle-like crystals of the complex salt will form at the alcohol-water boundary. Place a watch glass over the beaker.

Collect and wash crystals.

At the next laboratory period, stir the mixture GENTLY, but thoroughly. By stirring gently, you can avoid breaking the large needle-like crystals. Collect the crystals by filtration on a Büchner funnel. Wash them on the funnel with (a) a mixture of 10 mL of ethyl alcohol and 10 mL of concentrated aqueous ammonia, (b) 20 mL of alcohol, and (c) 20 mL of acetone. **You should have all three wash liquids ready to use before you begin the filtration. As each wash liquid disappears through the funnel, add the next wash liquid so that the crystals are not exposed to the air until all of the wash liquids have been used.**

Dry crystals quickly.

Press the crystals between two or three pieces of filter paper, quickly transfer the crystals to a dry, previously weighed container, and weigh as quickly as possible. Calculate the percent yield of

$[Cu(NH_3)_4]SO_4 \cdot H_2O$. Compare the appearance of these crystals with those obtained in the first part of the experiment. If requested, hand in the crystals to your laboratory instructor in a labelled container; otherwise, show your crystals to your instructor and ask him/her to initial your report form.

The formation of $[Cu(NH_3)_4]SO_4 \cdot H_2O$ can be represented by Eq. (2).

$$Cu^{2+} + SO_4^{2-} + 4 NH_3 + H_2O \longrightarrow [Cu(NH_3)_4]SO_4 \cdot H_2O \text{ (s)} \qquad (2)$$

Preparation of a Coordination Compound: $K_3[Fe(C_2O_4)_3] \cdot 3 H_2O$

You will start with a double salt, $Fe(NH_4)_2(SO_4)_2 \cdot 6 H_2O$, as a source of iron(II) ions. You will then add oxalic acid, a weak acid, and precipitate insoluble iron(II) oxalate dihydrate.

$$Fe^{2+} + H_2C_2O_4 + 2 H_2O \longrightarrow FeC_2O_4 \cdot 2 H_2O \text{ (s)} + 2 H^+ \qquad (3)$$

The insoluble $FeC_2O_4 \cdot 2 H_2O$ will then be oxidized by hydrogen peroxide to a soluble compound containing the complex ion, $[Fe(C_2O_4)_3]^{3-}$, in the presence of excess potassium oxalate [Eq. (4)].

$$2 FeC_2O_4 \cdot 2 H_2O \text{ (s)} + H_2O_2 + 4 C_2O_4^{2-} \longrightarrow$$
$$2[Fe(C_2O_4)_3]^{3-} + 4 H_2O + 2 OH^- \qquad (4)$$

An excess of oxalic acid will be added to destroy the OH^- ions produced in the reaction. Alcohol will then be added to decrease the polarity of the solvent (and the solubility of $K_3[Fe(C_2O_4)_3] \cdot 3 H_2O$, and then the solution will be cooled slowly to allow the coordination compound to form well-defined crystals.

$$3 K^+ + [Fe(C_2O_4)_3]^{3-} + 3 H_2O \longrightarrow K_3[Fe(C_2O_4)_3] \cdot 3 H_2O \text{ (s)} \qquad (5)$$

Place 5.0 g of $Fe(NH_4)_2(SO_4)_2 \cdot 6 H_2O$ in a 250-mL beaker containing 15 mL of warm distilled water and 3 drops of 6M H_2SO_4. Stir until the solid dissolves. Add 25 mL of 1M $H_2C_2O_4$, and heat the mixture to boiling. While the solution is being heated, you should stir it continuously to prevent "bumping." Remove the beaker from the heat, and allow the yellow precipitate, $FeC_2O_4 \cdot 2 H_2O$, to settle. Carefully pour off as much liquid as possible, while retaining the solid in the beaker. Add 20 mL of water to the solid, heat to approximately 80 °C, stir well, and then allow the precipitate to settle. Carefully pour off as much liquid as possible, but retain the solid in the beaker.

Combine reagents; stir; heat mixture.

Now add 10 mL of saturated $K_2C_2O_4$ (potassium oxalate) solution to the solid in the beaker, and heat the solution to 40 °C. VERY SLOWLY (over a 5-minute period) add 20 mL of 3% hydrogen peroxide solution while keeping the temperature as near 40 °C as possible. **Add just a few drops at a time.** Some red-brown $Fe(OH)_3$ may precipitate at this point. Heat the solution to boiling, and add 8 mL of 1M $H_2C_2O_4$ slowly (over a 3-minute period) with constant stirring. Keep the solution very near its boiling point.

Add $K_2C_2O_4$ solution.

Slowly add H_2O_2.

Filter the hot solution through an ordinary filter paper into a 100-mL beaker. Add 10 mL of alcohol, and if any cloudiness develops in the solution, heat it until it is clear (transparent, **not** colorless). Tie a short piece of thread to a wood splint or pencil, place the wood splint or pencil across the top of the beaker, and let the thread dip into the solution so that the end of the thread just touches the bottom of the beaker. Cover the beaker, and set it inside your desk until the next laboratory period. Most of the $K_3[Fe(C_2O_4)_3] \cdot 3 H_2O$ should crystallize on the thread.

Filter hot solution; add alcohol.

Suspend string in solution.

**Collect and
dry crystals.**   At the next laboratory period, collect the crystals on a Büchner
funnel (most can be scraped off the string), and wash them once with 10 mL
of alcohol followed by 10 mL of acetone (**Note 1**). Dry the crystals by
pressing them between two or three pieces of filter paper, transfer them
to a previously weighed container, and determine the weight of
$K_3[Fe(C_2O_4)_3] \cdot 3\ H_2O$. Calculate the percent yield based on the weight of
$Fe(NH_4)_2(SO_4)_2 \cdot 6\ H_2O$ used. An excess of all other reagents was used. If
requested, hand in the crystals to your laboratory instructor in a
labelled container; otherwise, show the crystals to your instructor, and
ask him/her to initial your report form.

NOTES

<u>Note 1</u>.   Keep flames from the area where you handle flammable organic solvents such as
alcohol and acetone.

REFERENCES

1.   Davis, Gailey, and Whitten, "Principles of Chemistry," Saunders College Publishing,
Philadelphia (1984), Chapter 23, Coordination Compounds.

2.   Whitten and Gailey, "General Chemistry" and "General Chemistry with Qualitative
Analysis," Saunders College Publishing, Philadelphia (1984), Chapter 27, Coordination
Compounds.

SYNTHESES OF THREE TRANSITION METAL COMPOUNDS

PRELABORATORY QUESTIONS

Name_____   Lab Instructor_____

Student ID No_____   Date_____

1. The double salt copper(II) potassium chloride dihydrate, $CuCl_2 \cdot 2\ KCl \cdot 2\ H_2O$, may be prepared from $CuCl_2 \cdot 2\ H_2O$ and KCl. Assume that aqueous solutions of $CuCl_2$ and KCl react to form $CuCl_2 \cdot 2\ KCl \cdot 2\ H_2O$ by the following equation.

$$CuCl_2 + 2\ KCl + 2\ H_2O \longrightarrow CuCl_2 \cdot 2\ KCl \cdot 2\ H_2O$$

   a. What weights of solid $CuCl_2 \cdot 2\ H_2O$ and solid KCl would be required to produce 0.20 mole of the double salt?

$$CuCl_2 \cdot 2\ H_2O = 170.48 \text{ g/mole}$$

$$KCl = 74.5510 \text{ g/mole}$$

$$CuCl_2 \cdot 2\ KCl \cdot 2\ H_2O = 245.03 \text{ g/mole}$$

   b. If 80% of the $CuCl_2 \cdot 2\ KCl \cdot 2\ H_2O$ is isolated from solution, what weight is obtained?

2. A classical inorganic preparation involves the preparation of ammonium hexachloro-
    stannate(IV), $(NH_4)_2[SnCl_6]$, starting with metallic tin. The reactions are:

    a. Tin reacts with an excess of chlorine to produce stannic chloride.

    $$Sn \text{ (solid)} + 2 Cl_2 \text{ (gas)} \longrightarrow SnCl_4 \text{ (liquid)}$$

    b. Stannic chloride reacts with an aqueous solution of ammonium chloride to form
        ammonium hexachlorostannate(IV) which is collected by filtration from cold
        solution.

    $$SnCl_4 + 2 NH_4Cl \longrightarrow (NH_4)_2[SnCl_6]$$

    aa. If 23.8 g of tin are converted to stannic chloride, what weight of stannic
        chloride would be formed?

    bb. If 26 g of $SnCl_4$ are converted to $(NH_4)_2[SnCl_6]$, what maximum weight of
        $(NH_4)_2[SnCl_6]$ would be formed?

    cc. If 30 g of $(NH_4)_2[SnCl_6]$ are isolated from the reaction described above (bb),
        what would be the percent yield of $(NH_4)_2[SnCl_6]$ (based on the weight of $SnCl_4$
        used)?

DETERMINATION OF THE FORMULA OF A COMPLEX ION

BY A SPECTROPHOTOMETRIC METHOD

Objective

To use spectrophotometry to determine the presence and formulas of complex ions in solution

Equipment Needed

Three burets; a pair of matched cuvettes or cells for the spectrophotometer; spectrophotometer; 10 small bottles or 25-mL test tubes fitted with stoppers; lens paper

Reagents Needed

Solution A, 3×10^{-3} M in $NH_4Fe(SO_4)_2$; solution B, 3×10^{-3} M in NH_4SCN; buffer solution, 0.25 M in $(NH_4)_2SO_4$ and 0.125 M in H_2SO_4

INTRODUCTION

Suppose that two species react to form a compound of unknown formula AB_n as illustrated in Eq. (1).*

$$A + nB \longrightarrow AB_n \tag{1}$$

If AB_n is a stable compound, it is a simple matter to prepare it, analyze it, and determine its formula by fundamental stoichiometric methods, as in Exps. 4 and 5. Often, however, AB_n is unstable and exists only in solution, and always in equilibrium with its components A and B. This is the case with many complex ions. Such ions cannot be isolated; they must be studied in solution, in the equilibrium mixture. To determine the formula of the complex ion, advantage may be taken of the fact that equilibrium is established.

The determination of the formula of the complex ion as it exists in solution is particularly simple if the compound is colored and its two components are colorless and if **one** of the possible complexes is considerably more stable than the others. (In such a case, the stable species is the only one present in appreciable concentrations.) Thus, for the reaction

$$A + nB \rightleftharpoons AB_n, \tag{2}$$
$$\text{(colorless)} \quad \text{(colorless)} \quad \text{(colored)}$$

the concentration of AB_n can be measured by the amount of light it absorbs at a particular wavelength. The change in concentration of AB_n, as the relative amounts of A and B are changed, can be used to determine the coefficient n in Eq. (2), assuming that there is only one atom or ion of A per formula unit of AB_n.

In this experiment the formula of the deep red thiocyanato-iron(III) complex will be determined by the **method of continuous variations**. This method involves measuring the absorbances of a series of solutions of varying composition at the wavelength at which

*In many cases, the species AB_n will have a net charge (e.g., AB_n^{+y} or AB_n^{-z}; for simplicity and generality, the charges have been omitted in the text.

the complex has maximum absorptivity. The **total number of moles** of Fe^{3+} and SCN^- in a given volume of the solution is kept constant while the **molar ratios** of the two reactants are varied. The absorbances are plotted against the fraction of the total moles represented by one reagent, and the values of n are determined from the fraction at which the maximum absorbance occurs. For example, in Fig. 27-1 the maximum absorbance is at 0.75; thus, the formula of the complex is MX_3^{n-y} since this solution contains 0.25 moles of M^{n+} ion for each 0.75 moles of X^{y-} ion. If the complex is somewhat unstable, the plots are curved near the maximum as in Fig. 27-1. In this case, one should extend the straight-line portions of the graph until they cross to determine the mole fraction at maximum absorbance.

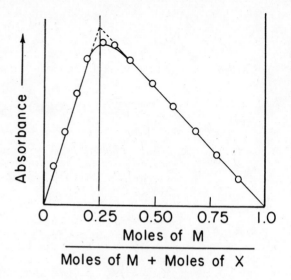

Figure 27-1. Absorbance as a function of mole fraction

Principles of Spectrophotometry[*]

We shall discuss briefly some important principles of spectrophotometry and equipment for the spectrophotometric technique.

Laws of Absorption. A property possessed by a beam of radiation is its **intensity** or **radiant power,** which is defined as the number of photons that strike a unit area per unit time. If the radiation is partly absorbed, the radiant power (I) measured by detectors, such as photocells or phototubes, is less than the incident power (I_o). The ratio of the radiant power transmitted through a sample to the radiant power incident on the sample is the transmittance, T.

$$T = I/I_o \tag{3}$$

The transmittance is often expressed as a percentage by multiplying by 100,

$$\%T = T \times 100\%.$$

The logarithm to the base 10 of the reciprocal of the transmittance is the absorbance.

$$A = \log_{10}(1/T) = \log_{10}(I_o/I) \tag{4}$$

The absorbance is more useful than the transmittance for quantitative work because it is directly proportional to concentration. If a monochromatic beam of radiation enters an absorbing medium, the rate of decrease in radiant power is proportional to the power of the incident radiation; that is, the light intensity is diminished in a geometric (not arithmetic) or exponential progression. Thus,

$$\frac{-dI}{I} = kdb. \tag{5}$$

Upon integrating and changing to logarithms of base 10 and putting $I = I_o$ when $b = 0$, one obtains

$$2.303 \log (I_o/I) = kb. \tag{6}$$

This is equivalent to stating that the radiant power of the unabsorbed light decreases exponentially as the thickness (b) of the absorbing medium increases arithmetically.

Beer's Law. This relationship indicates that the radiant power of a beam of monochromatic radiaton decreases in a similar manner as the concentration of the light-absorbing constituent increases. Thus,

---

[*]The terminology and abbreviations used in this section have been endorsed by the advisory board members of <u>Analytical Chemistry</u> in an attempt to obtain consistency in the field.

$$2.303 \log (I_o/I) = k'c. \tag{7}$$

Eqs. (6) and (7) may be combined and written as a single equation:

$$\log (I_o/I) = \varepsilon bc \tag{8}$$

$$I = I_o 10^{-\varepsilon bc} \tag{9}$$

in which I = power or intensity of radiation after passage through a sample.

I_o = power or intensity of radiation before passage through a sample. (It is assumed here that the solvent does not absorb radiation in the region discussed.)

ε = a constant for a given absorbing species, solvent, and temperature, dependent principally upon the intrinsic nature of the absorbing species and having a value dependent upon the wavelength, called the molar absorptivity.

c = the (stoichiometric) concentration of the absorbing species (moles/liter).

b = the radiation path length (centimeters) through the sample.

Absorbance is the product of the molar absorptivity, the optical path length, and the concentration of the absorbing species.

$$A = \varepsilon bc \tag{10}$$

From Eq. (10) it is evident that for a given absorbing species at a specific wavelength and for a given sample holder (**cuvette**) of fixed b, a plot of A against c is a straight line if Beer's Law is obeyed. Hence, the applicability of Beer's Law can be determined by measuring the absorbance as a function of concentration, using the same cuvette for all measurements and examining the linear character of the plot. Furthermore, after the slope of the line, b, has been determined, the concentration in any unknown solution can be calculated by measuring the absorbance and dividing this value by the slope. This is essentially the procedure of spectrophotometric analysis.

The Spectrophotometer. A spectrophotometer is a device for producing electromagnetic radiation (light) of rather precisely defined frequency (or wavelength). The frequency can be continuously varied over a range, and the intensity of the resulting radiation can be measured after its passage through a sample. The basic components of a spectrophotometer are briefly described in Appendix III.

Analysis by Spectrophotometry. Instruction will be given in the laboratory concerning the proper operation of the spectrophotometer. Read Appendix III before class. The instrument is a carefully constructed (and expensive) optical and electronic device. MAKE NO ADJUSTMENTS THAT YOU DO NOT THOROUGHLY UNDERSTAND.

Techniques of Spectrophotometry--PROCEDURE

Select matched pair of cuvettes.

First, select a pair of cuvettes that have approximately the same absorption and scattering characteristics, so that a proper comparison of the absorption of the thiocyanato-iron(III) solutons and the absorption of the solvent can be made. Examine several of them, and select two that, when filled with solvent and placed in the properly set instrument, each show 100 per cent transmittance when the aperture in front of the light source is adjusted so that the meter reading is 100 per cent for one of them. In using these cuvettes during the experiment, always carefully place them in the sample holder in the same orientation (etch mark toward the front). Precautions of cleanliness, no fingerprints, and so forth, are, of course, necessary. It is advisable to wipe each cuvette with lens paper just before inserting it in the sample holder. It is probably wise also to check the pair of cuvettes for likeness with the same solution of each, using a solution to give a transmittance of about 30 per cent to see that both read the same. Thereafter, always use one as the reference cell and the other as the solution cell. **Mark them** high on the neck above the area where the light will pass through the cell.

Clean and orient cuvettes properly.

The instrument gives the least error in the concentration of solute for a given error in the measurement of %T (the percentage transmittance on the meter) when %T is in the middle range, e.g., 20 to 60 or 70 per cent. Hence, to take advantage of the precision of the instrument, solutions should be diluted so that their absorbance values are in this range.

Having chosen matched cuvettes, it is then normally necessary to choose a wavelength for the absorbance measurements. The wavelength chosen should be one for which the molar absorptivity is high, i.e., ε large in Eq. (10), so that a slight change in concentration makes a great change in the absorbance, and it should be one for which the molar absorptivity changes as little as possible with a slight change in wavelength, so that the unavoidable mis-setting of the wavelength dial in repeated experiments does not result in a significant change in ε. Both of these criteria can be satisfied by choosing the wavelength that results in maximum absorbance by the chemical species being studied. At the maximum, the curve of absorbance versus wavelength is broad. For this reason, a slight error in setting the wavelength dial results in only a slight change in ε. But in Part A of this experiment, you do not know the identity of the light-absorbing species, and in fact the solutions may contain more than one light-absorbing species. Thus, in order to simplify your experimental problems, the wavelength resulting in maximum absorbance by the predominant thiocyanato-iron(III) complex has been found for you and is 450 nanometers.

Set wavelength dial at 450 nanometers (450 millimicrons).

Quantitative Basis of the Experiment

The equilibrium constant for the reaction that is represented by Eq. (2) is

$$K = \frac{[AB_n]_{eq}}{[A]_{eq}[B]_{eq}^n}. \tag{11}$$

Suppose that a series of experiments has been arranged in which the sum of the initial concentrations (before reaction) of A and B is always the same and equal to some value c. Let the initial concentration of A be x; then the intial concentration of B is c − x. When equilibrium is established, let the concentration of AB_n be y. Using information from the chemical Eq. (2), we then have

$$[AB_n]_{eq} = y \tag{12}$$

$$[A]_{eq} = x - y \tag{13}$$

$$[B]_{eq} = c - x - ny \tag{14}$$

and the equilibrium constant becomes

$$K = \frac{y}{(x - y)(c - x - ny)^n}. \tag{15}$$

The concentration of AB_n, that is, y, is proportional to the absorbance of the solution, by Beer's Law,

$$A = \log \frac{I_o}{I} = \varepsilon by, \tag{10}$$

if AB_n is the only absorbing species. Hence, we can measure changes in the concentration of AB_n, even though we may not know the value for ε, needed to determine its actual concentration, by Eq. (16).

$$y = \frac{A}{\varepsilon b} \qquad (16)$$

Eq. (16) shows that when the absorbance is zero, y is zero, and when the absorbance is a maximum, y is a maximum. A plot of the absorbance of various solutions against the values of x (the initial concentration of reactant A) for those solutions will, thus, have the same shape as a plot of y against x.

It can be shown that the maximum on such a plot appears at the point where the value of x is given by

$$x_{max} = \frac{c}{n + 1} \qquad (17)$$

regardless of the value for K (Fig. 27-2).

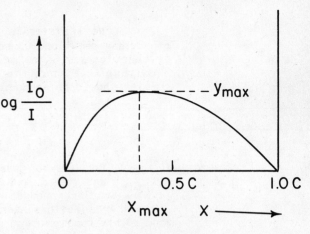

Figure 27-2

Absorbance as a function of concentration of A for a mixture of A and B which forms only one complex AB_n.

PROCEDURE

Make ten solutions by mixing reagents in the following quantities (to 0.02 mL) using three burets,

Prepare the ten solutions.

	Solution Number									
	1	2	3	4	5	6	7	8	9	10
Solution A (mL)	0	1	3	5	7	9	11	13	15	16
Solution B (mL)	16	15	13	11	9	7	5	3	1	0
Buffer (mL)	4	4	4	4	4	4	4	4	4	4

and determine their absorbance in the spectrophotometer at 450 nanometers (450 millimicrons), using a solution of 4 mL of buffer diluted to 20 mL with distilled water in the reference cell. Rinse the sample cell two or three times with small amounts of each new solution before taking the absorbance reading. Discard the wash solutions. This procedure should assure that the concentration of the solution in the cuvette is the same as that in the bottle.

Determine absorbance of each solution.

Note that solution 10 has slight absorbance at this wavelength, so that any unreacted iron(III) ion in the other solutions will also contribute to the absorption [i.e., the assumption in Eq. (2), that reagent A is colorless, is not correct]. To correct for this, we may make use of the fact that the total absorbance of the solution is the sum of the absorbances of the individual absorbing species, i.e.,

$$\text{Absorbance} = \varepsilon_i c_i b + \varepsilon_j c_j b + \varepsilon_k c_k b + \ldots \qquad (18)$$

If the absorbance of solution 10 (in which [B] = 0 and the complex ion is, of course, not present) is A_{10}, we have

$$A_{10} = \varepsilon_{Fe} c_{10} b = \varepsilon_{Fe}\left(\frac{MV_{10}}{20}\right) b \qquad (19)$$

in which c_{10} is the concentration of iron(III) in solution 10, V_{10} is the volume (milliliters) of solution A in solution 10, and M is the molarity of solution A. For any other solution, the absorbance due to iron(III) may then be approximated as $A_{10}\left(\frac{V_x}{V_{10}}\right)$ in which V_x is the volume (milliliters) of solution A, used in solution x.

355

Note that this is an overcorrection because in all solutions other than solution 10, some iron(III) has been removed from the solution by reaction (2). How much is thus removed depends upon the (unknown) magnitude of K, but the absorbance in the other solutions due to the complex should be approximately equal, from Eq. (18), to

$$A_{complex} = A_{measured} - \frac{A_{10}V_x}{V_{10}}. \qquad (20)$$

Correct absorbances.

Correct the measured absorbances according to Eq. (20), and plot $A_{complex}$ against x, or against some variable that is proportional to x. If more data are needed in order to define the maximum clearly, interpolate other solutions near the maximum. Find x_{max} and calculate the formula of the complex

$$Fe(NCS)_n^{(3 - n)+}.$$

NOTEBOOK AND REPORT

Write a brief report of the experiment, showing the tabulated data and representative calculations. Include the graph showing the absorbance plotted against mole fraction. Include sufficient discussion to answer any of the following questions assigned by the instructor.

REFERENCES

1. Day, R.A., and Underwood, A.L.: Quantitative Analysis. 4th edition. Prentice-Hall, Englewood Cliffs, NJ, 1980, pp. 376-406.
2. Carmody, W.R.: J. Chem. Ed., 41, 615 (1964).

Experiment 27

DETERMINATION OF THE FORMULA OF A COMPLEX ION

PRELABORATORY QUESTIONS

Name _____   Lab Instructor _____

Student ID _____   Date _____

1. What property of the thiocyanato-iron(III) complex ion is used in determining its
    formula in this experiment?

2. Why is the ion or its salt not isolated from solution and its composition determined
    by standard elemental analysis techniques?

3. What is Beer's Law? How will it be useful to you in this experiment?

357

4. What critical concentrations change in moving from one to another of the ten solutions used in this experiment? Why were the concentrations of these solutions chosen to be what they are?

5. How could you use the spectrophotometer to find the best wavelength to use in making your absorption measurements if this had not been given?

6. What would be the formula for the thiocyanato-iron(III) ion if the maximum absorption occurred in a solution in which the mole fraction of Fe^{3+} were 0.20?

Experiment 27

DETERMINATION OF THE FORMULA OF A COMPLEX ION

REPORT SHEET

Name _____   Lab Instructor _____

Student ID _____   Date _____

Initial Concentrations and Absorbances of Solutions (450 nanometers; 450 millimicrons)

	Solution Number				
	1	2	3	4	5
$x = [A]_{initial}$	_____	_____	_____	_____	_____
Total Absorbance	_____	_____	_____	_____	_____
Absorbance due to Fe^{3+} ($A_{10} \cdot V_x / V_{10}$)	_____	_____	_____	_____	_____
Absorbance due to the complex ion	_____	_____	_____	_____	_____

	Solution Number				
	6	7	8	9	10
$x = [A]_{initial}$	_____	_____	_____	_____	_____
Total Absorbance	_____	_____	_____	_____	_____
Absorbance due to Fe^{3+} ($A_{10} \cdot V_x / V_{10}$)	_____	_____	_____	_____	_____
Absorbance due to the complex ion	_____	_____	_____	_____	_____

Attach sheets to show sample calculations of the concentrations of the solutions and of the formula of the complex ion. Also, attach sheets to answer the assigned QUESTIONS--PROBLEMS on the next page.

QUESTIONS--PROBLEMS

1. What are some of the problems that would be encountered if you attempted to determine the formulas of the other thiocyanato-iron(III) complexes in equilibrium with $Fe(NCS)_n^{(3-n)+}$ by the method of continuous variations?

2. Although we have written the formula of the thiocyanato-iron(III) complex as $Fe(NCS)_n^{(3-n)+}$, in considering the normal coordination number of Fe^{3+} and the fact that it is in water, what is probably a more correct formula for the complex?

3. Another spectrophotometric technique for determining the formula of a complex is the **mole-ratio** method, involving a series of solutions in which the concentration of one reagent, such as Fe^{3+}, is constant and that of the other, such as SCN^-, is varied. The absorbances are plotted against the **ratio** of the moles of SCN^- to Fe^{3+}. What type of plot would you expect in this thiocyanato-iron(III) case? What difficulties could also be incurred with this method owing to the other thiocyanato-iron(III) complexes in equilibrium?

4. Derive Eq. (17), starting with Eq. (15). Procedure: Consider y as a function of x. Remember that at the maximum, the derivative of y with respect to x is zero. Write Eq. (15) in the form

$$y = K(x - y)(c - x - ny)^n \tag{21}$$

and differentiate implicitly. Set the derivative equal to zero, and solve the resulting equation for n in terms of c and x_{max}.

QUALITATIVE ANALYSIS OF IONIC MIXTURES

Objective

To determine the presence or absence of certain cations and anions in aqueous solutions; to study some of the methods used by chemists to make such analyses

Equipment Needed

Centrifuge; microburner; heating bath; 10-mL graduate; medicine dropping tubes or micropipets; semimicro spatula; 4-mL test tubes; small casserole; 7.5-cm watch glass; test tube brush; test tube holder; glass stirring rods; pH paper; water bath; 250-mL beaker

Reagents Needed

6 M and 12 M Hydrochloric acid, HCl; 6 M and 16 M nitric acid, HNO_3; 6 M acetic acid, CH_3CO_2H; 3 M and 6 M sodium hydroxide, NaOH; 6 M and 15 M aqueous ammonia, NH_3 or NH_4OH; 5% aqueous thioacetamide solution, CH_3CSNH_2; 3% aqueous hydrogen peroxide solution, H_2O_2; 3 M solutions of ammonium acetate, $NH_4CH_3CO_2$, ammonium chloride, NH_4Cl, ammonium thiocyanate, NH_4SCN; 0.1 M dimethylglyoxime solution in 95% ethanol; 0.10 M mercuric chloride, $HgCl_2$; saturated potassium dichromate, $K_2Cr_2O_7$; solid potassium ferrocyanide, $K_4Fe(CN)_6$; 0.5 M tin(II) chloride, $SnCl_2$ in 3 M HCl; acetone; ether; clean iron tacks; solid ammonium sulfate, $(NH_4)_2SO_4$; solid oxalic acid, $H_2C_2O_4$; solid ammonium chloride, NH_4Cl; aluminon test solution [0.1% aqueous solution of $C_{19}H_{11}(CO_2NH_4)_4$]; H_2SO_4 test solution, pH adjusted to pH = 0.4; methyl violet indicator solution; 1 M HCl; 1.5 M NH_3

Reagents for anion analysis are given in Exp. 3.

INTRODUCTION

As indicated in earlier experiments, qualitative analysis is the process of determining the substances or chemical species present in a sample of matter. The procedures used in such an analysis depend, of course, on the nature of the sample. For example, the analysis of blood for certain drugs or drug residues requires procedures and techniques different from those used for analysis of automotive exhausts for air pollutants. In this experiment you will be asked to determine the presence or absence of certain cations (and anions, in some cases) in various unknown mixtures. The analytical scheme and procedures will be made available to you, but you may not have to use all portions of the scheme in analyzing a given unknown. Once you have learned the analytical scheme, only a little thought and some common sense will enable you to select those portions and procedures that are appropriate for the particular unknown you are about to analyze.

The analytical scheme provided below will enable you to analyze for the following ions in aqueous solution:

Cations: Ag^+, Pb^{2+}, Hg_2^{2+}, Hg^{2+}, Bi^{3+}, Cu^{2+}, Sb^{3+} or Sb^{5+}, Sn^{2+} or Sn^{4+}, Fe^{2+} or Fe^{3+}, Al^{3+}, Cr^{3+}, Co^{2+}, Ni^{2+}, Zn^{2+}

Anions: CO_3^{2-}, SO_4^{2-}, F^-, Cl^-, Br^-, I^-.

Schemes are available for the analysis of a much larger group of anions. However, the present scheme contains many of the important features of traditional methods of ion analysis in aqueous solutions.

Before describing the scheme for the ions we have chosen, let us first consider how we can approach the overall problem of analyzing an aqueous mixture containing any or all of a rather large group of ions. For simplicity, let us assume that all of the ions present in the sample are dissolved in aqueous solution. How then do we proceed to ascertain the identity of these ions? Ideally, it would be desirable to have a chemical probe that when placed in the solution would simply indicate which ions were present or, failing this, to have a unique chemical test for each ion that could be performed on the solution. Unfortunately, no such chemical probe has been developed, and the presence of the other ions often interferes with the established tests for a given ion. Most tests for ions are valid only when that ion is separated from most other ions. Hence, an important part of qualitative analysis of ions in aqueous solution is the separation of the ions from one another. Once an ion has been separated--and isolated--specific chemical tests can then be performed.

Perhaps the simplest way to separate and isolate an ion from a complex mixture is to add a reagent that will cause this ion--and none of the others in the original mixture--to precipitate from the solution. The precipitate can then be physically separated from the solution and later caused to dissolve, forming a new solution--one in which the ion is said to be isolated. This new solution can then be tested to confirm the presence of the ion.

In practice it often is convenient to precipitate and separate groups of ions rather than single ions. The groups of precipitated ions can then be treated chemically so as to effect further separations and ultimate isolation and testing.

In designing procedures for separation, isolation, and testing of ions, the chemist makes use of the known properties of the ions such as the solubility or insolubility of certain of their compounds, their ability to form complex ions, to oxidize or not to oxidize with certain reagents, etc. In this experiment, the separations of one ion from another or of groups of ions are made on the basis of a difference in solubility, but this difference in solubility is obtained by making use of a variety of chemical facts. As you proceed with the experiments, you should look for the following chemical principles:

1. Although most chlorides are quite soluble in water, a very few are insoluble, and advantage may be taken of this gross difference in solubility.

2. Some compounds, although insoluble in the cold, are sufficiently soluble in hot water to make it possible to dissolve and separate them from other compounds which remain insoluble even at higher temperatures.

3. Compounds of some ions may be dissolved by causing the cation present to form a complex ion, thus making it possible to separate the cation from other cations which do not form soluble compounds containing complex ions.

4. In a manner similar to (3), some ions are amphoteric while others are not, and advantage of this may be taken to dissolve and separate compounds of the amphoteric ones while leaving behind the insoluble compounds of the ions which do not show the property of amphoterism.

5. Salts, M^+A^-, of a weak acid HA tend to be soluble in acidic solutions. If the equilibrium $M^+A^- + H_3O^+ \rightleftharpoons HA + H_2O + M^+$ can be pushed far enough to the right to bring $[A^-]$ to a sufficiently low value, the salt M^+A^- will dissolve, making it possible to separate it from a less soluble salt of a different metal ion.

6. Some cations undergo oxidation to form a soluble salt in the oxidized state, thus making it possible to separate an oxidizable cation from others which are not oxidized by the reagents used.

7. Some compounds dissolve more rapidly than others so that a timed procedure can separate the rapidly dissolving ones from slowly dissolving compounds.

While the sequence of reactions which leads to the **separation** of one kind of ion from other kinds often produces definite indications that a particular kind of ion is present, it is usually desirable to perform a special test for **identification** of the ion. Such an identifying or confirmatory test must be accomplished if the separation leads to a colorless solution of the ion—since it is then necessary to show that the ion is indeed present—and that the "solution" of the ion is not simply water containing only previously added reagents. As in the separation procedures discussed above, the identification tests involve several chemical procedures:

1. A precipitate of characteristic color or form may be produced without a change in oxidation state of the ion.

2. The metallic ion present may be (a) reduced to the metal or (b) reduced or oxidized to some insoluble compound, often of some characteristic color or form.

3. A complex ion of the metal ion to be identified is formed. This complex ion may give a characteristic color to the solution or it may form a precipitate.

4. The precipitate formed for identification as in (1) above may be of such a nature as to be almost invisible under ordinary conditions. To make it more visible, a dye may be added to the solution. Adsorption of the dye on the precipitate gives a color to it which makes it more readily seen.

IMPORTANT LABORATORY OPERATIONS

The procedures you will use in this experiment employ a laboratory technique known as semimicro--or very small scale--analysis. Semimicro methods were used in Exp. 3; they are faster and more conservative of materials than are the macro methods you have been using for most of the experiments. Please read the **Laboratory Techniques** on Semimicro Techniques (pp. 23-24) before starting Exp. 28.

NOTEBOOK AND REPORT

Good records are especially important in qualitative analysis. A highly useful approach is to record the procedure used and the observations made during each step of the analysis in the form of a flow sheet for each group (see p. 366). When a confirmatory test is inconclusive or the results otherwise ambiguous, a careful examination of the observations made throughout the analysis may clarify matters. Moreover, your instructor will require a report on each sample analyzed, and you will be expected to cite evidence to justify your conclusions.

GENERAL SUGGESTIONS

Before analyzing an unknown, you should work through the procedures with a sample that is known to contain all of the ions included in the scheme. In this way you can familiarize yourself with procedures, techniques, and the kinds of observations that can and must be made. As you work through the scheme, try to relate what you see to the chemistry that is taking place in the reaction mixture.

In analyzing an unknown sample, your main task is to identify the ions present. To do this, you should have a good idea of how the ions will behave at each point. Hence, you must have more than a cookbook comprehension of the scheme of analysis.

When your instructor issues an unknown, he may tell you that certain ions are not present in your sample. In such cases you may wish to omit or modify certain portions of the scheme. Considerable time and effort can be saved by planning each analysis in accordance with the special information provided with the unknown sample. If your unknown contains ions from only one specific group, omit the tests for ions in the other groups.

SCHEME FOR CATION ANALYSIS

The cations included in this scheme can be separated into three groups. The members of the analytical groups and the conditions for precipitation are summarized below. The group designations do **not** refer to the groups of the periodic table.

Anal. Group I Ions: Pb^{2+}, Ag^+, Hg_2^{2+} Precipitated as chlorides from acidic solution

Anal. Group II Ions: Hg^{2+}, Pb^{2+}, Bi^{3+}, Cu^{2+}, Sb^{3+} or $Sb(OH)_6^-$, Sn^{2+} or Sn^{4+} Precipitated as sulfides from 0.3 M acidic solution

Anal. Group III Ions: Fe^{3+}, Al^{3+}, Cr^{3+}, Co^{2+}, Ni^{2+}, Zn^{2+} Precipitated as hydroxides or sulfides from slightly basic solutions

PART A. ANALYSIS OF GROUP I

Of the cations included here, only lead, Pb^{2+}, silver, Ag^+, and mercury(I), Hg_2^{2+}, form insoluble chlorides. Addition of cold dilute hydrochloric acid to a solution containing any or all of these ions brings about the following reactions:

$$Pb^{2+} + 2\ Cl^- \rightleftharpoons \underline{PbCl_2} \quad \text{(white precipitate)}$$

$$Ag^+ + Cl^- \rightleftharpoons \underline{AgCl} \quad \text{(white precipitate)}$$

$$Hg_2^{2+} + 2\ Cl^- \rightleftharpoons \underline{Hg_2Cl_2} \quad \text{(white precipitate)}$$

A line under a formula in an equation will be used to indicate that this substance is present as a precipitate. The non-underlined formulas of other compounds or ions will indicate a soluble species. Actually, this group can be precipitated by any substance which provides chloride ions in solution (e.g., NaCl or KCl); HCl is used because the dilute acid environment prevents precipitation of Groups II and III ions as hydroxides (or as species produced by hydrolysis such as BiOCl) and assures more complete precipitation of the Group I chlorides. The mixture is kept cool since the solubility of $PbCl_2$ increases rapidly with increasing temperature. Addition of excess HCl (or Cl^-) must be avoided because it causes the chlorides to dissolve, forming the complex ions $PbCl_4^{2-}$, $AgCl_2^-$, and $Hg_2Cl_3^-$.

Once the chlorides have been precipitated, the mixture can be centrifuged (see p. 24) and the solution separated (or decanted) from the precipitate. The solution or decantate can be set aside to be analyzed later for Groups II and III if ions from these groups might be present. The precipitate can be analyzed to determine which members of Group I are present.

Separation of Lead. Lead ion can be separated from silver ion and mercurous ion by treating the precipitate of Group I chlorides with hot water. This will dissolve most or all of the lead chloride but not silver chloride or mercury(I) chloride.

$$\underline{PbCl_2} \underset{\text{hot water}}{\overset{\text{cold water}}{\rightleftharpoons}} Pb^{2+} + 2\ Cl^-$$

The hot water containing $PbCl_2$ can now be separated from the insoluble AgCl and Hg_2Cl_2 and this solution tested to confirm the presence of lead(II).

Confirmation of Lead. Potassium dichromate, $K_2Cr_2O_7$, is used to confirm the presence of Pb^{2+} ion. The reactions are:

$$Cr_2O_7^{2-} + 3 H_2O \rightleftharpoons 2 CrO_4^{2-} + 2 H_3O^+$$

$$PbCl_2(aq) + CrO_4^{2-} \rightleftharpoons \underline{PbCrO_4} \text{ (yellow precipitate)} + 2 Cl^-.$$

In the first step, the dichromate ion, $Cr_2O_7^{2-}$, reacts with water to establish an equilibrium in which chromate ion, CrO_4^{2-}, is produced. Lead(II) from $PbCl_2(aq)$ reacts with this ion to give yellow lead chromate, $PbCrO_4$, which is less soluble than $PbCr_2O_7$.

Separation of Silver and Mercury(I) Chlorides. The precipitate remaining after lead chloride is dissolved in hot water can be treated with ammonia solution to separate Ag^+ from Hg_2^{2+}. The important reactions are:

$$\underline{AgCl} + 2 NH_3 \rightleftharpoons Ag(NH_3)_2^+ + Cl^-$$

$$\underline{Hg_2Cl_2} + 2 NH_3 \rightleftharpoons \underset{\text{(white)}}{HgNH_2Cl} + \underset{\text{(black)}}{Hg} + NH_4^+ + Cl^-.$$

Silver chloride dissolves with the formation of the soluble complex ion $Ag(NH_3)_2^+$. Mercury(I) chloride undergoes a disproportionation reaction in which the white mercury(II) amido chloride, $HgNH_2Cl$, and black metallic mercury, Hg, are formed. The mixture of the two often is black; sometimes it has a salt and pepper appearance. Any remaining lead chloride reacts to form another white salt, $Pb(OH)Cl$, the appearance of which will not interfere with either of the other reactions.

Confirmation of Mercury(I) Ion. The black precipitate formed on treatment of Hg_2Cl_2 with NH_3 is usually sufficient to confirm Hg_2^{2+}. However, when silver is present, a small amount of the silver in AgCl may be reduced to metallic silver, Ag, which also appears black. To distinguish between silver and mercury, the black residue can be heated in aqua regia [a mixture of concentrated HCl (12 M) and concentrated HNO_3 (16 M)]. The reactions are:

$$Ag + 2 H_3O^+ \; 2 Cl^- + NO_3^- \rightleftharpoons NO_2\uparrow + AgCl_2^- + 3 H_2O$$

$$Hg + 4 H_3O^+ + 4 Cl^- + 2 NO_3^- \rightleftharpoons 2 NO_2\uparrow + HgCl_4^{2-} + 6 H_2O.$$

(The ↑ following the formula of a species indicates that it is produced as a gas.)

When this reaction mixture is cooled and added to water, a white precipitate of AgCl appears if some or all of the black residue was silver. Mercury, if present, can be confirmed by treating the resulting solution with tin(II) chloride. In this reaction Hg^{2+} is reduced to Hg_2^{2+} which precipitates with Cl^- as white Hg_2Cl_2.

$$Hg^{2+} + Sn^{2+} + 2 Cl^- \rightleftharpoons \underset{\text{(white)}}{\underline{Hg_2Cl_2}} + Sn^{4+}$$

Hence, a white precipitate at this point confirms the presence of mercury.

Confirmation of Silver Ion. If silver is present in the sample, it will now be in the form of the complex ion $Ag(NH_3)_2^+$ in the decantate from the treatment of the $AgCl/Hg_2Cl_2$ precipitate with ammonia. To confirm its presence, the complex ion must be decomposed and the silver ion allowed to reprecipitate as AgCl. This is accomplished by adding dropwise nitric acid, HNO_3, until the solution is acidic. The important reactions are:

$$Ag(NH_3)_2^+ + 2 H_3O^+ \rightleftharpoons Ag^+ + 2 NH_4^+ + 2 H_2O$$

$$Ag^+ + Cl^- \rightleftharpoons \underline{AgCl}.$$

The chloride ions for the second reaction above are present in the solution as a result of dissolving AgCl with NH_3.

A GRAPHICAL METHOD TO SHOW ION SEPARATION AND IDENTIFICATON

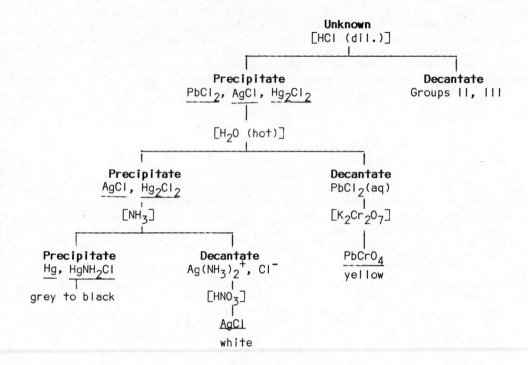

Unknown
[HCl (dil.)]

Precipitate
$PbCl_2$, $AgCl$, Hg_2Cl_2

Decantate
Groups II, III

[H_2O (hot)]

Precipitate
$AgCl$, Hg_2Cl_2

Decantate
$PbCl_2$(aq)

[NH_3]

[$K_2Cr_2O_7$]

Precipitate
Hg, $HgNH_2Cl$

grey to black

Decantate
$Ag(NH_3)_2^+$, Cl^-

[HNO_3]

$AgCl$
white

$PbCrO_4$
yellow

PROCEDURE

The solution to be analyzed may contain any or all of the cations of Groups I, II, III.* Add 5 drops of the cold solution to a 4-mL test tube and then add 1 drop of 3 M HCl. Mix thoroughly and centrifuge the mixture. Add another drop of HCl solution, and if precipitation is incomplete, add one more drop. Centrifuge the mixture and decant the supernatant liquid with a dropping tube. **This decantate is saved for the analysis of Groups II and III if this is a General Unknown.**

Wash the precipitate remaining in the test tube with 1 mL of cold water containing some HCl (1 drop of 3 M HCl in 4 mL of water), and add the washings to the previous decantate.

(Continue this procedure on the next page)

---

*If your unknown is a solid sample, follow the directions given below for a Group I or a General Unknown.

Group I: Prepare 1 mL of **cold** 12 M HCl to which has been added **1** drop (no more) of 3 M HNO_3. Place approximately 50-75 mg of the unknown powder into this solution, and stir vigorously for a **few** seconds (30 seconds **maximum**). If the precipitate is not completely white, add 1 more drop of 3 M HNO_3 and again stir vigorously for a **few** seconds (30 seconds maximum). Immediately dilute with an equal volume of water, stir, centrifuge, and decant. The precipitate is a mixture of Group I chlorides and is treated according to the procedure starting at the asterisk above.

General
Unknown: Treat 100 mg of the unknown powder with 1 mL of 12 M HCl. Immerse in boiling water, and stir continuously until all has been dissolved except Group I. Add 1 mL of water and stir. Cool thoroughly and centrifuge. The precipitate is a mixture of Group I chlorides and is treated as directed above at the asterisk. The decantate, which contains Groups II and III, is treated for Group II as directed on p. 376.

PROCEDURE--GROUP I
(continue from middle of previous page)

Precipitate: $PbCl_2$ (white), AgCl (white), Hg_2Cl_2 (white). Add one mL of water and heat in a bath of boiling water for 2-3 minutes. Quickly centrifuge (if necessary) and reheat the tube in the bath. Decant the hot solution and test it for $PbCl_2$ right away.

Decantate: Cations Groups II and III

Precipitate: AgCl, Hg_2Cl_2 (white). Repeat the hot water wash described above for 4 or 5 more times to remove all of the $PbCl_2$. (If $PbCl_2(aq)$ is present, the second and third washings each can be tested with saturated $K_2Cr_2O_7$ solution to reconfirm the presence of Pb^{2+}.) Add 5 drops of 15 M NH_3 to the test tube. Mix thoroughly, centrifuge, and decant.

Decantate: $PbCl_2$ (colorless solution). Add 1 or 2 drops of saturated $K_2Cr_2O_7$ solution and cool to room temperature. A yellow precipitate of $PbCrO_4$ indicates the presence of Pb^{2+}.

Precipitate: Hg (black) and $Hg(NH_2)Cl$ (white) confirm the presence of Hg_2^{2+}. If reduced silver was noted previously, an inconclusive result may occur here. To retest for the presence of mercury, perform the following:

Add 3 drops of 12 M HCl and 1 drop of 16 M HNO_3 and heat gently. Dilute the solution with 2 mL of water; any silver present will appear as white AgCl. Centrifuge if necessary, and add 2 drops of $SnCl_2$ solution to the decantate. A white or grey precipitate confirms the presence of Hg_2^{2+}.*

Decantate: $Ag(NH_3)_2^+$ (colorless solution). Add dilute HNO_3, drop by drop, with agitation of the solution until it is slightly acidic (test with pH paper). A white precipitate of AgCl confirms the presence of Ag^+.

---

*If silver is present and the test for Hg_2^{2+} is inconclusive, transfer the residue to a casserole. Add 3 drops of 12 M HCl and 1 drop of 16 M HNO_3 and heat gently. Dilute the solution with 2 mL of water; any silver present will appear as white AgCl. Centrifuge if necessary and add 4-6 drops of $SnCl_2$ solution to the decantate. A white or gray precipitate confirms the presence of Hg_2^{2+}.

1. Which of the separation procedures listed on pages 362 and 363 were involved in separation of the Group I cations from those of Groups II and III?

2. Which of the separation procedures listed on pages 362 and 363 were involved in the separation of lead chloride from the chlorides of mercury(I) and silver?

3. Which of the separation procedures listed on pages 362 and 363 were involved in the separation of silver ion from the mercury(I) ion?

4. Which of the identification items listed on page 363 was involved in identification of lead ion? Write the equation for the reaction that occurred on adding potassium dichromate to the lead ion solution.

5. Write the equation for the reaction which occurred in identification of silver ion. Does this identification correspond to any listed on page 363? If so, to which one?

6. Which of the identification items listed on page 363 was involved in identifying mercury(I) ion?

7. Using the information provided on Group I analysis, how would you distinguish between the substances in each of the following pairs (i) if both substances are in the same container? (ii) if each substance is in a separate container? Note that an answer to (i) requires a separation. An answer to (ii) requires only that you treat both substances in the same manner or with the same reagent and show that each behaves in a different characteristic manner.

   a. Hg_2Cl_2 and $AgCl$ d. $PbCrO_4$ and $AgCl$

   b. $PbCl_2$ and Hg_2Cl_2 e. KCl and Hg_2Cl_2

   c. $AgNO_3$ and $Hg_2(NO_3)_2$ f. $Pb(NO_3)_2$ and K_2CrO_4

8. You are given an aqueous solution that may contain any, all, or none of the ions given in each of the lettered items below. In each case, cite a reagent, reagents, or an operation that if added or performed would enable you to determine which, if any, of the ions are present. State the observations that would lead you to the various possible conclusions:

   a. Ag^+ and Pb^{2+} d. Sn^{2+} and Hg_2^{2+}

   b. Ag^+ and Hg_2^{2+} e. CrO_4^{2-} and Hg_2^{2+}

   c. Cu^{2+} and Pb^{2+} f. Hg_2^{2+} and Hg^{2+}

9. A solid sample is known to contain any or all of the following: $Pb(NO_3)_2$, $AgCl$, Hg_2Cl_2, K_2CrO_4, $CuCl_2$, and KCl. It gave a white precipitate and a colorless solution when treated with water. Approximately half of the precipitate dissolved when treated with concentrated ammonia, leaving a gray residue. On the basis of this information, classify each of the following ions as: **definitely present, definitely absent, or undetermined** in the original sample: Pb^{2+}, NO_3^-, Ag^+, Cl^-, Hg_2^{2+}, K^+, CrO_4^{2-}, Cu^{2+}.

Experiment 28

INTRODUCTION AND GROUP I

PRELABORATORY QUESTIONS

Name_____   Lab Instructor_____

Student ID No_____   Date_____

1. What is meant by the following terms, and how is each relevant in the qualitative analysis of ionic solutions?

    a. separation

    b. isolation

    c. identification

    d. confirmation

    e. semimicro

    f. 15-μL pipet

g.   decantation

h.   centrifuge

2.   Name the ions of Analytical Group I; how are they separated from those of Analytical Groups II and III?

3.   Draw a flow chart showing how Analytical Group I ions are analyzed.

Experiment 28

QUALITATIVE ANALYSIS OF IONIC MIXTURES

REPORT SHEET FOR GROUP I

Name_____   Lab. Instructor_____

Student ID No_____   Date_____

Results at Each Separation Part of the Flow Sheet

Ions Present in Unknown_____

Observations That Differed from the Text Presentation

Attach Your Answers to the Assigned Questions Shown on the Next Page

PART B.   ANALYSIS OF GROUP II

Following the removal of the cations of Group I as chlorides by precipitation and decantation, Group II cations may be separated from those of Group III by making use of the fact that the Group II cations form sulfides that are insoluble in dilute acidic solution. The concentration of acid in this solution is critical: too high a concentration will cause incomplete precipitation of the Group II cations and too low a concentration will cause some of the Group III cations to precipitate as sulfides. The optimum concentration here is 0.3 M, and the procedures have been developed so that, if followed, this concentration will be achieved.

The ions of Group II are: mercury(II), Hg^{2+}; lead, Pb^{2+} (which has not been completely removed by the Group I separation); bismuth, Bi^{3+}; copper, Cu^{2+}; antimony(II) and (V), $SbCl_4^-$ and $HSb(OH)_6$; and tin(II) and (IV), $SnCl_3^-$ and $SnCl_6^{2-}$.

Before proceeding to precipitate Group II, it is necessary to be certain that all of the tin present is in the IV oxidation state since Sn(II) can reduce Hg^{2+} to Hg_2^{2+}. In addition, a separation to come later--that of separating tin and antimony from the other Group II elements--will not be effective if tin is present as Sn(II). Tin(II) is oxidized to tin(IV) using aqua regia. This oxidizing agent also oxidizes antimony(II) to antimony(V). This latter oxidation will cause no problem.

Precipitation of Group II. Two reagents are needed to precipitate Group II. The first is nitric acid which, as has been indicated, needs to be present in 0.3 M concentration. The second is thioacetamide, CH_3CSNH_2. The latter reagent is used as a convenient source of H_2S which is formed by the following hydroysis reaction:

$$CH_3CSNH_2 \;+\; 2\,H_2O \;\overset{\Delta}{\rightleftharpoons}\; H_2S \;+\; NH_4^+ \;+\; CH_3CO_2^-.$$

The H_2S produced reacts to establish the following equilibria and gives sulfide ions:

$$H_2S \;+\; H_2O \;\rightleftharpoons\; H_3O^+ \;+\; HS^-$$

$$HS^- \;+\; H_2O \;\rightleftharpoons\; H_3O^+ \;+\; S^{2-}.$$

These equilibria indicate that the sulfide ion concentration may be controlled by adjustment of the hydronium ion concentration. Thus, if the hydronium ion concentration is increased, the sulfide ion concentration can be diminished and vice versa. By keeping the hydronium ion concentration at 0.3 M and using the amount of thioacetamide indicated in the procedures, the sulfide ion concentration can be controlled so as to precipitate the Group II cations effectively without precipitating those from Group III. However, if the hydronium ion concentration becomes too high, lead sulfide probably will not precipitate. Conversely, if the hydronium ion concentration is too low, the sulfide ion concentration in the H_2S equilibrium will be increased to the point that some sulfides of Group III-- sulfides of zinc, cobalt, and nickel--may precipitate.

While the equations for the precipitation reactions are complex in some cases, they may be represented simply as follows:

$$M^{2+} \;+\; S^{2-} \;\rightleftharpoons\; \underline{MS} \qquad\qquad \text{in which } M^{2+} = Hg^{2+},\ Pb^{2+},\ Cu^{2+}$$

$$2\,Bi^{3+} \;+\; 3\,S^{2-} \;\rightleftharpoons\; \underline{Bi_2S_3}$$

$$SnCl_6^{2-} \;+\; 2\,H_2S \;+\; 4\,H_2O \;\rightleftharpoons\; \underline{SnS_2} \;+\; 4\,H_3O^+ \;+\; 6\,Cl^-$$

$$2\,HSb(OH)_6 \;+\; 5\,H_2S \;\rightleftharpoons\; \underline{Sb_2S_5} \;+\; 12\,H_2O.$$

It is important to know the colors of the sulfides of Group II. By observing the colors formed on the precipitation of this group, it frequently is possible to get a hint as to which cations are present in an unknown. The colors of these sulfides are:

HgS	most often black, sometimes red	PbS	black
Bi_2S_3	dark brown	CuS	black
Sb_2S_5	orange red	SnS_2	yellow.

373

Separation of Group II into Subgroups. Because it is more convenient to work with smaller numbers of ions, Group II will be divided into subgroups known as the copper and antimony subgroups. The basis of this separation is the fact that antimony and tin are amphoteric elements; as a result, their sulfides will dissolve in excess base, whereas those of the other members of Group II--the copper subgroup--will not dissolve under these conditions. A 3 M sodium hydroxide solution will effect this separation. The sulfides insoluble under these conditions are

$$HgS, \ PbS, \ Bi_2S_3, \ and \ CuS$$

which constitute the copper subgroup. Equations for the dissolution of the antimony subgroup are:

$$4 \ Sb_2S_5 \ + \ 24 \ OH^- \ \rightleftarrows \ 5 \ SbS_4^{3-} \ + \ 3 \ SbO_4^{3-} \ + \ 12 \ H_2O$$

$$3 \ SnS_2 \ + \ 6 \ OH^- \ \rightleftarrows \ 2 \ SnS_3^{2-} \ + \ SnO_3^{2-} \ + \ 3 \ H_2O.$$

Copper Subgroup Analysis. A 4 M nitric acid solution will dissolve the sulfides of lead, bismuth, and copper but will not dissolve HgS. This is the basis for the separation of Hg^{2+} from the other cations of the copper subgroup. The reactions with HNO_3 are:

$$3 \ MS \ + \ 8 \ H_3O^+ \ + \ 2 \ NO_3^- \ \rightleftarrows \ 3 \ M^{2+} \ + \ 2 \ NO\uparrow \ + \ 12 \ H_2O \ + \ 3 \ S$$

in which MS = PbS, CuS;

$$Bi_2S_3 \ + \ 8 \ H_3O^+ \ + \ 2 \ NO_3^- \ \rightleftarrows \ 2 \ Bi^{3+} \ + \ 2 \ NO\uparrow \ + \ 12 \ H_2O \ + \ 3 \ S.$$

Confirmation of Mercury. Mercury is confirmed by first oxidizing the sulfide using aqua regia. The key reaction is:

$$3 \ HgS \ + \ 8 \ H_3O^+ \ + \ 2 \ NO_3^- \ + \ 12 \ Cl^- \ \rightleftarrows \ 3 \ HgCl_4^{2-} \ + \ 3 \ S \ + \ 2 \ NO\uparrow \ + \ 12 \ H_2O.$$

The solution is then evaporated carefully to a paste to get rid of excess HCl and HNO_3 and to convert $HgCl_4^{2-}$ to $HgCl_2$. The residue is redissolved in water. This water solution is then treated with excess tin(II) chloride which reduces the mercury to the +1 and subsequently to the 0 oxidation state.* Under these conditions, mercury(I) precipitates initially as white Hg_2Cl_2, which is then reduced to metallic mercury which appears black. The confirmatory test for mercury then is observed as a white precipitate turning to gray as the black mercury is formed and mixes with the white Hg_2Cl_2. Ultimately, the mixture turns black since all mercury present is reduced to the 0 oxidation state. The important equations are:

$$2 \ HgCl_2 \ + \ Sn^{2+} \ + \ 4 \ Cl^- \ \rightleftarrows \ SnCl_6^{2-} \ + \ Hg_2Cl_2 \ (white)$$

$$Hg_2Cl_2 \ + \ Sn^{2+} \ + \ 4 \ Cl^- \ \rightleftarrows \ SnCl_6^{2-} \ + \ 2 \ Hg \ (black).$$

Separation and Confirmation of Lead. Pb^{2+}, Bi^{3+}, and Cu^{2+}, if present in the sample, are in the decantate resulting from the treatment of the copper subgroup precipitate with the nitric acid. Lead ion can be precipitated in the presence of the bismuth and copper ions by using sulfate ion which forms white insoluble lead sulfate, $PbSO_4$. The reagent used to supply sulfate ions is ammonium sulfate, $(NH_4)_2SO_4$.

This reagent is added as a solid and stirred into the solution to provide a high concentration of sulfate ions. After stirring for a few minutes, the solution is cooled to minimize the possibility of lead sulfate forming supersaturated solutions. If no precipitate forms at this point, the solution should be allowed to stand for several minutes before it is concluded that lead is not present. Even small amounts of white precipitate at this point should be carried over to the confirmatory tests for lead. Since lead sulfate is highly granular and very efficiently packed, small amounts of this material often give voluminous precipitates of $PbCrO_4$ in the confirmatory test for lead. Lead ion is confirmed by separating the lead sulfate from its decantate and dissolving it in a solution of ammonium acetate, $CH_3CO_2NH_4$. Acetate ion forms a soluble covalent compound with lead which displaces the equilibrium to the right, causing the lead sulfate to

---

*Excess $SnCl_2$ is necessary because some oxidizing capacity remains from the aqua regia.

$$\underline{PbSO_4} + 2\ CH_3CO_2^- \rightleftharpoons Pb(CH_3CO_2)_2(aq) + SO_4^{2-}$$

dissolve. Once the lead sulfate is dissolved, Pb^{2+} is reprecipitated as the brilliant yellow lead chromate, $PbCrO_4$, by adding potassium dichromate reagent, $K_2Cr_2O_7$, to the solution. The important reaction is

$$2\ Pb(CH_3CO_2)_2(aq) + Cr_2O_7^{2-} + H_2O \rightleftharpoons 2\ CH_3CO_2H + \underline{2\ PbCrO_4}\ (yellow).$$

Separation and Confirmation of Bismuth. The decantate from the precipitation of lead sulfate may contain Bi^{3+} and Cu^{2+} ions. Bismuth ions are separated from copper ions by addition of concentrated ammonia which leads to the formation of insoluble bismuth hydroxide, $Bi(OH)_3$, and the formation of the soluble complex ion, $Cu(NH_3)_4^{2+}$. Bismuth hydroxide is a white precipitate; the tetraammine copper(II) ion is deep blue. Normally, a white precipitate at this point indicates the presence of bismuth, and a deep blue solution characteristic of the $Cu(NH_3)_4^{2+}$ ion is an indication of the presence of copper. The key reactions are:

$$NH_3 + H_2O \rightleftharpoons NH_4^+ + OH^-$$

$$Bi^{3+} + 3\ OH^- \rightleftharpoons \underline{Bi(OH)_3}$$

$$Cu^{2+} + 4\ NH_3 \rightleftharpoons [Cu(NH_3)_4]^{2+}\ (blue).$$

Bismuth ion is confirmed by adding a specific reducing agent which will reduce bismuth(III) ion to metallic bismuth. This will appear as a black precipitate in the reaction mixture. The specific reducing agent used for this is sodium stannite solution. The important reaction is

$$\underline{2\ Bi(OH)_3} + 3\ HSnO_2^- + 3\ OH^- \rightleftharpoons \underline{2\ Bi}\ (black) + 3\ SnO_3^{2-} + 6\ H_2O.$$

Confirmation of Copper. This is accomplished by treating the decantate from the separation of bismuth with acetic acid to destroy the ammine complex. The reaction is

$$Cu(NH_3)_4^{2+} + 4\ CH_3CO_2H \rightleftharpoons Cu^{2+} + 4\ NH_4^+ + 4\ CH_3CO_2^-.$$

The copper ion can now be precipitated as the reddish brown copper ferrocyanide, $Cu_2Fe(CN)_6$, by addition of potassium ferrocyanide reagent, $K_4Fe(CN)_6$. The key reaction is

$$2\ Cu^{2+} + [Fe(CN)_6]^{4-} \rightleftharpoons \underline{Cu_2[Fe(CN)_6]}\ \begin{array}{l}\text{deep rose to}\\ \text{reddish brown color.}\end{array}$$

Antimony Subgroup Analysis. At this point in the analysis, the members of the antimony subgroup are found dissolved in a basic solution in the form of their anions, SbS_4^{3-}, SbO_4^{3-}, SnS_3^{2-}, or SnO_3^{2-}. Because the confirmatory tests for antimony and tin are much more easily performed on the chloro complex ions of these elements than on their oxo- or thio-anions, concentrated hydrochloric acid is added to the solution. This reagent functions first to neutralize the base and then to convert the anions of antimony and tin, if present, to the corresponding chloro anions of these elements, $SbCl_6^-$ and $SnCl_6^{2-}$. The reactions can be represented as:

$$SbS_4^{3-} + 8\ H_3O^+ + 6\ Cl^- \longrightarrow SbCl_6^- + 4\ H_2S + 8\ H_2O$$

$$SbO_4^{3-} + 8\ H_3O^+ + 6\ Cl^- \longrightarrow SbCl_6^- + 12\ H_2O$$

$$SnS_3^{2-} + 6\ H_3O^+ + 6\ Cl^- \longrightarrow SnCl_6^{2-} + 3\ H_2S + 6\ H_2O$$

$$SnO_3^{2-} + 6\ H_3O^+ + 6\ Cl^- \longrightarrow SnCl_6^{2-} + 9\ H_2O.$$

The solution formed as a result of the treatment with concentrated hydrochloric acid can now be divided into two parts, one part to be used to test for the precence of tin and the other for the presence of antimony.

To confirm tin, it is necessary to remove the antimony, if present, from solution and also to reduce the tin from the IV to the II oxidation state. A clean iron nail placed in the solution will serve as the reducing agent and will give rise to a large black precipitate if antimony is present. The reactions are:

375

$$SnCl_6^{2-} + Fe \rightleftharpoons Fe^{2+} + 6\ Cl^- + Sn^{2+}$$

$$2\ SbCl_6^- + 5\ Fe \rightleftharpoons 5\ Fe^{2+} + \underline{2Sb}\ \text{(black)} + 12\ Cl^-.$$

A heavy black precipitate at this point is definite evidence that antimony is present. After separating the black residue of antimony and the iron nail, the solution can be tested for the presence of tin. If tin is present, it is now in its II oxidation state. In this state, it can reduce mercury from the II to the I and finally to the 0 oxidation state. This is accomplished by adding mercury(II) chloride, $HgCl_2$, and observing the white to gray to black color changes as the mercury is converted to mercury(I) and precipitated as Hg_2Cl_2, and this is further reduced to black metallic mercury according to the equations:

$$Sn^{2+} + 2\ HgCl_2 + 2\ Cl^- \rightleftharpoons SnCl_4 + \underline{Hg_2Cl_2}\ \text{(white)}$$

$$Sn^{2+} + Hg_2Cl_2 + 2\ Cl^- \rightleftharpoons SnCl_4 + \underline{2\ Hg}\ \text{(black)}.$$

The second portion of the solution containing the antimony subgroup ions can be tested for the presence of antimony. To do this, the tin ions present must be complexed in such a way that they will not precipitate under the conditions created to precipitate the antimony. This is accomplished by adding oxalic acid, $H_2C_2O_4$. While both antimony and tin form complex ions with this substance, the tin complexes are somewhat more stable than those of antimony; hence, it is possible to add thioacetamide and to cause orange antimony sulfide, Sb_2S_5, to precipitate without having tin sulfide precipitate. The reactions are:

$$SbCl_6^- + 3\ C_2O_4^{2-} \rightleftharpoons Sb(C_2O_4)_3^- + 6\ Cl^-$$

$$SnCl_6^{2-} + 3\ C_2O_4^{2-} \rightleftharpoons Sn(C_2O_4)_3^{2-} + 6\ Cl^-$$

$$2\ Sb(C_2O_4)_3^- + 5\ S^{2-} \rightleftharpoons \underline{Sb_2S_5} + 6\ C_2O_4^{2-}.$$

PROCEDURES FOR GROUP II ANALYSIS

Precipitation and Separation into Subgroups; Analysis of Copper Subgroup. The decantate from the separation of Group I may contain any or all of the cations of Groups II and III.* Pour this decantate into a casserole and evaporate to a paste (not to dryness). Add 8 to 10 drops of 12 M HCl and 8 to 10 drops of 16 M HNO_3 and evaporate again to a paste. Dissolve the residue in 8 drops of water and 6 drops of 6 M HNO_3. Add enough 5% thioacetamide solution (about 26 drops) to bring the volume of the mixture to 2 mL (**Note 1**). Heat the mixture in a boiling water bath in the hood for 5 minutes, stirring well. Centrifuge, decant the liquid, and save the solid. Divide the decantate, place half of it in a 4-mL test tube and the other half in a second test tube. To each of these test tubes, add 10 drops of 5% thioacetamide solution and 10 drops of H_2O. Check the pH of each tube and adjust if necessary as in Note 1. Heat 5 minutes more in a hood. To assure complete precipitation, again add 10 drops of 5% thioacetamide and 10 drops of water to each of the tubes and heat for 5 more minutes. Centrifuge, decant, and combine all of the precipitate (**Note 2**). Save the decantate for analysis of Group III and use the combined precipitate in the analysis of Group II.

---

*If your unknown is a solid sample of Group II ions only, treat 50 mg of the unknown powder with 1 mL of 12 M HCl. Immerse the test tube in boiling water and stir continuously for two minutes or until the powder is dissolved entirely. The resultant solution is treated according to the procedure starting at the asterisk above. The test tube should be rinsed with distilled water.

Precipitate: <u>HgS</u> (black), <u>PbS</u> (black), Bi_2S_3 (brown), <u>CuS</u> (black), Sb_2S_5 (orange), SnS_2 (yellow). Wash the precipitate <u>once</u> with 2 mL of distilled water and discard the washing. Now add 10 drops of 3 M NaOH and stir vigorously for 20-30 seconds. Centrifuge and decant the clear liquid.

Decantate: Stopper tightly and save for analysis of Group III.

Precipitate: <u>HgS</u>, <u>PbS</u>, Bi_2S_3, <u>CuS</u>. Wash the precipitate once with 2 mL of water and discard the washing. Now add 6 drops of 6 M HNO_3 and heat on a boiling water bath in a hood for 3 minutes. Centrifuge and decant the liquid into a clean test tube. Repeat this procedure using another 6 drops of 6 M HNO_3, and add this decantate to the above decantate.

Decantate: Antimony subgroup. Stopper tightly and save for analysis of the antimony subgroup.

Precipitate: <u>HgS</u> (black or red) and <u>S</u> (yellow). Dissolve this precipitate in 3 drops of 12 M HCl and 1 drop of 16 M HNO_3, using moderate heat. Add 1 mL of water and evaporate the solution to a paste. Redissolve in 1 mL of water, and evaporate the solution to a paste. Redissolve in 1 mL of water, centrifuge to remove any sulfur, and add 2 drops of 0.5 M $SnCl_2$. A white to gray to black precipitate confirms the presence of mercury(II).

Decantate: Pb^{2+}, Bi^{3+}, Cu^{2+}. To this decantate, add 0.4 grams of solid $(NH_4)_2SO_4$. Stir until this is dissolved, and allow this mixture to stand for 3-5 minutes. If no precipitate forms, cool the mixture in an ice bath for another 5 minutes to see if a precipitate will form. Centrifuge and decant.

Precipitate: $PbSO_4$ (white). Wash the residue with hot water three times and discard these washings. Then dissolve it in 4 drops of 3 M $CH_3CO_2NH_4$, heating if necessary. Add 1 drop of 6 M CH_3CO_2H and 2 drops of saturated $K_2Cr_2O_7$. A voluminous yellow precipitate confirms the presence of Pb^{2+}.

Decantate: Bi^{3+} and Cu^{2+}. Add 15 M NH_3 dropwise until the solution is strongly basic. Centrifuge and decant.

Precipitate: $Bi(OH)_3$ (white). Wash this residue <u>once</u> with water and discard the wash solution. Add to the precipitate 2 drops of freshly prepared sodium stannite solution.* A black precipitate of metallic bismuth confirms the presence of Bi^{3+}.

Decantate: $Cu(NH_3)_4^{2+}$. If Cu^{2+} is present, this solution should now be a deep blue color. Make the solution acid with 6 M CH_3CO_2H, and add a few crystals of solid $K_4Fe(CN)_6$. A red precipitate of $Cu_2Fe(CN)_6$ confirms the presence of Cu^{2+}.

---

*The sodium stannite solution is prepared by adding 6 M NaOH drop by drop, with stirring, to two drops of a solution containing 0.5 M $SnCl_2$ in 6 M HCl until the first precipitate just dissolves. The equation is: $3\ OH^- + Sn^{2+} \longrightarrow Sn(OH)_3^-$.

Antimony Subgroup Analysis. The decantate resulting from the addition of sodium hydroxide to the Group II precipitate should contain the oxo- and thio-anions of antimony and tin if either of these elements is present. To this solution, add 3 M HCl dropwise and with constant stirring until the solution is barely acidic. Centrifuge, discard the decantate, wash the precipitate with 1 mL of water, and discard the washing. To the precipitate, add 10 drops of 12 M HCl and place in a boiling water bath for at least 3 minutes. Centrifuge the mixture, decant, save the decantate, and discard the residue which may consist of sulfur and traces of mercury sulfide if Hg^{2+} is present. **Now divide this decantate into equal parts.** Test one part for antimony, the other for tin.

Test for Tin

Add a clean iron nail to the mixture in the test tube, and heat for 5 minutes on the water bath. The appearance of a voluminous black precipitate at this point indicates the presence of antimony. Centrifuge, if necessary, and decant the clear liquid into a test tube containing 4 drops of 0.1 M $HgCl_2$. A white to gray to black precipitate confirms the presence of tin.

Test for Antimony

Add 0.5 gram of oxalic acid and 5 mL of water to the solution. Stir and heat until the oxalic acid is dissolved. Add 5 drops of thioacetamide and heat for 2 minutes. An orange-red precipitate of Sb_2S_5 indicates the presence of antimony. When tin is present, a slowly forming brown precipitate may also appear.

NOTES

Note 1. Because the pH of this solution is critical, you should check it, and adjust it if necessary, as follows:

Obtain a small piece of filter paper. Using methyl violet solution, make 5 or 6 small spots on the filter paper. Put one drop of the pH 0.4 H_2SO_4 test solution on one of the spots and note the color. Before this spot dries, place one drop of your solution on another spot. Compare the colors. If your solution makes the methyl violet more yellow than the pH 0.4 test solution, then your solution is too acidic. If the result is more blue, then your solution is too basic. For a solution that is too acidic, add 3 M NaOH drop by drop until the pH is correct. If the solution is too basic, add 6 M HNO_3 drop by drop until the pH is correct.

Note 2. Use 2 mL of water from your wash bottle to wash the precipitate into a single test tube.

REFERENCES

1. Whitten and Gailey, General Chemistry with Qualitative Analysis, Saunders College Publishing, Philadelphia, PA, 1984, Chapter 31-36.

2. Garrett, Sisler, Bonk, and Stoufer, Semimicro Qualitative Analysis, Blaisdell Publishing Company, Waltham, MA, 1966.

3. Layde and Busch, Introduction to Qualitative Analysis, 2nd Ed., Allyn and Bacon, Inc., Boston, MA, 1971.

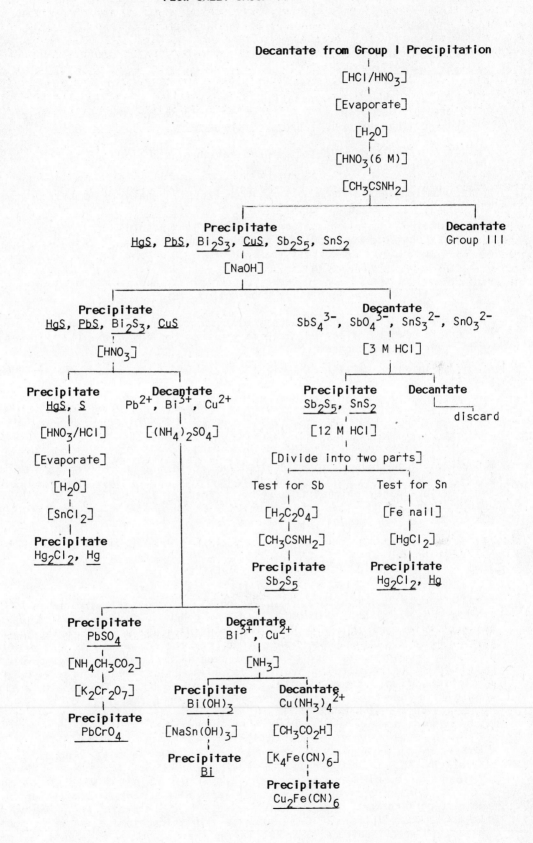

Decantate from Group I Precipitation

[HCl/HNO$_3$]

[Evaporate]

[H$_2$O]

[HNO$_3$ (6 M)]

[CH$_3$CSNH$_2$]

Precipitate
HgS, PbS, Bi$_2$S$_3$, CuS, Sb$_2$S$_5$, SnS$_2$

Decantate
Group III

[NaOH]

Precipitate
HgS, PbS, Bi$_2$S$_3$, CuS

Decantate
SbS$_4^{3-}$, SbO$_4^{3-}$, SnS$_3^{2-}$, SnO$_3^{2-}$

[HNO$_3$]

[3 M HCl]

Precipitate
HgS, S

Decantate
Pb^{2+}, Bi^{3+}, Cu^{2+}

Precipitate
Sb$_2$S$_5$, SnS$_2$

Decantate
discard

[HNO$_3$/HCl]

[(NH$_4$)$_2$SO$_4$]

[12 M HCl]

[Evaporate]

[Divide into two parts]

[H$_2$O]

Test for Sb

Test for Sn

[SnCl$_2$]

[H$_2$C$_2$O$_4$]

[Fe nail]

Precipitate
Hg$_2$Cl$_2$, Hg

[CH$_3$CSNH$_2$]

[HgCl$_2$]

Precipitate
Sb$_2$S$_5$

Precipitate
Hg$_2$Cl$_2$, Hg

Precipitate
PbSO$_4$

Decantate
Bi^{3+}, Cu^{2+}

[NH$_4$CH$_3$CO$_2$]

[NH$_3$]

[K$_2$Cr$_2$O$_7$]

Precipitate
Bi(OH)$_3$

Decantate
Cu(NH$_3$)$_4^{2+}$

Precipitate
PbCrO$_4$

[NaSn(OH)$_3$]

[CH$_3$CO$_2$H]

Precipitate
Bi

[K$_4$Fe(CN)$_6$]

Precipitate
Cu$_2$Fe(CN)$_6$

1. Why is 0.3 M acid used in the precipitation of the Group II cations? Calculate the equilibrium concentration of S^{2-} present in a 0.10 M H_2S solution that also contains 0.3 M H_3O^+ aqueous solution.

2. In analyzing Group II unknowns, several students in one class used sulfuric acid and several others used hydrochloric acid instead of the nitric acid prescribed in the procedure for the precipitation of Group II. Some of these students obtained white precipitates upon adding the acid. Account for the white precipitates and for the fact that not all students obtained them.

3. What is the chemical basis for the separation of the sulfides of Group II cations into the copper and antimony subgroups?

4. Write equations based on procedures from Group II analysis to illustrate each of the following:

   a) control of the concentration of sulfide ion in solution
   b) the amphoteric behavior of a metal sulfide
   c) the formation of a complex ion
   d) oxidation by aqua regia
   e) removal of one cation in order to precipitate another
   f) reduction of a cation to its 0 oxidation state

5. How would you distinguish between the substances in each of the following pairs (i) if both members of the pair are in the same container and (ii) if each member of the pair is in a separate container?

   a) lead sulfide and tin(IV) sulfide
   b) bismuth sulfide and copper sulfide
   c) mercury(II) sulfide and lead sulfide
   d) antimony(V) sulfide and tin(IV) sulfide
   e) lead sulfate and bismuth sulfate
   f) lead chloride and lead sulfate

6. You are given an aqueous solution that may contain any, all, or none of the ions given in each of the lettered items below. In each case, cite a reagent, reagents, or an operation that if added or performed would enable you to determine which, if any, of the ions are present. State the observations that would lead you to the various possible conclusions.

   a) Pb^{2+} and Cu^{2+} d) Hg^{2+} and Sn^{4+} g) Sn^{2+} and Hg^{2+}
   b) Bi^{3+} and Cu^{2+} e) Hg^{2+} and Hg_2^{2+} h) Pb^{2+} and Zn^{2+}
   c) Sn^{4+} and Sb^{5+} f) Bi^{3+} and Sb^{5+}

7. A solid sample is known to contain any or all of the following compounds, but no others: $Hg_2(NO_3)_2$, $SbCl_3$, $Bi(OH)_3$, $CuCl_2$, and $HgCl_2$. It gave a white precipitate and a colorless solution (A) when treated with enough water to bring about solution. The precipitate (B) was separated from the decantate A. The precipitate was unchanged by the addition of concentrated NH_3, but it dissolved completely in dilute HCl. Addition of thioacetamide gave a bright orange precipitate. This precipitate dissolved completely when treated with NaOH. The decantate A gave no precipitate when treated with thioacetamide. On the basis of these observations, indicate whether each of the following ions was **definitely present, definitely absent,** or **undetermined** Hg^{2+}, NO_3^-, Sb^{3+}, Cl^-, Bi^{3+}, OH^-, Cu^{2+}, Hg_2^{2+}.

8. A solid sample is known to contain any or all of the following salts, but no others: $Hg_2(NO_3)_2$, $CuCl_2$, $PbCl_2$, $Bi(NO_3)_3$, and $SnCl_4$. It gave a white precipitate and a blue solution (A) when treated with sufficient water to bring about solution. A major portion of the precipitate (B) dissolved in hot water, with the remaining portion turning dark when treated with concentrated NH_3. The solution A gave a black precipitate (C) when treated with thioacetamide. A major portion of C dissolved when treated with NaOH. On the basis of these observations, classify each of the following ions as being **definitely present, definitely absent,** or **undetermined:** Hg_2^{2+}, NO_3^-, Cu^{2+}, Cl^-, Pb^{2+}, Bi^{3+}, Sn^{3+}.

GROUP II ANALYSIS

PRELABORATORY QUESTIONS

Name_____   Lab Instructor_____

Student ID No_____   Date_____

1. What is the basis for the separation of Group II cations from those of Group III?
    Why is the pH important in this separation?

2. List the cations in each of the Group II subgroups.

3. How are the subgroups separated from one another? What chemical principle forms
    the basis for this separation?

4. How would you separate the substances in each of the following pairs if both members of the pair are in the same container?

    a. Lead sulfide and zinc sulfide, both solids

    b. Lead sulfide and mercury(II) sulfide, both solids

    c. Lead nitrate and copper(II) nitrate, both in water solution

    d. Bismuth(III) nitrate and tin(IV) nitrate, both in water solution

5. What is aqua regia? What role does it play in Group II analysis?

6. What is thioacetamide? What role does it play in Group II analysis?

QUALITATIVE ANALYSIS OF IONIC MIXTURES

REPORT SHEET FOR GROUP II

Name_____   Lab Instructor_____

Student ID No_____   Date_____

Results of Each Separation Part of the Flow Sheet

Ions Present in Unknown _____

Observations That Differed from the Text Presentation

Attach Your Answers to the Assigned Questions Shown on the Next Page.

PART C. ANALYSIS OF GROUP III CATIONS

The Group III cations include: iron(II and III), Fe^{2+} and Fe^{3+}; aluminum, Al^{3+}; chromium, Cr^{3+}; cobalt, Co^{2+}; nickel, Ni^{2+}; and zinc, Zn^{2+}. Any or all of these ions present in the original sample will be found in the decantate from the precipitation of Group II. They are precipitated from this decantate in two groups of three. Iron, aluminum, and chromium hydroxides are initially precipitated by adding a concentrated ammonia solution to the decantate. These hydroxides are separated and analyzed as the aluminum subgroup. The remaining Group III cations are precipiated as sulfides using ammonium sulfide, $(NH_4)_2S$. They are analyzed as the nickel subgroup.

Before attempting to precipitate iron, aluminum, and chromium hydroxides, it is necessary to remove hydrogen sulfide from the solution; otherwise, the sulfides of the nickel subgroup will precipitate. This is accomplished by evaporating the decantate to a paste. Addition of concentrated ammonia then precipitates the aluminum subgroup hydroxides. The separation of the subgroups is accomplished in this step since ammonia also forms soluble complex ions with cobalt, nickel, and zinc. The important reactions are:

$$Al^{3+} + 3 NH_3 + 3 H_2O \rightleftharpoons 3 NH_4^+ + \underline{Al(OH)_3} \text{ (white)}$$

$$Fe^{3+} + 3 NH_3 + 3 H_2O \rightleftharpoons 3 NH_4^+ + \underline{Fe(OH)_3} \text{ (rust)}$$

$$Cr^{3+} + 3 NH_3 + 3 H_2O \rightleftharpoons 3 NH_4^+ + \underline{Cr(OH)_3} \text{ (blue-gray)}$$

$$Ni^{2+} + 6 NH_3 \rightleftharpoons [Ni(NH_3)_6]^{2+} \text{ (blue solution)}$$

$$Co^{2+} + 6 NH_3 \rightleftharpoons [Co(NH_3)_6]^{2+} \text{ (blue solution)}$$

$$Zn^{2+} + 4 NH_3 \rightleftharpoons [Zn(NH_3)_4]^{2+} \text{ (colorless solution)}.$$

The hydroxides of nickel subgroup members are prevented from precipitating not only through the formation of the complex ammine ions but also because the hydroxide ion concentration is carefully controlled by an ammonium ion/ammonia buffer system. This equilibrium is represented by the equation:

$$NH_3 + H_2O \rightleftharpoons NH_4^+ + OH^-.$$

By means of this equilibrium, the hydroxide ion concentration can be maintained at a level high enough to precipitate the aluminum subgroup hydroxides but too low (because of the added ammonium ion) to permit precipitation of the nickel subgroup.

Aluminum Subgroup Analysis. Aluminum and chromium hydroxides are separated from iron(III) hydroxide by making use of their amphoteric properties. Thus, the addition of sodium hydroxide and hydrogen peroxide solutions and subsequent heating of the mixture result in the dissolution of aluminum hydroxide through formation of hydroxo complexes. Iron(III) hydroxide does not form such complexes. The equation is:

$$Al(OH)_3 + OH^- \rightleftharpoons Al(OH)_4^-.$$

At the same time, chromium hydroxide is dissolved through oxidation of chromium from the III to the VI oxidation state, using hydrogen peroxide in a basic solution. Iron(III) hydroxide is not oxidized under these conditions. The key reaction is:

$$2 Cr(OH)_3 + 3 H_2O_2 + 4 OH^- \rightleftharpoons 2 CrO_4^{2-} \text{ (yellow)} + 8 H_2O.$$

Confirmation of Aluminum. Aluminum ion is confirmed by allowing it to pre-cipitate as the hydroxide in the presence of a red organic dye called aluminon. As the aluminum hydroxide precipitate forms in this solution, the dye is absorbed on it, thereby enhancing and concentrating the color of the dye and giving a specific test for aluminum.

Because the conditions for the absorption of the dye must be carefully con-trolled, the decantate containing the hydroxo complex of aluminum is treated with a series of reagents prior to bringing the aluminum ions in contact with the dye. Thus, the decantate is first neutralized to convert the hydroxo complex to Al^{3+}, according to the reaction:

$$Al(OH)_4^- + 4 H_3O^+ \rightleftharpoons Al^{3+} + 8 H_2O.$$

Under these conditions, the yellow solution, because of the chromate ion, CrO_4^{2-}, will turn orange as the dichromate ion, $Cr_2O_7^{2-}$, is produced.

$$2 CrO_4^{2-} + 2 H_3O^+ \rightleftharpoons Cr_2O_7^{2-} + 3 H_2O.$$

Then aluminum hydroxide is carefully precipitated again by using ammonia and ammonium chloride. Under these conditions, the CrO_4^{2-} ion will be regenerated, but no chromium species should precipitate. The purpose of these reagents is to control the hydroxide ion concentration in the solution so as to get a maximum volume of aluminum hydroxide precipitate. The use of ammonium ion avoids dissolving some of the aluminum as $[Al(OH)_4]^-$ by controlling the amount of excess hydroxide ion.

Aluminum hydroxide is then dissolved in a mixture of acetic acid and ammonium acetate, $CH_3CO_2H/CH_3CO_2NH_4$, and the aluminon dye is added to this solution. Finally, the solution is made basic by adding ammonia. This provides hydroxide ions for still another precipitation of aluminum hydroxide. This time, as aluminum hydroxide precipitates, it carries the dye with it, giving the enhanced and concentrated color.

Chromium is confirmed by reconverting chromate ion, CrO_4^{2-}, to dichromate ion, $Cr_2O_7^{2-}$, by making the solution acidic. Treatment of the dichromate ion with hydrogen peroxide in acid solution produces a peroxy acid of chromium having the formula, H_2CrO_5. This acid is blue in color and is reasonably stable in ether. Thus, a few drops of ether are added to the solution following the oxidation of chromium to chromate and its conversion to dichromate. The presence of a blue color congregating in the ether layer is indicative of the presence of chromium. The important reactions in these procedures are:

$$2 CrO_4^{2-} + 2 H_3O^+ \rightleftharpoons Cr_2O_7^{2-} + 3 H_2O$$

$$Cr_2O_7^{2-} + 2 H_3O^+ + 2 H_2O_2 \rightleftharpoons 2 H_2CrO_5 \text{ (blue in ether)} + 3 H_2O.$$

Confirmation of Iron. $Fe(OH)_3$ is dissolved in HCl and the solution treated with ammonium thiocyanate, NH_4SCN; this forms a blood red complex having the formula $Fe(NCS)^{2+}$. The important reactions are:

$$Fe(OH)_3 + 3 H_3O^+ \rightleftharpoons Fe^{3+} + 6 H_2O$$

$$Fe^{3+} + SCN^- \rightleftharpoons Fe(NCS)^{2+} \text{ (blood red).}$$

Nickel Subgroup Analysis. The cations of the nickel subgroup are found as their ammine complexes, $Ni(NH_3)_6^{2+}$, $Co(NH_3)_6^{2+}$, and $Zn(NH_3)_4^{2+}$ in the decantate from the precipitation of the aluminum subgroup hydroxides at the beginning of the analysis of Group III. The nickel subgroup members are first precipitated as sulfides by adding ammonium sulfide, $(NH_4)_2S$ to this solution and heating. The key reactions are:

$$Ni(NH_3)_6^{2+} + S^{2-} \rightleftharpoons \underline{NiS} \text{ (black)} + 6 NH_3$$

$$Co(NH_3)_6^{2+} + S^{2-} \rightleftharpoons \underline{CoS} \text{ (black)} + 6 NH_3$$

$$Zn(NH_3)_4^{2+} + S^{2-} \rightleftharpoons \underline{ZnS} \text{ (white)} + 4 NH_3.$$

Separation of Zinc from Cobalt and Nickel. This is accomplished by first heating the sulfides so as to convert those of nickel and cobalt to less soluble crystalline modifications that dissolve very slowly in acid. Then the mixture is treated with 3 M HCl which permits the zinc sulfide to dissolve without affecting the NiS or CoS. The important reaction is

$$ZnS + 2 H_3O^+ \rightleftharpoons Zn^{2+} + H_2S + 2 H_2O.$$

The zinc ion, having been dissolved and separated, can now be reprecipitated as white ZnS by use of thioacetamide.

Analysis of Nickel and Cobalt. At this point in the analysis, cobalt and nickel are present as a precipitate containing NiS and CoS. These sulfides are readily soluble in aqua regia. The important reactions are:

$$\underline{3\ NiS} + 8\ H_3O^+ + 2\ NO_3^- \rightleftharpoons 3\ Ni^{2+} + 2\ NO + 3\ S + 12\ H_2O$$

$$\underline{3\ CoS} + 8\ H_3O^+ + 2\ NO_3^- \rightleftharpoons 3\ Co^{2+} + 2\ NO + 3\ S + 12\ H_2O.$$

Following the treatment with aqua regia, the solution must be evaporated just to a paste to remove this strong oxidizing agent and any excess sulfur that may be present. The paste is then treated with dilute hydrochloric acid and the solution divided into equal parts. One is tested for nickel, the other for cobalt.

The test for nickel involves making the solution basic with ammonia and then adding a small amount of dimethylglyoxime, a specific and sensitive test reagent for nickel. This substance on contact with nickel ion gives a brilliant red color. The reaction is:

$$(\text{green})\ Ni^{2+} + 2\ NH_3 + 2\ (CH_3)_2C_2(NOH)_2 \rightleftharpoons 2\ NH_4^+ + \underline{Ni(C_4H_7N_2O_2)_2}\ (\text{red}).$$

Cobalt(II) forms a brownish, soluble complex, $[Co(DMG)_3]^-$. Although this complex does not interfere with identification of Ni^{2+}, its color is noted more quickly, and excess dimethylglyoxime reagent may have to be added.

The test for cobalt ions involves their reaction with thiocyanate ion, SCN^-, which gives a blue complex ion having the formula $Co(NCS)_4^{2-}$. The color of this ion is more pronounced if a small amount of acetone is added to the solution. The reaction is

$$Co^{2+} + 4\ SCN^- \rightleftharpoons Co(NCS)_4^{2-}\ (\text{blue in acetone}).$$

PROCEDURE FOR GROUP III ANALYSIS

We are now ready to analyze the decantate from the precipitation of Group II which may contain any or all of the ions, Al^{3+}, Cr^{3+}, Fe^{2+} or Fe^{3+}, Co^{2+}, Ni^{2+}, Zn^{2+}.* These ions are in an acid solution containing H_2S and S^{2-} ions. Pour the decantate from the precipitation of Group II into a casserole and evaporate just to a paste (not to dryness). Add 2 drops of 6 M HCl and 25 drops of 3% H_2O_2, and again evaporate to a paste. Dissolve the residue in 10 drops of water to which has been added 2 drops of 6 M HCl. To this, add 3 drops of 3 M NH_4Cl and enough 15 M NH_3 to make the solution distinctly basic. Do not add a large excess. Stir well, centrifuge quickly, and decant the clear liquid. Add 1 drop of 6 M NH_3 to the decantate to test for completeness of precipitation.

---

*If your unknown is a solid sample of Group III ions only, treat 50 mg of the unknown powder with 1 mL of 12 M HCl. Immerse the test tube in boiling water and stir continuously for a few seconds. When the powder is dissolved entirely, treat the solution according to the procedure starting at the asterisk above.

Separation of Aluminum and Nickel Subgroups

Precipitate: Aluminum subgroup $Al(OH)_3$ (white), $Cr(OH)_3$ (blue-gray), $Fe(OH)_3$ (rust). Wash the precipitate once with 0.5 mL of 1.5 M ammonia and proceed as described under the aluminum subgroup on the next page.

Decantate: $Ni(NH_3)_6^{2+}$, $Co(NH_3)_6^{2+}$, $Zn(NH_3)_4^{2+}$. To the decantate add 10 drops of 6 M NH_3. Then add 10 drops of thioacetamide. Heat in a boiling water bath for at least 10 minutes with occasional stirring. Centrifuge and decant the clear liquid. Save the precipitate. To the decantate, add 2 drops of thioacetamide, CH_3CSNH_2, and heat as before. If no additional precipitate is produced, discard this decantate. Combine the precipitates and proceed as described under the nickel subgroup.

Nickel Subgroup Analysis

Precipitate: Nickel subgroup <u>NiS</u> (black), <u>CoS</u> (black), <u>ZnS</u> (white). Wash this precipiate once with water and discard the washings. To the precipitate add 10 drops of cold 1 M HCl, and stir constantly for 1 minute. Centrifuge and decant the clear liquid.

Precipitate: <u>NiS</u>, <u>CoS</u>. Wash the precipitate once with water, and discard the washings. Now treat the precipitate with 6 drops of 12 M HCl and 2 drops of 16 M HNO_3. Heat the mixture until the black residue dissolves, discarding any white or yellow residue of sulfur which remains. Transfer the solution to a casserole and evaporate to a paste. Add 10 drops of water and 1 drop of 6 M HCl. Divide the solution into 2 equal parts. Test one part for nickel, the other for cobalt.

Test for Nickel: Drop 6 M NH_3 into the solution until it is basic. Do not add an excess of NH_3. Then add 2 drops of dimethylglyoxime solution and mix. A red precipitate of nickel dimethylglyoxime indicates the presence of Ni^{2+}. If a brownish solution forms initially, cobalt(II) is quite likely present. Add several more drops of dimethylglyoxime to ensure complete precipitation of the red nickel compound. Centrifuge and decant, if necessary, to observe the red precipitate.

Test for Cobalt: Add 5 drops of 1 M NH_4SCN and 25-30 drops of acetone to the solution, and mix well. The appearance of blue solution due to $Co(NCS)_4^{2-}$ confirms the presence of Co^{2+}.

Decantate: Zn^{2+}. Add 6 M NH_3 dropwise until the solution is basic to litmus. Add 10 drops of thioacetamide and heat in a boiling water bath for 5 minutes while the top of the test tube is stoppered loosely with cotton. *Centrifuge the white ZnS precipitate and decant. To confirm that the precipitate is not sulfur, transfer it to a casserole and add 1 mL of 3 M HCl with gentle heating. (Sulfur will not dissolve.) Boil the solution down to 0.5 mL, and add 3 M NaOH with vigorous stirring until the solution is alkaline to litmus and then add 5 more drops. Transfer to a 4-mL test tube. If the solution is cloudy, centrifuge and decant. Discard the precipitate. Add 5 drops of thioacetamide to the decantate, and heat in a boiling water bath for 5 minutes, again having the test tube loosely stoppered with cotton. A white precipitate of ZnS confirms the presence of Zn^{2+}. A dark precipitate may indicate incomplete separation from nickel and cobalt. To complete the separation, redissolve and precipitate in HCl and reprecipitate the ZnS (start at *). If the precipitate becomes lighter after each of two or three repeated dissolving/precipitation cycles, then Zn may be inferred as being present.

Aluminum Subgroup Analysis. We find the aluminum subgroup as a precipitate containing any or all of the hydroxides of iron, aluminum, and chromium. To this precipitate add 6 drops of 6 M NaOH and 10 drops of 3% H_2O_2 and stir vigorously. When the evolution of gases has ceased, add 3 more drops of H_2O_2 and boil gently until the evolution of gases again ceases. Dilute the solution to 2 mL with thorough mixing, centrifuge, and remove the decantate.

Precipitate: $Fe(OH)_3$. Wash the precipitate once with distilled water and discard the washings. Dissolve the precipitate in 6 M HCl, and add 2 drops of NH_4SCN with stirring. A deep red color due to $FeNCS^{2+}$ confirms the presence of Fe^{3+}. A light pink color due to cobalt ion may be observed. If cobalt is present, the addition of 2 mL of acetone would turn the solution blue. If iron is in the sample, the addition of acetone would have no effect on the color.

Decantate: $Al(OH)_4^-$, CrO_4^{2-} Acidify this decantate with 6 M HNO_3, add 0.4 gram of NH_4Cl, and mix well. Now add 15 M NH_3 until the solution is distinctly alkaline. Approximately 1-2 mL may be needed. Heat the mixture for one minute. Centrifuge and remove the decantate.

Precipitate: $Al(OH)_3$. Add 10 drops of 6 M CH_3CO_2H and heat the mixture for 2-3 minutes. Discard any residue which remains. Now add to the solution 10 drops of 3 M $CH_3CO_2NH_4$ and 5 drops of aluminon test solution. While stirring the mixture, make it basic by adding 6 M NH_3. Heat the mixture for one minute. Formation of a red precipitate confirms the presence of Al^{3+}

Decantate: CrO_4^2 (yellow solution). Pour the decantate into a casserole and boil down to approximately 0.5 mL; acidify this solution with 6 M HNO_3 and cool to room temperature. Add 15 drops of ether and 5 drops of 3% H_2O_2 to a test tube. Then quickly pour the above decantate into the test tube containing the ether and H_2O_2. A sky blue coloration in the ether layer which disappears on standing a few seconds confirms the presence of Cr^{3+}.

ANION ANALYSIS

Procedures for identifying the ions NO_3^-, CO_3^{2-}, SO_4^{2-}, F^-, Cl^-, Br^-, and I^- are given in Exp. 3. A fresh sample of the unknown should be used for each of the anion identification tests.

FLOW SHEET: GROUP III

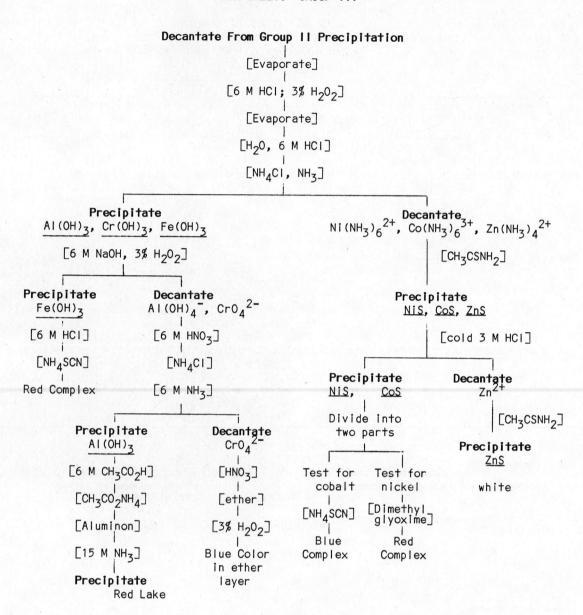

Decantate From Group II Precipitation

[Evaporate]

[6 M HCl; 3% H_2O_2]

[Evaporate]

[H_2O, 6 M HCl]

[NH_4Cl, NH_3]

Precipitate
$\underline{Al(OH)_3}$, $\underline{Cr(OH)_3}$, $\underline{Fe(OH)_3}$

[6 M NaOH, 3% H_2O_2]

Decantate
$Ni(NH_3)_6^{2+}$, $Co(NH_3)_6^{3+}$, $Zn(NH_3)_4^{2+}$

[CH_3CSNH_2]

Precipitate
$\underline{NiS}$, $\underline{CoS}$, $\underline{ZnS}$

[cold 3 M HCl]

Precipitate
$\underline{Fe(OH)_3}$

[6 M HCl]

[NH_4SCN]

Red Complex

Decantate
$Al(OH)_4^-$, CrO_4^{2-}

[6 M HNO_3]

[NH_4Cl]

[6 M NH_3]

Precipitate
$\underline{Al(OH)_3}$

[6 M CH_3CO_2H]

[$CH_3CO_2NH_4$]

[Aluminon]

[15 M NH_3]

Precipitate
Red Lake

Decantate
CrO_4^{2-}

[HNO_3]

[ether]

[3% H_2O_2]

Blue Color
in ether
layer

Precipitate
$\underline{NiS}$, $\underline{CoS}$

Divide into
two parts

Test for   Test for
cobalt   nickel

[NH_4SCN]   [Dimethyl
                glyoxime]

Blue   Red
Complex   Complex

Decantate
Zn^{2+}

[CH_3CSNH_2]

Precipitate
$\underline{ZnS}$

white

REFERENCES

1. Whitten and Gailey, _General Chemistry with Qualitative Analysis_, Saunders College Publishing, Philadelphia, PA, 1984, Chapters 31-36.

2. Garrett, Sisler, Bonk, and Stoufer, _Semimicro Qualitative Analysis_, Blaisdell Publishing Company, Waltham, MA, 1966.

3. Layde and Busch, _Introduction to Qualitative Analysis_, 2nd Ed., Allyn and Bacon, Inc., Boston, MA, 1971.

GROUP III ANALYSIS

PRELABORATORY QUESTIONS

Name_____   Lab Instructor_____

Student ID No_____   Date_____

1. How are the Group III cations precipitated for analysis?

2. List the cations in each of the Group III subgroups.

3. How can $Fe(OH)_3$ be separated from $Al(OH)_3$?

4. How can CoS be separated from ZnS?

5. If, upon precipitation of the aluminum subgroup, a white precipitate forms and if, upon precipitation of the nickel subgroup, a white precipitate forms, which Group III cations do you expect to be present and which absent from your unknown?

6. If a water solution containing some or all of the Group III cations were colorless, which Group III cations do you expect to be absent and which could be present?

7. A solid sample is known to contain two or more of the following salts in equivalent amounts, but no others: $Al(NO_3)_3$, $CrCl_3$, $Cu(NO_3)_2$, $SnCl_2$, and $CoCl_2$. It was completely soluble in concentrated NH_3, giving a colored solution (A). Solution A was neutralized and the NH_3 boiled out. It was then made 0.30 M in HNO_3 and thioacetamide was added, whereupon a black precipitate (B) and a colored solution (C) was observed. On the basis of these observations, classify each of the following ions as: **definitely absent, definitely present,** or **undetermined:** Al^{3+}, NO_3^-, Cr^{3+}, Cl^-, Cu^{2+}, Sn^{2+}, Co^{2+}.

Experiment 28

QUALITATIVE ANALYSIS OF IONIC MIXTURE

REPORT SHEET FOR GROUP III

Name_____   Lab Instructor_____

Student ID No_____   Date_____

Results at Each Separation Part of the Flow Sheet

Ions Present in Unknown _____

Observations That Differed from the Text Presentation

Attach Your Answers to the Assigned Questions Shown on the Next Page.

1. What property of the ions of cobalt, nickel, and zinc is used to separate them from the ions of iron, aluminum, and chromium?

2. If the sulfides of Group II were not all removed in the Group II precipitation procedure, would they precipitate with the Group III ions in the precipitation of Group III? Why or why not?

3. Write equations based on Group III procedures to illustrate each of the following:

    a) the separation of iron(III) ions from nickel(II) ions
    b) the separation of aluminum ions from chromium(III) ions
    c) the separation of zinc ions from cobalt(II) ions
    d) the oxidation of chromium from the III to the VI state
    e) the separation of iron ions from chromium ions
    f) the formation of three complex ions, each of which has different ligands (groups bonded to the metal ion)

4. How would you distinguish between the substances in each of the following pairs (i) if both are in the same container and (ii) if each is in a separate container?

    a) $Al(NO_3)_3$ and $Zn(NO_3)_2$ e) $Ni(NO_3)_2$ and $Co(NO_3)_2$
    b) $ZnCl_2$ and $NiCl_2$ f) $Al(OH)_3$ and $Cr(OH)_3$
    c) $Cr(OH)_3$ and $Fe(OH)_3$ g) $NiCl_2$ and $CuSO_4$
    d) CoS and ZnS h) $AlCl_3$ and $PbCl_2$

5. You are given an aqueous solution that may contain any, all, or none of the ions given in each of the lettered items below. In each case, cite a reagent, reagents, or an operation that if added or performed would enable you to determine which, if any, of the ions are present. State the observations that would lead you to the various possible conclusions.

    a) Cr^{3+} and Zn^{2+} e) Ni^{2+} and Bi^{3+}
    b) Cr^{3+} and Fe^{3+} f) Ag^+ and Al^{3+}
    c) Ni^{2+} and Co^{2+} g) Zn^{2+} and Hg^{2+}
    d) Al^{3+} and Cr^{3+} h) Sn^{2+} and Zn^{2+}

6. A solid sample is known to contain any or all of the following salts but no others: $Hg_2(NO_3)_2$, $HgCl_2$, SnS, $NiCl_2$, and $ZnCl_2$. It gave a brown precipitate and a colorless solution A when treated with water. The precipitate was completely soluble in NaOH. Solution A gave a white precipitate when treated with thioacetamide in basic solution. On the basis of these observations, classify each of the following ions as **definitely absent, definitely present,** or **undetermined:** Hg_2^{2+}, Hg^{2+}, Sn^{2+}, Ni^{2+}, Zn^{2+}, NO_3^-, Cl^-, S^{2-}.

7. A solid sample is known to contain any or all of the following compounds but no others: $PbCl_2$, $AgNO_3$, $BiCl_3$, $CoCl_2$, and $Fe(OH)_3$. It gave a white precipitate and a colored solution when treated with water. The white precipitate (A) was insoluble in hot water but soluble in NH_3. The colored solution (B) gave a white precipitate (C) when treated with concentrated NH_3. On the basis of these observations, classify the following ions as being **definitely absent, definitely present,** or **undetermined:** Pb^{2+}, Cl^-, Ag^+, NO_3^-, Co^{2+}, Fe^{3+}, OH^-.

8. Give the name or formula of a reagent that if added to each of the following pairs would bring about a separation of the cations:

    a) $HgCl_2$ and $PbCl_2$ f) $SbCl_3$ and $Bi(OH)_3$
    b) $Hg_2(NO_3)_2$ and $Hg(NO_3)_2$ g) $NiCl_2$ and $NaCl$
    c) $Pb(NO_3)_2$ and $Bi(NO_3)_3$ h) $Cu(NO_3)_2$ and $SnCl_2$
    d) $Cu(NO_3)_2$ and $Bi(NO_3)_3$ i) $AlCl_3$ and $HgCl_2$
    e) $Hg(NO_3)_2$ and $Fe(NO_3)_3$ j) $AlCl_3$ and $ZnCl_2$

ANALYSIS OF A MIXTURE OF SALTS

Experiments 29, 30, and 31

The purpose of this series of three experiments (nos. 29, 30, and 31) is to illustrate a method for quantitatively determining the concentrations of components of a mixture and to provide experience with the important analytical methods known as ion exchange chromatography, ion-selective electrodes, and complexometric titrations. More specifically, you will be asked to analyze a mixture of sodium chloride, sodium iodide, and zinc chloride to determine the concentration of sodium, zinc, and iodide ions in the mixture. You will do this by exchanging the sodium and zinc ions in solution for hydrogen ions (hydronium) using a cation exchange resin. You will then determine the total concentration of cations by titrating the hydronium ions with standard sodium hydroxide. Then the zinc ion concentration can be determined with an EDTA complexometric titration. The sodium ion concentration is the difference between the total cation concentration and the zinc ion concentration. Finally, iodide will be determined by the use of an iodide-selective electrode.

You will be given an unknown sample that is to be used for each of the Experiments 29, 30, and 31. Be careful not to contaminate the solution with dirty pipets or other solutions, and do not waste the sample solution.

ION EXCHANGE CHROMATOGRAPHY

Analysis for Total Cationic Charge

Objective

To use ion exchange chromatography to determine the total cation concentration of a solution containing sodium and zinc ions

Equipment Needed

25-mL Buret; 10-mL pipet; pipet bulb; cation exchange column; two 125-mL Erlenmeyer flasks

Reagents Needed

3 M HCl Solution; standardized solution of sodium hydroxide ($\sim$0.1 M); phenolphthalein; Dowex 50W-4X cation exchange resin; solutions of unknowns made from 1 M NaCl, 1 M NaI, and 1 M ZnCl$_2$

INTRODUCTION

Chromatography (Exp. 8) is a method of separation in which the components to be separated are distributed between two phases. In ion exchange chromatography charged ions are exchanged between a mobile solution phase and a stationary solid phase. Such exchange processes have been known for a long time. They are important in the interaction of soils with fertilizers and plant roots; also, they are used with naturally occurring mineral or man-made solid phases in various industrial operations, such as water softening.

Synthetic ion exchange resins are very insoluble polymers of high molecular weight. They have open netlike molecular structures which water and ions in solution can readily penetrate. Commercial resins may be divided into two main groups, acidic and basic; the names indicate their chemical nature. The acidic cation exchange resins are composed of organic polymers with acidic groups such as the strongly acidic sulfonic acid groups (-SO$_3$H) or the more weakly acidic carboxyl group (-CO$_2$H). The negative part of each sulfonate radical remains fixed to the resin molecule, but the hydrogen ions are free to move; thus, the ionizable hydrogen ions can be replaced by cations in the aqueous solution that permeates the pores of the resin. For example,

$$\text{Resin} \cdot \text{SO}_3\text{H} + \text{H}_2\text{O} + \text{Na}^+ \longrightarrow \text{resin} \cdot \text{SO}_3^-\text{Na}^+ + \text{H}_3\text{O}^+.$$

The extent to which a cation displaces the hydronium ion of such a resin depends upon several factors, among them the temperature and pH value of the solution. Of greater effect, however, is the relative concentration of the cation of the electrolyte because the cation exchange is a reversible one. Le Chatelier's principle applies here, just as it does to other chemical equilibria. The foregoing equilibrium can, therefore, be displaced to the left, and the original resin compound can be regenerated if acid of moderately high concentration is introduced into the system.

For many ion exchange equilibria, the equilibrium can be most conveniently and efficiently established by allowing a solution to percolate slowly through a tube containing a sufficiently long column of resin. As the solution percolates down the column, it continually contacts fresh resin, and the exchange occurs before the solution emerges from the end of the column. Thus, the concentration of a neutral salt in solution can be quantitatively determined by exchanging hydronium ions for the cation and then determining the acidity of the resulting solution by titration. Usually washing the column with pure solvent is necessary to assure that all ions that should be displaced from the column have actually been removed. Thus, after the solution has been percolated, follow it with pure solvent until the solvent comes through unchanged [i.e., when the effluent is neutral to pH paper]. You can then assume that the ion exchange resin has been returned to its stoichiometrically neutral state.

In this experiment, we shall use a cation exchange resin to determine the total concentration of positive charge in an unknown solution; the solution may contain any, or all, of the compounds sodium iodide, sodium chloride, and zinc chloride. The resin absorbs all of the cations from a sample of the solution and liberates hydronium ion, H_3O^+, which one can titrate with standardized sodium hydroxide.

PROCEDURE

Before starting this experiment, you should study "Use of Volumetric Glassware" (pp. 16-19) in the **Laboratory Techniques** section.

Regenerate the column to the H-form using 3 M HCl.

The equipment required for ion exchange chromatography is generally very simple. Obtain from your instructor a small glass column filled with cation resin and equipped with a rubber tube and screw clamp at the bottom. Treat the column with 30 mL of 3 M HCl solution. Pass the acid solution through the column at a rate not exceeding 3 mL per minute. **Never treat ion exchange resins with nitric acid or other oxidizing acids.** Then wash the resin column with distilled water until the effluent from the column tests neutral to pH paper. **Never allow the water level to fall below the level of the top of the resin.** The rate of flow of the wash solution can be 6 to 7 mL per minute.

If a large number of air bubbles appear in the column, repack the column. If necessary, the ion exchange column, filled with distilled water and tightly stoppered, can be kept in the laboratory locker until the next laboratory period. **The column must be returned to the instructor or the stock room when you have finished Exp. 29.**

Carefully pipet 10 mL of unknown solution onto the resin column.

Pipet 10 mL (**Note 1**) (accurate to 0.02 mL) of the unknown solution onto the resin column and collect the effluent in a clean 125-mL Erlenmeyer flask. Wash the column with distilled water, which has been boiled (to remove carbon dioxide) and cooled, until the effluent is neutral, i.e., until you have washed all of the liberated H_3O^+ from the column (**Note 2**).

Repeat with a second sample.

Titrate with standard base.

Pipet a second sample onto the column and begin collecting the effluent in a second clean flask. If you are careful to watch both the column and your titration, you can begin titrating the first solution while collecting the second. Titrate with standardized sodium hydroxide ($\sim$ 0.1 M), using four to five drops of phenolphthalein as an indicator. The results of the two titrations should agree to within 0.10 mL; if they do not, regenerate the column with hydrochloric acid and make one or two additional trials.

All data for this experiment should be recorded in your notebook and transferred later to the report sheet. Calculate and report the moles of hydronium ion liberated per liter of sample taken (or what can be called the molarity of positive charge in your unknown solution) using the equation

$$M_{PC} = \frac{\text{moles of positive charge}}{\text{volume of sample in liters}}$$

REFERENCES

1. Day, R.A., and Underwood, A.L.; <u>Quantitative Analysis</u>. 4th Edition. Prentice-Hall, Englewood Cliffs, NJ, 1980, Chapter 8.

2. Davis, Gailey, Whitten, <u>Principles of Chemistry</u>, Saunders College Publishing, Philadelphia, PA, 1984, Chapter 18 (Acid-Base Titrations).

3. Whitten and Gailey, <u>General Chemistry 2nd Ed.</u>, Saunders College Publishing, Philadelphia, PA, 1984, Chapter 16 (Equilibria in Aqueous Solutions--I).

NOTES

<u>Note 1</u>.   To avoid accidentally spilling the unknown sample during the pipeting, place the sample bottle in a 600-mL beaker. A still better technique would be to pour a sample of the unknown into a clean, dry 100-mL beaker, and pipet the unknown from the beaker. This procedure avoids possible contamination of the original unknown from a dirty pipet.

<u>Note 2</u>.   A common error is to pipet 10 mL of unknown onto the column and then to collect only 10 mL of solution from it. Of course, the column must be washed with distilled water until the pH of the effluent is again the same as that of the distilled wash water. (Approximately 30-40 mL of wash water will be required.)

ION EXCHANGE CHROMATOGRAPHY

PRELABORATORY QUESTIONS

Name_____   Lab Instructor_____

Student ID No._____   Date_____

1. If a solution was known to contain 0.1 M zinc ion, Zn^{2+}, and 0.15 M sodium ion, Na^+, what would be the molarity of positive charge in this solution, as defined at the end of the procedure?

2. What error will be introduced in M_{PC} if the ion exchange resin absorbs all of the zinc ion but only 90% of the sodium ion from the solution described in Question 1?

3. Why is phenolphthalein a satisfactory indicator for the titration in this experiment?

on exchange resin columns be used more than once without regeneration of the
ιn? Explain.

5. Write equations to illustrate the reactions that occur:

a. for the exchange of Na^+ and Zn^{2+} with H^+ on the resin.

b. for the neutralization reaction resulting from the NaOH titration.

Experiment 29

ION EXCHANGE CHROMATOGRAPHY

REPORT SHEET

Name_____   Lab Instructor_____

Student ID No._____   Date_____

Data

	Trial		
	1	2	3
Volume of sample used (mL)	_____	_____	_____
Molarity of standardized NaOH used	_____	_____	_____
Volume of NaOH used (mL)	_____	_____	_____
Molarity of positive charge in the sample	_____	_____	_____
Averaged value of molarity of positive charge	_____		

Examples of Calculations

QUESTIONS

1. Could an aqueous mixture of hydrochloric acid, HCl, and barium chloride, $BaCl_2$, be analyzed as in this experiment by ion exchange chromatography? Why or why not?

2. Suppose that your unknown sample had contained three metal cations, e.g., Na, Ca^{2+}, and Zn^{2+}. Would you still be able to determine the molarity of positive charge in the sample? Explain if the presence of three cations would change the nature of the procedure or of the calculation.

DETERMINATION OF IODIDE ION BY AN ION SELECTIVE ELECTRODE

Objective

To determine the concentration of iodide ion in a mixture of salts using an ion selective electrode

Equipment Needed

One 50-mL, one 100-mL, four 150-mL beakers; one 10-mL pipet; one plastic squeeze bottle for distilled water; three small magnetic stirring bars, magnetic stirrer, pH meter fitted with iodide selective electrode*

Reagents Needed

1×10^{-1} M, 1×10^{-2} M, 1×10^{-3} M, and 1×10^{-4} M standardized KI solutions; unknown salt solutions from Exp. 29; Kemwipes or other blotting paper

INTRODUCTION

Certain chemical reactions can be carried out so as to produce electricity. The batteries in our calculator, flashlight, and tape recorder function in this way. In arranging a reaction so it produces electricity, a potential difference or voltage is established between the electrodes of the electrochemical cell or battery. Instruments

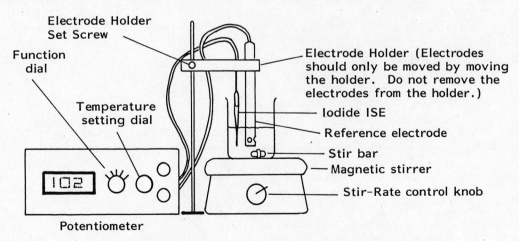

Figure 30-1. Diagram of the Experimental Setup

---

*Instructions for preparation of the iodide selective electrodes are given in the Teacher's Guide.

called potentiometers have been developed to measure this potential. The potentiometers used in many electrochemical experiments measure the potential in volts or millivolts. They are also called voltmeters.

Since the cell potential is produced by a chemical reaction, changing the concentrations of reactants or products of the reaction changes the potential. This means that a certain potential is associated with a certain concentration of reactants and products of the cell reaction.

The relationship between potential and concentration can be used to determine how much of a reactant is present in certain cases. Perhaps the most common use of this concept is the pH meter. This is simply an electrochemical cell in which the cell reaction involves H_3O^+ (or H^+_{aq}) ions, and the cell potential depends upon the concentration of H^+_{aq}. Therefore, when the cell is connected to a potentiometer, the potentiometer reading can be converted directly to pH.

To make them easy to use, pH meters consist of a potentiometer connected by cables to two electrodes. The electrodes are placed in the solution whose pH is to be measured. One of these electrodes--called the indicator electrode--is sensitive to H^+_{aq} ions. The other--called the reference electrode--is insensitive to these and other ions in solution. The potential generated by the reference electrode is constant; that generated by the indicator electrode varies with the concentration of H^+_{aq} in solution.

Electrodes sensitive to ions other than H^+_{aq} have been developed. When used in place of the H^+_{aq} indicator electrode in a pH meter, they make it possible to determine the concentration of these ions in solution. Such electrodes are called **ion selective electrodes** (ISE).

The iodide ion selective electrode you will use in this experiment consists of a copper wire coated with a plastic. The plastic is polyvinylchloride impregnated with an iodide salt. The reaction occurring at this electrode generates a potential that depends upon the concentration of iodide ions in solution.

By use of this electrode to replace the H^+_{aq} indicator electrode in a pH meter, you can determine the concentration of iodide ions in the mixture of salts you began analyzing in Exp. 29.

BACKGROUND

The voltage or potential measured by the potentiometer is the sum of three terms:

$$E = E_{ind} + E_{ref} + E_{interface} \tag{1}$$

in which
  E is the observed potential
  E_{ind} is the potential of the indicating electrode
  E_{ref} is the potential of the reference electrode
  $E_{interface}$ is the potential generated at the region
      where solution and electrodes make contact.

The potential of the indicating electrode as a function of concentration is quantitatively described by the Nernst equation.

$$E_{ind} = E^O + \frac{RT}{nF} \ln[x] \tag{2}$$

where
  E^O = equilibrium potential of the system
  R = molar gas constant
  n = the charge on ion x
  F = Faraday's constant
  $\ln[x]$ = the natural log of the concentration of ion x

By combining Eqs. (1) and (2), we find that

$$E = \frac{RT}{nF} \ln x + E^O + E_{ref} + E_{interface}. \qquad (3)$$

For a given electrode system E^O, $E_{ref} + E_{interface}$ are constant, so we may combine them into a single constant k. Now Eq. (3) becomes

$$E = \frac{RT}{nF} \ln x + k. \qquad (4)$$

It is often convenient to deal in common (base 10) rather than natural logs (base e). For this reason, Eq. (4) is often given as

$$E = \frac{2.3 \ RT}{nF} \log x + k. \qquad (5)$$

Note that Eq. (5) is the form

$$y = mx + b.$$

It is a linear function of slope 2.3 RT/nF. For an ion of $\pm$ 1 charge and at 25 ^{O}C, calculation of this slope gives 59.2 mV. Therefore, Eq. (5) may be written as

$$E = 59.2 \log x + k. \qquad (6)$$

For this experiment, Eq. (6) gives the relationship between the voltmeter (potentiometer) reading and the concentration of iodide ions in solution. It shows that a plot of voltmeter reading at various values of the logarithm of iodide ion concentration should be a straight line.

Since a plot can be made by:

1.   measuring the potentials of a series of standard solutions--solutions containing known concentrations of iodide ion

2.   looking up and recording the logarithms of these iodide ion concentrations

3.   plotting potential vs. log $[I^-]$.

This plot is a calibration curve of this electrode. It can be used to determine the concentration of iodide ions in a solution with unknown concentration of iodide.

NOTEBOOK AND REPORT

Prepare a data table similar to that on page 413 to record your raw data.

Your report should include all of the information listed on page 413. The concentration of iodide ion in your unknown should be reported with the concentrations of the other ions in your unknown solution as determined in Exps. 29 and 31.

PROCEDURE

There are three important parts to this experiment:

1.   becoming proficient in the use of a volumetric pipet

2.   preparing and assembling the solutions whose potentials are to be measured

3.   making the measurements.

Parts (1) and (2) should be completed before moving to the pH meter assembly and making the meaurements.

Use of Volumetric Pipet. Read carefully the section on pipetting on pages 17-18 in the **LABORATORY TECHNIQUES** section. Using a 10-mL pipet and tap water, practice transferring 10-mL portions of water from an Erlenmeyer flask to a beaker until you can do it with precision. This should not take more than 15 minutes.

Preparing and Assembling Solutions. In this and the next part of the experiment, you should work in pairs. However, each member of the pair must prepare and make measurements on his/her unknown solution. Identify the person you will work with and proceed together as follows:

Clean and add standard KI solutions to four beakers.

1. Each person should clean two 150-mL, one 100-mL and one 50-mL beaker (8 beakers in all) by washing them with plenty of tap water and then with some distilled water.

2. One person should label his/her 150-mL beakers 10^{-1} M KI (first beaker); 10^{-2} M KI (second beaker). The second person should label his/her 150-mL beakers 10^{-3} M KI (first beaker); 10^{-4} M KI (second beaker). Place a clean, dry magnetic stirring bar in each of the 100-mL and 150-mL beakers.

3. Carry the four 150-mL beakers to the reagent table. Rinse each beaker with a small amount ($\sim$3 mL) of the standard KI solution that has the same concentration as that on its label. (Rinse the beaker marked 10^{-1} M KI with the 10^{-1} M KI solution; the beaker marked 10^{-2} M KI with 10^{-2} M KI solution; etc.) Discard the rinsing solutions.

Now add about 75 mL of each of the standard KI solutions to the appropriate beakers. Return to your lab bench and set these beakers aside until you have prepared your unknown solution for measurement.

4. Each person should prepare his/her own unknown solution as follows:

Prepare "unknown" solution for analysis.

Label your 100-mL beaker with your initials and the word "unknown." Pour about 5 mL of your unknown solution into your 50-mL beaker and use this to rinse a clean 10-mL pipet. Discard the rinse solution. Now fill this beaker to about the 30-mL mark with your unknown solution. By use of the rinsed pipet, transfer exactly 10.00 mL of this solution from the 50-mL beaker to the 100-mL beaker that you just labeled. Rinse the same pipet with distilled water, and then transfer exactly 20.00 mL of distilled water to the 100-mL beaker. Keep the pipet because you will need it one more time.

Making Measurements

1. Carry the six solutions (three for each partner), a plastic squeeze bottle filled with distilled water, an empty 50-mL beaker, and a 10-mL pipet to the pH meter assembly.

Prepare the instrument for making measurements.

2. Carefully remove the Iodide-Ion Selective Electrode (IISE) from the storage beaker by loosening the holder, raising the assembly, and then reclamping the holder. Carefully remove the protective plastic cap from the combination electrode (CE) and set it and the storage beaker aside where you will not lose them. Place the empty 50-mL beaker under the electrodes. Rinse the electrodes with distilled water from the squeeze bottle and blot them dry with a Kimwipe. **Blot, do not wipe, the electrodes to avoid scratching the surface.** Remove the 50-mL beaker.

3. Position the beaker marked "10^{-4} M KI" in the center of the magnetic stirrer, turn on the stirrer, and adjust the speed so that the stirring bar rotates smoothly at a moderate rate that does not produce splashing.

4. Lower the electrodes into the solution so that the solution covers the electrodes as shown in the diagram below. Note the time, to the

nearest second, so that you can make a voltage reading at the end of one minute.   DO NOT ALLOW THE STIRRING BAR TO TOUCH THE ELECTRODES!

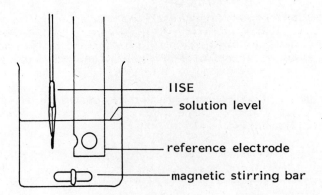

Figure 30-2. Placement of electrodes in solution

Make
measurements
at prescribed
time intervals.

5.   Make sure that no bubbles are trapped on the electrodes.   If they are, gently move the electrodes in circles to release them.

6.   Turn the function mode knob of the electronic voltmeter from "standby" to "Mv" (millivolts). **Under no circumstances should you touch or move the temperature or other control knobs on the instrument.**

7.   **Exactly** one minute after the electrodes were lowered into the solution, record the voltmeter reading.

8.   Turn the function mode knob on the instrument to "standby."

9.   Repeat steps (2) through (8) with the beakers labeled 10^{-3} M KI, 10^{-2} M KI, and 10^{-1} M KI **in this order.**   Always rinse and blot the electrodes before placing them in a new or different solution.

10.   One partner should now repeat steps (2) through (7) with his/her unknown solution.

11.   Immediately after recording the voltmeter reading on the unknown solution, pipet exactly 10.00 mL of distilled water into the beaker.   Wait two minutes, and again record the voltmeter reading.

12.   The other partner should now repeat steps (10) and (11) on his/her unknown solution.

13.   When you have made the measurements, rinse the electrodes with distilled water, and blot them dry.   Replace the protective cap on the combination electrode and lower the IISE into the storage beaker so that the setup is left as you found it.

Restore
instrument to
its original
state.

TREATMENT OF DATA

1.   Record the voltmeter readings at the appropriate points in the data table.

2.   Determine the logarithms of the iodide concentrations for each standard solution, and record them in the table.

3.   Plot potential in millivolts against $\log[I^-]$ on graph paper.   Draw the best straight line through the points.

4. Determine the iodide concentrations in your once- and twice-diluted unknown solutions by reading from the graph the log[I⁻] corresponding to the voltmeter readings for each of these solutions.

5. Take the antilog of the log[I⁻] values obtained in (4) above.

6. Use these values and the fact that 10.00 mL of the unknown was diluted first with water and then with another 10.00 mL of water to calculate the iodide concentration in your undiluted unknown. Report the average of the two calculations.

7. Calculate the slope of your graph of potential against log[I⁻] and compare this with the expected value.

REFERENCES

Day, R.A., Jr.; Underwood, A.L. Qualitative Analysis, 4th Ed., Prentice-Hall, Inc., Englewood Cliffs, NJ, 1980, Chapter 12.

DETERMINATION OF IODIDE ION BY AN ION SELECTIVE ELECTRODE

PRELABORATORY QUESTIONS

Name_____   Lab Instructor_____

Student ID_____   Date_____

1. What is an ion selective electrode? Describe the scientific principle upon which it functions.

2. Why is it necessary to become proficient in the use of the pipet before beginning this experiment?

3. Why is it necessary to measure the iodide ion concentration in four standard solutions in addition to that in your unknown solution?

4. Describe how you will determine the iodide ion concentration in your unknown solution once you have measured the potential (voltage) of this solution.

5. What is the purpose of diluting your unknown solution and measuring the potential of the diluted solution?

6. Why is it important that the dilution referred in in (5) above be done carefully?

DETERMINATION OF IODIDE ION BY AN ION SELECTIVE ELECTRODE

REPORT SHEET

Name_____   Lab Instructor_____

Student ID_____   Date_____

DATA TABLE

KI Solution	log[I⁻]	voltmeter reading (mv)
10^{-4} M	_____	_____
10^{-3} M	_____	_____
10^{-2} M	_____	_____
10^{-1} M	_____	_____

xxxxxxxxxxxxxxxxxxxxxxxxxxxxxxxxxxxxxxxxxxxxxxxxxxxxxxxxxxxxxxxxxxxxxxxxxxxxx

	voltmeter reading	log [I⁻]	[I⁻]	[I⁻] in undiluted unknown
once-diluted unknown	_____	_____	_____	
twice-diluted unknown	_____	_____	_____	
				_____

slope of your calibration curve_____; expected slope_____

Plot of graph should appear below, and a description of how you used this graph in arriving at your results should be included in your report.

Attach sheets of paper to answer the assigned Questions and Problems on the reverse side.

QUESTIONS AND PROBLEMS

1. Could you have determined the I^- concentration in your unknown solution without the use of standard solutions? Justify your answer.

2. If your plot of potential against log $[I^-]$ is not a straight line, but a well-defined curve, can you still use it to determine the I^- concentration in your unknown? Why or why not?

3. Suppose you failed to rinse your pipet with your unknown solution and the pipet contained a few drops of water. Then you used it to transfer the unknown. How will this affect the concentration of I^- you report?

4. Will the presence of chloride ions in your unknown solution interfere with a reliable determination of the iodide concentration by this procedure? Why or why not?

5. If the value of the I^- concentration you report is 50% higher than that actually present in your unknown, how will this affect:

    a. the value of the M_{pc} concentration you report for your unknown solution for Exps. 29, 30, 31?

    b. the value of the Na^+ concentration you report for your unknown solution for Exps. 29, 30, 31?

A COMPLEXOMETRIC TITRATION

Ethylenediaminetetra-acetic Acid (EDTA)

Determination of Zinc Ion

Determination of Hardness in Water

Objective

To determine zinc ion in the presence of sodium ion using a complexometric titration

Equipment Needed

25-mL buret; 10-mL pipet; 1-mL pipet (instructor); aspirator bulb for pipeting; two 125-mL Erlenmeyer flasks; 10-mL graduated cylinder

Reagents Needed

Standardized solutions of EDTA (0.025 M); buffer solution 0.5 M ammonium chloride plus 0.5 M aqueous ammonia buffered at pH$\sim$10); Eriochrome Black T-potassium chloride mixture; standardized unknown solutions of zinc (for Exps. 29, 30, and 31)

INTRODUCTION

In this experiment the concentration of zinc ion in an unknown sample will be determined by titration of a portion of the mixture with a solution containing ethylenediaminetetraacetate.

EDTA-Metal Complexes

Titration of a solution containing a metal ion with a suitable standard solution of a complexing agent or ligand is an important method of analysis for metal ions. To be suitable for such a titration, the complex-formation reaction must proceed rapidly and according to a well-defined stoichiometry. It also must lend itself to a sensitive end-point detection.

Ethylenediaminetetraacetic acid, EDTA, is an important and well known tetraprotic acid.

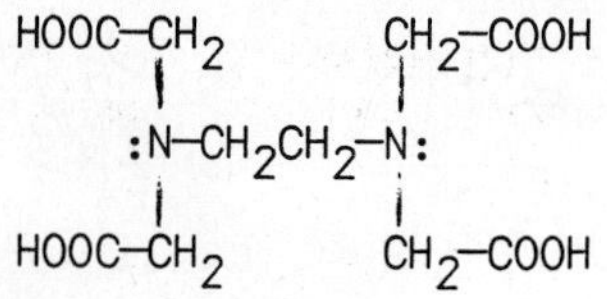

$$HOOC-CH_2 \qquad CH_2-COOH$$

$$:N-CH_2CH_2-N:$$

$$HOOC-CH_2 \qquad CH_2-COOH$$

Its four pK_a values are 1.99, 2.67, 6.16, and 10.26, respectively. In the form of its anion, ethylenediaminetetraacetate, $EDTA^{4-}$, or simply Y^{4-}, it acts as a hexadentate ligand, forming very stable one-to-one complexes with nearly every metal ion. The reaction may be represented as

$$M^{n+} + Y^{4-} \rightleftharpoons MY^{(n-4)+}$$

and the equilibrium constant for this reaction is given by

$$K_{MY} = \frac{[MY^{(n-4)+}]}{[M^{n+}][Y^{4-}]}.$$

Values of this equilibrium constant for several metal complexes at 25 $^{\circ}C$ are:

Table 31-1

Metal Ion	K_{MY}	Metal Ion	K_{MY}
Ca^{2+}	$10^{10.70}$	Fe^{2+}	$10^{14.33}$
Co^{2+}	$10^{16.31}$	Mg^{2+}	$10^{8.69}$
Cu^{2+}	$10^{18.80}$	Zn^{2+}	$10^{16.50}$

The very large values for K_{MY} indicate that the complexes are very stable, particularly for Zn^{2+} and Cu^{2+}. (For example, the $10^{10.70}$ value for Ca^{2+} is equivalent to 5×10^{10}.) The high stability of the complex ion formed and the fact that the reaction has a one-to-one stoichiometry are the reasons for sharp breaks at the end points in the titration of EDTA with metal ions. The value of K_{MY} for the sodium salt is very small, indicating that the sodium complex is unstable. Hence, zinc ion can be titrated successfully in the presence of sodium ion.

Infrared and X-ray studies have shown that the EDTA complex of cobalt(III) ion has a structure that may be represented as shown at the right. The Zn^{2+}, Ca^{2+}, Fe^{2+}, and Mg^{2+} complex ions presumably have similar structures and an overall charge of 2- for the complex.

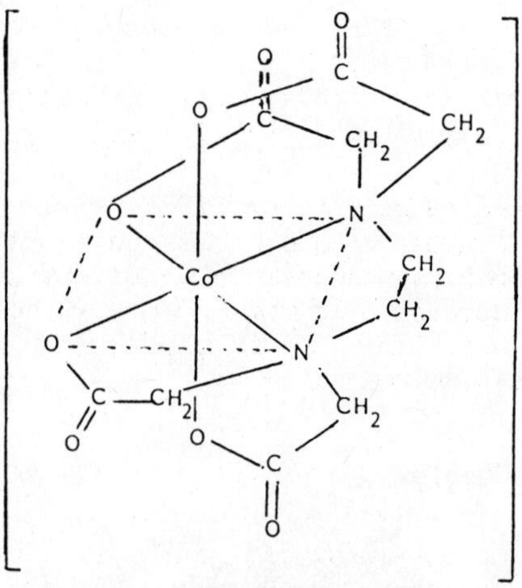

Metal Ion Indicators

Some organic compounds react with metal ions to form colored complexes in reactions analogous to those of acid-base indicators which have already been studied in Exps. 11 and 12. Some of these compounds are useful for indicators in EDTA titrations of metal ions. Eriochrome Black T (ErioT) is a dye molecule that has suitable properties to serve as an indicator for Zn^{2+}, Mg^{2+}, Ca^{2+}, Co^{2+}, and Fe^{2+} ions. $ErioT^-$ has the structure given in Fig. 31-1.

Metal chelates are formed with $ErioT^-$ by loss of hydrogen ions from the phenolic (-OH) groups and the formation of bonds between the metal ions and the oxygen atoms as well as the azo (-N=N-) group (Fig. 31-2). The molecule is usually represented in abbreviated form as a triprotic acid, H_3In. The sulfonic acid group (RSO_3^-) is shown in Figs. 31-1 and 31-2 as being ionized; this is a strong acid group which is dissociated in aqueous solution regardless of pH; thus, the structure shown is that of the ion H_2In^-. This form of the indicator is red. The pK_a value for the dissociation of H_2In^- to form HIn^{2-} is 6.3. The latter species is blue. The pK_a value for the ionization of HIn^{2-} to form In^{3-} is 11.6; the latter ion is yellowish orange.

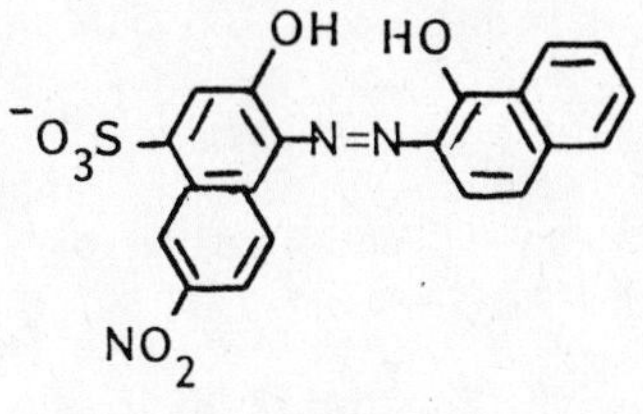

Figure 31-1

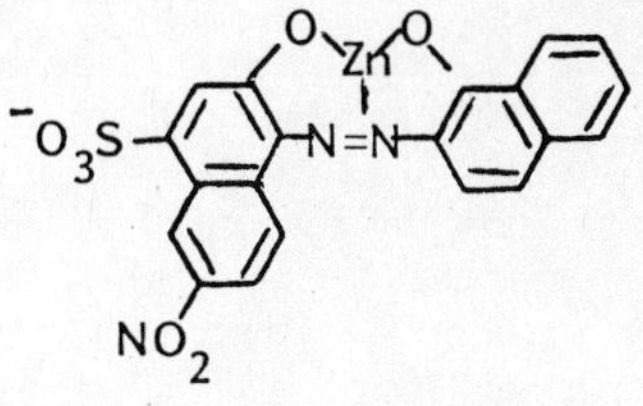

Figure 31-2

The color of the uncomplexed dye depends upon its degree of ionization; for the discussion below, assume $In = ErioT^{3-}$.

$$H_2In^- \rightleftharpoons HIn^{2-} \rightleftharpoons In^{3-}$$

(red) (blue) (yellow-orange)

The color of the zinc complex $ZnIn^-$ is red.

On addition of EDTA to a solution containing Zn^{2+} and the indicator (Eriochrome Black T) (ErioT), a sharp color change of wine-red to blue occurs when the zinc ions have been removed by EDTA. Zinc forms a more stable complex with EDTA than it does with $ErioT^-$.

$$ZnIn^- + H_2Y^{2-} \rightleftharpoons ZnY^{2-} + HIn^{2-} + H^+$$

(wine-red) (colorless) pH 10 (colorless) (blue)

The hydrogen ion on the right side of the equilibrium is neutralized in the basic buffer solution, and the equilibrium shifts to the right. The color reaction for zinc and ErioT is sharpest in solutions buffered at pH 10 with aqueous ammonia and ammonia chloride. Because the stabilities of both the zinc EDTA complex and the zinc indicator complex are affected by pH changes, the titrations of zinc with EDTA are performed in solutions of controlled pH.

Hardness in Water

One of the oldest and most common analyses done by chemists is the measurement of water hardness. The "hardness" of a water solution is a measure of the amount of divalent metal cations, such as Ca^{2+} or Mg^{2+}, present in that solution. "Soft" water contains few, if any, of these ions. Very "hard" water has high concentrations of such ions. The hardness of water is a very important factor when that water is to be used with a soap or detergent. Soaps (and detergents) are primarily long-chain hydrocarbons that have an acid group attached to one end.

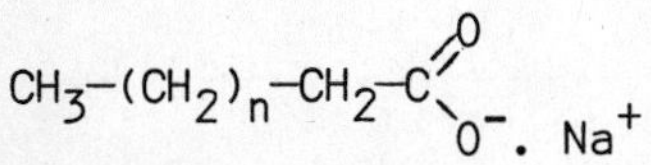

$$CH_3-(CH_2)_n-CH_2-C{\overset{O}{\underset{O^-}{\Big\langle}}} \cdot Na^+$$

a "soap" molecule

417

Divalent metal cations tend to form water-insoluble complexes with the acid part of soap molecules which reduces the molecule's ability to react with "dirt." As a result, hard water requires more soap to produce the same cleaning effect as soft water.

$$[CH_3-(CH_2)_n-CH_2-C(O)-O]_2Mg$$

a Mg-"soap" complex

The vast majority of divalent metal cations present in natural water samples are calcium (Ca^{++}) and magnesium (Mg^{++}). As you might imagine, the relative hardness of a water sample can best be determined by measuring the amount of these ions present in the sample, which you will do in Part B of the experiment.

Part A of this experiment is concerned with the measurement of the concentration of Zn^{2+} in an unknown solution by titration with the organic complexing agent, EDTA. From Table 31-1 you can see that both Mg^{2+} and Ca^{2+} form fairly strong complexes with EDTA. Note that the Ca-EDTA complex is somewhat stronger than the Mg-EDTA complex, but both are weaker than the Zn-EDTA complex. Thus, it should be possible to measure the total concentration of Ca^{2+} and Mg^{++} by performing the EDTA titration. Let's see what will happen if we do such a titration on a sample of hard water. On addition of the indicator (ErioT Black) to the water sample, the Mg-indicator complex will form, causing the solution to take on its pink color. As the EDTA titrant is added, it will first react with Ca^{2+} present in the sample. Once all of the Ca^{2+} has been complexed, further addition of EDTA will result in the formation of the Mg-EDTA complex. As the Mg^{2+} is used, the pink Mg-indicator complex will begin to dissociate, producing free indicator molecules which are blue. The disappearance of the last trace of the pink color (leaving a blue solution) indicates that all of the Ca^{2+} and Mg^{2+} ions have been complexed with EDTA. Thus, the endpoint is the same as for the titration of Zn^{2+} in Part A. This titration is the classical technique for hard-water analysis.

PROCEDURE

PART A. DETERMINATION OF ZINC ION

Determine the zinc ion concentration of your unknown solution directly, i.e., without treating it with a cation exchange resin, as in Experiment 29.

Pipet 10-mL aliquots of unknown solution.

Carefully pipet 10-mL portions of your unknown solution into two clean 125-mL Erlenmeyer flasks and dilute each with 10 mL of distilled water from a graduated cylinder. Add enough buffer solution to give a pH of approximately 10. Ten milliliters of buffer probably will suffice; test with pH paper. Obtain the Eriochrome Black T solid mixture at the instructor's desk, and add approximately 20 mg or more (about one third of a microspatula, enough to produce a slight color). Return the indicator mixture to the desk immediately so that other students may use it. Titrate the Zn^{2+} solution with standardized EDTA solution, swirling the flask gently and constantly, until the color changes from wine-red to grey to pure blue. The equivalence point occurs with the disappearance of the last trace of red. Neither red nor purple should be visible at the end point. If, during the titration, the end point is not sharp or the ErioT indicator color appears to be fading, the pH may have dropped below 10. In this case, add 2 to 3 mL of the NH_3-NH_4Cl buffer and continue the titration. Record the volume of EDTA solution to the nearest 0.01 mL.

Test with pH paper.

Titrate solution with EDTA until red color is gone.

Repeat the titration 2 times.

Repeat the titration procedure two more times. However, you should choose a 20-mL sample of Zn^{2+} if the amount of EDTA used in your first titration was less than half the capacity of the buret. If 20 mL is used, add 40 mL of distilled water and 20 mL of the buffer. Obtain a sufficient quantity of EDTA solution for your two additional trials. Repeat the trials until two subsequent volumes agree to within 0.10 mL.

PART B. DETERMINATION OF HARDNESS IN WATER

In this part, you will determine the hardness of both the tap water and the distilled water available in the lab.

Clean and thoroughly rinse your 400-mL beaker with distilled water. Fill the clean beaker with tap water. This will be your source of "samples" for the following titrations. Fill your buret with the standardized EDTA solution, and record the intial buret reading. To a clean 125-mL Erlenmeyer flask, add 10 mL of the pH 10 buffer (use your graduated cylinder to measure this). Obtain a 50-mL pipet from your instructor, carefully fill the volumetric pipet to the mark with your tap water sample, and then carefully transfer the 50-mL sample into the Erlenmeyer flask. Return the pipet to your instructor when finished since the stockroom has only a limited number of these volumetric pipets available.

Measure 50-mL sample of tap water with volumetric pipet.

Add approximately 20 mg of the ErioT Black indicator to the Erlenmeyer flask and swirl to mix. Titrate to the blue endpoint using the standardized EDTA solution. (**CAUTION:** This titration should not require more than 5 mL and may use less than 1 mL of EDTA solution.) Record the volume of EDTA used. Repeat the titrations of tap water until you obtain two results that agree to within 0.10 mL.

Titrate tap water.

Empty your 400-mL beaker and rinse it thoroughly with distilled water; then fill the beaker with distilled water. Repeat the EDTA titrations, using this distilled water sample.

Repeat titrations with distilled water.

CALCULATIONS

PART A. From the data obtained, calculate and report the molar concentration of zinc ions in the sample. Using this information and the results of Exps. 29 and 30, calculate the concentrations of the three salts--sodium iodide, sodium chloride, and zinc chloride--in the original sample and include the results in your report.

PART B. Because the EDTA forms a 1:1 complex with divalent metal cations, the total moles of such ions can be determined from the titration. At the end point,

moles of EDTA added = total moles of divalent metal ions.

Using this equality and the volume of the sample, the concentration of such ions can be determined.

Water hardness is generally reported in one of two ways. Both methods make the assumption that <u>all</u> of the divalent metal cations present are calcium ions. Even though this is a false assumption, it does work well as a means of comparing the hardness of various water samples.

The first method is to report the hardness in terms of milligrams of calcium per milliliter of sample [(mg of Ca^{2+})/(mL of sample)]. This is done by converting the value for moles of divalent metal ions into milligrams of Ca^{2+}, using the atomic weight of calcium. The resultant number is then divided by the sample size in milliliters. The other method is to report hardness as parts per million (ppm). Again, the moles of metal ions are converted to a mass of calcium. This mass is then divided by the mass of the sample and the result multiplied by 1,000,000.

$$ppm = \frac{\text{mass of calcium}}{\text{mass of sample}} \times 1,000,000 \text{ ppm}$$

For the purpose of this exercise, you may assume that the density of your sample is 1.0000 g/mL. You are expected to report the hardness of your samples using both of these methods.

REFERENCES

1. Day, R. A., and Underwood, A. L.: <u>Quantitative Analysis</u>. 4th edition. Prentice-Hall, Englewood Cliffs, NJ, 1980, Chapter 8.

2. Davis, Gailey, and Whitten, <u>Principles of Chemistry</u>, Saunders College Publishing, Philadelphia, PA, 1984, pp. 311-323, 762-772 (Coordination Chemistry and Volumetric Analysis).

3. Whitten and Gailey, <u>General Chemistry</u>, 2nd Ed., Saunders College Publishing, Philadelphia, 1984, pp. 398-404, 801-811 (Coordination Chemistry and Volumetric Analysis).

QUESTIONS--PROBLEMS

1. Briefly discuss the chemistry of the indicator used in this experiment.

2. What is the function of the ammonium chloride/aqueous ammonia hydroxide buffer used in this experiment?

3. How would one prepare 1.5 L of the ammonium chloride/aqueous ammonia buffer so that it would be pH 10 (show calculations)?

4. Before you took the initial buret reading, suppose you forgot to fill the buret tip below the stopcock. Would this error make your results too high or too low? Explain logically your answer.

5. To obtain quantitative information from the titration, why isn't it necessary that the molarity of the EDTA solution be <u>exactly</u> 0.025000 M?

Experiment 31

A COMPLEXOMETRIC TITRATION

PRELABORATORY QUESTIONS

Name_____   Lab Instructor_____

Student ID No._____   Date_____

1. Why is it possible in this experiment to titrate zinc ions accurately even though
    sodium and iodide ions also are present in the solution?

2. Is it possible to use this procedure to titrate magnesium ions quantitatively in the
    presence of an unknown quantity of zinc ions? Why or why not?

3. What difficulties would you expect to encounter in this titration if tap water (containing Ca^{2+}, Fe^{3+}, Mg^{2+}, and other dissolved metal ions) were used to dilute the solutions for the determination of zinc ion?

4. Devise a procedure by which you could test the assumption that EDTA and Zn^{2+} form a one-to-one complex ion.

Experiment 31

A COMPLEXOMETRIC TITRATION

REPORT SHEET

Name_____   Lab Instructor_____

Student ID No._____   Date_____

	Trial		
	1	2	3

DATA, PART A

Molarity of EDTA solution used   _____ _____ _____

Initial buret reading (mL)   _____ _____ _____

Final buret reading (mL)   _____ _____ _____

Volume of EDTA delivered (mL)   _____ _____ _____

Moles of EDTA delivered   _____ _____ _____

Moles of Zn^{2+} titrated   _____ _____ _____

Volume of Zn^{2+} solution used (mL)   _____ _____ _____

Molarity of Zn^{2+} _____ _____ _____

Average molarity of Zn^{2+} _____

Sample Calculations

DATA, PART B

	Trial		
	1	2	3

Tap Water

Molarity of EDTA solution used _____ _____ _____

Initial buret reading (mL) _____ _____ _____

Final buret reading (mL) _____ _____ _____

Volume of EDTA delivered (mL) _____ _____ _____

Moles of M^{2+} titrated _____ _____ _____

Volume of M^{2+} solution used (mL) _____ _____ _____

mg of Ca^{2+}/mL* _____ _____ _____

ppm of Ca^{2+} _____ _____ _____

Averaged mg of Ca^{2+}/mL _____

Averaged ppm of Ca^{2+} _____

Distilled Water

Molarity of EDTA solution used _____ _____ _____

Initial buret reading (mL) _____ _____ _____

Final buret reading (mL) _____ _____ _____

Volume of EDTA delivered (mL) _____ _____ _____

Moles of M^{2+} titrated _____ _____ _____

Volume of M^{2+} solution used (mL) _____ _____ _____

mg of Ca^{2+}/mL* _____ _____ _____

ppm of Ca^{2+} _____ _____ _____

Averaged mg of Ca^{2+}/mL _____

Averaged ppm of Ca^{2+} _____

---

*Calculated, assuming all of the M^{2+} is Ca^{2+}.

ORGANIC SYNTHESIS

Preparation of Medicinally Useful Compounds

Objective

To illustrate several aspects of synthetic organic chemistry by preparing several medicinally useful compounds from a given starting material

Equipment Needed

Two 250-mL Erlenmeyer flasks; 100-, 250-, 600-, or 800-mL beakers; boiling chips; condenser; Büchner funnel; suction filter flask; 125-mL separatory funnel; hot plate; long scoopula or spatula; Meker burner; melting point tubes, 25 x 200 mm test tubes, rubber bands, plastic bag; cork stopper; 300 $^{\circ}$C or 400 $^{\circ}$C thermometer

Chemicals Needed

Salicylic acid, thionyl chloride, concentrated ammonia, methanol, ether, acetic anhydride, concentrated H_2SO_4, 95% ethanol, phthalic anhydride, dilute sodium hydroxide solution, 1.0 M $NaHCO_3$ solution, 12 M HCl, ice; dibutylphthalate for melting point bath

INTRODUCTION

One reason organic chemistry has made considerable contributions to our health and welfare is the very highly developed skill of the organic chemist in synthesizing complex and uniquely structured compounds in high purity and often in large quantities from plentiful and readily available starting materials. Among the important synthetic compounds prepared by organic chemists are many of the medicinal products we use regularly.

In this experiment, we shall illustrate several aspects of synthetic organic chemistry by preparing compounds that have known medicinal applications. The synthetic principles illustrated here include: (1) the selection of appropriate organic reactions such as substitution, condensation, acetylation, decarboxylation, and esterification; (2) the concept of multistep syntheses whereby the chemist, using a given starting material, must convert it by appropriate reactions into several intermediate substances before synthesizing the final product; (3) the choice of suitable procedures for working up reaction mixtures and isolating and purifying products of a reaction.

Starting material for the reactions in this experiment is salicylic acid. This is a solid, melting at 157-159 $^{\circ}$C. Its esters occur naturally in certain plants, notably in the bark of sweet birch and in wintergreen.

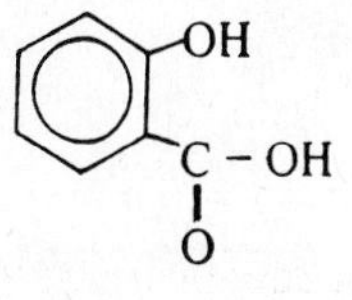

In one part of the experiment, the acid will be converted to the acyl chloride by reaction with thionyl chloride.

salicylic acid

Substitution

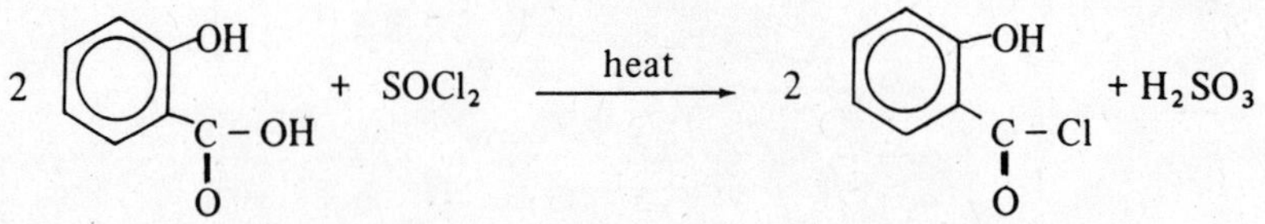

$$2 \quad \text{[benzene ring with OH and C-OH (O double bond)]} + SOCl_2 \xrightarrow{\text{heat}} 2 \quad \text{[benzene ring with OH and C-Cl (O double bond)]} + H_2SO_3$$

The acid chloride can then be treated with ammonia to give the amide or with methanol to give the methyl ester, commonly known as oil of wintergreen.

Acylation of ammonia to form an amide

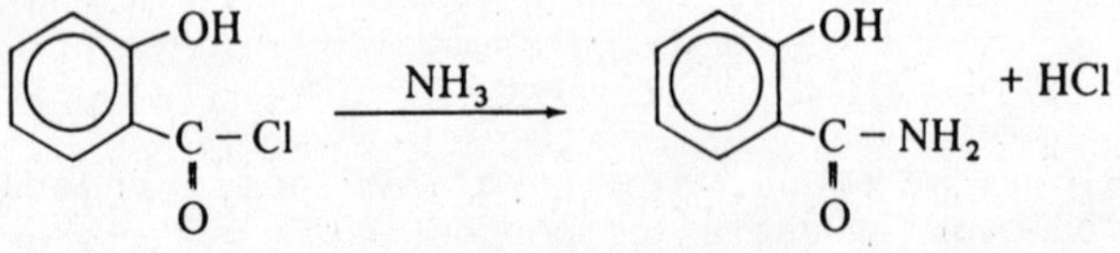

$$\text{[benzene ring with OH and C-Cl (O double bond)]} \xrightarrow{NH_3} \text{[benzene ring with OH and C-NH}_2\text{ (O double bond)]} + HCl$$

Salicylamide (m.p. 140°)

Esterification by acylation of an alcohol

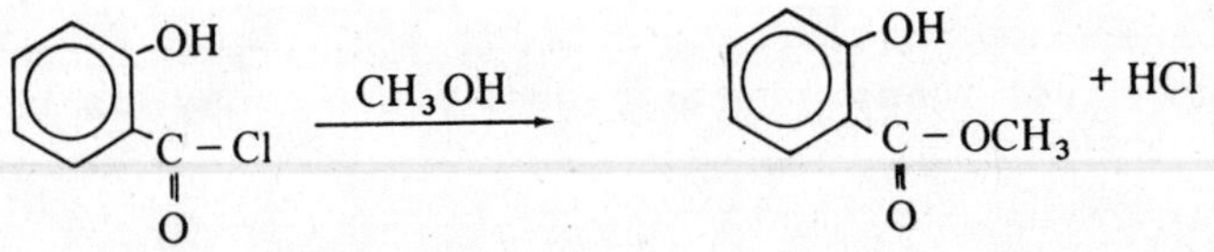

$$\text{[benzene ring with OH and C-Cl (O double bond)]} \xrightarrow{CH_3OH} \text{[benzene ring with OH and C-OCH}_3\text{ (O double bond)]} + HCl$$

methyl salicylate (b.p. 220-224°)

In another part of the experiment, salicylic acid will be converted to acetyl-salicylic acid, commonly known as aspirin, by treatment with acetic anhydride.

Acetylation

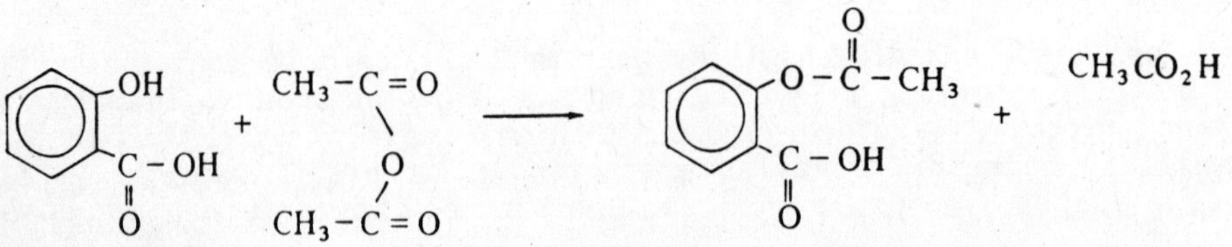

$$\text{[benzene ring with OH and C-OH (O double bond)]} + \begin{array}{c} CH_3-C=O \\ \backslash \\ O \\ / \\ CH_3-C=O \end{array} \longrightarrow \text{[benzene ring with O-C(=O)-CH}_3\text{ and C-OH (O double bond)]} + CH_3CO_2H$$

acetyl salicylate (m.p. 129°)

In a third part of the experiment, salicylic acid will be converted to phenol and the phenol allowed to react with phthalic anhydride to give phenolphthalein. The first of these reactions is a decarboxylation; the second is a condensation.

Decarboxylation

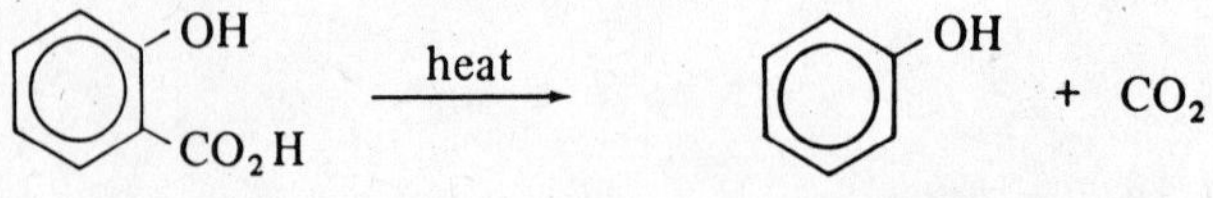

$$\text{[benzene ring with OH and CO}_2\text{H]} \xrightarrow{\text{heat}} \text{[benzene ring with OH]} + CO_2$$

phenol (m.p. 43°)

426

Condensation

phthalic anhydride   phenolphthalein (m.p. 258-262°)

The products of each of these reactions have important uses. Salicylamide is used to relieve pain, reduce fever, and as an antirheumatic. Methyl salicylate is used medicinally to reduce inflammation of muscles. It also is used for flavoring candies and in perfumery. Aspirin, of course, is used to reduce pain, fever, and inflammation. Phenol is used in 1% solutions for ointments to relieve itching. In full strength, it is very escharotic. Phenolphthalien is used as a cathartic; it also is used as an indicator in acid-base titrations.

Salicylic acid is used in ointments and alcohol solutions for fungus and ring-worm infections.

TECHNIQUES

Some of the reactions selected for this exercise proceed readily at room temperature; others require only heating. The equipment used is much simpler than that which might be employed in many organic syntheses. The reactions that occur readily at room temperature require that certain **safety precautions be strictly and constantly adhered to.** These include the addition of small amounts of material at reasonable intervals so as to prevent the reactions from getting out of hand and, in some cases, the ready availability of ice baths in which the reaction flask can be placed should the reaction become too violent. Two reagents, thionyl chloride and acetic anhydride, must be kept away from moisture and the skin at all times. Open flames in the vicinity of organic vapors should be avoided, and safety glasses must be worn at all times.

The techniques used in separating the product from the other components of the reaction mixture and the purification of the product may include extraction, followed by recrystallization or distillation. In extraction, use is made of the fact that the organic product ordinarily will be more soluble in a nonpolar solvent such as ether than in water, whereas many of the inorganic products of the reaction will be more soluble in water than in ether. The technique of **extraction** is discussed in the **Laboratory Techniques** section on p. 12 and illustrated in Fig. 13. Read that section before performing this experiment.

In Part A of this experiment, methyl salicylate will be extracted from the reaction mixture by using ether. In Parts B and C, the products will be removed by crystallizing them from ice water or from ethanol. Here, the product that is formed is separated from the solvent and further purified by dissolving it in a small amount of a solvent in which the impurities present in the crude solid are soluble and again either evaporating some of the solvent or reducing its temperature to the point at which the pure cyrstals will form. These are then separated and dried and their melting points determined. As indicated in earlier experiments, the melting range of a solid is an indication of its purity. Samples that melt over a 0.1-degree range are usually quite pure. Samples that melt over a 1- to 1.5-degree range can be considered acceptable for most work. Procedures for determining the melting points of substances are given on p. 21 of the **Laboratory Techniques** section.

427

PART A. PREPARATION OF SALICYLAMIDE AND METHYL SALICYLATE

Assemble apparatus.

In a hood, support a 125-mL Erlenmeyer flask in an 800-mL beaker in such a way that the beaker can be used as a water bath to heat the contents of the flask. Put a few boiling chips in the water in the beaker. Using a cork stopper, attach a condenser to the top of the flask, and arrange for the flow of water through the condenser (Fig. 32-1).

Add salicylic acid.

Remove the condenser, and add 4 g of salicylic acid (weighed to the nearest 0.1 g) to the flask. **Carefully and using precautions to avoid**

Add thionyl chloride.

contact of the reagent with the skin, nasal passages, clothing, or with moisture,* add 6 mL of thionyl chloride to the flask. Replace the

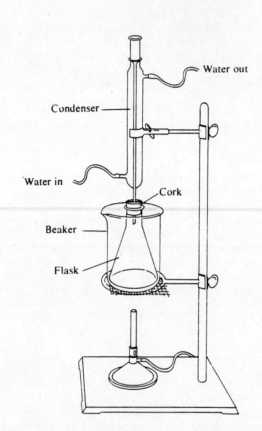

Water out

Condenser

Water in

Cork

Beaker

Flask

Figure 32-1. Diagram of apparatus for reaction of salicylic acid with thionyl chloride

condenser, and heat the water in the bath. When the liquid in the flask begins to boil, reduce the heat slightly but keep the reaction liquid

Reflux.

boiling and condensing back into the flask (refluxing) for 30 minutes. Remove the condenser from the flask and the flask from the beaker. Allow the reaction mixture to cool (**Note 1**).

Cool the ammonia.

Meanwhile, add about 25 mL of concentrated ammonia to a beaker or an Erlenmeyer flask, and cool it by placing the flask in a beaker of crushed ice. Add 10 mL of methanol to a second flask.

Carefully transfer half of reaction mixture.

Carefully, using precautions to avoid contact of the reaction mixture with the skin, pour half of it--with the aid of a long spatula or scoopula--to the flask containing the methanol. Allow the mixture to stand while the remaining half of the reaction mixture is treated with ammonia and the product isolated, as in the following paragraphs.

*If $SOCl_2$ makes contact with the skin or clothing, wash the affected area immediately with large quantities of water.

Carefully, with cautious swirling, transfer the second half of the reaction mixture to the ice-cold ammonia solution. [Caution: If added too rapidly, the reaction will get out of hand, and considerable splattering of material may occur.] Stir this mixture with a stirring rod for 2 minutes; allow the solid to settle, and decant the liquid from it. Discard the solid. Heat the liquid in a hood, maintaining a gentle boil for 5 minutes. Cool the solution, and carefully neutralize it by adding, a little at a time, about 30 mL of concentrated hydrochloric acid. Cool the mixture by placing it in a beaker of ice. Separate the solid that forms by suction filtration; that is, pour the contents of the flask into a Büchner funnel attached to a filter flask, and using an aspirator attached by suction tubing to the filter flask, pull the liquid through the filter (see Fig. 11 on p. 11 for set up).

Transfer second half of mixture in hood.

Discard solid.

Add HCl.

Filter.

Wash the precipitate on the filter once with water, and discard this washing and the solution from which the solid was separated. Dissolve the precipitate in 10 mL or less of hot water. Allow the mixture to cool and once again separate the solid product. Set it aside to dry in the air and, when dry, determine its mass and its melting point. Pure salicylamide melts at 140 $^{\circ}$C.

Wash the precipitate and dissolve it in hot water.

While the amide is drying, return to the flask containing methanol and the crude salicylyl chloride. Gently heat this on a hot plate in a hood for five minutes. DO NOT use an open flame because methanol may burn on contact with it.

Allow the contents of the flask to cool, and pour them carefully into 50 mL of a 1 M NaHCO$_3$ solution in a separatory funnel. Extract the methyl salicylate from this mixture, using three 10-mL samples of ether as follows (also see Fig. 13 on p. 13). Add 10 mL of ether to the separatory funnel. Stopper the funnel, shake gently, and relieve the pressure. Repeat with more vigorous shaking, relieving pressure periodically. Allow the mixture to separate, and remove and save the ether layer. Return the water layer to the separatory funnel, and repeat the extraction with a second, and then a third, 10-mL portion of ether. Combine the three ether extracts. Allow the ether to evaporate, using a procedure to be suggested by your instructor. Determine the mass, and note other physical properties such as odor, color, and viscosity of the resulting product.

Extract with water.

The crude methyl salicylate obtained here can be further purified by distillation or chromatography. Because these require more elaborate equipment than is available to us, we shall not purify the product further.

Submit both products to your instructor in labeled vials when you submit your report.

Submit samples.

PART B. ACETYLATION OF SALICYLIC ACID-- PREPARATION OF ASPIRIN

Arrange a 250-mL Erlenmeyer flask in an 800-mL beaker in such a way that the beaker can be used as a water bath to heat the contents of the flask as in Part A (Fig. 32-1). [The reflux condenser shown in Fig. 32-1 is not needed for this part of the experiment and should be removed.] Put a few boiling chips in the water in the beaker. Remove the flask from the water bath, and place a known amount (approximately 2 g) of salicylic acid in it. Obtain 8 mL of acetic anhydride and add this to the flask. [Caution: acetic anhydride is irritating to the skin and eyes. It should be used only in the hood or with adequate ventilation. Should this get on your skin, the affected area should be washed immediately with large amounts of water.]

In the apparatus, combine salicylic acid and acetic anhydride.

To the mixture, add carefully and slowly 5 drops of concentrated sulfuric acid, swirling the flask gently after each addition. [Caution:

concentrated sulfuric acid is extremely irritating to the skin and eyes. It is destructive to clothing, and it reacts violently with water. It should be handled with extreme care. Affected areas of the skin should be washed immediately with large amounts of water.] After the sulfuric acid has been added, place the flask in the beaker of boiling water for 10 minutes. Remove the flask from the water bath, and carefully add 25 mL of an ice-water slush to the flask. This will destroy any unreacted acetic anhydride and dilute the sulfuric acid present. Set the flask in a beaker of ice until crystallization appears to be complete. Use a Büchner funnel and suction filtration to separate the crystals from the liquid.

Cool the reaction mixture.

With the crude product still in the Büchner funnel, draw air over the product to dry it as much as possible. Transfer this solid material to a clean, dry 100-mL beaker, and add about 5 mL of ethanol. Heat slowly, with stirring, on a hot plate to dissolve the product. Add more ethanol, if necessary, but use only the smallest amount possible to dissolve the product. When all solid material has dissolved, place the warm beaker in an ice bath to which some rock salt has been added. Rapid cooling of the beaker is very important. Using a glass stirring rod, scratch the inside of the beaker below the surface of the ethanol. This will promote crystal formation. Leave the beaker in the ice bath until crystal formation is complete. Again separate the crystals from the liquid using a Büchner funnel and suction filtration, drawing air over the crystals to dry them. Weigh the dried product and record the weight. Calculate the yield of aspirin based on the amount of salicylic acid used as starting mterial.

Recrystallize the aspirin.

Submit the product to your instructor in a labeled vial with your report.

PART C. DECARBOXYLATION OF SALICYLIC ACID; PREPARATION OF PHENOLPHTHALEIN

To a large (25 x 200 mm) test tube, add about 2 g of salicylic acid. Heat this rapidly on a Meker burner flame under a hood until it melts. Continue heating the liquid acid for 5 minutes, moving it in and out of the flame to prevent splattering or boiling over. Cool the test tube and its contents and carefully note the odor of the product after cooling. This is the characteristic odor of phenol.

In a large test tube, heat the salicylic acid.

Add about 2 g of phthalic anhydride and 2 drops of concentrated sulfuric acid (**CAUTION**) to the test tube, and once again gently heat the mixture under a hood until it melts. Continue heating the liquid and moving it in and out of the flame until the liquid becomes dark red, but not black.

Add phthalic anhydride and sulfuric acid.

Allow the test tube and contents to cool. Crystals will begin to form on the inside walls of the test tube near the top. As the test tube cools, crystals will form further and further down the walls. When crystal formation has reached 1 in. above the liquid, rapidly add, with swirling, 20 mL of distilled water. Allow the test tube to cool for another 5 minutes, and then decant and discard the liquid. Add 3 mL of ethanol to the solid that remains and warm it until it dissolves. Add more ethanol, if necessary, but use the smallest amount needed to dissolve the product. Pour the ethanol solution into a 100-mL beaker, and rapidly place this beaker in a rock salt/ice bath. Again, use your stirring rod to scratch the inside of the beaker to promote crystallization. When crystal formation is complete, use the Buchner funnel and suction filtration to separate and dry the crystals. Weigh the dried product and record the weight. DO NOT discard the liquid from the filtration, but use it as follows:

Cool the test tube and add water.

Add a few drops of the ethanol solution to a dilute solution of sodium hydroxide and explain your observations.

430

CALCULATIONS

To calculate the percent yield of your recrystallized product, use the equation:

$$\% \text{ yield } = \frac{\text{experimental yield}}{\text{theoretical yield}} \times 100\%.$$

NOTE

<u>Note 1.</u>   The top of the reflux condenser may fume badly. If so, arrange a tube leading from the condenser to within 1 cm of the surface of 3 M NaOH contained in an open flask or to an open soda lime tube.

NOTEBOOK AND REPORT

Record the amounts of all starting materials, any changes in procedure, unusual observations and the masses, melting points, and yields of all isolated products.

In the report include (balanced) equations for all reactions, and describe the method used in calculating yields of products.

SUGGESTIONS FOR ADDITIONAL STUDIES

At room temperature, phenol reacts with salicylyl chloride, acetic anhydride and phthalic anhydride. One of the products from these reactions is phenyl salicylate. This is used in medicine as an intestinal antiseptic. It passes through the stomach unchanged and is slowly hydrolyzed in the intestinal tract. It also is used as a coating for pills that are intended to pass through the stomach before dissolving. As an additional project, you may wish to carry out some of the reactions described above and isolate the products. You should plan your work carefully and discuss it with your instructor before proceeding.

REFERENCES

1.   Davis, Gailey, and Whitten, <u>Principles of Chemistry</u>, Saunders College Publishing, Philadelphia, PA, 1984, Chapter 25 (Organic Chemistry).

2.   Whitten and Gailey, <u>General Chemistry</u>, 2nd Ed., Saunders College Publishing, Philadelphia, PA, 1984, Chapter 30 (Organic Chemistry II: Functional Groups).

QUESTIONS

Attach a sheet of paper with answers to the assigned questions from the list below.

1. Why is the extraction with several portions of ether more efficient than a single extraction with a larger volume?

2. Write equations for

   (a) the reaction of base with each of the following:
   salicylic acid, methyl salicylate, and aspirin

   (b) the reaction of water with each of the following:
   thionyl chloride, acetic anhydride, and salicylyl chloride

   (c) the reaction of ethanol with each of the following:
   phthalic anhydride, acetic anhydride, and salicylic acid

   (d) the reaction of phenol with each of the following:
   phthalic anhydride, acetic anhydride, and salicylic acid

3. Why is the reaction of salicylic acid with thionyl chloride not carried out in the presence of a solvent such as water or ethanol? Would any solvent be suitable for this reaction? Explain.

4. What is the role of sulfuric acid in the acetylation of salicylic acid? Suggest a "mechanism" for its involvement in this reaction.

5. Why does the acetylated product in Part B not contain acetyl groups at both the $-CO_2H$ and $-OH$ functions on salicylic acid?

Experiment 32

ORGANIC SYNTHESIS

PRELABORATORY QUESTIONS

Name_____   Lab Instructor_____

Student ID No._____   Date_____

1. Write equations containing structural formulas to illustrate the synthesis of (a)
    salicylamide; (b) methylsalicylate; (c) acetylsalicylic acid (aspirin); (d)
    phenolphthalein.

2. Describe briefly how and why each of the following techniques is performed in the
    laboratory.

    (a) **extraction**

         how?

         why?

    (b) **recrystallization**

         how?

         why?

3. List the operations in this experiment that must be performed

    (a) in a hood.

    (b) to avoid contact of reagents with parts of your body.

4. Why is ether a commonly used extraction solvent?

5. If you started the synthesis of aspirin with 1.00 g of salicylic acid and isolated 1.00 g of acetylsalicylic acid, what is the percent yield of aspirin in your synthesis?

Experiment 32

ORGANIC SYNTHESIS

REPORT SHEET

Name________________________________ Lab Instructor______________________

Student ID No.____________________ Date______________________________

PART A

Mass of salicylic acid taken (g) ____________________

Volume of thionyl chloride taken (mL) ____________________

Mass of salicylamide obtained (g) ____________________

Your melting point of salicylamide (^{o}C) ____________________

Mass of methyl salicylate obtained (g) ____________________

Yield of products (%): salicylamide ____________________

methyl salicylate ____________________

PART B

Mass of salicylic acid used (g) ____________________

Volume of acetic anhydride used (mL) ____________________

Mass of aspirin obtained (g) ____________________

Your melting point of aspirin (^{o}C) ____________________

Yield of aspirin obtained (%) ____________________

PART C

Mass of salicylic acid used (g)   _____

Mass of phthalic anhydride used (g)   _____

Your melting point of phenolphthalein ($^{\circ}$C) _____

Yield of phenolphthalein (%)   _____

AMINO ACIDS ON HUMAN SKIN

Objective

To separate and identify some amino acids from human skin and from food proteins. To illustrate the sensitivity and effectiveness of partition chromatography

Equipment Needed

Whatman 3MM chromatography paper 8 x 6 in. sheets; development tank or jar; rubber band; small casserole; 600- or 800-mL beaker; 15-μL pipet; staples and staple gun; spray bottle; hotplate; ruler; oven (optional)

Chemicals Needed

6 M Acetic acid; acetonitrile developing solvent (60 parts acetonitrile, 40 parts 0.1 M aqueous ammonium acetate, V/V); n-butanol developing solvent (40 parts n-butanol, 10 parts glacial acetic acid, 10 parts water, V/V/V); ninhydrin spray solution (0.5% ninhydrin in 95 mL of n-butanol and 5 mL of 60% aqueous acetic acid); samples of reference amino acids fitted with toothpicks as applicators (0.5% by weight solutions of each of the following: leucine, tyrosine, valine, alanine, glutamic acid, glycine, histidine, asparagine, arginine, serine, and phenylalanine); soap; plastic film; casein, wheat gluten, soybean meal, and other protein materials

INTRODUCTION

The amino acids in the proteins of human skin include alanine, arginine, asparagine, glutamic acid, glycine, histidine, leucine, phenylalanine, proline, serine, tyrosine, and valine. In this experiment you will obtain some amino acids from the palm of your hand and from food proteins, separate them using paper chromatography, and identify them by comparing their rates of movement across the paper with that of known amino acids used as references.

TECHNIQUES

The principal technique used is known as ascending paper chromatography. It is similar to that described for thin-layer chromatography in Exp. 8, except that the stationary phase here is water on a cellulose surface. As with ascending thin-layer chromatography, the sample of the mixture to be separated is placed near the bottom of the strip of chromatography paper, and this strip is dipped into a solution of a developing solvent. The developing solvent is then allowed to rise by capillary action up the paper strip where it eventually hits the sample and moves the components with it. The components move at various rates depending upon their relative solubilities in the water of the stationary phase and in the components of the developing mixture. Either of two developing mixtures can be used here: 60 parts acetonitrile to 40 parts of 0.1 M aqueous ammonium acetate, or 40 parts n-butanol to 10 parts glacial acetic acid and 10 parts water. The acetonitrile solvent is faster; the n-butanol mixture gives a better separation.

To aid in identification of the amino acids after they are separated, samples of known amino acids will be chromatographed on the same paper and simultaneously with the mixture to be separated. For example, a single sheet of chromatography paper 8-in. wide will be prepared by spotting separate samples at one-half-inch intervals along a line 1-in. from the bottom edge of the paper and starting 1.5 in. from the left edge. Four of these samples will contain the skin and food mixtures to be separated. Each of the others will be a different amino acid to be used as a reference. When the samples have been spotted and dried, the paper is bent to form a cylinder and placed in the development tank.

The chromatogram is allowed to develop until the solvent front has moved upward approximately 6 in. It is then removed, allowed to dry, sprayed carefully with a ninhydrin solution, and heated at 60 °C for about 10 minutes. The colored spots on each of the samples are circled with a pencil since the color may change upon standing.

The amino acids in the original samples can be identified by associating a given spot in the unknown samples with that of a known amino acid that has moved the same distance during development or by comparing its R_f value with those in Table 33-1. Spraying the sample with a ninhydrin solution and heating will make the locations of the amino acid visible.

Table 33-1. R_f Values for Amino Acids Using Acetonitrile and Ammonium Acetate

Amino Acid	R_f Value*
leucine	0.76
valine	0.64
proline	0.57
alanine	0.52
glutamic acid	0.44
glycine	0.43
histidine	0.40
asparagine	0.31

$$*R_f = \frac{\text{distance the component moves}}{\text{distance the solvent moves}}$$

PROCEDURE

Obtaining Amino Acids from Your Hand. DO NOT WASH YOUR HANDS. Gently boil about 100 mL of water in a 250-mL beaker. Place 5 mL of distilled water and 2 drops of 6 M acetic acid in an evaporating dish. Set the dish on top of the beaker and immediately, using an eye dropper, flush your palm and fingers repeatedly, letting the water drop back into the evaporating dish. Continue this flushing until the water is too hot for comfort. Let the 5 mL of water cool, adding more distilled water if too much has evaporated. Repeat this heating and flushing for 10 minutes, then let the 5 mL of water evaporate completely. Dissolve the resultant residue in 6 drops of 6 M acetic acid and heat on the water bath for another 5 minutes. If all of the liquid evaporates, add a couple more of 6 M acetic acid. The resultant solution is your "skin sample." Save it until required later.

Obtain sample of amino acids from your hand.

Preparing the Developing Tank. Pour 70 mL of the developing solvent (butanol/acetic acid/water) into a 400- or 800-mL beaker. Cover the beaker with plastic wrap, and secure it with a rubber band. Set the beaker aside until called for later.

Prepare developing tank and saturate the tank air with solvent vapor.

Preparing the Chromatography Paper. Obtain a piece of chromatography paper from your instructor. Touch it as little as possible and

438

only at the corners since the dirt, oil, and water on your fingers will soil the paper. **KEEP THE PAPER FREE OF ALL DIRT AND CHEMICALS.** With a straight edge, make a light **pencil** mark across the sheet parallel to the longer side, ~1 in. from the edge. Make 11 dots on this line, evenly spaced and at least 1.5 in. from the ends of the paper. Later you will spot your samples on these dots. Your paper should look like this:

Prepare chromatography paper and place samples on it.

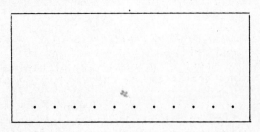

$\updownarrow$ 1 in.

Since you will be putting 11 different samples on the chromatography paper, you must label the spots. The system you choose is up to you as long as you can later identify each sample spot. Label (lightly and in PENCIL, below the line) 4 of the dots near the center of the line for 2 skin samples and 2 food samples. For food samples, use 2 of the following: (1) peanut, (2) soy, corn, or egg, and (3) wheat or milk. Label the remaining 7 spots for the known amino acid samples. You may wish to use the first 2 letters of the names as symbols. The 7 known amino acids are: arginine, aspartic acid, glutamic acid, leucine, phenylalanine, proline, and valine.

Spotting the Samples onto the Paper. Using the toothpicks in the sample vials, put one small spot of each sample on the appropriate pencil dot. **Do not mix the toothpicks,** or the experiment will be meaningless for the next student. The toothpick must **not** have any solution hanging as a drop from the end. This will give too big a spot. Due to separating, the spots will get bigger as the development proceeds so you want to make your initial spots as small as possible. After spotting, wave the paper in the air to dry the spots. Repeat the spotting procedure **four more times,** drying after each application. All 5 spots for a sample must be in **exactly** the same place, on the pencil dot you labeled for that sample. When spotting is complete, hold the paper by the corners, turn it into a cylinder so that the line becomes a circle, and staple the top and bottom without overlapping the ends.

Development. Remove the plastic wrap from your large beaker and quickly place the cylinder into the beaker with the sample spots at the bottom. **Make sure that the paper does not touch the sides of the beaker and that the solvent is not in contact with your sample spots.** Quickly replace the plastic wrap and rubber band. Do not move the beaker until development is complete. As development proceeds, the solvent will climb up the paper. Ideally, the solvent should climb to within 1 in. of the top of the paper; however, you probably won't have enough time for this. Allow the development to proceed for **at least** 60 minutes and longer, if possible. When development is complete, remove the paper. **Immediately, mark the level the solvent has reached** and allow the paper to dry in the oven. Put the solvent into the waste bottle; **do not pour it down the drain!**

Develop the chromatogram.

Locating the Spots. At this point, the amino acid spots are not visible to the naked eye. To see the spots, we spray the paper with a dye that will react with the amino acids to make them visible. When the paper has dried, remove it from the oven, and detach the staples. Take the paper to your instructor who will spray it with the dye ninhydrin. (Ninhydrin is toxic and is absorbed through the skin, so avoid touching or breathing it!) Put the paper back into the oven for 5 minutes. Remove the paper, and immediately circle the spots since they will begin to fade in about 15 minutes. Also draw a line through the

Spray to make spots of amino acids visible.

center of mass of each spot and record the color of each spot. The colors will fade with time.

Determine R_f value.

Computation of R_f Values. Use a ruler to measure the distance that the solvent moved past the original dot for each spot. Also measure the distance of the center of mass of each spot from the original dot. Calculate the R_f value for each spot and then, using these values and the colors of the spots, determine which amino acids were present in each protein sample.

NOTEBOOK AND REPORT

Record your observations in the notebook, and try to explain any unusual observations in the report. The report should also include the Report Sheet and answers to the questions that are assigned by your instructor.

REFERENCES

1. Brinkman, U.A. Th., and DeVries, G. J. Chem. Educ. (1972), 49, 545.

2. Heimer, E.P. J. Chem. Educ. (1972), 49, 547.

Experiment 33

AMINO ACIDS ON HUMAN SKIN

PRELABORATORY QUESTIONS

Name______________________________ Lab Instructor____________________

Student ID No.____________________ Date______________________________

1. Why would you expect to obtain amino acids from the palm of your hand?

2. From a biochemistry textbook or a chemistry handbook, obtain the structural formulas for three amino acids that might be obtained from your hand.

3. Offer a brief explanation of how you will determine which amino acids are obtained from your skin.

4. What is an R_f value? What is its importance in this experiment?

5.   What does it mean to "develop a chromatogram"?

6.   What is the role of ninhydrin in this experiment?   What precautions must be observed
     in using it?

7.   Why would you expect to find amino acids in peanuts, casein (from milk and cheese),
     wheat gluten, and soybeans? Would you expect to find amino acids in potatoes and
     apples? Why or why not?

AMINO ACIDS ON HUMAN SKIN

REPORT SHEET

Name_____   Lab Instructor_____

Student ID No._____   Date_____

Data

Developing Solvent_____

	Spot No.					
	1	2	3	4	5	6
Color with anhydrin	_____	_____	_____	_____	_____	_____
Reference acid at comparable position	_____	_____	_____	_____	_____	_____
R$_f$ value	_____	_____	_____	_____	_____	_____
Identification	_____	_____	_____	_____	_____	_____

	Spot No.				
	7	8	9	10	11
Color with anhydrin	_____	_____	_____	_____	_____
Reference acid at comparable position	_____	_____	_____	_____	_____
R$_f$ value	_____	_____	_____	_____	_____
Identification	_____	_____	_____	_____	_____

QUESTIONS

Attach a sheet of paper with answers to the assigned questions from the list below.

1. What assumption is made in identifying the amino acids in the sample by associating their positions on the developed chromatogram with those of reference amino acids? How could the validity of this assumption be tested?

2. Why can an R_f value never be greater than 1.0?

3. What would happen if you made the original line and dots with ink rather than with pencil? How would this affect your results?

4. Make a table listing the 7 known amino acids in order of increasing R_f values. Include the measured R_f values and the chemical structures (obtain from a biochemistry textbook or a chemistry handbook) of the amino acids. Explain how the chemical structures can account for the observed order of R_f values. Hint: you will need to think about solubilities.

5. Do you expect all students to obtain the same amino acids from their skin sample? Why or why not? Compare the amino acids present in your skin sample with those of three other students.

6. Name 3 additional sources of amino acids from the human body that could be readily obtained and identified as you did in this experiment.

7. Suppose you found that using the procedure you used here on the skin of pigs, chickens, and fish gave the same amino acids as you found from your own skin. What conclusion or conclusions could you draw?

8. The effectiveness of the acetonitrile developing solvent can be improved for certain combinations of amino acids if it is buffered at a lower or higher pH. For example, by adding acetic acid it can be buffered at pH 4, or by adding ammonia it can be buffered at pH 9.2. What structural features of the amino acids of skin proteins are expected to be important in bringing about better separations at the lower pH? at the higher pH?

EVALUATION OF EXPERIMENTAL DATA

Now that you have gained experience in calibrating and using instruments that measure temperature, mass, and spectra, we will examine the way in which one scientifically evaluates experimental data. In all of the experiments you should be aware of the precision required, the accuracy of the data, and the sources of systematic and random errors. (These topics are treated in the following sections.) Then you will be asked to evaluate the data obtained in some of the previous experiments.

MEASUREMENT

Most scientific discoveries begin as a personal experience for the investigator. In order to study this experience objectively and to communicate it accurately to others, the investigator usually finds it necessary to use instruments to measure the factors involved. For example, centuries ago, man first realized that he had a heartbeat. Perhaps he realized that the rate of heartbeat seemed to change at different times of the day. Upon comparing his heartbeat with that of another person, man undoubtedly discovered differences in rates between the two. Then came the question: How can we communicate to others what we have found? One way to do this would be to design an instrument to measure heartbeat rates objectively so that differences between persons or differences in one person at different times of the day could be measured precisely. Of course, this instrument is the clock! Perhaps this legend of its inception is convincing justification for the importance scientists give to measurement.

Measurement makes it possible to obtain more exact information about the properties of matter, such as the size, shape, mass, temperature, or composition of a sample Measuring instruments are merely extensions or refinements of our senses. For example, the balance makes it possible to determine the mass of an object more accurately than we could by lifting it, and the clock allows us to measure time more accurately than we could by observing with the naked eye the position of the sun in the sky.

Although great importance is given to measurement, equal importance should be given to recognizing the limitations of the measuring instrument and the reliability of the data obtained from an instrument. Viewed broadly, the limitations of instruments are summarized in two questions:

1. **Is the instrument suitable for making the measurement under consideration?** For example, is an ordinary meter stick, which can be read to the nearest millimeter, suitable for measuring the thickness of a human hair which is approximately 0.1-mm thick? The distance between the smallest interval ruled on the meter stick is 1 mm. If the meter stick were used for this purpose, the result would not be very reliable. It is unlikely that one could detect a difference in thickness between one hair and another with the meter stick. Therefore, the meter stick is not a suitable instrument for this purpose. Such measurements are much more valid when they are made with the aid of a microscope and a rule calibrated to 0.01 mm.

2. **Given a suitable measuring instrument, can the measurements with it be made with the required precision?** As an illustration, consider the results of measuring the length of this laboratory manual by using a meter stick. We can read without difficulty to the nearest millimeter, and with care can estimate the length to the nearest 0.5 mm. With difficulty, much squinting, and proportionate

uncertainty, we might be able to estimate the length to the nearest 0.1 mm. But we cannot go further than this because of the limitation inherent in our instrument and in our vision. Therefore, measurement of length with the meter stick is reliable at best to ± 0.1 mm. If we need to know the length more precisely than this, a different measuring instrument is required.

Accuracy and Precision. There is some degree of uncertainty in every measurement, which may come from either limitations of accuracy or limitations of precision. One should note carefully the difference between the terms accuracy and precision. **Accuracy** involves a comparison of the average result found for a measurement with that of a true or accepted value. **Precision,** on the other hand, involves comparison of a series of measurements made in the same way to one another (Fig. 34-1). We can always obtain an exact value for the precision on a given set of measurements, but a true or accepted value must be known in order for the accuracy to be determined. Otherwise, the accuracy can only be estimated.

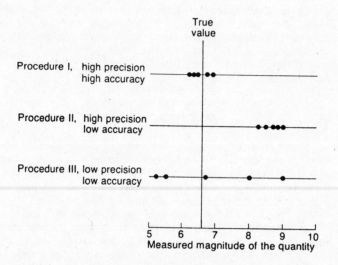

Figure 34-1. Accuracy and precision illustrated

Most of the experiments in this laboratory program have a quantitative basis; they rely on measurements of factors such as temperature, mass, and volume. In order to evaluate quantitatively the accuracy and precision of a set of measurements, one needs to consider a set of N replicate measurements, X_1, X_2, X_3, ..., X_N. The mean (sometimes called the average or arithmetic mean) is defined as

$$\overline{X} = \frac{X_1 + X_2 + X_3 + ... + X_N}{N} \tag{1}$$

For each measurement (and for the mean value), there is a difference between the observed value (e.g., X_1) and the true value, T. This difference is the **error** of the measurment.

$$\text{Error} = \text{observed value} - \text{true value} \tag{2}$$

The difference between the true value and a single measurement is called the absolute error. A better estimate of the error can be made if the mean error (the difference between the mean value of the measurement and the true value) is calculated.

Often it is even more meaningful to express error as a value **relative** to the magnitude of the quantity being measured, i.e.,

$$\text{Relative error} = \frac{\text{error}}{\text{true value}}. \tag{3}$$

This ratio is often multiplied by 100, 1000, or 1,000,000 and expressed as percentage (%), parts per thousand (ppt), or parts per million (ppm), respectively.

A quantitative representation of the precision of a given measurement is the **deviation,** defined as the difference between the mean of a set of measurements and the individual measurement. Thus,

$$\text{Deviation,} \quad \delta = \bar{X} - X_i. \tag{4}$$

In any experimental science, we are more often concerned with the precision of a set of measurements than with the deviation of a single measurement. We are interested in the **average deviation,** $\bar{\delta}$, which is the average value of all of the individual deviations,

$$\bar{\delta} = \frac{|\delta_1| + |\delta_2| + |\delta_3| + \ldots + |\delta_N|}{N} \tag{5}$$

δ, in which the vertical bars, $||$, signify that the absolute value of the enclosed quantity is used. The average deviation, $\bar{\delta}$, is easy to calculate, but two other measures of deviation, the **range** and the **standard deviation,** are also useful. The **range,** W, is merely the difference between the largest measured value and the smallest measured value, i.e.,

$$W = X_{largest} - X_{smallest}.$$

The **standard deviation,** σ, is defined for a finite set of data as

$$\sigma = \sqrt{\frac{\delta_1{}^2 + \delta_2{}^2 + \delta_3{}^2 + \ldots + \delta_N{}^2}{N - 1}}. \tag{6}$$

Comparisons of the actual deviation of a measurement with the standard deviation of the set of measurements provides a criterion for discarding a given measurement or evaluating the precision of a set of measurements.

ERRORS

The numerical results obtained in an experiment are never completely accurate but are always in error by variable amounts. The magnitude of the error depends upon the skill of the experimenter and the precision of his or her measuring instruments. Errors are divided for convenience into two broad categories, determinate (systematic) and indeterminate (random) errors. **Determinate (systematic) errors** are those that are introduced as a result of some inherent error in the method of measurement or in the calibration or manufacturing specifications of the measuring device. Determinate errors affect every measurement of a set to the same extent. They do not alter the precision but do, of course, affect the accuracy of the measurement. For example, if an experimenter measured all lengths with a "yardstick" which was actually a "meterstick"--a trap into which unwary carpenters sometimes fall when working in a chemistry laboratory--it is evident that all of the measurements would be systematically in error.

Indeterminate (random) errors, on the other hand, are those that are present in spite of the experimenter's best efforts. It is difficult, for example, to repeat a procedure in exactly the same way and under the same conditions that it is carried out the first time. In the simple operation of heating a crucible which is then to be cooled and weighed, for example, the heating time may be inadvertently changed by a few minutes or the temperature in the flame may be changed because of unrecognized changes in the composition of the gas/air mixture. These differences may be reflected in a slightly changed weight for the crucible. One should not be disturbed, therefore, if the results of two measurements are not exactly the same. On the other hand, the results should not vary so much that the differences cannot be reasonably accounted for on the basis of chance.

Normal Distribution Curve. If a large number of measurements are performed on a quantity having a true value of T, all individual measurements will not be identical to T but will be scattered about T, owing to random error. If we plot the absolute error of each instrument against the frequency with which a given absolute error and sign occurs, a **normal distribution curve (or error curve)** (Fig. 34-2) results. Two important consequences are apparent from the curve of Fig. 35-2. (1) Both positive and negative errors are equally probable. Thus, the arithmetical mean (or average) of a series of single measurements represents the most reliable value, and the reliability (precision) increases as the number of measurements in the series increases. However, in doing an experiment,

447

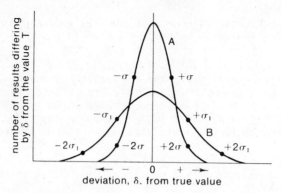

Figure 34-2. Normal distribution curves. Curves A and B represent the determination of the same quantity by two methods with inherently different reliability; method A is much more precise than method B.

one must consider the amount of time required to perform a large number of measurements. In the interest of progress, the experimenter must make some rational judgment between the time required to collect a large number of measurements and the reliability. Except in the most precise work, the average of three or four measurements is usually sufficient. (2) Small errors occur frequently, but the occurrence of a large error is relatively improbable.

The breadth or spread of the error curve indicates the precision of the measurements. A precise method gives a curve that is sharply peaked and drops off rapidly for large errors, e.g., curve **A** in Fig. 34-2; for imprecise measurements the curve is broad, e.g., curve **B** in Fig. 34-2. For a normal distribution, 68.3% of the results will differ from the arithmetical mean by less than one standard deviation ($\pm$ 1σ), 95.5% by less than 2 ($\pm$ 2σ), and 99.7% by less than 3 ($\pm$ 3σ).

SIGNIFICANT FIGURES

All measuring instruments have limits to their suitability and precision. **Consequently, all measurements and calculations reported in scientific work must reflect the limitations of the instruments used.** This is done by expressing the measurement to the correct number of significant figures.

The meaning of significant figures may be illustrated by considering the following data for the weight of a crucible:

A	B	C
12.8 g	12.86g	12.864 g

The first result tells the reader that the crucible was weighed with an accuracy of 0.1 g; the weight is closer to 12.8 g than to 12.7 or 12.9 g. Hopefully, it lies between 12.75 and 12.85 g, but the reader cannot be sure because the balance used may not have enabled one to distinguish values in the second decimal place. Similarly, in result **B** the weight is placed between 12.85 and 12.87 g, and in weight **C** it is between 12.863 and 12.865 g. Result **A** is recorded to three significant figures, result **B** is recorded to four significant figures, and result **C** is recorded to five significant figures. The third result is, of course, much more precise than either of the others. The weighing in result **C** is made to within 1 mg, or 0.001 g, in a total weight of approximately 13 g. Thus, the **absolute uncertainty** of the experimental weight is 0.001 g, whereas the **relative uncertainty** is 0.001/12.864, which may be expressed as 1 part in 12,864, or approximately 1 in 13,000. Weight **A** has a relative uncertainty of 1 part in only 128 (0.1/12.8), and weight **B** has a relative uncertainty of 1 part in 1286, or approximately 1 in 1300.

The relative error is often more important than the absolute error, as shown in the following example. The absolute error in result **C** is 0.001 g, and the value 12.864 g is very precise (to 1 part in ∿13,000) for the object weighing about 13 g. However, a weighing made with the same absolute error (0.001 g) for an object weighing only 0.013 g would have a relative uncertainty of 1 part in 13.

In reporting the result of a set of measurements, we should give the best value for the set, i.e., the arithmetical mean, **and** an indication of the precision observed between the individual values used to calculate the mean. We have already indicated that the latter may be expressed in terms of the range, average deviation, or standard deviation. One should determine and report all numbers that are known with certainty and, in addition, the first uncertain digit should be reported.

For example, assume the values reported for an experiment were 21.24, 21.01, 21.22, and 21.15. The mean is 21.155 and the average deviation from the mean is ± 0.075. Clearly, the number in the second decimal place is uncertain, and we should round the mean value accordingly. Next, we must decide between 21.15 and 21.16, the value 21.155 being spaced equally between them. In a case of a remaining 5, round the number to the nearest **even** number. Thus, we should report these results as 21.16 ± 0.08.

The **significant figures** of a number are all digits having values known with certainty plus the first digit having uncertain value. The position of the decimal point is irrelevant. Thus, 0.43214, 4.3214, 432.14, and 43,214 all contain five significant figures.

In some cases, the uncertainty in the final significant figure may be more than one unit. Suppose, for example, that the balance scale is divided by lines into 0.01 g units, and the needle comes to rest between 2 lines. The experimenter then visually divides each space into 10 parts, and estimates the position of the needle in terms of these imaginary marks. In Fig. 34-3, for example, the recorded value would be 0.164, because the experimenter would estimate the needle to be four-tenths of the way from 16 to 17. Such an estimate cannot be made with a precision greater than about 0.2 unit, and the result might be recorded as 0.164 ± 0.002 g to indicate that the uncertainty in the final significant figure was greater than one unit.

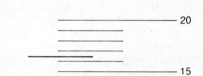

Figure 34-3. Estimating the space between graduations

Zero as a Significant Figure. The zero digit occupies an ambiguous position with regard to significant figures. In the numbers 10.7, 17.03, and 17.0233 the zero is a significant figure. Zeros enclosed by digits other than zero **are always significant.** They are called imbedded zeroes. Thus, 10.01 contains four significant figures.

The zero is not a significant figure in the number .033 since it merely serves to locate the position of the decimal point. A zero is **never** a significant figure when it appears between the decimal point and the first number on the right side of the decimal. They are called leading zeroes. In the number 0.033 neither zero is a significant figure. It may be helpful to note that when the number is written as a fraction (33/1000), the zero is not a significant figure but simply designates the magnitude.

When the zero comes last in a whole number but before the decimal point, it may or may not be a significant figure. In the number 730, for example, the zero is not a significant figure if the precision of the measurement is ± 10 units and the intention of the information is that the number lies between 720 and 740. However, if 730 represents a number between 729 and 731, the zero is a significant figure. In the first case the number is expressed to only two significant figures, and the zero merely indicates that the decimal point is to be placed one place farther to the right than the last significant figure, thus, 730 and not 73. **Modern scientific notation requires that a number like 730 but containing only two significant figures be written as 7.3** 10^2. This removes the ambiguity previously associated with numbers ending in zero.

Propagation of Errors

It is often important to estimate the error of a final result that is calculated from several different measurements, each possessing a degree of uncertainty. It is evident that the precision of the final result can be no greater than that of the least precise measurement from which it was calculated.

Addition and Subtraction. The preceding point may be illustrated by the following determinations of the weight of a salt, based on the gain in weight of a crucible on the balance.

	A	B	C	D
Weight of crucible and salt	17.13 g	17.033 g	17.0 g	17.033 g
Weight of crucible	12 g	12.1 g	12.13 g	17.020 g
Weight of salt	5 g	4.9 g	4.9 g	.013 g

In each of the examples, the number of reliable, i.e., significant, figures that can be carried to the answer is determined by the least precise measured value.

This generalization is important in two ways. In the first place, it shows that it is wasteful of laboratory time to make one measurement with extreme precision when the precision of the final result is fixed by a second measurement that is inherently less precise. In the determination of the density of a common liquid (for example, Exp. 1), there would be no point in weighing the liquid to the nearest milligram if the volume could be measured only in a cylinder graduated in 2-mL units (0, 2, 4, 6, 8, 10 mL, etc.). Even if the volume could be measured with the same precision as the weight, there would be little point in doing so unless the temperature measurement could be made with a similar precision. Since the volume of a liquid changes with change in temperature, the experimenter might have a very precise value of the density but not know to what temperature that value corresponds. Thus, it is often useful to consider what precision is necessary or possible for the several measurements before starting an experiment.

The second way in which the preceding sums are important is in showing that in subtractions the absolute error is often more important than the relative error. For result **A**, since the crucible was weighed only to the nearest gram, the weight of the salt is also known only to the nearest gram; the relative error is 1 part in 5, a very imprecise result. This effect is particularly marked when there is a small difference between two large numbers. Thus, the result of the two weighings of **D** has a precision of only 1 part in 13, although each weighing was reliable to 1 part in ∿17,000.

Multiplication and Division. In calculated results involving multiplication or division, the **relative error is more important than the absolute error.** and the final result will be in error by the amount of the largest relative error. Suppose, for example, you wish to determine the value for the product of pressure and volume for a gas in a case in which the pressure can be measured to the nearest 0.1 cm of mercury (i.e., 1 torr) and the volume to the nearest 0.1 mL. Assume the experimental values were 74.5 cm and 15.5 mL; the numerical product would be 1154.75 mL x cm. But the volume is measured to 1 part in 155 (0.1 in 15.5) and the pressure to 1 part in 745 (0.1 in 74.5). Since the result is precise only to within the amount of the least precise measurement, it will be reliable to 1 part in 155, or about 1 in the third digit. The value of the pressure-volume product must then be reported with only 3 significant figures; the numerical answer must be rounded to 1150 mL $\times$ cm or, less ambiguously, to 1.15×10^3 mL·cm.

These examples illustrate two important rules for determining the number of significant figures in the result derived from experimental data:

1. **In addition or subtraction,** the **absolute** uncertainty of the component is considered. Round the answer so that it has the same precision as the least precise component.

2. **In multiplication or division,** the **relative** uncertainty of the component quantities governs the number of significant figures in the product or quotient. The answer should reflect a relative uncertainty that is of the same order as that of the least precise component.

Calculation of Percentage Error. The percentage error is calculated by dividing the difference between the accepted value and the experimenter's measured value by the accepted value and multiplying by 100%. For example, an experimenter determines the percentage of oxygen in pure potassium chlorate to be 38.7%. The correct value is 39.6%. The percentage error is calculated as

$$\frac{39.6 - 38.7}{39.6} \times 100\% = 2.3\%.$$

In calculations such as these, the difference in the numerator is always considered to be positive. Had the measured value been 40.5%, the percentage error would have been calculated as

$$\frac{40.5 - 39.6}{39.6} \times 100\% = 2.3\%.$$

UNITS AND DIMENSIONS

Every measurement involves relating the particular quantity measured to some reference scale. The reference scale is usually composed of arbitrarily chosen standards of measurement called units. A given dimension, such as length, may be expressed in a variety of units such as angstroms, millimeters, centimeters, meters, kilometers, or light-years. The unit used is usually determined by its convenience for the kind and magnitude of measurement to be made. For example, if a small length such as the diameter of an atom is to be measured, it is more convenient to express that value in terms of angstroms than in terms of centimeters or meters. For most objects used in the laboratory, the convenient unit of length is the centimeter. For greater distances, kilometers or miles are used; in considering distances in interstallar space, the light-year is the unit usually employed. A light-year is about 10^{16} meters.

Scientific convention requires that units be indicated for every measurement or derived result reported. Students in science should follow this rule not only in the laboratory but also in problem solving and on examinations.

Carrying Units in Mathematical Operations

When two or more measured quantities are used in mathematical operations, attention must be given to the proper handling of units. The following rules apply to such manipulations.

1. In addition and substraction, all quantities must be expressed in the same units before the operation is performed. For example, in adding 1.22 cm and 10.3 mm, both quantities must be expressed in centimeters or in millimeters before the addition is performed. Converting 1.22 cm to 12.2 mm and adding this to 10.3 mm gives 22.5 mm. If both numbers are expressed in centimeters, the answer would be 2.25 cm which is, of course, the same length as 22.5 mm.

2. In multiplication and division, the units are multipled or divided in the same way as the numbers are treated. For example, in multiplying the 10.2 mm by 4.00 mL, the product is 40.8 mm·mL (expressed as millimeter milliliters); in dividing 14.4 g by 1.20 mL, the quotient is 12.0 g/mL (expressed as grams per milliliter); in multiplying 10.2 cm by 5.0 cm, the product is 51 cm·cm or 51 cm^2 (expressed as centimeters squared or square centimeters).

Conversion of Units

Often a quantity expressed in one set of units must be expressed in a different set as in Item 1 preceding, in which 1.22 cm is changed to 12.2 mm. This change is effected by using the conversion factor or unit factor, which indicates that 1 cm is equivalent to 10 mm. It is convenient to write such conversion factors as fractions (in which both numerator and denominator represent the same amount, hence the term **unit** factor) and to use them as such, **retaining the unit labels.** Thus, the conversion of 1.22 cm to 12.2 mm can formally be expressed as

$$? \text{ mm} = 1.22 \text{ cm} \times \frac{10 \text{ mm}}{1 \text{ cm}} = \frac{1.22 \text{ cm} \times 10 \text{ mm}}{1 \text{ cm}} = \frac{1.22 \times 10 \text{ mm}}{1}$$

Note that the centimeter units are cancelled, just as if they were numerical factors. For a less trivial case, consider converting a density of 340 mg per cubic centimeter to the corresponding value in pounds per cubic foot. We need the conversion factors for milligrams to grams, grams to pounds, centimeters to inches, and inches to feet, as shown in the following formal arrangement:

$$\frac{? \text{ lb}}{\text{ft}^3} = \frac{340 \text{ mg}}{1 \text{ cm}^3} \times \frac{1 \text{ g}}{1000 \text{ mg}} \times \frac{1 \text{ lb}}{454 \text{ g}} \times \left(\frac{2.54 \text{ cm}}{1 \text{ in}}\right)^3 \times \left(\frac{12 \text{ in}}{1 \text{ ft}}\right)^3 =$$

$$\frac{340 \times 1 \times 1 \times (2.54)^3 \times (12)^3 \times mg \times g \times \text{lb} \times cm^3 \times in^3}{1 \times 1000 \times 454 \times 1^3 \times 1^3 \times cm^3 \times mg \times g \times in^3 \times \text{ft}^3} = 21.2 \text{ lb/ft}^3$$

In writing the conversion factor, the ratio of one unit to another can always be written two (i.e., correct and incorrect) ways. It is very important that fractions representing conversion factors be written in such a way that the unwanted units cancel. The factor for changing milligrams to grams is written $\frac{1 \text{ g}}{1000 \text{ mg}}$ so that "mg" in the demoninator of the conversion factor can cancel the "mg" that appears in the numerator in the given data. Had the factor been written in the reciprocal manner, i.e., $\frac{1000 \text{ mg}}{1 \text{ g}}$, "mg" would not cancel, and "mg^2" would have appeared in the answer. If properly arranged, all unit labels except those desired cancel in the answer. Thus, one can feel confident that he or she has worked a problem in a correct manner if he or she carried through the units and arrives at the answer with the desired units on the numerical part of the answer.

As a further example of the use of conversion factors, consider the following problem. How many liters of oxygen at standard temperature and pressure (STP) can be obtained by heating 61.25 g of $KClO_3$ which decomposes according to the equation

$$2 \text{ } KClO_3 \longrightarrow 2 \text{ } KCl + 3 \text{ } O_2?$$

Here, one of the conversion factors comes from the (calculated or known) formula weight of potassium chlorate, and another comes from the chemical equation which gives the relation between the number of moles of oxygen formed and the number of moles of potassium chlorate decomposed. The problem is set up with the given information as follows:

$$61.25 \text{ g of } KClO_3 \times \frac{1 \text{ mole of } KClO_3}{122.5 \text{ g of } KClO_3} \times \frac{3 \text{ moles of } O_2}{2 \text{ moles of } KClO_3} \times \frac{22.4 \text{ liters of } O_2 \text{ at STP}}{1 \text{ mole of } O_2} =$$

$$\frac{61.25 \times 1 \times 3 \times 22.4}{122.5 \times 2 \times 1} \quad \frac{\text{g of } KClO_3 \times \text{mole of } KClO_3 \times \text{mole of } O_2 \times \text{liters of } O_2 \text{ at STP}}{\text{g of } KClO_3 \times \text{mole of } KClO_3 \times \text{mole of } O_2} =$$

16.8 liters of O_2 at STP

Note again that the conversion factors are arranged so that only the units of the desired answer "liters of O_2 at STP" remain uncancelled.

REFERENCES

1. Davis, Gailey, and Whitten, *Principles of Chemistry*, Saunders College Publishing, Philadelphia, PA, 1984, pp. 11-24

2. Whitten and Gailey, *General Chemistry*, 2nd Ed., Saunders College Publishing, Philadelphia, PA, 1984, pp. 12-25.

EVALUATION OF EXPERIMENTAL DATA

PRELABORATORY REPORT

Name_____   Lab Instructor_____

Student ID No._____   Date_____

1. Perform the following operations, observing the number of significant figures.

    a.   (0.092)(16.000) =

    b. $\dfrac{0.491}{6.022 \times 10^{23}}$ =

    c. $\left(\dfrac{5.00}{1.0}\right)$ (20) =

    d.   (500) $\left(\dfrac{1}{1000}\right)\left(\dfrac{1}{4.71}\right)$ =

2. Perform the following operations, observing the number of significant figures.

    a. $1.0 \times 10^3 \times 2.0 \times 10^4 \times 3.0 \times 10^{-7}$ =

    b. $\dfrac{1.00 \times 10^{-2} \times 4.0 \times 10^{-8}}{3.00 \times 10^9}$ =

    c. $\dfrac{1.00 \times 10^{-4} \times 3.00 \times 10^{-5}}{5.0 \times 10^3 \times 7.00 \times 10^{-2}}$ =

453

3. Perform the following operations, carrying units and the proper number of significant figures in the answer.

a. 3.48 cm + 3.43 cm + 11.47 mm =

b. $\dfrac{2.056 \text{ g}}{9.26 \text{ mL}}$ =

c. 49.1 cm × 10.0 cm =

d. 3.4×10^{-14} cm + 2.0×10^{-15} m =

e. $\dfrac{(4/3) \times \pi \times (1.49 \text{ Å})^3}{1 \text{ atom}} \times \dfrac{6.022 \times 10^{23} \text{ atoms}}{1 \text{ mole}}$ =

4. Make the following conversions, observing significant figures.

a. 9.63 ergs to joules

b. 4.184×10^5 joules to calories

c. 30.0 amu to grams

d. 22.7×10^{-22} g to amu

Experiment 34

EVALUATION OF EXPERIMENTAL DATA

REPORT

Name_____   Lab Instructor_____

Student ID No._____   Date_____

1. Perform the following operations, observing the number of significant figures.

    a. $\left(\dfrac{3000}{40}\right)\left(\dfrac{4000}{80}\right) =$

    b. 149.3 + 7.21 + 0.1987 =

    c. 1.0046 - 0.0042 =

    d. 3.0 - 0.0031 =

2. Perform the following operations, observing the number of significant figures.

    a. $\dfrac{5.6 \times 10^{12}}{1.8 \times 10^{-12}} + \dfrac{1.3 \times 10^{7}}{2.6 \times 10^{-17}} =$

    b. $5.1 \times 10^{-6} + 2.5 \times 10^{-7} - 6.2 \times 10^{-5} =$

    c. $4 \times 10^{-6} \times 8.46 \times 10^{5} =$

3. Perform the following operations, carrying units and the proper number of significant figures in the answer.

    a. 3.1×10^8 coulombs/g $\times 2.05 \times 10^{-16}$ g/s =

    b. $\dfrac{14.2 \text{ feet}}{3.7 \text{ feet/year}}$ =

    c. 14.2 amperes $\times$ 8.5 volts =

4. Make the following conversions, observing the number of significant figures.

    a. 56 g of nitrogen to moles of nitrogen atoms (1 mole of nitrogen atoms is 14.0067 g)

    b. 6.63 ergs to kilocalories

    c. 32 amu to pounds (1 lb equals 453.59 g)

    d. 9.3143×10^7 ergs·mole^{-1} to calories per mole

5. From a table of logarithms, determine the logarithms of:

    a. 5.862   e. 6.83×10^2

    b. 692.9   f. 7.829×10^{-3}

    c. 0.502   g. 3.16×10^{-14}

    d. 0.00905   h. 5.093×10^{22}

6. From a table, determine the numbers y described as indicated:

    a. $\log y = 5.0868$ c. $\log y = -2.8468$

    b. $\log y = 0.7042$ d. $\log y = -0.8262$

ANALYTICAL BALANCES

ELECTRONIC ANALYTICAL BALANCES

Many of you will have access to electronic balances that have greatly simplified weighing operations. These balances differ from the older mechanical balances in that the load from the object to be weighed is balanced by a magnetic force rather than by the mechanical manipulation of balance weights.[1]

Operating procedures are similar for most electronic balances regardless of whether they are designed to be read to 0.1 mg or to 0.1 g. Fig. AI-1 shows an analytical electronic balance designed to be read to 0.1 mg; Fig. AI-2 shows balance designed to to be read to 0.1 mg or to 0.1 g. Fig. AI-1 shows an analytical electronic balance designed to be read to 0.I mg; Fig. AI-2 shows a balance designed to be read to 1 mg.

Figure AI-1 (Courtesy of Mettler Instrument Corp., Hightstown, NJ)   **Figure AI-2** (Courtesy of Ohaus Scale Corp.)

----

[1]   For a readable, detailed description of the principles of electronic balances, see: R. M. Schoonover, Anal. Chem. 1982, 54, 973A.

Operation

Single Weighing

1. Turn **on** the display by depressing the power switch **or** the single bar (the tare bar) at the front of the case, depending on the model balance you have. Balances with switches need to warm for about 15 minutes for stable readings. Single-bar balances are "on" all the time; only the display is off. These are ready immediately. In both cases, the whole display will light up and then rapidly change until it reads zero. If a zero reading is not obtained, depress the tare bar again to produce a zero reading.

2. Place the object to be weighed on the center of the balance pan and read its weight directly from the display.

3. Remove the object from the balance and depress the tare bar to produce a zero display.

Setting a Tare Weight

The tare weight is the weight of the empty container in which you will weigh a chemical. The balance will provide you with the weight of the chemical alone by subtracting the weight of the container from the total weight of the container and compound.

1. Weigh the empty container as above.

2. Depress the tare bar; this puts the balance to zero.

3. Add the chemical to be weighed to the container; the weight of the chemical alone appears on the display.

4. Remove the filled container and depress the tare bar to return the display to zero.

Subtractive Weighing

1. Place the container with the substance to be weighed on the balance pan.

2. Depress the tare bar to set the display to zero.

3. Remove the desired quantity of substance from the container.

4. Read the weight of the substance removed with a negative sign in front on the display.

5. To do successive weighings, simply repeat steps 2-4.

6. Remove the container and reset the display to zero.

MECHANICAL SINGLE-PAN BALANCES

Mechanical single-pan analytical balances were marketed by a number of firms, but all are quite similar in construction. The weighing mechanism consists of a beam resting near its middle upon a sapphire knife-edge. The end of the beam toward the front of the balance carries a stirrup and hanger device which supports the balance pan, contact again being made on a jewelled knife-edge. Also at the front and rigidly attached to the beam is a rod which carries weights of several denominations adding to a total corresponding to the maximum load of the balance, 99 g, for a nominal maximum of 100 g, for example. The end of the beam toward the back of the balance carries a counter weight equal to the combined mass of weights, rod, and balance pan so that when all of the weights are on the rod and nothing is on the pan, the beam balances horizontally on the central knife-edge (Fig. A1-3). The mass of an object placed on the balance pan is determined by counting the weights which must be lifted off the rod to compensate for the object's mass and restore the beam to its horizontal, balanced position. Also attached to the beam is a dash-pot to damp motion of the beam so that it does not rock back and forth indefinitely but comes quickly to rest and a marker that, through an optical device, registers and translates into milligrams and tenths of milligrams the small differences from absolute horizontal that are caused by fractional differences of these magnitudes between the mass of the object and the mass of the weights removed.

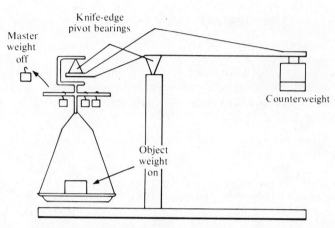

Single-arm substitution balance

Figure AI-3. Diagram for the beam of a single-pan analytical balance

For reproducible weighings, the beam and knife-edges must always be in the same relation to each other, so each balance carries a leveling mechanism and devices to prevent rubbing of the knife-edges and their opposite bearing plates, with subsequent dulling of the knife-edges, when the balance is not in use, and which will drop the bearing plates onto the knife-edges in the same position each time the balance is used. Balances of different manufacture differ in the position on the balance case of the knobs or levers which operature these knife-edge-protecting devices and the fingers which lift the weights from the rod attached to the beam. They also differ in the optical mechanism and the nature of the read-out which reports the third and fourth decimal place; sometimes this appears as a reference mark which points to a number and sometimes as a number which appears in a gap.

Your instructor will give you directions for operating the particular make of balance in your laboratory, but you should note and look for the following features.

1. **The Level Indicator.** This is usually a small disc on the floor or top of the balance which carries a bubble. When the balance is level, the bubble should be directly in the circle at the top of the disc. It is usually not necessary to adjust the level more than once or twice a day to compensate for temperature changes which change the position of the building or change unequally the length of the legs on the balance table.

2. **The Weight Manipulation Knobs.** These knobs, usually two, control the fingers which lift weights from the beam to balance the mass of the object on the pan. One knob will remove weights in 10-g increments, the other removes weights in 1-g increments. Turning the knobs also turns a dial so that the magnitude of the weight removed can be read. It is important that these knobs be turned **slowly and gently** and only when the beam and balance pan are supported free of the knife-edges. Rapid turning may cause the weights to bounce off their supports, and adding or removing weights when the beam and pan are resting on the knife-edges will dull the knife-edges and make the balance useless.

3. **The Zero Line Adjustment Knob.** This knob changes the position of the optical scale so that it rests on zero when the pan is empty and the beam is at equilibrium. This control also should need only infrequent adjustment but should be checked before each weighing.

4. **The Optical Scale, Micrometer, or Vernier Adjustment Device.** This control positions the optical scale relative to a reference line or pointer so that a reading to 0.0001 g can be obtained. On some makes it is not necessary to make this adjustment; the final reading appears automatically when the weights are set in the optical range.

5. **The Pan and Beam Control Knob.** This knob keeps the knife-edges separated from the beam when the balance is not in use and, if turned **gently**, will lower the beam and pan reproducibly when weighing. It should be emphasized that contact with the knife-edges should be made softly and smoothly by gentle turning of this knob. Turning this knob also switches on the light source for the optical scale. There are commonly three positions:

    a. **Arrest Position.** The beam is completely supported, and the knife-edges are not in contact. The balance should be put in the arrest position whenever the operator is placing objects on or removing them from the pan and between weighings.

    b. **Partial Arrest Position.** In this position, the beam is free to move, but contact with the fragile knife-edges is restricted. Weights can be removed (with care) when the beam is in the partial arrest position without harm to the balance mechanism. The partial arrest position is used in obtaining the approximate weight needed to balance the mass of the object being weighed.

    c. **Fully Released Position.** This is the position in which the beam is freely swinging, and it and the pan are supported only on the knife-edges. The balance is particularly vulnerable in this position and should never be touched except for careful and gentle adjustment of the zero line or optical scale. Final weighings are taken in the fully released position.

    d. Fig. AI-4 shows a diagram of a representative single-pan balance, and instructions for the use of a typical balance follow.

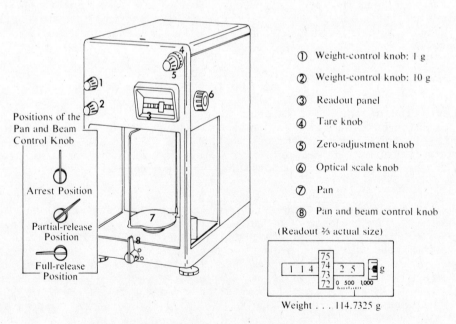

Figure AI-4. A typical single-pan balance

460

1. Before weighing, be sure that:

    a. The balance is arrested.
    b. There is nothing on the pan, the pan is clean, and the doors are closed.
    c. The weight-control knobs, optical-scale knob, and tare knob are set at zero.

2. Setting the zero point; the zero point must be rechecked before each weighing:

    a. Turn the pan and beam-control knob to the full-release position.
    b. When the numbered scale stops moving, turn the zero-adjustment knob until the line is perfectly centered at the zero position.
    c. Arrest the balance by turning the pan and beam control.

3. Weighing the sample:

    a. Place sample on pan with forceps. Use a container or weighing paper.
    b. Close the doors.
    c. Turn the pan and beam control to the partial-release position.
    d. Turn the 10-g weight-control knob until the beam is nearly balanced.
    e. Repeat with the other weight-control knob.
    f. Turn the pan and beam-control knob to the arrest position, and, after a slight pause, turn it (gently!) to the full-release position.
    g. Turn the optical-scale knob (after the numbered scale stops moving) until a line is perfectly centered in the indicator slit or aligned with the pointer.

4. Completing the weighing:

    a. Record the results.
    b. Arrest the balance.
    c. Remove sample from pan with forceps.
    d. Return all knobs to zero.
    e. If you spilled anything on the pan or in the balance, clean it up.

DIAGRAMS AND BRIEF INSTRUCTIONS

FOR USING SPECTROPHOTOMETERS

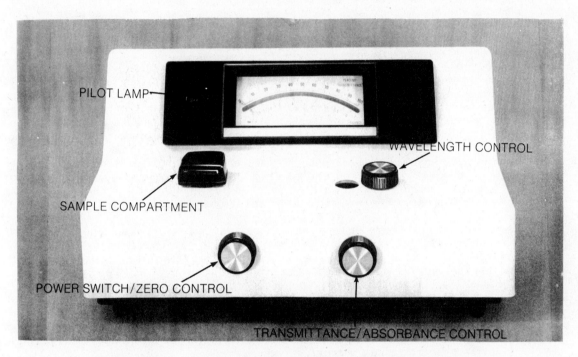

PILOT LAMP

WAVELENGTH CONTROL

SAMPLE COMPARTMENT

POWER SWITCH/ZERO CONTROL

TRANSMITTANCE/ABSORBANCE CONTROL

Figure AII-1. Spectronic 20 showing key operating features

Our purpose here is to give operating instructions for using simple spectrophotometers rather than to develop the theory behind them. It is enough to say that they work by comparing the light absorbed by a solution of a colored substance with the light absorbed by a reference solution **at a single wavelength.** Note that this means we will need to contain the solutions in a sample **cell,** be able to select a **wavelength,** and **compare** the reference and sample. We will consider each of these in turn for the Bausch & Lomb Spectronic 20 which is the most common spectrophotometer for general chemistry laboratories.

Operating Instructions

1. Turn **on** the instrument, using the **power switch.** The red pilot lamp will light up; allow at least a 15-minute warm-up period.

2. **Wavelength.** Set the desired wavelength using the wavelength control knob. The Spectronic 20 covers the visible region of the spectrum from 340 to 650 nm. The range can be extended to 950 nm in the near infrared region with a suitable phototube and filter. Note that a nanometer, nm, is 10^{-9} m and is equivalent to a millimicron, mμ. The wavelength dial on your instrument may be marked "mμ" rather than nm.*

―――――― *To convince yourself that the instrument really does cover the visible spectrum, put a piece of white chalk in one of the sample tubes provided. Put the tube in the sample compartment and **leave the cover** open. Now turn the wavelength control slowly from 340 to 650 nm and watch the colors on the chalk.

3. **Cell.** Sample tubes for the Spectronic 20 will be provided. They are essentially test tubes; any good-quality, appropriately sized test tubes are acceptable sample cells. Sample cells must be **clean** and **free from fingerprints.** Wipe the cells with tissue before readings. Since the tubes are not perfectly cylindrical, you will need to mark a line on top of them with a grease pencil to be sure they are always inserted the same way.

4. **Comparison.**

   A. **Zero Setting.** When there is no tube in the sample holder, a shutter automatically falls into the path of the light. With **no** sample in the holder and with the sample compartment cover closed, adjust the zero control (the lower left knob) until the meter reads zero percent transmittance. This adjustment compensates for stray light inside the instrument and is also called setting the dark current.

   B. **Reference and Full-Scale Setting.** Fill two sample tubes with the reference solution--probably the solvent. Wipe the tubes with tissue and place one in the sample compartment. You will feel the shutter being moved aside. **Close the cover.** Now use the transmittance control (lower right knob) to set the meter at 100% T. Mark the alignment of the tube with a grease pencil. Replace this tube with the other one, **close the cover,** and note the meter reading. Turn the tube in the holder and take another reading, again with the cover closed. Repeat this procedure until the reading for this second tube is also 100% T. (It will not take long to find a match.) Now mark the alignment of this tube. You now have a pair of matched cells. One will be used for the reference and the other for the sample solutions.

   C. **Sample Reading.** Empty one of the marked test tubes, rinse it several times with the sample solution, fill it half full with sample solution, and wipe the outside with tissue. Insert the tube in the sample holder, close the cover, and line it up, using the marks you made previously. Now read the meter as either % T or absorbance, A.

   Repeat this process for multiple samples. Between sample readings, insert the reference cell containing the reference solution. As before, close the cover and check to see that the reading is still 100% T. If it is not, readjust it, using the transmittance control.

Note: If you change wavelengths, you must repeat step 4, including matching the cells.

Summary of the Steps

   1. Turn on the instrument
   2. Set the wavelength
   3. Set the 0% T
   4. Set the 100% T and match the reference and sample cells
   5. Insert sample
   6. Read the % T or absorbance value

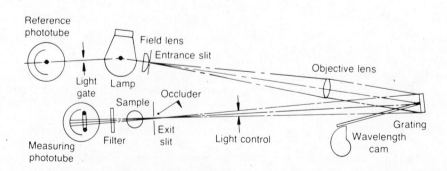

Figure AII-2. Light path as viewed from a point directly above the instrument
(courtesy of Bausch & Lomb)

These newer (and somewhat more expensive) models have automatically interchanged phototubes and cover the range of 325 to 925 nm. The photometric readout on the Spectronic 70 is on an 8-in., mirror-scale meter, whereas the Spectronic 100 has a digital readout. The operational steps for taking a measurement are similar to those for the Spectronic 20. The design of the two instruments is similar; the Spectronic 70 is shown in Fig. AII-3. The digital readout of the Spectronic 100 is shown in Fig. AII-4.

Figure AII-3.   (Courtesy of Bausch & Lomb)

Figure AII-4.   (Courtesy of Bausch & Lomb)

CONVERSION FACTORS

THE METRIC SYSTEM

Basic Units

length: meter
weight: kilogram
volume: liter

Length

1 kilometer (km) = 1000 m
     1 meter (m) = 100 cm = 1000 mm
1 centimeter (cm) = 10 mm
1 millimeter (mm) = 10,000,000 Å
     1 angstrom (Å) = 1 × 10^{-8} cm = 1 × 10^{-10} m

Weight

1 kilogram (kg) = 1000 g
    1 gram (g) = 1000 mg
1 milligram (mg) = 0.001 g

Volume

1 liter (ℓ) = 1000 mL = 1000.027 cm^3
.1 milliliter (mL) = 0.001
     1 mL = 1 cm^3
          = 1 cc

Prefixes Used with Base Units

Submultiple	Prefix	Symbol	Multiple	Prefix	Symbol
10^{-1}	deci	d	10	deca	da
10^{-2}	centi	c	10^{2}	hecto	h
10^{-3}	milli	m	10^{3}	kilo	k
10^{-6}	micro	μ	10^{6}	mega	M
10^{-9}	nano	n	10^{9}	giga	G
10^{-12}	pico	p	10^{12}	tera	T
10^{-15}	femto	f	10^{15}	peta	P
10^{-18}	atto	a	10^{18}	exa	E

THE SYSTEM INTERNATIONAL (S I)

SI Base Units

Physical Quantity	Name of Unit	Symbol
length	meter	m
mass	kilogram	kg
time	second	s
electric current	ampere	A
thermodynamic temperature	kelvin	K
luminous intensity	candela	cd
amount of substance	mole	mol

Special Names and Symbols for Certain SI Derived Units

Physical Quantity	Name of SI Unit	Symbol for SI Unit	Definition of SI Unit
force	newton	N	$kg \cdot m \cdot s^{-2}$
pressure	pascal	Pa	$kg \cdot m^{-1} \cdot s^{-2}$ $(= N \cdot m^{-2})$
energy	joule	J	$kg \cdot m^{2} \cdot s^{-2}$ $(= N \cdot m)$
power	watt	W	$kg \cdot m^{2} \cdot s^{-3}$ $(= J \cdot s^{-1})$
electric charge	coulomb	C	$A \cdot s$
electric potential difference	volt	V	$kg \cdot m^{2} \cdot s^{-3} \cdot A^{-1}$ $(= J \cdot A^{-1} \cdot s^{-1}) = JC^{-1}$
electric resistance	ohm	Ω	$kg \cdot m^{2} \cdot s^{-3} \cdot A^{-2}$ $(= V \cdot A^{-1})$
electric conductance	siemens	S	$kg^{-1} \cdot m^{-2} \cdot s^{3} \cdot A^{2}$ $(= A \cdot V^{-1} = \Omega^{-1})$
electric capacitance	farad	F	$A^{2} \cdot s^{4} \cdot kg^{-1} \cdot m^{-2}$ $(= A \cdot s \cdot V^{-1})$ $(= CV^{-1})$
frequency	hertz	Hz	s^{-1}

Symbols for SI Derived Units without Special Names

Physical Quantity	Symbol for Quantity	Name of SI Unit	Symbol for SI Unit
area	A	square metre	m^{2}
volume	V	cubic metre	m^{3}
density	ρ	kilogram per cubic metre	$kg\ m^{-3}$
velocity	u, v, w, c	metre per second	$m\ s^{-1}$
concentration*	$\tilde{c}$	mole per cubic metre	$mol\ m^{-3}$
electric field strength	E	volt per metre	$V\ m^{-1}$

*For concentration in $mol/L = mol/dm^{3}$, we use c. Thus, $\tilde{c} = 1000$.

SOME CONVERSION RELATIONSHIPS

Electric Charge

one coulomb = 2.778×10^{-4} A·h
= 1.036×10^{-5} Faraday
= 2.998×10^{9} statcoul

Electric Dipole Moment

one debye (D) = 1×10^{-18} statcoulomb·cm
= 3.336×10^{-20} C·Å
= 0.21 electron·Å

Energy and Work
(Mass units are included
as energy equivalents.)

one erg = 10^{-7} J
= 2.389×10^{-8} cal
= 6.242×10^{11} eV
= 1.113×10^{-24} kg
= 670.5 amu

one calorie (cal) = 4.1840×10^{7} erg
= 4.184 J
= 2.613×10^{19} eV
= 4.659×10^{-17} kg
= 2.807×10^{10} amu

one electron volt (eV) = 1.602×10^{-12} erg
= 1.602×10^{-19} J
= 3.827×10^{-20} cal
= 1.783×10^{-36} kg
= 1.074×10^{-19} amu

one kilogram (kg) = 8.987×10^{23} erg
= 8.987×10^{-16} J
= 2.142×10^{16} cal
= 5.610×10^{35} eV
= 6.025×10^{26} amu

one atomic mass unit
(amu) = 1.492×10^{-3} erg
= 1.492×10^{-10} J
= 3.564×10^{-11} cal
= 9.31×10^{8} eV
= 1.660×10^{-27} kg

Force

one newton (N) = 10^{5} dyn = 10^{5} g cm s^{-2}
= 0.2248 lb

one pound (lb) = 4.448×10^{5} dyn
= 4.448 N

Length

one meter (m) = 39.37 in.
= 3.281 ft
= 6.214×10^{-4} mi

one inch (in.) = 2.540 cm

one Angstrom (Å) = 10^{-10} m = 10^{-8} cm

one micron = 10^{-6} m

one light-year = 9.4600×10^{12} km

Mass and Weight
(Mass-weight equivalents are valid
for terrestrial use only.)

one gram (g) = 6.852×10^{-5} slug
= 6.024×10^{23} amu
= 3.27×10^{-2} oz
= 2.205×10^{-3} lb

one atomic mass unit
(amu) = 1.6602×10^{-24} g

one pound (lb) = 453.6 g

one ton = 2000 lb
= 907.2 kg

Pressure

one atmosphere (atm) = 1.013×10^{6} dyn/cm^2
= 1.013×10^{5} N·m^{-2}
= 76.0 cm Hg
= 14.70 lb/in.^{2}
= 2116 lb/ft^2
= 760 torr

one centimeter
mercury (cm Hg) = 10 torr
= 1.316×10^{-2} atm
= 1.333×10^{4} dyn/cm^2
= 5.353 in. H_2O
= 0.1934 lb/in.^{2}
= 27.85 lb/ft^2

INSTRUCTIONS FOR pH METERS

INTRODUCTION

Specific operating instructions vary slightly from one manufacturer's pH meter to another but some features are common to all. Pictures of four common types of pH meters are given below.

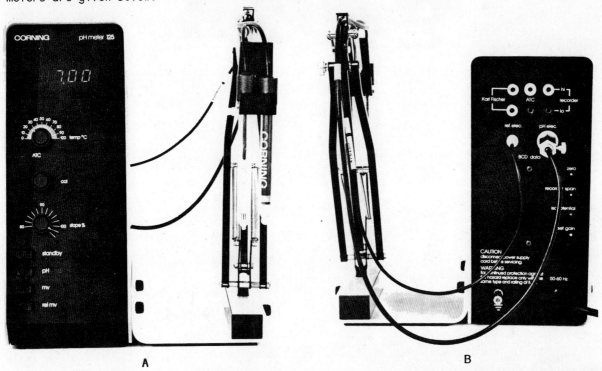

Figure AIV-1. Front (A) and back (B) views of the Corning Model 125 and 130 pH meters. (Courtesy of Corning Glass Works.)

Figure AIV-2a. Front view of the Beckman 3500 pH meter. (Courtesy of Beckman Instruments, Inc.)

Figure AIV-2b.   Front view of the Zeromatic IV pH meter.
(Courtesy of Beckman Instruments, Inc.)

Measuring pH

Two electrodes are used with the pH meter: a standard calomel electrode (SCE) and a glass electrode. The SCE should always be checked to be sure it is filled with a saturated solution of potassium chloride. If the water level is more than one inch from the top, distilled water should be added. If excess salt crystals are not in the bottom, solid potassium chloride should be added. The glass electrode should be checked for breakage since the tip is **very** fragile. Some plastic electrodes are also available; they are factory sealed and no KCl or water needs to be added. They contain both the calomel and glass electrode in a single casing.

Stirring during titration is achieved by use of a stirplate and a magnetic stirring bar in the solution. Ideally, electrodes should be submerged about 4 cm to reduce effects of the atmosphere, but they must be high enough to be out of the way of the rotating spin bar.

Do not wait longer than ten seconds to take a reading in a stirred solution. Do not worry about variation in the second decimal place of the reading. If the pH meter is unstable, change electrodes first. Only rarely is the problem with the pH meter.

OPERATING INSTRUCTIONS FOR CORNING MODELS 125 AND 130 pH METERS

A.   **Determining the pH of a Solution:**
     One-Point Calibration Method

   1.   Immerse the electrodes into a pH buffer to be used for calibration; release the STANDBY button and depress the pH button. Choose a buffer whose pH is near that expected for the solution to be measured. Measure the temperature of the buffer solution and set the Temperature Control to this value. Turn outer slope knob to 100 and inner knob fully clockwise.*

   2.   Adjust the CALIBRATION control until the readout displays the pH value of the buffer solution.

   3.   Remove the electrodes from the buffer solution by moving the electrode holder up. Rinse the electrodes with distilled water from a plastic squeeze bottle to prevent carryover of the buffer. **Blot**, do not wipe, the excess water with Kimwipes or tissue.

     *Inner knob is only on Model 130.

4. Assure that the temperature of the sample solution is the same as that of the buffer solution for calibration. If it is not, adjust the Temperature Control to the temperature of the unknown sample.

5. Lower the electrodes into the unknown sample solution. The display now indicates the pH of the unknown. If the pH value of the unknown is not within ± 3 units of the pH value of the calibrating buffer, a two-point calibration should be performed.

6. After measurement, raise and rinse the electrodes with distilled water. Repeat Step 5 for additional unknowns.

B. pH Titrations: Two-Point Calibration Method

In this procedure, two buffer solutions of different pH values are utilized. The first-point calibration is performed at pH 7 as outlined above and a second calibration is performed at a different pH.

1. Perform the one-point calibration at pH 7; rinse and blot the electrodes.

2. Immerse the electrodes into the second buffer solution of known pH value.

3. Adjust both the outer and inner Slope knobs (as required) until the readout displays the pH value of the second buffer.

4. Raise electrodes, rinse them, and make measurements of unknown solutions.

C. Potentiometric Titrations

A standard calomel electrode and a platinum electrode are used for potentiometric titrations. Either relative millivolt or absolute millivolt measurement can be used to obtain the endpoint in the experiment on the Potentiometric Determination of Iron (Exp. 21).

1. Relative Millivolt Measurements

a. Connect the electrodes; release the STANDBY button and press the REL MV button.

b. Immerse the electrodes into a pH 7 buffer solution and adjust the CALIBRATE control until the meter reads zero. The temperature and slope controls are inactive in this mode.

c. Remove the electrodes from the buffer and rinse with distilled water. Relative millivolt measurements may now be made on test solutions.

2. Absolute Millivolt Measurements

If absolute millivolt measurement is desired, simply release the STANDBY button and press the MV button. The TEMPERATURE, SLOPE, and CALIBRATE controls are inactive in this mode.

TABLES OF DATA

TABLE AV-A. IONIZATION CONSTANTS OF WEAK ELECTROLYTES

Acids	Ionization Equation	K_{ion} at $25°C$
Acetic	$CH_3CO_2H \rightleftharpoons H^+ + CH_3CO_2^-$	1.85×10^{-5}
Aqueous carbon	$CO_2 + H_2O \rightleftharpoons H^+ + HCO_3^-$	4.2×10^{-7}
dioxide	$HCO_3^- \rightleftharpoons H^+ + CO_3^{2-}$	4.8×10^{-11}
Hydrogen cyanide	$HCN \rightleftharpoons H^+ + CN^-$	4.0×10^{-10}
Hydrogen sulfate	$HSO_4^- \rightleftharpoons H^+ + SO_4^{2-}$	1.3×10^{-2}
Hydrogen sulfide	$H_2S \rightleftharpoons H^+ + HS^-$	1.1×10^{-7}
	$HS^- \rightleftharpoons H^+ + S^{2-}$	1×10^{-14}
Hypochlorous	$HClO \rightleftharpoons H^+ + ClO^-$	3.2×10^{-8}
Nitrous	$HNO_2 \rightleftharpoons H^+ + NO_2^-$	4.5×10^{-4}
Phosphoric	$H_3PO_4 \rightleftharpoons H^+ + H_2PO_4^-$	7.5×10^{-3}
	$H_2PO_4^- \rightleftharpoons H^+ + HPO_4^{2-}$	6.2×10^{-8}
	$HPO_4^{2-} \rightleftharpoons H^+ + PO_4^{3-}$	1.0×10^{-12}
Phosphorous	$H_3PO_3 \rightleftharpoons H^+ + H_2PO_3^-$	1.6×10^{-2}
	$H_2PO_3^- \rightleftharpoons H^+ + HPO_3^{2-}$	7×10^{-7}
Sulfurous	$H_2SO_3 \rightleftharpoons H^+ + HSO_3^-$	1.3×10^{-2}
	$HSO_3^- \rightleftharpoons H^+ + SO_3^{2-}$	5.6×10^{-8}
Bases		
Aqueous ammonia	$NH_3 + H_2O \rightleftharpoons NH_4^+ + OH^-$	1.8×10^{-5}

TABLE AV-B. DISSOCIATION CONSTANTS OF COMPLEX IONS

Dissociation Equilibrium	K_d
$[AgBr_2]^- \rightleftharpoons Ag^+ + 2\ Br^-$	7.8×10^{-8}
$[AgCl_2]^- \rightleftharpoons Ag^+ + 2\ Cl^-$	4.0×10^{-6}
$[Ag(CN)_2]^- \rightleftharpoons Ag^+ + 2\ CN^-$	1.8×10^{-19}
$[Ag(S_2O_3)_2]^{3-} \rightleftharpoons Ag^+ + 2\ S_2O_3^{2-}$	5.0×10^{-14}
$[Ag(NH_3)_2]^+ \rightleftharpoons Ag^+ + 2\ NH_3$	6.3×10^{-8}
$[Ag(en)]^+ \rightleftharpoons Ag^+ + en^*$	1.0×10^{-5}
$[AlF_6]^{3-} \rightleftharpoons Al^{3+} + 6\ F^-$	2.0×10^{-24}
$[Al(OH)_4]^- \rightleftharpoons Al^{3+} + 4\ OH^-$	1.3×10^{-34}
$[Au(CN)_2]^- \rightleftharpoons Au^+ + 2\ CN^-$	5.0×10^{-39}
$[Cd(CN)_4]^{2-} \rightleftharpoons Cd^{2+} + 4\ CN^-$	7.8×10^{-18}
$[CdCl_4]^{2-} \rightleftharpoons Cd^{2+} + 4\ Cl^-$	1.0×10^{-4}
$[Cd(NH_3)_4]^{2+} \rightleftharpoons Cd^{2+} + 4\ NH_3$	1.0×10^{-7}
$[Co(NH_3)_6]^{2+} \rightleftharpoons Co^{2+} + 6\ NH_3$	1.3×10^{-5}
$[Co(NH_3)_6]^{3+} \rightleftharpoons Co^{3+} + 6\ NH_3$	2.2×10^{-34}
$[Co(en)_3]^{2+} \rightleftharpoons Co^{2+} + 3\ en^*$	1.5×10^{-14}
$[Co(en)_3]^{3+} \rightleftharpoons Co^{3+} + 3\ en^*$	2.0×10^{-49}
$[Cu(CN)_2]^- \rightleftharpoons Cu^+ + 2\ CN^-$	1.0×10^{-16}
$[CuCl_2]^- \rightleftharpoons Cu^+ + 2\ Cl^-$	1.0×10^{-5}
$[Cu(NH_3)_2]^+ \rightleftharpoons Cu^+ + 2\ NH_3$	1.4×10^{-11}
$[Cu(NH_3)_4]^{2+} \rightleftharpoons Cu^{2+} + 4\ NH_3$	8.5×10^{-13}
$[Fe(CN)_6]^{4-} \rightleftharpoons Fe^{2+} + 6\ CN^-$	1.3×10^{-37}
$[Fe(CN)_6]^{3-} \rightleftharpoons Fe^{3+} + 6\ CN^-$	1.3×10^{-44}
$[HgCl_4]^{2-} \rightleftharpoons Hg^{2+} + 4\ Cl^-$	8.3×10^{-16}
$[Ni(CN)_4]^{2-} \rightleftharpoons Ni^{2+} + 4\ CN^-$	1.0×10^{-31}
$[Ni(NH_3)_6]^{2+} \rightleftharpoons Ni^{2+} + 6\ NH_3$	1.8×10^{-9}
$[Zn(OH)_4]^{2-} \rightleftharpoons Zn^{2+} + 4\ OH^-$	3.5×10^{-16}
$[Zn(NH_3)_4]^{2+} \rightleftharpoons Zn^{2+} + 4\ NH_3$	3.4×10^{-10}

* en represents ethylenediamine, $H_2NCH_2CH_2NH_2$

TABLE AV-C. SOLUBILITY PRODUCT CONSTANTS FOR SOME INORGANIC COMPOUNDS AT 25 °C

Substance		K_{sp}
Aluminum hydroxide	$Al(OH)_3$	3×10^{-33}
Antimony(III) sulfide	Sb_2S_3	2.9×10^{-59}
Barium carbonate	$BaCO_3$	5.0×10^{-9}
Barium chromate	$BaCrO_4$	1.8×10^{-10}
Barium fluoride	BaF_2	1.0×10^{-5}
Barium oxalate	BaC_2O_4	1.7×10^{-7}
Barium sulfate	$BaSO_4$	1.1×10^{-10}
Bismuth sulfide	Bi_2S_3	6.8×10^{-97}
Cadmium carbonate	$CdCO_3$	2.2×10^{-13}
Cadmium hydroxide	$Cd(OH)_2$	2.2×10^{-14}
Cadmium sulfide	CdS	7.8×10^{-27}
Calcium carbonate	$CaCO_3$	7.5×10^{-9}
Calcium chromate	$CaCrO_4$	7.1×10^{-4}
Calcium fluoride	CaF_2	9.6×10^{-11}
Calcium oxalate	CaC_2O_4	2.0×10^{-9}
Calcium phosphate	$Ca_3(PO_4)_2$	1×10^{-25}
Calcium sulfate	$CaSO_4$	2.4×10^{-5}
Cobalt(II) hydroxide	$Co(OH)_2$	2.5×10^{-16}
Cobalt(II) sulfide	CoS	5.9×10^{-21}
Cobalt(III) hydroxide	$Co(OH)_3$	3.0×10^{-43}
Chromium(III) hydroxide	$Cr(OH)_3$	7×10^{-31}
Copper(I) chloride	$CuCl$	4×10^{-7}
Copper(I) iodide	CuI	1×10^{-12}
Copper(I) sulfide	Cu_2S	1.6×10^{-48}
Copper(II) iodate	$Cu(IO_3)_2$	1.4×10^{-7}
Copper(II) sulfide	CuS	8.7×10^{-36}
Iron(II) hydroxide	$Fe(OH)_2$	2.0×10^{-15}
Iron(II) sulfide	FeS	4.9×10^{-18}
Iron (III) hydroxide	$Fe(OH)_3$	6.0×10^{-38}
Lead(II) bromide	$PbBr_2$	5.0×10^{-6}
Lead(II) carbonate	$PbCO_3$	1.2×10^{-13}
Lead(II) chloride	$PbCl_2$	1.6×10^{-5}
Lead(II) chromate	$PbCrO_4$	2×10^{-15}
Lead(II) fluoride	PbF_2	3.0×10^{-8}
Lead(II) hydroxide	$Pb(OH)_2$	9×10^{-15}
Lead(II) iodate	$Pb(IO_3)_2$	1.9×10^{-13}
Lead(II) iodide	PbI_2	9.6×10^{-9}
Lead(II) phosphate	$Pb_3(PO_4)_2$	3×10^{-44}
Lead(II) sulfate	$PbSO_4$	1.4×10^{-8}
Lead(II) sulfide	PbS	8.4×10^{-28}

All solubility products for sulfides are from Waggoner, *J. Chem. Educ.*, 35, 339 (1958). Averaged values from the literature are used for other compounds.

TABLE AV-C. SOLUBILITY PRODUCT CONSTANTS FOR SOME INORGANIC COMPOUNDS AT 25 °C (continued)

Substance		K_{sp}
Lithium phosphate	Li_3PO_4	3.5×10^{-13}
Magnesium ammonium phosphate	$MgNH_4PO_4$	2.5×10^{-13}
Magnesium carbonate	$MgCO_3$	4×10^{-5}
Magnesium fluoride	MgF_2	8×10^{-8}
Magnesium hydroxide	$Mg(OH)_2$	1.2×10^{-11}
Magnesium oxalate	MgC_2O_4	8.6×10^{-5}
Manganese(II) carbonate	$MnCO_3$	8.8×10^{-11}
Manganese(II) hydroxide	$Mn(OH)_2$	6×10^{-14}
Manganese(II) sulfide	MnS	5.1×10^{-15}
Mercury(I) bromide	Hg_2Br_2	1.0×10^{-22}
Mercury(I) chloride	Hg_2Cl_2	1.3×10^{-18}
Mercury(I) iodide	Hg_2I_2	3.3×10^{-25}
Mercury(I) sulfide	Hg_2S	5.8×10^{-44}
Mercury(II) sulfide	HgS	8.6×10^{-53}
Nickel carbonate	$NiCO_3$	1.4×10^{-7}
Nickel hydroxide	$Ni(OH)_2$	2×10^{-16}
Nickel sulfide	NiS	1.8×10^{-21}
Silver acetate	AgO_2CCH_3	2.5×10^{-3}
Silver arsenate	Ag_3AsO_4	1×10^{-22}
Silver bromide	$AgBr$	4.8×10^{-13}
Silver carbonate	Ag_2CO_3	8×10^{-12}
Silver chloride	$AgCl$	1.2×10^{-10}
Silver chromate	Ag_2CrO_4	2.2×10^{-12}
Silver cyanide	$AgCN$	1.5×10^{-14}
Silver iodide	AgI	1.4×10^{-16}
Silver nitrite	$AgNO_2$	2.5×10^{-4}
Silver phosphate	Ag_3PO_4	1.0×10^{-18}
Silver sulfide	Ag_2S	6.8×10^{-50}
Silver thiocyanate	$AgSCN$	1×10^{-12}
Strontium carbonate	$SrCO_3$	1.0×10^{-9}
Strontium chromate	$SrCrO_4$	3.6×10^{-5}
Strontium fluoride	SrF_2	7.9×10^{-10}
Strontium oxalate	SrC_2O_4	5.6×10^{-8}
Strontium sulfate	$SrSO_4$	3.0×10^{-7}
Tin(II) hydroxide	$Sn(OH)_2$	5×10^{-26}
Tin(II) sulfide	SnS	1.2×10^{-25}
Zinc carbonate	$ZnCO_3$	1×10^{-10}
Zinc hydroxide	$Zn(OH)_2$	4×10^{-17}
Zinc sulfide	ZnS	1.1×10^{-21}

All solubility products for sulfides are from Waggoner, *J. Chem. Educ.*, 35, 339 (1958). Averaged values from the literature are used for other compounds.

TABLE AV-D.   STANDARD REDUCTION POTENTIALS IN AQUEOUS SOLUTION AT 25 °C

Acidic Solution	Standard Reduction Potential, $E°$ (volts)
Ba^{2+} (aq) + $2e^-$ → Ba (s)	−2.90
Sr^{2+} (aq) + $2e^-$ → Sr (s)	−2.89
Ca^{2+} (aq) + $2e^-$ → Ca (s)	−2.87
Na^+ (aq) + e^- → Na (s)	−2.714
Mg^{2+} (aq) + $2e^-$ → Mg (s)	−2.37
H_2 (g) + $2e^-$ → $2H^-$ (aq)	−2.25
Al^{3+} (aq) + $3e^-$ → Al (s)	−1.66
Zr^{4+} (aq) + $4e^-$ → Zr (s)	−1.53
ZnS (s) + $2e^-$ → Zn (s) + S^{2-} (aq)	−1.44
CdS (s) + $2e^-$ → Cd (s) + S^{2-} (aq)	−1.21
V^{2+} (aq) + $2e^-$ → V (s)	−1.18
Mn^{2+} (aq) + $2e^-$ → Mn (s)	−1.18
FeS (s) + $2e^-$ → Fe (s) + S^{2-} (aq)	−1.01
Cr^{2+} (aq) + $2e^-$ → Cr (s)	−0.91
Zn^{2+} (aq) + $2e^-$ → Zn (s)	−0.763
Cr^{3+} (aq) + $3e^-$ → Cr (s)	−0.74
HgS (s) + $2H^+$ (aq) + $2e^-$ → Hg (ℓ) + H_2S (g)	−0.72
Ga^{3+} (aq) + $3e^-$ → Ga (s)	−0.53
$2CO_2$ (g) + $2H^+$ (aq) + $2e^-$ → $(COOH)_2$ (aq)	−0.49
Fe^{2+} (aq) + $2e^-$ → Fe (s)	−0.44
Cr^{3+} (aq) + e^- → Cr^{2+} (aq)	−0.41
Cd^{2+} (aq) + $2e^-$ → Cd (s)	−0.403
Se (s) + $2H^+$ (aq) + $2e^-$ → H_2Se (aq)	−0.40
$PbSO_4$ (s) + $2e^-$ → Pb (s) + SO_4^{2-} (aq)	−0.356
Tl^+ (aq) + e^- → Tl (s)	−0.34
Co^{2+} (aq) + $2e^-$ → Co (s)	−0.28
Ni^{2+} (aq) + $2e^-$ → Ni (s)	−0.25
$[SnF_6]^{2-}$ (aq) + $4e^-$ → Sn (s) + $6F^-$ (aq)	−0.25
AgI (s) + e^- → Ag (s) + I^- (aq)	−0.15
Sn^{2+} (aq) + $2e^-$ → Sn (s)	−0.14
Pb^{2+} (aq) + $2e^-$ → Pb (s)	−0.126
N_2O (g) + $6H^+$ (aq) + H_2O + $4e^-$ → $2NH_3OH^+$ (aq)	−0.05
$2H^+$ (aq) + $2e^-$ → H_2 (g) **(reference electrode)**	0
AgBr (s) + e^- → Ag (s) + Br^- (aq)	0.10
S (s) + $2H^+$ (aq) + $2e^-$ → H_2S (aq)	0.14
Sn^{4+} (aq) + $2e^-$ → Sn^{2+} (aq)	0.15
Cu^{2+} (aq) + e^- → Cu^+ (aq)	0.153
SO_4^{2-} (aq) + $4H^+$ (aq) + $2e^-$ → H_2SO_3 (aq) + H_2O	0.17
SO_4^{2-} (aq) + $4H^+$ (aq) + $2e^-$ → SO_2 (g) + $2H_2O$	0.20
AgCl (s) + e^- → Ag (s) + Cl^- (aq)	0.222
Hg_2Cl_2 (s) + $2e^-$ → 2Hg (ℓ) + $2Cl^-$ (aq)	0.27
Cu^{2+} (aq) + $2e^-$ → Cu (s)	0.337
$[RhCl_6]^{3-}$ (aq) + $3e^-$ → Rh (s) + $6Cl^-$ (aq)	0.44
Cu^+ (aq) + e^- → Cu (s)	0.521
TeO_2 (s) + $4H^+$ (aq) + $4e^-$ → Te (s) + $2H_2O$	0.529
I_2 (s) + $2e^-$ → $2I^-$ (aq)	0.535
H_3AsO_4 (aq) + $2H^+$ (aq) + $2e^-$ → H_3AsO_3 (aq) + H_2O	0.58
$[PtCl_6]^{2-}$ (aq) + $2e^-$ → $[PtCl_4]^{2-}$ (aq) + $2Cl^-$ (aq)	0.68
O_2 (g) + $2H^+$ (aq) + $2e^-$ → H_2O_2 (aq)	0.682

TABLE AV-D. STANDARD REDUCTION POTENTIALS IN AQUEOUS SOLUTION AT 25 °C (continued)

Acidic Solution	Standard Reduction Potential, E (volts)
$[PtCl_4]^{2-}$ (aq) + $2e^-$ → Pt (s) + $4Cl^-$ (aq)	0.73
$SbCl_6^-$ (aq) + $2e^-$ → $SbCl_4^-$ (aq) + $2Cl^-$ (aq)	0.75
Fe^{3+} (aq) + e^- → Fe^{2+} (aq)	0.771
Hg_2^{2+} (aq) + $2e^-$ → 2Hg (ℓ)	0.789
Ag^+ (aq) + e^- → Ag (s)	0.7994
Hg^{2+} (aq) + $2e^-$ → Hg (ℓ)	0.855
$2Hg^{2+}$ (aq) + $2e^-$ → Hg_2^{2+} (aq)	0.920
NO_3^- (aq) + $3H^+$ (aq) + $2e^-$ → HNO_2 (aq) + H_2O	0.94
NO_3^- (aq) + $4H^+$ (aq) + $3e^-$ → NO (g) + $2H_2O$	0.96
Pd^{2+} (aq) + $2e^-$ → Pd (s)	0.987
$AuCl_4^-$ (aq) + $3e^-$ → Au (s) + $4Cl^-$ (aq)	1.00
Br_2 (ℓ) + $2e^-$ → $2Br^-$ (aq)	1.08
ClO_4^- (aq) + $2H^+$ (aq) + $2e^-$ → ClO_3^- (aq) + H_2O	1.19
IO_3^- (aq) + $6H^+$ (aq) + $5e^-$ → $\frac{1}{2}I_2$ (aq) + $3H_2O$	1.195
Pt^{2+} (aq) + $2e^-$ → Pt (s)	1.2
O_2 (g) + $4H^+$ (aq) + $4e^-$ → $2H_2O$	1.229
MnO_2 (s) + $4H^+$ (aq) + $2e^-$ → Mn^{2+} (aq) + $2H_2O$	1.23
$N_2H_5^+$ (aq) + $3H^+$ (aq) + $2e^-$ → $2NH_4^+$ (aq)	1.24
$Cr_2O_7^{2-}$ (aq) + $14H^+$ (aq) + $6e^-$ → $2Cr^{3+}$ (aq) + $7H_2O$	1.33
Cl_2 (g) + $2e^-$ → $2Cl^-$ (aq)	1.360
BrO_3^- (aq) + $6H^+$ (aq) + $6e^-$ → Br^- (aq) + $3H_2O$	1.44
ClO_3^- (aq) + $6H^+$ (aq) + $5e^-$ → $\frac{1}{2}Cl_2$ (g) + $3H_2O$	1.47
Au^{3+} (aq) + $3e^-$ → Au (s)	1.50
MnO_4^- (aq) + $8H^+$ (aq) + $5e^-$ → Mn^{2+} (aq) + $4H_2O$	1.51
$NaBiO_3$ (s) + $6H^+$ (aq) + $2e^-$ → Bi^{3+} (aq) + Na^+ (aq) + $3H_2O$	1.6
Ce^{4+} (aq) + e^- → Ce^{3+} (aq)	1.61
$2HClO$ (aq) + $2H^+$ (aq) + $2e^-$ → Cl_2 (g) + $2H_2O$	1.63
Au^+ (aq) + e^- → Au (s)	1.68
PbO_2 (s) + SO_4^{2-} (aq) + $4H^+$ (aq) + $2e^-$ → $PbSO_4$ (s) + $2H_2O$	1.685
NiO_2 (s) + $4H^+$ (aq) + $2e^-$ → Ni^{2+} (aq) + $2H_2O$	1.7
H_2O_2 (aq) + $2H^+$ (aq) + $2e^-$ → $2H_2O$	1.77
Pb^{4+} (aq) + $2e^-$ → Pb^{2+} (aq)	1.8
Co^{3+} (aq) + e^- → Co^{2+} (aq)	1.82
F_2 (g) + $2e^-$ → $2F^-$ (aq)	2.87

TABLES OF BOILING OR MELTING POINTS OF ALCOHOLS, ALDEHYDES, KETONES, CARBOXYLIC ACIDS AND DERIVATIVES

ACIDS-LIQUID

Compound	B.p.	M.p. of Amide
Acetic	118	82
Propionic	141	81
Isobutyric	155	128
n-Butyric	163	115
Crotonic (cis)	169	101
Ethylmethylacetic	176	112
Isovaleric	176	135
n-Valeric	186	106
Dichloroacetic	194	98 subl.
Diethylacetic	195	112
Isocaproic	199	120
n-Caproic	205	100
Ethoxyacetic	206	81

ACIDS-SOLID

Compounds	M.p.	M.p. of Amide
Oleic	16	76
Methacrylic	16	106
dl-Lactic	18	74
Caproic	31.5	108
Levulinic	33	107
Lauric	43	99
β-Phenylpropionic (Hydrocinnamic)	48	105
Myristic	54	103
Chloroacetic	61	121
Stearic	70	109
Phenylacetic	76.5 subl.	156
o-Toluic	104	143
Azelaic	106.5	175
m-Toluic	112	97
p-Isopropylbenzoic	117	133
Benzoic	122	130
o-Benzoylbenzoic	128	165

ACIDS-SOLID (Continued)

Compounds	M.p.	M.p. of Amide
2, 5-Dimethylbenzoic	132	186
Sebacic	133	210
Acetylsalicylic	135	138
Diphenylacetic	145	168
p-Hydroxyphenylacetic	148	175
Adipic	152	220
2, 5-Dichlorobenzoic	153	155
Salicylic	158	139
p-Toluic	179	158
β-Naphthoic	185	195
Succinic	188	242
Phthalic	206	149

ALCOHOLS-LIQUID

Compounds	B.p.	M.p. of 3,5-Dinitrobenzoate
Methyl	65	108
Ethyl	78	93
Isopropyl	82	123
n-Propyl	97	74
Isobutyl	108	87
3-Pentanol	116	101
n-Butyl	117	64
2,3-Dimethyl-2-butanol	118	111
3,3-Dimethyl-2-butanol	120	107
2-Methyl-2-pentanol	121	72
3-Methyl-3-pentanol	123	96.5
2-Methylbutanol	129	70
4-Methyl-2-pentanol	132	65
Isoamyl (3-Methylbutanol)	132	61
2-Ethoxyethanol	135	75
3-Hexanol	136	77
n-Amyl (1-Pentanol)	138	46
Cyclopentanol	141	115
2,3-Dimethylbutanol	145	51.5
2-Methylpentanol	148	50.5
2-Ethylbutanol	148	51.5

ALCOHOLS-SOLID

Compound	M.p.	M.p. of 3,5-Dinitrobenzoate
α-Methylbenzyl (α-Phenylethyl)	20	95
2-Methylcyclohexanol (trans or α)	21	115
Dodecyl (Lauryl)	24	60
Cyclohexanol	25	113
tert-Butyl	25	(142
Cinnamyl	33	121
α-Terpineol	35	79
L-Menthol	44	153
Cetyl (Hexadecanol)	49	66
Octadecanol (Stearyl)	60	66
p-Methylbenzyl p-Tolylcarbinol)	60	117
Benzhydrol (Diphenylcarbinol)	68	141
Ergosterol (anh.)	165	202

ALDEHYDES-LIQUID

Compounds	B.p.	M.p. of 2,4-Dinitrophenylhydrazone
Acetaldehyde (Ethanal)	20	168
Propionaldehyde (Propanal)	48	148
Isovaleraldehyde	64	187
n-Butyraldehyde (Butanal)	75	123
Pivaldehyde (Trimethylacetaldehyde)	75	209
Isovaleraldehyde	92.5	123
2-Methyl-1-butanal (α-Methyl-n-butyraldehyde)	92	120
Chloral	98	131
n-Pentanal (Valeraldehyde)	103	98
n-Hexanal (Caproaldehyde)	131	104
n-Heptanal	153	108

ALDEHYDES-SOLID

Compounds	M.p.	M.p. of 2,4-Dinitrophenylhydrazone
Palmitaldehyde	34	108
Phenylacetaldehyde	34	121
Piperonal (Heliotropin)	37	266
o-Methoxybenzaldehyde	38	253
Stearaldehyde	38	101
Lauraldehyde	44	106
p-Chlorobenzaldehyde	48	254
2-Napthaldehyde	60	270
Vanillin	81	271
p-Nitrobenzaldehyde	106	320
p-Hydroxybenzaldehyde	116	280

KETONES-LIQUID

Compound	B.p.	M.p. of 2,4-Dinitrophenylhydrazone
Acetone	56	126
2-Butanone (Ethyl methyl)	80	116
2-Methyl-3-butanone	94	120
3-Pentanone (Diethyl)	102	156
2-Pentanone (Methyl propyl)	102	143
4-Methyl-2-pentanone	117	95
2,4-Dimethyl-3-pentanone	124	88
3-Hexanone	125	130
2-Hexanone	128	106
Cyclopentanone	131	146
4-Heptanone (Dipropyl)	144	75
Cyclohexanone	156	160

KETONES-SOLID

Compound	M.p.	M.p. of 2,4-Dinitrophenylhydrazone
Acetophenone	20	238
Benzyl methyl ketone	27	156
p-Methylacetophenone	28	260
p-Methoxyacetophenone	38	220
Benzalacetone	41	227
Benzophenone	48	238
Phenyl p-tolyl ketone	55	199
β-Naphthyl methyl ketone	56	262
Benzalacetophenone	58	244
p-Methoxybenzophenone	63	180
p-Toluquinone	69	269
p-Chlorobenzophenone	78	185
m-Nitroacetophenone	81	228
Fluorenone	83	283
Benzil	95	189
p-Hydroxyacetophenone	96	261

NOMENCLATURE (NAMING) OF SIMPLE INORGANIC COMPOUNDS*

Since millions of compounds are known, it is important to be able to associate names and formulas unambiguously and in a systematic way. The rules for naming inorganic compounds were established in 1957 by the Committee on Inorganic Nomenclature of the International Union of Pure and Applied Chemistry (IUPAC). To make naming easier, we classify simple compounds in two major categories. These are **binary compounds,** those consisting of two elements, and **ternary compounds,** those consisting of three elements.

A. BINARY COMPOUNDS

Binary compounds may be either ionic or covalent. In both cases, the general rule is to name the less electronegative element first and the more electronegative element second. The more electronegative element is named by adding an "-ide" suffix to the element's characteristic (unambiguous) stem, which is derived from the name of the element. Stems for the <u>nonmetals</u> are given below:

IIIA	IVA	VA	VIA	VIIA
				H hydr
B bor	C carb	N nitr	O ox	F fluor
	Si silic	P phosph	S sulf	Cl chlor
		As arsen	Se selen	Br brom
		Sb antimon	Te tellur	I iod

Binary ionic compounds contain metal cations and nonmetal anions. The cation is named first and the anion second, according to the rule above. Some examples are:

Formula	Name	Formula	Name
KBr	potassium bromide	Rb_2S	rubidium sulfide
$CaCl_2$	calcium chloride	Al_2Se_3	aluminum selenide
NaH	sodium hydride	SrO	strontium oxide

The above method is sufficient for naming binary ionic compounds containing metals that exhibit only one oxidation number (oxidation state) other than zero. However, most transition elements, and a few of the more electronegative representative metals, exhibit more than one oxidation number. These metals can form two or more binary compounds with the same nonmetal. In order to distinguish among all possibilities, the oxidation number of the metal is indicated by a Roman numeral in parentheses following its name. Some typical examples follow.

Formula	Oxidation Number of the Metal	Name	Formula	Oxidation Number of the Metal	Name
Cu_2O	+1	copper(I) oxide	$SnCl_4$	+4	tin(IV) chloride
CuF_2	+2	copper(II) fluoride	SnS_2	+4	tin(IV) sulfide
FeS	+2	iron(II) sulfide	PbO	+2	lead(II) oxide
Fe_2O_3	+3	iron(III) oxide	PbO_2	+4	lead(IV) oxide
$SnCl_2$	+2	tin(II) chloride			

*This section is taken from: Davis, Gailey, Whitten, <u>Principles of Chemistry</u>, Saunders Publishing Co., Philadelphia, PA, 1984, pp. 205-209. For naming more complicated examples and rules, read this section.

Roman numerals are <u>not</u> necessary for metals that commonly exhibit only one oxidation number.

An older method, still in use but not recommended by the IUPAC, involves the use of "-ous" and "-ic" suffixes to indicate lower and higher oxidation numbers, respectively. This system can distinguish between only two different oxidation numbers for a metal and therefore is not as useful as the Roman numeral system. However, the older system is still widely used in many scientific, engineering, and medical fields; some examples are illustrated below.

Formula	Oxidation Number of the Metal	Name	Formula	Oxidation Number of the Metal	Name
CuCl	+1	cuprous chloride	SnF_2	+2	stannous flouride
$CuCl_2$	+2	cupric chloride	SnF_4	+4	stannic fluoride
FeO	+2	ferrous oxide	Hg_2Cl_2	+1	mercurous chloride
$FeBr_3$	+3	ferric bromide	$HgCl_2$	+2	mercuric chloride

The advantage of the IUPAC system is that if you know the formula you can write the exact and unambiguous name, and if you are given the name you can write the formula at once.

Nearly all **binary covalent compounds** involve two <u>nonmetals</u> bonded together. Although many nonmetals can exhibit different oxidation numbers, their oxidation numbers properly are <u>not</u> indicated by Roman numerals or suffixes. Instead, elemental proportions in binary covalent compounds are indicated by using a prefix system for both elements. The Greek or Latin prefixes used are **mono, di, tri, tetra, penta, hexa, hepta, octa, nona, deca, undeca,** and **dodeca.** The prefix mono is omitted except in the common (trivial) name for CO, carbon monoxide. The minumum number of prefixes required to name a compound unambiguously is used.

Formula	Name	Formula	Name
SO_2	sulfur dioxide	Cl_2O_7	dichlorine heptoxide
SO_3	sulfur trioxide	CS_2	carbon disulfide
N_2O_4	dinitrogen tetroxide	As_4O_6	tetraarsenic hexoxide

Chemists sometimes name binary covalent compounds that contain two nonmetals by the same system used to name compounds of metals that show variable oxidation states; i.e., the oxidation state of the less electronegative element is indicated by a Roman numeral in parentheses. However, we do not recommend this procedure because it is incapable of naming compounds <u>unambiguously</u>, which is the principal requirement for a system for naming compounds. For example, both NO_2 and N_2O_4 are called nitrogen(IV) oxide by this system, and the name does not distinguish between the two compounds. The compound P_4O_{10} is tetraphosphorus decoxide, which indicates clearly its composition. Using the Roman numeral system, it would be called phosphorus(V) oxide, which could lead to the incorrect formula, P_2O_5. The simplest formula for P_4O_{10} is P_2O_5, but the name for a covalent compound must indicate clearly the composition of its molecules, not just its simplest formula.

Binary acids are compounds containing hydrogen bonded to one of the more electronegative nonmetals. These compounds act as acids when dissolved in water. The pure compounds are named as typical binary compounds. Their aqueous solutions are named by modifying the characteristic stem of the nonmetal with the prefix "hydro-" and the suffix "-ic", followed by the word "acid." The stem for sulfur in this instance is "sulfur" rather than "sulf." Some typical binary acids are listed below.

Formula	Name of Compound	Name of Aqueous Solution
HCl	hydrogen chloride	hydrochloric acid, HCl(aq)
HF	hydrogen fluoride	hydrofluoric acid, HF(aq)
H_2S	hydrogen sulfide	hydrosulfuric acid, H_2S(aq)
HCN	hydrogen cyanide	hydrocyanic acid, HCN(aq)

B. TERNARY COMPOUNDS

Ternary acids (oxyacids) are compounds of hydrogen, oxygen, and a nonmetal. A nonmetal that can exhibit more than one oxidation state can form more than one ternary acid. These ternary acids differ in the number of oxygen atoms they contain (the higher the oxidation state of the central element, the greater the number of oxygen atoms). As with binary compounds, the suffixes "-ous" and "-ic" indicate lower and higher oxidation states, respectively. These follow the stem name of the central element. One common ternary acid of each nonmetal is (somewhat arbitrarily) designated as the "-ic acid." That is, it is named "stem-ic acid/" The common ternary "ic acids" are:

Periodic Group of Central Elements	IIIA	IVA	VA	VIA	VIIA
	H_3BO_3 boric acid	H_2CO_3 carbonic acid	HNO_3 nitric acid		
		H_4SiO_4 salicic acid	H_3PO_4 phosphoric acid	H_2SO_4 sulfuric acid	$HClO_3$ chloric acid
			H_2AsO_4 arsenic acid	H_2SeO_4 selenic acid	$HBrO_3$ bromic acid
				H_6TeO_6 telluric acid	HIO_3 iodic acid

There are no common ternary "-ic" acids for the omitted nonmetals. It is important to learn the names and formulas of these acids since the names of all other ternary acids and salts are derived from them.

Acids containing <u>one fewer oxygen</u> atom per central atom are named in the same way except that the "-ic" suffix is changed to "-ous" as in the following examples. Notice that the central element has a lower oxidation number in the "-ous" acid than in the "ic" acid.

Formula	Oxidation Number	Name	Formula	Oxidation Number	Name
H_2SO_3	+4	sulfur**ous** acid	H_2SO_4	+6	sulfur**ic** acid
HNO_2	+3	nitr**ous** acid	HNO_3	+5	nitr**ic** acid
H_2SeO_3	+4	selen**ous** acid	H_2SeO_4	+6	selen**ic** acid
$HBrO_2$	+3	brom**ous** acid	$HBrO_3$	+5	brom**ic** acid

Ternary salts are compounds that result from replacing the hydrogen in a ternary acid with another ion. They usually contain metal cations or the ammonium ion. As with binary compounds, the cation is named first. The name of the anion is based on the name of the ternary acid from which it is derived. An anion derived from a ternary acid with an "-ic" ending is named by dropping the "-ic acid" and replacing it with "-ate" ion. An anion derived from an "-ous acid" is named by replacing the suffix "-ous acid" with "-ite" ion.

Formula	Name	Formula	Name
$(NH_4)_2SO_4$	ammonium sulfate (SO_4^{2-} derived from H_2SO_4)	$NaBrO_2$	sodium bromite (BrO_2^- derived from $HBrO_2$)
KNO_3	potassium nitrate (NO_3^- derived from HNO_3)	$FePO_4$	iron(III) phosphate (PO_4^{3-} derived from H_3PO_4)
$Ca(NO_2)_2$	calcium nitrite (NO_2^- derived from HNO_2)		

TABLE AVII-1. FORMULAS, IONIC CHARGES, AND NAMES FOR SOME COMMON IONS

A. Common Cations		
Formula	Charge	Name
Li^+	1+	lithium ion
Na^+	1+	sodium ion
K^+	1+	potassium ion
NH_4^+	1+	ammonium ion
Ag^+	1+	silver ion
Mg^{2+}	2+	magnesium ion
Ca^{2+}	2+	calcium ion
Ba^{2+}	2+	barium ion
Cd^{2+}	2+	cadmium ion
Zn^{2+}	2+	zinc ion
Cu^{2+}	2+	copper(II) ion or cupric ion
Hg_2^{2+}	2+	mercury(I) ion or mercurous ion
Hg^{2+}	2+	mercury(II) ion or mercuric ion
Mn^{2+}	2+	manganese(II) ion or manganous ion
Co^{2+}	2+	cobalt(II) ion or cobaltous ion
Ni^{2+}	2+	nickel(II) ion or nickelous ion
Pb^{2+}	2+	lead(II) ion or plumbous ion
Sn^{2+}	2+	tin(II) ion or stannous ion
Fe^{2+}	2+	iron(II) ion or ferrous ion
Fe^{3+}	3+	iron(III) ion or ferric ion
Al^{3+}	3+	aluminum ion
Cr^{3+}	3+	chromium(III) ion or chromic ion

B. Common Anions		
Formula	Charge	Name
F^-	1−	fluoride ion
Cl^-	1−	chloride ion
Br^-	1−	bromide ion
I^-	1−	iodide ion
OH^-	1−	hydroxide ion
CN^-	1−	cyanide ion
ClO^-	1−	hypochlorite ion
ClO_2^-	1−	chlorite ion
ClO_3^-	1−	chlorate ion
ClO_4^-	1−	perchlorate ion
CH_3COO^-	1−	acetate ion
MnO_4^-	1−	permanganate ion
NO_2^-	1−	nitrite ion
NO_3^-	1−	nitrate ion
SCN^-	1−	thiocyanate ion
O^{2-}	2−	oxide ion
S^{2-}	2−	sulfide ion
HSO_3^-	1−	hydrogen sulfite ion or bisulfite ion
SO_3^{2-}	2−	sulfite ion
HSO_4^-	1−	hydrogen sulfate ion or bisulfate ion
SO_4^{2-}	2−	sulfate ion
HCO_3^-	1−	hydrogen carbonate ion or bicarbonate ion
CO_3^{2-}	2−	carbonate ion
CrO_4^{2-}	2−	chromate ion
$Cr_2O_7^{2-}$	2−	dichromate ion
PO_4^{3-}	3−	phosphate ion
AsO_4^{3-}	3−	arsenate ion

Acid salts are salts containing anions derived from ternary acids in which one or more acidic hydrogen atoms remain. These salts are named in the same way as they would be if they were the usual type of ternary salt, except that the word "hydrogen," or "dihydrogen," is inserted after the name of the metal cation to indicate the number of acidic hydrogen atoms:

Formula	Name
$NaHSO_4$	sodium hydrogen sulfate
$NaHSO_3$	sodium hydrogen sulfite
KH_2PO_4	potassium dihydrogen phosphate

Formula	Name
K_2HPO_4	potassium hydrogen phosphate
$NaHCO_3$	sodium hydrogen carbonate

MOLECULAR AND IONIC CHEMICAL EQUATIONS

A **molecular equation** shows the complete formulas of all substances in a reaction; that is, formulas are written as if all substances were present as undissociated molecules. For example, the molecular equation for the metathesis reaction of sodium sulfide with iron(II) nitrate (both compounds are soluble in water) to form insoluble iron(II) sulfide and soluble sodium nitrate is

$$Na_2S \text{ (aq)} + Fe(NO_3)_2 \text{ (aq)} \longrightarrow FeS \text{ (s)} + 2 NaNO_3 \text{ (aq)}.$$

Molecular equations are especially useful in stoichiometry where one must deal with formula weights and, therefore, must know the entire formulas of compounds.

Ionic equations show each species in its predominant form in aqueous solution. All compounds in the previous reaction except FeS are soluble and ionic. Thus, the **total ionic equation** is

$$[2 Na^+ \text{ (aq)} + S^{2-} \text{ (aq)}] + [Fe^{2+} \text{ (aq)} + 2 NO_3^- \text{ (aq)}] \longrightarrow FeS \text{ (s)} + 2 [Na^+ \text{ (aq)} + NO_3^- \text{(aq)}].$$

Since $2 Na^+$ (aq) and $2 NO_3^-$ (aq) appear on both sides of the equation, they are not involved in the net reaction and are called **spectator ions**. Cancellation of spectator ions gives the net ionic equation, which shows the essence of the reaction, the formation of the precipitate from its ions.

$$S^{2-} \text{ (aq)} + Fe^{2+} \text{ (aq)} \longrightarrow FeS \text{ (s)}$$

In general, you must answer two questions about a substance to determine whether or not to write the formula in the ionic form.

(1) Is it soluble in water?
(2) If it is soluble, is it highly ionized or dissociated in water?

If both answers are yes, the substance is a soluble strong electrolyte and its formula is written in ionic form. If **either** answer is no, its formula is written as if the substance exists as molecules. To answer these questions, it is helpful to know the strong acids and strong soluble bases. These acids and bases are completely, or nearly completely, ionized in dilute aqueous solutions. Other common acids and bases are either insoluble or only slightly ionized. In addition, the solubility rules allow you to determine which salts are soluble in water. Most salts that are soluble in water are also strong electrolytes. Exceptions such as lead acetate, $Pb(CH_3COO)_2$, which is soluble but predominantly un-ionized, will be noted as they are encountered.

Two further examples illustrate molecular and ionic equations. Consider the displacement and oxidation-reduction reaction in which metallic magnesium reacts with hydrochloric acid, a strong acid, to form soluble magnesium chloride and gaseous hydrogen.

molecular equation: $Mg \text{ (s)} + 2 HCl \text{ (aq)} \longrightarrow MgCl_2 \text{ (aq)} + H_2 \text{ (g)}$

total ionic
equation: $Mg \text{ (s)} + 2 [H^+ \text{ (aq)} + Cl^- \text{ (aq)}] \longrightarrow [Mg^{2+} \text{ (aq)} + 2 Cl^- \text{ (aq)}] + H_2 \text{ (g)}$

net ionic equation: $Mg \text{ (s)} + 2 H^+ \text{ (aq)} \longrightarrow Mg^{2+} \text{ (aq)} + H_2 \text{ (g)}$

Consider also the acid-base (metathesis) reaction of carbonic acid, a weak acid, with sodium hydroxide, a strong soluble base, to form sodium carbonate, a soluble salt, and (covalent) water.

molecular
equation: H_2CO_3 (aq) + 2 NaOH (aq) $\longrightarrow$ Na_2CO_3 (aq) + 2 H_2O

total ionic
equation: H_2CO_3 (aq) + 2 [Na^+ (aq) + OH^- (aq)_] $\rightarrow$ [2 Na^+ (aq) + CO_3^{2-} (aq)] + 2 H_2O

net ionic
equation: H_2CO_3 (aq) + 2 OH^- (aq) $\longrightarrow$ CO_3^{2-} (aq) + 2 H_2O